W9-AEX-317

THE ANALYTIC ART

The Analytic Art

Nine Studies in Algebra, Geometry and Trigonometry from the *Opus Restitutae Mathematicae Analyseos, seu Algebrâ Novâ*

by
FRANÇOIS VIETE

translated by
T. Richard Witmer

The Kent State University Press

The publisher is indebted to A. K. Rajappa for his technical assistance in the late stages of production of this book.

Library of Congress Cataloging in Publication Data

Viète, François, 1540–1603.
    The analytic art.

    Includes index.
    1. Algebra—Early works to 1800. 2. Geometry—
Early works to 1800.   3. Trigonometry—Early works to
1800. I. Title.
QA33.V4813 1983   512   82-21381
ISBN O-87338-282-X

Contents

TRANSLATOR'S INTRODUCTION

François Viète was born in 1540 in Fontenay-le-Comte, which lies in what is now the department of the Vendée and in the historical province of Poitou.[1] He was a son of Etienne Viète, a lawyer and a first cousin by marriage of Barnabé Brisson, who for a while was president of the Parlement de Paris. The younger Viète studied first with the Franciscans at their cloister in Fontenay—the same place in which, fifty years earlier, François Rabelais had lived and studied for 15 years—and then, when he was 18, at the University of Poitiers. Returning to Fontenay in 1559 with his bachelor's degree in law, he began the practice of that profession. His practice appears to have flourished—he numbered among his clients, we are told, Mary Stuart and Queen Eleanor of Austria—and he acquired the title of Sieur de la Bigotière. More important for his future, however, was his taking on the legal affairs of the Soubise family in 1564 and, as a consequence of that, his becoming private secretary to Antoinette d'Aubeterre, a member of that family. Antoinette had married Jean de Parthenay-l'Archeveque in 1553 and he, a staunch Huguenot, had been in command at the time Lyon was besieged by the Catholic forces. The loss of Lyon led to strong recriminations against him. One of the things for which Antoinette particularly wanted the services of Viète was as an advocate to help her husband defend himself against these recriminations. Another was as a tutor to her eleven-year-old daughter, Catherine de Parthenay, who, we are

[1]There is no full-scale biography of Viète of which I am aware. This and what follows are pieced together largely from the sketches by Frederic Ritter, *François Viète, Inventeur de l'Algebre Moderne* (Paris, 1895) and Joseph E. Hofmann's introduction to the facsimile reprint of Viète's *Opera Mathematica* (Frans van Schooten, originally Leyden, 1646; reprint Georg Olms Verlag, Hildesheim, 1970). A note appended to the Ritter piece says that he had prepared a complete biography, intended to accompany a translation into French of Viète's complete works, which would run to 350 pages. The whereabouts of this manuscript is unknown.

told, was particularly interested in astrology and, therefore, in astronomy, with which Viète had to acquaint himself thoroughly.[2]

Four years after Viète's employment with the Soubise family began, Catherine (then fifteen years old) married a nobleman. Trouble developed between him and his mother-in-law, who packed up and took her whole household, including Viète, to La Rochelle. Here Viète became acquainted with Jeanne d'Albret, a first cousin of Françoise de Rohan, who was Henri III's aunt and a sister of René de Rohan, whom Catherine married after her first husband was killed in the St. Bartholomew's Massacre. Viète left La Rochelle in 1570 to go to Paris, where the next year, he became legal adviser to the Parlement de Paris. Paris was home for a number of then prominent mathematicians and, says Ritter, Viète soon became acquainted with them.

From Paris, Viète moved to Brittany in 1574, where he became an adviser to the Parlement which sat at Rennes. The work there was light, and being, so to speak, next door to Poitou, he no doubt spent a good deal of time in his native stamping grounds tending to his outside interests, among them mathematical studies. He had, however, attracted the attention of Henri III, who came to the throne in 1574 upon the death of Charles IX. Viète was recommended to Henri by such personages as Barnabé Brisson (then the *avocat générale* of the Parlement de Paris), Françoise de Rohan, and Henri de Navarre. Within a short time, Henri III was calling upon Viète for private advice and for confidential missions and negotiations. This, and Viète's success in finding a way out of an unhappy dispute between Françoise de Rohan and Anne de Ferrara, otherwise Anne d'Esté,[3] led to Viète's appointment as *maître des réquètes* at the court and a member of the privy council in 1580. This, of course, brought him back to Paris where he stayed until the end of 1584 or the beginning of 1585, when he was dismissed through the machinations of the Guise and Nemours families, whom he had offended by his handling of the Françoise de Rohan–Anne de Ferrara affair. He returned first to Garnache for a short while, and then to Fontenay and his nearby place at Bigotière. In April

---

[2]Viète remained a friend and adviser to Catherine throughout his life. The 1591 edition of his *Introduction to the Analytic Art* carries a glowing dedication to her.

[3]Françoise had been engaged to Jacques de Savoy, the duke of Nemours. An illegitimate son was born to them, but Nemours refused to marry her and instead married Anne d'Esté, the widow of François de Guise. Françoise demanded that this marriage be declared illegal, that Anne's children be declared bastards, and that she be held to be the wife of Jacques de Nemours. Both parties had powerful friends at court, so Henri III, doing all he could to escape the unpleasantness, called on Viète to solve the problem. In 1580 the Parlement de Paris found Françoise to have been the rightful wife of Nemours and awarded her the title of duchess of Loudinois. The marriage of Jacques to Anne, however, was explained away as having been dissolved, so that Anne's honor and the honor of her children were not impaired.

1589, Henri III moved his seat of government from Paris to Tours. Viète was recalled to the court but, because Tours is not far from Fontenay, he could still spend a good deal of time at the latter. One of his tasks at Tours was that of acting as a cryptanalyst of messages passing between the enemies of Henri III. He was so successful at this, we are told, that there were those, particularly in Rome, who denounced him by saying that the decipherment could only have been the product of sorcery and necromancy.

On 31 July 1589 Henri III was killed. He was succeeded on the throne by Henri IV. Viète's negotiating abilities and his prior acquaintance with Henri made him one of the most influential men at court, but he did his best to remain in the background. (It was at Tours, says Ritter, that Viète probably married at a no longer youthful age.)[4] The court returned to Paris in 1594 and Viète, called upon to be a privy councillor, went there with it. Apparently, ill health overtook him and the story closes with his being given a delicate mission in Poitou, which enabled him to live in Fontenay. In 1602 he retired, and he died the next year.

Such, in brief, was Viète's professional life. If this were all that he accomplished, his name would long since have disappeared from all the books except those that deal with the minutiae of local and family history. But alongside his professional life he led another—a contemplative life, if you will.[5] It was this life that produced his mathematical works, both those that are contained in this translation and others besides, and thus assured him a lasting name.

His life as a mathematician falls, as nearly as we can judge today, into two fairly distinct periods. The first probably began with or shortly after his full-time employment by the Soubise family in 1564, and ended in 1571 when Jean Mettayer, the royal printer, made his press available for publication of the *Canon Mathematicus* and the *Universalium Inspectionum Liber Singularis,* both published in Paris in 1579. These works, two of a projected four, consisted primarily of tables of the trigonometric func-

---

[4]*Francois Viète, op. cit.,* p. 31. Ritter also thinks that Viète had only one child, a daughter, who died without having been married (p. 5). Hofmann belives that he married twice and that he had three children by his first wife and another by his second (in *Opera Mathematica*).

[5]Contemplative, indeed, it must have been, unless Jacques de Thou was indulging a completely wild excess of imagination in his *Historiarum Sui Temporis,* vol. 5, 1060 (Geneva, 1620), where he says: "So profound was his meditation that he was often seen fixed in thought for three whole days in a row, seated at his lamp-lit dining room table, with neither food nor sleep except what he got resting on his elbow, and not stirring from his place to revivify himself from time to time." This passage, along with its context, is also set out at the head of the *Opera Mathematica* of 1646.

tions on an ambitious scale, for Viète made his computations for every minute of arc and to one part in 10,000,000. His computation for the sine of one minute of arc was based on an inscribed polygon of 6,144 sides and a circumscribed polygon of 12,288 sides. The value he derived was 29.083,819,59 on a base of 10,000,000. Though he speedily tried to withdraw his work from circulation because, he said, of its many errors, parts of it, particularly those dealing with spherical triangles, were reprinted in his *Variorum de Rebus Mathematicis Responsorum Liber VIII.*[6]

Viète's second active mathematical period began, as nearly as we can surmise, about 1584. It was during this period that the greater part of the works contained in this volume, plus some others, were produced. Their publication came piecemeal, in spite of Viète's apparently thinking of them as a whole. The earliest was published in 1591, again by Jean Mettayer, and the latest were posthumous.

Both in reading these works and in assessing Viète's contributions to the development of mathematics, it is good to remember that, as his dates (1540–1603) indicate, he comes one generation after Girolamo Cardano (1501–1576) and little more that a generation before René Descartes (1596–1650) and Pierre de Fermat (1601–1665).[7]

Clearly his best-known contribution to the development of algebra

---

[6]Tours, 1593, ch. XIX. Also to be found in the *Opera Mathematica,* p. 400ff.

[7]Though Viète is quite explicit about his indebtedness to the Greek writers on mathematics, particularly Diophantus, he leaves to surmise the answer to the question of how fully acquainted he was with the works of Cardano, Lodovico Ferrari, Nicolo Tartaglia, Simon Stevin, and others of their time. We find, in the works included in this volume, only two references to Cardano's *Practica Arithmeticae* (Milan, 1539) and none at all to the vastly more important *Ars Magna* (Nürnberg, 1545; 2d ed., Basel, 1570). Yet it seems entirely likely that he was acquainted with at least some of their works. Ritter (François Viète, p. 11), for instance, mentioned among the names of a number of prominent mathematicians living in Paris while Viète was there that of Georges Gosselin, who translated Tartaglia's works into French. If, as Ritter believes, Viète became acquainted with Gosselin, an altogether likely event, he could hardly have failed to know about Tartaglia's work and, knowing about this, could hardly have failed to know about Cardano's *Great Art,* since Tartaglia and Cardano were rivals and, indeed, upon the publication of the *Great Art,* enemies, and Tartaglia did not spare himself in heaping aspersions on Cardano. Moreover, Moritz Cantor concludes (*Vorlesungen über Geschichte der Mathematik,* 2d ed., Leipzig, 1900, vol. II, p. 636) that Viète's solution of cubic equations from a four-part proportion so closely resembles that of the Italian school that he must have been familiar with their work and (ibid., p. 638) that his working out of the solution of the biquadratic betokens the same, with particular reference to the Ferrari-Cardano exposition of it. (Cf. J. F. Montucla, *Histoire de Mathematiques,* vol. I [New printing Paris, 1960, from nouvelle edition of Paris, 1796], p. 601: 'A l'égard des équations cubiques, M. Viète les resoud d'une manière différente de celle de Cardan et de Bombelli.') Yet Viète so completely overlooks some of Cardano's contributions (cf. p. 6 infra) that one is led to wonder how thorough his acquaintance with the latter's works was.

was his espousal and consistent utilization of the letters of the alphabet—he called these *species*—to represent both the constant and the variable terms in all equations. Though, as Cardano had demonstrated, it was not impossible to state the formulae for solving cubic and biquadratic equations with the older nomenclature, Viète's new way of doing it had the great advantage of making more visible the operations which went into building up or solving a complex series of terms. This is due more to his substitution of letters for the givens—a substitution which, as far as is known, was Viète's own contribution—than to the use of letters to represent the variables. (After all, Cardano's *res, positio,* and *quantitas,* all of which he used to represent the first power of the unknown or unknowns, are quite simple and not much less economical than Viète's *A, E* or *O.*) But numerical coefficients tend, first, to obscure the generality of what is being proposed and, second, to merge with each other as letters do not when a given expression is subjected to processing.[8]

Yet still another step had to be taken before the full economy of Viète's lettering system could be fully realized. For although in Viète such a term as the *quadrato-quadratum* in *A quadrato-quadratum*—or, as he frequently abbreviated it, *A quad-quad* or even *Aqq* or, as we might abbreviate it, A^{qq}—had become for all intents and purposes an exponent, a pure number, it still retained something of the flavor of a multidimensional object it had in Cardano and others of his time, where it was not the exponent alone but the unknown-cum-exponent. As we look back on it, we wonder that Viète did not himself take the next step—that of converting his verbal exponents into numerical exponents, or even (though this would have been, perhaps, too radical a step) into letters analogous to those he used for the basic terms of his operations. The fact that he did not do so may well indicate that he was not familiar with the works of Raffaello Bombelli and Simon Stevin, his near-contemporaries, for both of them, in works antedating Viète's (except for his *Canon Mathematicus* and *Universalium Inspectionum*), used superior figures attached to coefficients to show the powers of the unknown to which the coefficients belonged.[9]

<hr/>

[8]To use the language of John Wallis in his *Treatise of Algebra, Both Historical and Practical* (London, 1675): The advantage of symbolic algebra over numerical is this, "that whereas there [i.e., in numerical algebra] the Numbers first taken, are lost or swallowed up in those which by several operations are derived from them, so as not to remain in view, or easily be discerned in the Result: Here [i.e., in symbolic algebra] they are so preserved, as till the last, to remain in view with the several operations concerning them, so as they serve not only for a Resolution of the particular Question proposed, but as a general Solution of the like Questions in other Quantities, however changed."

[9]See David Eugene Smith, *History of Mathematics* (Boston, Ginn & Co. 1925), vol. II, pp. 428, 430 for examples. See also Viète's *Ad Problema Quod Omnibus Mathematicis Totius Orbis Construendum Proposuit Adrianus Romanus* (Paris, 1795) reprinted in the

In addition to this, another important advance that Viète made on his predecessors flowed from, or was made feasible by, his adoption of the *species* as the primary means of expressing himself. That is, he was able to free himself almost entirely from the geometric diagrams on which Cardano's proofs of almost every algebraic proposition hinged. In fact, Viète does not use such diagrams even as illustrative matter except where he is dealing with triangles. Reliance on diagrams for proof was not only awkward—see, for instance, the Ferrari-Cardano solution for the biquadratic in *The Great Art*[10]—but it could and would be inhibiting for progress in the higher powers.

A third point of interest in his work is his insistence that the key to knowing how to solve equations is to understand how they are built up in the first place[11]—an idea that, looked at through today's eyes, would seem to be so obvious as not even to need stating. But his insistence on it and his constant practice of it loom large in his works, and undoubtedly led him to many of his most important results.

A subsidiary to this insistence and practice was his attempt, in the cases of quadratic and cubic equations, to state their components—the unknown, the affecting parts, and the given, in terms of the components of a proportion.[12] Though the possibility of converting proportions to equations and vice versa was not original with him, he regarded the equation-proportion relationship as fundamental. It was an interesting exercise, but not one that bore much fruit.

These methodological advances, particularly the first two, were accompanied by a striving for generalizations that frequently exceeded Viète's reach but that, given the further developments of the next generation, were very fruitful. Three examples will make this clear. The first is his near approach to the biquadratic formula as Descartes developed it. We can see this in the *Preliminary Notes*.[13] This, in turn, led him, we may believe, to his method—again almost generalized, but not quite—set out in his *Amendment of Equations*[14] for getting rid of the next-to-highest power in any equation. The third example, which also comes from the *Preliminary Notes*,[15] is that of the rules for multiplying an angle of a right triangle and

---

Opera Mathematica, pp. 305ff.), in which Adriaen van Roomen used circled superior figures in setting out his problem and Viète his familiar *Q, C, QQ, QC*, etc., in his response.

[10] Girolamo Cardano, *The Great Art,* trans. T. Richard Witmer (Cambridge, Mass., M.I.T. Press, 1958), pp. 237ff.

[11] See p. 159.

[12] See pp. 161–70

[13] Proposition XI, p. 39

[14] Chapter I.

[15] Propositions XLVIII–LI, pp. 72–74.

for finding the functions of the new angle that results. Thus, putting his conclusions into modern terms, he almost, but not quite, reached the formulae

$$\cos n\alpha = \cos^n\alpha - \frac{n(n-1)}{1 \cdot 2} \cos^{n-2}\alpha \sin^2\alpha$$

$$+ \frac{n(n-1)(n-2)(n-3)}{1 \cdot 2 \cdot 3 \cdot 4} \cos^{n-4}\alpha \sin^{4\alpha} - \cdots$$

$$\sin n\alpha = n \cos^{n-1}\alpha \sin\alpha - \frac{n(n-1)(n-2)}{1 \cdot 2 \cdot 3} \cos^{n-3}\alpha \sin^3\alpha$$

$$+ \frac{n(n-1)(n-2)(n-3)(n-4)}{1 \cdot 2 \cdot 3 \cdot 4 \cdot 5} \cos^{n-5}\alpha \sin^5\alpha - \cdots$$

Beyond these rather general contributions to the study of mathematics, the historians and others who have written about Viète have singled out a number of specific outstanding contributions of his. If he himself were asked what he considered the most important, he would probably point (as he did toward the end of the *Introduction to the Analytic Art*[16]) to his methods of trisecting an angle,[17] of finding two or more proportionals between given quantities,[18] and of discovering the value of a regular heptagon inscribed in a circle.[19] Another great mathematician, commenting on his contributions, laid particular stress on his application of algebra to geometry, thus reversing the historic role of geometry as the mother of algebra and its great nurturer.[20] And Henry Percy, Earl of Northumberland, a student of his works, who edited and brought out Thomas Harriot's *Artis Analyticae Praxis,*[21] a direct descendant of Viète's work, was particularly impressed with the Viète's method for the numerical solution of equations.[22] Others have pointed to his discovery of the solution of the

[16]Introduction, p. 28.

[17]Supplement to Geometry, Proposition IX, p. 398.

[18]Ibid., Propositions V–VII, p. 392–96.

[19]Ibid., Proposition XXIV, p. 413.

[20]Said Joseph Fourier of Viète: "He resolved questions of geometry by algebraic analysis and from the solutions deduced geometric problems. His researches led him to the theory of angular sections and he formulated general rules to express the values of chords. . . ." Quoted in *La Grande Encyclopedie,* vol. 31, p. 972 (Paris, Societé Anonyme de la Grande Encyclopedie, 1901).

[21]London, 1631.

[22]The connecting link between Viète and Henry Percy, and hence Thomas Harriot, appears to have been Nathaniel Torporley, a student of Viète's who, upon his return to England, was employed by Percy.

"irreducible case" of the cubic, to his statement of the law of tangents,

$$\frac{a + b}{a - b} = \frac{\tan \frac{1}{2}(a + b)}{\tan \frac{1}{2}(a - b)},\ [23]$$

to his demonstration that

$$2/\pi = \sqrt{\tfrac{1}{2}} \times \sqrt{\tfrac{1}{2} + \tfrac{1}{2}\sqrt{\tfrac{1}{2}}} \times \sqrt{\tfrac{1}{2} + \tfrac{1}{2}\sqrt{\tfrac{1}{2} + \tfrac{1}{2}\ \sqrt{\tfrac{1}{2}}}} \cdots,\ [24]$$

to his exposition of the various ways in which given equations can be transformed into more usable forms,[25] and to his tour de force in providing almost overnight twenty-three answers to the equation posed for solution by Adriaen van Roomen:[26]

$$45x - 3795x^3 + 95,634x^5 - 1,138,500x^7 \ldots$$

$$+ 945x^{41} - 45x^{43} + x^{45} = N$$

To say all this is, however, not enough. Not everything that Viète proposed has stood the test of time. One item in particular in his insistence on endowing coefficients with dimensions such that all terms in any given equation will be of the same degree.[27] Though he lays great store by this, it quickly became merely an unnecessary encumbrance and was dropped.

In addition, the one great lack in Viète's work is his disregard for the possibility of negative solutions for equations. Though he recognized that equations, or at least certain types of equations, may have multiple solutions, he gives no hint as to why he disregarded or overlooked or rejected—choose whichever verb you will—the possibility of negative solutions and, except in one or two instances which seem to have been inadvertent, he studiously avoids cases which clearly lead to them, and eschews any discussion of them. This makes one wonder, other evidence to the contrary notwithstanding, how carefully he had studied Cardano, for in this regard he obviously fell several steps behind his great predecessor and fell far short of contributing to the theory of equations as much as he was capable of contributing.

[23] In the *Canon Mathematicus*. I owe this reference to Morris Kline, *Mathematical Thought from Ancient to Modern Times* (New York, Oxford University Press, 1972), p. 239. I cannot, however, supply a page reference since Kline does not do so and no copy of the *Canon* is available to me.

[24] See Chapter XVIII, Proposition II, of the *Variorum de Rebus Mathematicis Responsorum Liber VIII* (Tours, 1593); reprinted in the *Opera Mathematica*, pp. 400.

[25] This is the subject of the book on the *Understanding and Amendment of Equations*, pp. 159–311.

[26] See the *Ad Problema Quod Omnibus Mathematicis Totius Orbis Construendum Proposuit Adrianus Romanus*, supra n. 9, p. 5.

[27] See particularly Chapter III of the *Introduction to the Analytic Art*, pp. 15–17 infra.

All of the works contained in this volume are included in the *Opera Mathematica* of Viète, edited by Frans van Schooten and published in Leyden in 1646.[28] In addition to the van Schooten edition, there are the following prints of the individual works contained in this volume:

Isagoge in Artem Analyticem[29] *(Introduction to the Analytic Art)*— Tours, 1591; Paris, 1624; Paris, 1631, with extensive notes by Jean de Beaugrand, many of which were carried into van Schooten's edition; Leyden, 1635.[30]

Ad Logisticem Speciosam Notae Priores (Preliminary Notes to Symbolic Logistic)—Paris, 1631, with notes by Jean de Beaugrand.

Zeteticorum Libri Quinque (Five Books of Zetetica)—Tours, 1591 or 1593.[31]

De Aequationum Recognitione et Emendatione Tractatus Duo (Two Treatises on the Understanding and Amendment of Equations)—Paris, 1615, with an introduction by Alexander Anderson.

De Numerosa Potestatum ad Exegesin Resolutione (On the Numerical Resolution of Powers by Exegetics)—Paris, 1600, with an afterword by Marino Ghetaldi.

Effectionum Geometricarum Canonica Recensio (A Canonical Survey of Geometric Constructions)—Tours, 1593.[32]

Supplementum Geometriae (A Supplement to Geometry)—Tours, 1593.

Ad Angularium Sectionum Analyticen Theoremata[33] *(Universal Theorems on the Analysis of Angular Sections)*—Paris, 1615, with proofs supplied by Alexander Anderson.

In preparing this translation, I have seen and used all the above editions with the exception of the *Supplementum Geometriae,* which was not available to me. References in the footnotes to the translation to these editions as well as to the *Opera Mathematica* are by date alone.

In addition, there have been four translations of the *Introduction* into

---

[28] A facsimile reprint was published in Hildesheim in 1970.

[29] As noted at the heads of the text of the translation of this work and the next, the title varies slightly from one edition to another.

[30] The copy of this edition that I have seen lacks the first four chapters.

[31] 1593 is the date given by both Ritter and Hofmann. The copy that I have seen from the Harvard University Library lacks a title page, but the library catalog lists it as 1591. So also for the listing in the catalog of the Bibliotheque Nationale, Paris. In the introduction to his translation of Diophantus, *Les Six Livres Arithmétiques* (Bruges, Desclee, De Brouwer et Cie, 1926), Paul Ver Ecke gives 1591 as the date on p. lxxix and 1593 as the date on p. xxxviii.

[32] The copy I have seen lacks a title page with place and date; these have been supplied from other sources.

[33] Title varies slightly from one edition to another.

French: those of Jean-Louis Vaulezard,[34] Antoine Vasset,[35] Nicholas Durret,[36] and Frederic Ritter.[37] Ritter also published a French translation of the *Preliminary Notes*;[38] Vaulezard and Vasset translations of the *Zetetica*;[39] and Durret a translation of the *Geometric Constructions* and part of the *Numerical Resolution.*[40]

Except for the *Introduction,* there have been no translations into English of which I am aware. The *Introduction* was translated by J. Winfree Smith and published as an appendix to Jacob Klein's *Greek Mathematical Thought and the Origin of Algebra.*[41]

These French and English translations are referred to in the footnotes in this book by the name of the translator alone.[42]

In addition to the above, I have occasionally found helpful Carlo Renaldini's *Opus Algebricum,*[43] a work which contains generous chunks of Viète practically intact, but with occasional explanatory interpolations, and James Hume's *Algèbre de Viète, d'une Methode Nouvelle, Claire et Facile.*[44] These are referred to by the authors' names.

This translation was begun many years ago at the suggestion of the late Professor Frederic Barry of Columbia University. Its initial stage was supported by a grant from the Columbia University Council for Research in the Humanities.

---

[34]*Introduction en l'Art Analytic, ou Novelle Algèbre* (Paris, 1630), with annotations by the translator.

[35]*L'Algèbre Nouvelle de Mr Viete* (Paris, 1630), with a lengthy introduction (which includes many criticisms of Vaulezard's translation) by the translator.

[36]*L'Algèbre, Effections Geometriques et Partie de l'Exegetique Nombreuse de Viète* (Paris, 1694), with accompanying notes.

[37]*Introduction a l'Art Analytique,* in *Bullettino di Bibliographa e di Storia delle Scienze Matematiche e Fisiche,* vol. I, pp. 228 (Rome, 1868).

[38]*Première Série de Notes sur la Logistique Spécieuse,* in ibid p. 245ff.

[39]See nn. 34 and 35 above.

[40]See n. 36 above.

[41]Cambridge, Mass., M.I.T. Press, 1968.

[42]In the case of Ritter, references to his sketch of Viète's life are distinguished from his translation by appending "biog." to his name.

[43]Ancona, 1644.

[44]Paris, 1636.

INTRODUCTION TO THE ANALYTIC ART[1]

CHAPTER I

On the Meaning and Components of Analysis and on Matters Useful to Zetetics

There is a certain way of searching for the truth in mathematics that Plato is said first to have discovered. Theon called it analysis, which he defined as assuming that which is sought as if it were admitted [and working] through the consequences [of that assumption] to what is admittedly true, as opposed to synthesis, which is assuming what is [already] admitted [and working] through the consequences [of that assumption] to arrive at and to understand that which is sought.[2]

Although the ancients propounded only [two kinds of] analysis, zetetics and poristics,[3] to which the definition of Theon best applies, I have

[1] The title varies slightly in the different editions of this work: 1591, 1624, and 1631 have *In Artem Analyticem Isagoge*, 1635 has *In Artem Analyticam Isagoge*, and 1646 has *In Artem Analyticen Isagoge*.

[2] T. L. Heath, in vol. III, p. 442, of his second edition of Euclid's *Elements* (Cambridge, The University Press, 1925) points out that these definitions were interpolated in Book XIII before Theon's time and have been variously attributed to Theaetetus, Eudoxus, and Heron. See also the definitions of the same terms by Pappus as translated by Heath in his essay on "Mathematics and Astronomy" in *The Legacy of Greece*, ed. R. W. Livingstone (Oxford University Press, 1921), p. 102.

[3] ζητητιὴν καὶ ποριστικὴν. Viète apparently borrowed these two terms, but not the meanings he attributes to them, from Pappus who, in *The Treasury of Analysis*, said: "Now analysis is of two kinds, one, whose object is to seek the truth [ζητητικὸν], being called theoretical, and the other, whose object is to find something set for finding [ποριστικὸν], being called problematical. . . ." Quoted in *Selections Illustrating the History of Greek Mathematics*, tr. Ivor Thomas (Cambridge, Mass., Loeb Classical Library, 1941), p. 599. Compare Beaugrand's notes to his edition of this work of Viète's (1631, p. 25): "Porro Analysis veterum duplex, una theorematica, qua Theorematis oblati veritas examinatur. Altera Problematica, cuius dua sunt partes; prior qua propositi Problematis solutio inquiritur Zetetice vocatur;

added a third, which may be called rhetics or exegetics.[4] It is properly zetetics by which one sets up an equation or proportion[5] between a term that is to be found and the given terms, poristics by which the truth of a stated theorem is tested by means of an equation or proportion,[6] and exegetics by which the value of the unknown term in a given equation or proportion is determined. Therefore the whole analytic art, assuming this three-fold function for itself, may be called the science of correct discovery in mathematics.

Now whatever pertains to zetetics begins, in accordance with the art of logic, with syllogisms and enthymemes the premises of which are those

---

posterior quae determinat quando, qua ratione, et quot modis fieri possit Problema Poristice dici potest." This definition is picked up and followed by Durret in the notes to his translation (p. 6), by Jacques Ozanam in his *Dictionaire Mathematique* (Amsterdam, 1691) and, as far as it concerns poristics, by Alexandre Saverein in his *Dictionnaire Universel de Mathematique et de Physique* (Paris, 1753), vol. II, p. 314.

[4]The vagaries of sixteenth-century punctuation and the ambiguity of the word *constitui* make the reading of the end of this sentence and the beginning of the next uncertain. In the Latin we have *constitui tamen etiam tertiam speciem, quae dicitur* ῥητικὴ ἢ ἐξηγητικὴ *consentaneum est, ut sit Zetetice qua invenitur*, etc. An alternative reading to the one adopted above, would be, ". . . it is proper to add a third type which may be called rhetics or exegetics. Hence it is zetetics by which. . . ." Ritter, Vasset, and Smith so read the passage; Vaulezard and Durret read it as given above.

[5]1624 has *aequalitas proportione*, an error for *aequalitas proportiove*.

[6]*Poristice, qua de aequalitate vel proportione ordinati Theorematis veritas examinatur.* The question arises whether Viète is speaking of testing a theorem derived from an equation or proportion or of testing a theorem by means of an equation or proportion. Either fits his language and its context. Vaulezard translates this passage, "Le Poristique, par lequel est enquis de la verité du Theoreme ordonné, par l'egalité ou proportiõ"; Vasset, "La Poristicque est celle par laquelle on examine la verité d'un Theoreme déja ordonné, par le moyen de l'égalité ou proportion"; Durret, "La Poristique, celle par le moyẽ de laquelle on examine la verité du Theoréme ordonné touchant l'egalité, ou proportion"; Ritter, "par la méthode Poristique on examine, au moyen de l'égalité ou de la proportion, la verité d'un théorème enoncé"; and Smith, "a poristic art by which from the equation or proportion the truth of the theorem set up is investigated." Vaulezard offers a further explanation that the task of poristics is to "examiner & tenter si les Theoremes & consequences trouvées par le Zetetique sont veritables." Compare the passage from Beaugrand, n. 3 supra, and the illustrations he gives on pp. 75ff. of his edition of Viète's work.

Thomas Harriot, in his *Artis Analyticae Praxis* (London, 1631), p. 2, throws a little further light on his century's understanding of the difference between the zetetic and the poristic processes: "Veteres Analystae praeter Zeteticen quae ad problematum solutionem proprie pertinet aliam Aanlycices [sic] speciem fecerunt poristicen. . . . Methodus enim utriusque Analytica est, ab assumpto probando tanquam concesso per consequentia ad verum concessum. In hoc tamen inter se differunt, quod Zetetice quaestionem deducit ad aequale datum scil. quaesito, poristice autem ad idem, vel concessum. . . . Unde et altera inter eas oritur differentia quod in poristice, cum processus eius terminetur in identitate vel concesso, ulterior resolutione non sit opus (ut fit in Zetetice) ad propositi finalem verificationem."

No work of Viète's on poristics is extant and there is no certainty that he ever wrote one.

fundamental rules[7] with which equations and proportions are established. These are derived from axioms and from theorems created by analysis itself. Zetetics, however, has its own method of proceeding. It no longer limits its reasoning to numbers, a shortcoming of the old analysts, but works with a newly discovered symbolic logistic[8] which is far more fruitful and powerful than numerical logistic for comparing magnitudes with one another. It rests on the law of homogeneous terms first and then sets up, as it were, a formal series or scale of terms ascending or descending proportionally from class to class in keeping with their nature[9] and, [by this

---

At two places in his work on *A Supplement to Geometry,* however, (p. 388ff. infra) he uses the expression *inventum est in Poristicis* with the possible implication that there was once such a work. It is not out of the question that he treated of poristics at length in the now-lost *Ad Logisticem Speciosam Notae Posteriores.*

[7] *symbola*

[8] *per logisticem sub specie.* In Chapter III this becomes *Logistice speciosa* (algebra) in contrast to *Logistice numerosa* (arithmetic). On the history of the word "logistic," see David Eugene Smith, *History of Mathematics* (Boston, 1925), vol. II, pp. 7, 392, and Jacob Klein, *Greek Mathematical Thought and the Origin of Algebra,* tr. Eva Brann (Cambridge, Mass., 1968), passim.

Viète's curious words *sub specie* and *speciosa* have called forth a variety of comments and explanations: One, by John Wallis in his *Treatise of Algebra* (London, 1685), p. 66, is to the effect that Viète's use of *species* reflects his familiarity with the civil law where the word, Wallis says, is used to designate unknown or indefinite defendants in what we today would call "John Doe" cases; Wallis's view appears to be an expansion of that of Harriot, op. cit., supra n. 6, p. 1, that the meaning of the phrase *in specie* derives *ex usu forensi recepto speciei vocabulo.* Another, by Samuel Jeake in his Λογιστικηλογία (London, 1696), p. 334, has it that this "name . . . with the Latins serveth for the Figure, Form or shape of any thing" and that, accordingly, "*Species* are Quantities or Magnitudes, denoted by Letters, signifying Numbers, Lines, Lineats, Figures Geometrical, &c." Alexandre Saverein's *Dictionnaire Universel de Mathematique et de Physique* (Paris, 1753), vol. I, p. 17, says that the expression "algébre spécieuse" derives from that fact that quantities are represented by letters which designate "leur forme et leur espece," adding "d'ou vient le mot spécieuse." Ritter (p. 232, n. 3), on the other hand, thinks Viète coined a new meaning for an old word, the new meaning having no connection with its meanings in Latin or French. Still another explanation is offered in such modern French dictionaries as Littré's, for example, where the word "spécieux" is said to come directly from the Latin *speciosa* with its meaning of "beautiful in appearance" and the phrase "Arithmétique spécieuse" is explained by saying that it is "ainsi dite à cause de la beauté de l'algèbre par rapport à l'arithmétique." Smith thinks Diophantus "the most likely source for Vieta's use of the word 'species' " and that it is, in effect, his substitute for Diophantus' εἶδος. I am inclined to believe that Viète chose to give the noun *species,* with its meanings of "appearance," "semblance," "likeness," etc. and no doubt with an appreciation of its ancillary overtones, the somewhat enlarged meaning of a representation or symbol and have translated accordingly.

[9] *ex genere ad genus vi sua proportionaliter.* The phrase *vi sua proportionaliter* in this context is troublesome. Vaulezard translates it as "de leur propre puissance," Vasset as "d'elles-meme proportionellement," Durret as "proportionellement par leur force," Ritter as "proportionellement pour leur propre puissance," and Smith as "by their own nature."

series,] designates and distinguishes the grades and natures of terms used in comparisons.

CHAPTER II

On the Fundamental Rules of Equations and Proportions

Analysis accepts as proven the well-known fundamental rules of equations and proportions that are given in the *Elements*. They are these:

1. The whole is equal to [the sum of] its parts.
2. Things equal to the same thing are equal to each other.
3. If equals are added to equals, the sums are equal.
4. If equals are subtracted from equals, the remainders are equal.
5. If equals are multiplied by equals, the products are equal.
6. If equals are divided by equals, the quotients are equal.
7. Whatever are in proportion directly are in proportion inversely and alternately.
8. If similar proportionals are added to similar proportionals, the sums are proportional.
9. If similar proportionals are subtracted from similar proportionals, the remainders are proportional.
10. If proportionals are multiplied proportionally, the products are proportional.
11. If proportionals are divided proportionally, the quotients are proportional.
12. An equation or ratio is not changed by common multiplication or division [of its terms].
13. The [sum of the] products of the several parts [of a whole] is equal to the product of the whole.
14. Consecutive multiplications of terms and consecutive divisions of terms yield the same results regardless of the order in which the multiplication or division of the terms is carried out.[10]

A sovereign rule,[11] moreover, in equations and proportions, one that is of great importance throughout analysis, is this:

---

[10]*Facta continue sub magnitudinibus, vel ex iis continue orta, esse aequalia quocumque magnitudinum ordine ductio vel adplicatio fiat.*

[11]*κύριον . . . symbolum.*

15. If there are three or four terms such that the product of the extremes is equal to the square of the mean or the product of the means, they are proportionals. Conversely,

16. If there are three or four terms and the first is to the second as the second or third is to the last, the product of the extremes will be equal to the product of the means.

Thus a proportion may be said to be that from which an equation is composed and an equation that into which a proportion resolves itself.[12]

CHAPTER III

On the Law of Homogeneous Terms and on the Grades and the Kinds of Magnitudes of Comparison

[1] The prime and perpetual law of equations or proportions which, since it deals with their homogeneity, is called the law of homogeneous terms, is this:

Homogeneous terms must be compared with homogeneous terms,[13]

for, as Adrastos said,[14] it is impossible to understand how heterogeneous terms [can] affect each other. Thus,

If one magnitude is added to another, the latter is homogeneous with the former.

If one magnitude is subtracted from another, the latter is homogeneous with the former.

If one magnitude is multiplied by another, the product is heterogeneous to [both] the former and the latter.

---

[12] *Itaque proportio dici cõstitution aequalitatis. Aequalitas, resolutio proportionis.* This cryptic sentence summarizes a good deal of Viète's approach to algebra, as will become apparent later on. In addition, the word *constitutio* is one of his favorites. Vasset and Ritter translate it in this place by "établissement" or "establissement," Vaulezard and Durret by "constitution," and Smith by "composition." In many other places in this book, I have rendered it by "structure" or the like.

[13] *Homogenea homogeneis comparari.*

[14] Viète's source for Adrastos's dictum was probably Theon's Euclid. It is quoted by Jacob Klein, op. cit. supra n. 8, p. 276, n. 253. See p. 173 for Klein's appraisal of the use Viète makes of it. On Adrastos himself—he lived in Aphrodias in the first half of the second century—see George Sarton, *Introduction to the History of Science* (Baltimore, 1927), vol. I, p. 271.

If one magnitude is divided[15] by another, [the quotient] is heterogeneous to the former [i.e., to the dividend].

Much of the fogginess and obscurity of the old analysts is due to their not
having been attentive to these [rules].

2. Magnitudes that ascend or descend proportionally in keeping with
their nature from one kind to another are called scalar terms.

3. The first of the scalar magnitudes is the side or root.[16] [Then
follow:]

2. The square
3. The cube
4. The square-square
5. The square-cube
6. The cubo-cube
7. The square-square-cube
8. The square-cubo-cube
9. The cubo-cubo-cube

and so on, naming the others in [accordance with] this same series and by
this same method.[17]

4.[18] The kinds of magnitudes of comparison,[19] naming them in the
same order as the scalar terms, are:

1. Length or breadth
2. Plane
3. Solid
4. Plano-plane

---

[15]*adplicatur,* Viète's usual term for the verb "divide," though he sometimes uses
dividere. Durret (p. 14) comments on the difference between "application" and "division"
thus: "car l'application differe de la division, en ce que le genre de la grandeur engendrée, ou
quotient, est tousiours heterogene au genre de la grandeur appliquée; mais au contraire le
quotient de la division est tousiours homogene au genre de la grandeur divisée." In the latter
case, for instance, the division of a line into, say, three parts, gives three lines that are
homogeneous with the original line, whereas the "application" of a plane by a length gives
another length which is not homogeneous with the plane.

[16]*Latus, seu Radix.* Viète's more usual term is *latus.* Elsewhere he uses *radix* with a
somewhat different meaning; see n. 54 infra.

[17]In most places in this translation, I have replaced Viète's nomenclature by the more
familiar terms "first power" ... "fourth power," "fifth power," etc., or, when his terms are
attached to letters, by the use of numerical exponents in the modern form.

[18]In the text this and the next three paragraphs are misnumbered 7, 8, 9 and 10.

[19]*magnitudinum comparatorum.* Viète usually uses *homogeneum comparationis* for the
singular form of this expression. In either case it means the purely numerical terms with which
the variable terms are equated or compared. The same length-plane-solid-etc. terminology
that Viète uses here is also used by him for his coefficients, but he calls these *subgraduales.*

5. Plano-solid
6. Solido-solid
7. Plano-plano-solid
8. Plano-solido-solid
9. Solido-solido-solid

and so on, naming the others in [accordance with] the same series and by the same method.[20]

5. In a series of scalar terms, the highest, counting up from the root, is called the power. The term of comparison [must be] consistent with this. The other lower scalar terms are [referred to as] lower-order terms.[21]

6. A power is pure when it lacks any affection. It is affected when[22] it is associated [by addition or subtraction] with a homogeneous term that is the product of a lower-order term and a supplemental term [or] coefficient.[23]

7. A supplemental term the product of which and a lower-order term is homogeneous with the power it [i.e., the product] affects is called a coefficient.[24]

CHAPTER IIII[25]

On the Rules of Symbolic Logistic

Numerical logistic is [a logistic] that employs numbers, symbolic logistic one that employs symbols or signs for things[26] as, say, the letters of the alphabet.

---

[20]Later on it will often be convenient to abbreviate these rather clumsy terms by showing them as exponents. For instance *B plano-solidum* will appear as B^{ps} and *X solido-solidum* as X^{ss}, and so forth.

[21]*gradus parodici ad potestatem.*

[22]The text has *cui*, which I read as a misprint for *cum.*

[23]*adscita coefficiente magnitudine.* Ritter translates this as "une grandeur étrangère coefficiente," Vasset as "une grandeur coëfficiente empruntée," Vaulezard as "une grandeur adscitice coeficiente," and Durret as "la grandeur coeficiente adiointe."

[24]*Subgraduales.* I take it that, rather than using *sub* to indicate that the "subgradual" is of lower degree than the "gradual," Viète here uses it to indicate multiplication (cf. n. 29 infra)—that is, a "subgradual" is a multiplier of a "gradual," i.e., of a degree of the unknown lower than the power.

[25]1591 and other early editions of Viète's works use this form of the Roman numeral.

[26]*Logistice numerosa est quae per numeros, Speciosa quae per species seu formas exhibitur.* The translations of this passage vary greatly. Vasset has "La Logistique nombreuse est celle qui s'exerce par les nombres. Et la specieuse est celle qui se pratique par les especes ou

There are four basic rules for symbolic logistic just as there are for numerical logistic:

RULE I

To add one magnitude to another

Let there be two magnitudes, A and B. One is to be added to the other.

Since one magnitude is to be added to another, and homogeneous and heterogeneous terms do not affect each other, the two magnitudes proposed are homogeneous. (Greater or less do not constitute differences in kind.) Therefore they will be properly added by the signs of conjunction or addition and their sum will be A plus B, if they are simple lengths or breadths. But if they are higher up in the series set out above or if, by their nature, they correspond to higher terms, they should be properly designated as, say, A^2 plus B^p, or A^3 plus B^s, and so forth for the rest.

Analysts customarily indicate a positive affection by the symbol $+$.

RULE II

To subtract one magnitude from another

Let there be two magnitudes, A and B, the former the greater, the latter the less. The smaller is to be subtracted from the greater.

Since one magnitude is to be substracted from another and homogeneous and heterogeneous magnitudes do not affect one another, the two given magnitudes are homogeneous. (Greater or less do not constitute differences in kind.) Therefore the subtraction of the smaller from the larger is properly made by the sign of disjunction or subtraction, and the disjoint terms will be A minus B if they are only simple lengths or breadths. But if they are higher up in the series set out above or if, by their nature, they correspond to higher terms, they should be properly designated as, say, A^2 minus B^p, or A^3 minus B^s, and so forth for the rest.

The process is no different if the subtrahend is affected, since the whole and its parts ought not to be thought of as being subject to different

---

formes, mesmes des choses"; Vaulezard has "Le Logistique Numerique est celui qui est exhibé & traité par les nombres, le Specifique par especes ou formes des choses"; Durret has "La logistique nombreuse est celle, qui se fait par les nombres; la specieuse, par les especes, ou formes des choses"; Ritter has "Logistique numérale est celle qui est exposée par des nombres. Logistique spécieuse est celle qui est exposée par des signes ou de figures"; and Smith has "The numerical reckoning operates with numbers; the reckoning by species operates with species or forms of things."

rules. Thus if B plus D is to be subtracted from A, the remainder will be A minus B minus D, the terms B and D having been subtracted individually.

But if D should be subtracted from this same B and B minus D is to be subtracted from A, the remainder will be A minus B plus D, since in substracting the magnitude B, more than enough, to the extent of D, has been taken away and compensation must therefore be made by adding it.

Usually analysts indicate a negative affection by the symbol $-$. And this is what Diophantus calls λεῖψ's, as he calls the affection of addition ὕπαρξ's.[27]

If, however, it is not stated which term is greater and which smaller and yet a subtraction is to be made, the sign of difference is $=$, i.e., an undetermined negative. Thus supposing we had A^2 and B^p, the difference would be $A^2 = B^p$, or $B^p = A^2$.[28]

RULE III

To multiply one magnitude by another

Let there be two magnitudes, A and B. One is to be multiplied by the other.

Since one magnitude is to be multiplied by another, they will produce a magnitude heterogeneous to themselves. The product may conveniently be designated by the word *times* or *by*,[29] as in A *times* B which means that the latter is multiplied by the former or, otherwise, that the result is A *by* B.

[The magnitudes are stated] simply if A and B are simple lengths or breadths, but if they are higher up on the scale or if, by their nature, they correspond to higher terms, it is well to give them the proper designations of the scalar terms or of those of corresponding nature, as, say, A^2 times B or A^2 times B^p or B^s, and so on for the others.

The operation is no different if the magnitudes to be multiplied or either of them consist of two or more terms, since the whole is equal to [the sum of] its parts and, therefore, the [sum of the] products of the parts of any magnitude is equal to the product of the whole.

If a positive term of one quantity is multiplied by a positive term of

---

[27]These two Greek terms have been variously translated as "defection" and "existence" (Vaulezard), "diminution" and "adionction" (Vasset), "diminution" and "augmentation" (Durret), "soustraction" and "addition" (Ritter), "defect" and "presence" (Smith), and "deficiency" and "forthcoming" or "minus" and "plus" (Ivor Thomas, op. cit., supra n. 3).

[28]In order to avoid confusion hereafter, the symbol $=$ will be used as it is normally used today (Viète had no sign for equality) and the modern symbol $\sim$ will be substituted for Viète's $=$.

[29]The Latin terms are *in* and *sub*.

another quantity, the product will be positive and if by a negative the result will be negative. The consequence of this rule is that multiplying a negative by a negative produces a positive, as when $A - B$ is multiplied by $D - G$.[30] The product of $+A$ and $-G$ is negative, but this takes away or subtracts too much[31] since A is not the exact magnitude to be multiplied. Similarly the product of $-B$ and $+D$ is negative, which takes away too much since D is not the exact magnitude to be multiplied. The positive product when $-B$ is multiplied by $-G$ makes up for this.

The names of the products of the magnitudes ascending proportionally from one kind to another are these:

x times itself yields x^2
x times x^2 yields x^3
x times x^3 yields x^4
x times x^4 yields x^5
x times x^5 yields x^6.

Likewise the other way around: That is, x^2 times x produces x^3; x^3 times x produces x^4; and so forth.

Again,

x^2 times itself yields x^4
x^2 times x^3 yields x^5
x^2 times x^4 yields x^6

and likewise the other way around.

Again,

x^3 times itself yields x^6
x^3 times x^4 yields x^7
x^3 times x^5 yields x^8
x^3 times x^6 yields x^9

and likewise the other way around, and beyond this in the same order.

Similarly with the homogeneous terms:

A breadth times a length produces a plane
A breadth times a plane produces a solid
A breadth times a solid produces a plano-plane
A breadth times a plano-plane produces a plano-solid
A breadth times a plano-solid produces a solido-solid

and likewise the other way around.

[30] 1646 has $A \sim B$ and $D \sim G$.

[31] 1624 has *quod est minus negare minuereve;* 1591, 1631, and 1646 have *quod est nimium negare minuereve.*

A plane times a plane produces a plano-plane
A plane times a solid produces a plano-solid
A plane times a plano-solid produces a solido-solid

and likewise the other way around.

A solid times a solid produces a solido-solid
A solid times a plano-plane produces a plano-plano-solid
A solid times a plano-solid produces a plano-solido-solid[32]
A solid times a solido-solid produces a solido-solido-solid

and likewise the other way around, and beyond this in the same order.

RULE IIII

To divide one magnitude by another.

Let there be two magnitudes, A and B. One is to be divided by the other.

Since one magnitude is to be divided by another and higher terms are [always] divided by lower and homogeneous by heterogeneous, the magnitudes are heterogeneous. Let A be a length and B a plane. Accordingly, it is convenient for a line to be drawn between B, the higher term, which is to be divided, and A, the lower, by which the division is to be made.

These magnitudes should be labeled in accordance with their grades or the grades to which they are carried either on the scale of proportionals or on that of the homogeneous terms, as B^p/A. This symbol identifies the breadth that results from dividing the plane B by the length A. If B were given as a cube and A as a plane, it would be shown as B^3/A^p, which symbol indicates the breadth that results from dividing the cube B by the plane A. And if B were assumed to be a cube and A a length, it would be shown as B^3/A, which symbol indicates the plane that results from dividing the cube B by A. And so on in this order to infinity.

Nothing different will be observed for binomial or polynomial magnitudes.

The names of the quotients derived from dividing the magnitudes ascending proportionally from one kind to another are these:

x^2 divided by x yields x
x^3 divided by x yields x^2
x^4 divided by x yields x^3
x^5 divided by x yields x^4
x^6 divided by x yields x^5

[32] 1624 has "solido-solid"; 1591's similar error is corrected in its errata notes. 1624 also omits the next line completely.

and the other way around. That is, x^3 divided by x^2 yields x, x^4 divided by x^3 yields x, and so on.

Again,

x^4 divided by x^2 yields x^2
x^5 divided by x^2 yields x^3
x^6 divided by x^2 yields x^4

and the other way around.

Again,

x^{733} divided by x^3 yields x^4
x^8 divided by x^3 yields x^5
x^9 divided by x^3 yields x^6

and the other way around, and so on in the same order.

Likewise in the homogeneous terms,

A plane divided by a breadth yields a length
A solid divided by a breadth yields a plane
A plano-plane divided by a breadth yields a solid
A plano-solid divided by a breadth yields a plano-plane
A solido-solid divided by a breadth yields a plano-solid

and the other way around.

A plano-plane divided by a plane yields a plane
A plano-solid divided by a plane yields a solid
A solido-solid divided by a plane yields a plano-plane

and the other way around.

A solido-solid divided by a solid yields a solid
A plano-plano-solid divided by a solid yields a plano-plane
A plano-solido-solid divided by a solid yields a plano-solid

A solido-solido-solid[34] divided by a solid yields a solido-solid

and the other way around, and so on in the same order.

Division does not foreclose the addition or subtraction of magnitudes or their multiplication or division in accordance with the foregoing rules. But notice that when the upper and lower magnitudes in a division are multiplied by the same magnitude, nothing is added to and nothing is taken

---

[33] 1591, 1624, and 1646 have x^6; 1631 is correct and also inserts another line reading "x^6 divided by x^3 yields x^3."

[34] 1624 has "plano-solido-solid."

away from the kind or value of the quotient since division resolves what multiplication effects, as BA/B equals A and BA^p/B equals A^p.

Thus in the case of addition: Suppose Z is to be added to A^p/B; the sum will be $(A^p + ZB)/B$. Or if Z^2/G is to be added to A^p/B, the sum will be $(GA^p + BZ^2)/BG$.

In subtraction: Z is to be subtracted from A^p/B; the remainder will be $(A^p - ZB)/B$. Or Z^2/G is to be subtracted from A^p/B; the remainder will be $(A^pG - Z^2B)/BG$.

In multiplication: A^p/B is to be multiplied by B; the result will be A^p. Or A^p/B is to be multiplied by Z; the result will be A^pZ/B. Or, finally A^p/B is to be multplied by Z^2/G; the result will be A^pZ^2/BG.

In division: A^3/B is to be divided by D; having multiplied both magnitudes by B, the quotient will be A^3/BD. Or BG is to be divided by A^p/D; both magnitudes being multiplied by D, the quotient will be BGD/A^p. Or, finally, B^3/Z is to be divided by A^3/D^p;[35] the quotient will be B^3D^p/ZA^3.

CHAPTER V

On the Rules of Zetetics

The manner of working in zetetics is, in general, contained in these rules:

1. If it is a length that is to be found and there is an equation or proportion latent in the terms proposed,[36] let x be that length.

2. If it is a plane that is to be found and there is an equation or proportion latent in the terms proposed, let x^2 be that plane.

3. If it is a solid that is to be found and there is an equation or proportion latent in the terms proposed, let x^3 be that solid.

What is to be found will, in short, rise or fall, in keeping with its nature, through the various grades of the magnitudes of comparison.

4. Magnitudes, both given and sought, are to be combined and compared, in accordance with the given statement of a problem, by adding, subtracting, multiplying and dividing, always observing the law of homogeneous terms.

Hence it is evident that in the end something will be found that is

---

[35] 1624 has A^3/A^p.

[36] *lateat autem aequalitas vel proportio sub involucris earum quae proponuntur.*

equal to the unknown or one of its powers. This may be made up entirely of given terms or it may be the product of given terms and the unknown or of those terms and a lower-order grade.

5. In order to assist this work by another device, given terms are distinguished from unknown by constant, general and easily recognized symbols, as (say) by designating unknown magnitudes by the letter A and the other vowels E, I, O, U and Y and given terms by the letters B, G, D and the other consonants.

6. Terms made up exclusively of given magnitudes are added to or subtracted from one another in accordance with the sign of their affection and consolidated into one. Let this be the homogeneous term of comparison or the constant[37] and put it on one side of the equation.

7. Likewise, terms made up of given quantities and the same lower-order grade are added to or subtracted from one another in accordance with the sign of their affection and consolidated into one. Let this be the homogeneous term of affection or the lower-order homogeneous term.[38]

8. Keep these lower-order homogeneous terms with the power they affect or by which they are affected and place them and the power on the other side of the equation. Hence the constant term will be designated in keeping with the nature and order of the power. It will be called pure if [the power] is free from affection. But if [the power] is accompanied by homogeneous terms of affection, show this by the [proper] symbols of affection and of degree along with any supplementary terms that are their coefficients.[39]

---

[37] *homogeneum comparationis, seu sub data mensura.* Cf. Hume p. 36: "La partie de l'equation sans voyelles est appellee par Viete *l'Homogene de comparaison,* ou contenu sous la grandeur donnee, parce que toutes les grandeurs signifiees par les consones sont cognuës; et partant toute ceste partie de l'equation est cognuë."

[38] *homogeneum adfectionis, seu sub gradu.*

[39] *Atque ideo homogeneum sub data mensura de potestate a suo genere vel ordine designata enuncietur, puro si quidem ea pura est ab adfectione, sin eam comitantur adfectionum homogenea indicat tum adfectionis, tum gradus symbolo, una cum ipsa, quae cum gradu coefficiet, adscititia magnitudine.* This passage is not without its difficulties. I think that what Viète is saying is that if, for instance, $x^3 = N$, N will be known as a pure cube and that if $x^3 + a^2x = N$, N will be known as a cube affected positively by a linear term with a coefficient of the second degree. This is borne out by the phraseology he employs in the books on the *Numerical Resolution of Pure and Affected Powers.* Smith, however, reads the passage this way: "And thus, the element that is homogeneous under a given measure will be equated to a power designated in its own genus or order; simply, if that power is free from all conjunction with other magnitudes, but if magnitudes homogeneous in conjunction accompany it, which magnitudes are indicated both by the symbol of conjunction and by the rung of the lower ladder magnitudes, then the magnitude homogeneous under a given measure will be equated not only to it, but to it along with the magnitudes that are products of rungs and coefficient magnitudes." Cf. the French translators. Vasset puts it thus: "& partant l'Homogene produict soubs la mesure donnee, sera énoncé de la puissance, laquelle puissance

9. If the constant happens to be associated with a subordinate homogeneous term, carry out a transposition.[40]

Transposition is a removal of affecting or affected terms from one side of an equation to the other with the contrary sign of affection. That an equation is not altered by this operation is now to be demonstrated:

PROPOSITION I

An equation is not changed by transposition.

Let

$$A^2 - D^p = G^2 - BA.$$

I say that

$$A^2 + BA = G^2 + D^p$$

and that the equation is not changed by this transposition with contrary signs of affection. For since[41]

$$A^2 - D^{p\,[42]} = G^2 - BA,$$

add $D^p + BA$ to both sides. Then by common agreement

$$A^2 - D^p + D^p + BA = G^2 - BA + D^p + BA.$$

The negative affection on each side of this equation cancels a positive: on one side the affection D^p vanishes, on the other the affection BA. This

---

prendra sa designation de son gendre, ou ordre purement, si elle est sans affection ou meslange; autrement si elle est affectee par des Homogenes d'affection, il la faudra designer, tant elle, que le genre de l'affection, qui pareillement le degré, que la qualité de la grandeur, qui sert de coëfficiente au degré." Vaulezard has: "C'est pourquoy l'Homogene sous la mesure donnee sera enoncé de la puissance de son genre ou ordre, sçavoir, purement si elle est pure et exempte d'affection, si elle est affectee, lors seront indiquees tant les Homogenes d'affection que les degrez, par les symboles d'iceux, ensemble ceste grandeur laquelle avec le degre faict l'adsitice." Durret translates this way: "Et partant l'homogene sous la mesure donnée sera énoncé de la puissance designée par son genre, ou par son ordre, sçavoir purement, si la puissance est pure, ou exêpte d'affectiõ; si ce n'est que les homogenes des affections l'accompagnent, étant indiquée, tant par la marque d'affection, que du degré avec la mesme grandeur adioodite, laquelle coaffecte avec le degré." And Ritter has: "et par conséquent l'homogène sous la mesure donnée sera énoncé de la puissance désignée par son genre ou ordre, purement si elle est pure d'affection, et, si elle n'est pas pure, les homogènes d'affection l'accompagneront et on indiquera le symbole soit de l'affection, soit du dégré avec la grandeur étrangère qui est coefficiente avec le dégré."

[40]*fiat Antithesis.*
[41]1591, 1624, and 1631 have *Quoniam cum;* 1635 has simply *Quoniam;* 1646 has *Quoniam enim.*
[42]1591, 1624, and 1635 have $B^p;$ 1631 and 1646 have D^p.

leaves

$$A^2 + BA = G^2 + D^p.$$

10. If it happens that all the magnitudes given are multiplied by a grade and that, therefore, no pure constant term is immediately apparent, carry out a depression.[43]

Depression is an equal lowering of the power and the lower-order terms in the observed order of the scale until the lowest variable term becomes a pure constant to which the others can be compared. That an equation is not changed by this operation is now to be demonstrated:

PROPOSITION II

An equation is not changed by depression

Let

$$A^3 + BA^2 = Z^p A.$$

I say that by depression

$$A^2 + BA = Z^p,$$

for all of these solids have been divided by a common divisor, [a process] that, it has been settled, does not change an equation.

11. If it happens that the highest grade of the unknown does not stand by itself but is multiplied by some given magnitude, carry out a reduction.[44]

Reduction is a common division[45] of the homogeneous magnitudes making up an equation by the given magnitude by which the highest grade of the unknown is multiplied so that this grade may lay claim to the title of power by itself and that from this an equation [in proper form] may finally remain. That an equation is not impaired by this operation is now to be demonstrated:

PROPOSITION III

An equation is not changed by reduction

Let

$$BA^2 + D^p A = Z^s.$$

---

[43] *fiat Hypobibasmus*
[44] *fiat Parabolismus.*
[45] 1624 and 1635 have "multiplication." The same error occurs in 1591 but is corrected in its errata notes.

I say that by reduction

$$A^2 + \frac{D^p A}{B} = \frac{Z^s}{B}$$

for all the solids have been divided by a common divisor, [a process] which, it has been settled, does not change an equation.

12. Following all this, an equation may be said to be clearly expressed and in proper order. [It may be] restated, if you wish, as a proportion, but with this particular warning: the product of the extreme terms [of the proportion] corresponds to the power plus the homogeneous terms of affection and the product of the mean terms corresponds to the constant.

13. Hence a properly constructed proportion may be defined as a series of three or four magnitudes so expressed in terms, either pure or affected, that all of them are givens except the one that is being sought or its power and its lower-order grades.

14. Finally, when an equation or proportion has been set up, zetetics may be said to have fulfilled its task.

Diophantus used zetetics most subtly of all in those books that have been collected in the *Arithmetic*. There he assuredly exhibits this method in numbers but not in symbols, for which it is nevertheless used. Because of this his ingenuity and quickness of mind are the more to be admired,[46] for things that appear to be very subtle and abstruse in numerical logistic are quite familiar and even easy in symbolic logistic.

CHAPTER VI

On the Examination of Theorems by Poristics

Zetetics having completed [its work], the analyst moves from hypothesis to thesis and presents the theorems derived from his discovery in the

---

[46]*Eam vero tanquam per numeros, non etiam per species, quibus tamen usus est, institutam exhibuit, quo sua esset magis admirationi subtilitas & solertia.* Smith translates this, "But he presented it as if established by means of numbers and not also by species (which, nevertheless, he used), in order that his subtlety and quickness of mind might be the more admired. . . ." The French translations are as follows: "Il l'a toutesfois laisee, comme l'ayant exercee par nombres, (encores qu'il se soit servy de la specieuse) affin de rendre sa subtilité plus recommendable. . . ." (Vasset); "mais comme il a donné son institut par les nombres et non par especes; (desquelles toutefois il s'est servi:) c'est en quoy la subtilité et ingeniosité de son esprit est grandement à admirer. . . ." (Vaulezard); "Il là instituée comme par nombres, &

form prescribed by the art comformably to the laws[47] κάτὰ παντὸς, καθ αὐτὰ, καθόλου πρῶτον.[48]

Such [theorems], although they are demonstrated by and grounded in zetetics, are still subject to the rules of synthesis, which is rated the most rational method of demonstration.[49] If necessary, they are confirmed by it, this being a great miracle of the inventive art. So the footsteps of analysis are retraced. This is itself [a form of] analysis and, thanks to the introduction of symbolic logistic, is no longer difficult. But if some unfamiliar discovery is presented or has been stumbled on fortuitously and its truth must be weighed and inquired into, the poristic way should first be tried. It will be easy to return to synthesis later on. Examples of this are given by Theon in the *Elements*, by Apollonius of Perga in the *Conics*, and by Archimedes in his various books.

CHAPTER VII

On the Function of Rhetics

An equation having been set up with a magnitude that is to be found, rhetics or exegetics, which is the remaining part of analysis and[50] pertains

---

non par les especes, desquelles toutesfois il s'est servy, pour faire admirer d'avantage l'industrie et subtilité de son esprit. . . ." (Durret); "Cependant il l'a représentée établie par des nombres et non par espèces, dont cependant il a fait usage, ce qui doit faire admirer d'avantage sa subtilité et son talent. . . ." (Ritter).

[47]These "laws," set out by Aristotle in the *Posterior Analytics,* Book I, Part IV, govern the relation of attribute to subject. An attribute is κάτὰ παντὸς if it is predicated in every instance in which the subject occurs; it is καό αὐτὰ if it is an essential, not an accidental, element of the subject; and it is καθόλου πρῶτον if, to use Smith's phrasing, it is "completely convertible with the subject."

[48]*Perfecta Zetesi confert se ab hypothesi ad thesim Analysta, conceptaque suae inventionis Theoremata in artis ordinationem exhibet, legibus . . . obnoxia.* Several phrases and clauses of this sentence are open to a variety of translations. Vaulezard reads the sentence thus: "La parfaicte Analitique du Zetese, est celle qui se confere de l'hypotese à la these; & exibe les Theoremes conceus de son invention en l'ordre de l'art, par les lois. . . ." Vasset gives us, "La Zetese estant achevee, l'analiste passe de l'hypothese à la these, & arrange les theoremes de son invention en art formé, & s'assubiectist aux lois. . . ." Durret's rendering is this: "La Zetese accomplie, l'Analyste va de l'hypothese à la these, et fait voir les theoremes conceus de son invention, pour la disposition, et ordere de l'art subiets aux lois. . . ." Ritter has, "La Zètèse achevée, l'Analiste passe de l'hypothèse à la thèse, et montre que les Théorèmes découverts par lui pour le règlement de l'art sont soumis aux lois. . . ." And Smith reads it this way: "When the zetesis has been completed, the analyst turns from hypothesis to thesis and presents theorems of his own finding, theorems that obey the regulations of the art and are subject to the laws. . . ."

[49]λογικωτέρη

[50]1591, 1624, and 1631 have *eaque;* 1635 and 1646 have *atque.*

most especially to the general ordering of the art[51] (as it logically should since the other two [are more concerned with] patterns than with rules),[52] performs its function. It does so both with numbers, if the problem to be solved concerns a term that is to be extracted numerically, and with lengths, surfaces or bodies, if it is a matter of exhibiting a magnitude itself. In the latter case the analyst turns geometer by executing a true construction after having worked out a solution that is analogous to the true. In the former he becomes an arithmetician, solving numerically whatever powers, either pure or affected, are exhibited. He brings forth examples of his art, either arithmetic or geometric, in accordance with the terms of the equation that he has found or of the proportion properly derived from it.

It is true that not every geometric construction is elegant, for each particular problem has its own refinements. It is also true that [that construction] is preferred to any other that makes clear not the structure of a work from an equation but the equation from the structure; thus the structure demonstrates itself.[53] So a skillful geometer, although thoroughly versed in analysis, conceals the fact and, while thinking about the accomplishment of his work, sheds light on and explains his problem synthetically. Then, as an aid to the arithmeticians, he sets out and demonstrates his theorem with the equation or proportion he sees in it.

CHAPTER VIII

On the Nomenclature of Equations, and an Epilogue to the Art

[1] In analysis the word "equation," standing by itself, means an equality properly constructed in accordance with [the rules of] zetetics.

2. Thus an equation is a comparison of an unknown magnitude and a known magnitude.

---

[51]*ad artis ordinationem:* Smith translates this as "to the application of the art," Vaulezard as "a l'ordonnance de l'art," Vasset as "à l'establissement de l'art," and Ritter as "les règles générales de l'art."

[52]*cum reliquae duae exemplorum sint potius quam praeceptorum ut Logicis jure concedendum est.*

[53]As Ritter observes, this passage is obscure. He illustrates Viète's meaning thus: "To find a rectangle equal to a given square, the sum of its dimensions being equal to a given line. One could find the sides by resolving the equations $xy = k^2$, $x + y = l$, but Viète prefers a solution like the following which is indicated by the composition of the equations. From an examination of them, it results in effect that k is a mean proportional between x and y, segments of a given diameter l, whence [follows] the known geometric construction by means of which one can determine the values of x and y in algebraic form."

3. The unknown magnitude may be a root or a power.[54]

4. A power may be pure or affected.

5. An affection may be either positive or negative.

6. When an affecting homogeneous term is subtracted from a power, the negation is direct.

7.[55] When, on the contrary, the power is subtracted from an affecting homogeneous term on a lower-order grade, the negation is inverse.

8. In a homogeneous term of affection, the coefficient tells how many [units to be counted or units of measurement there are] and the lower-order term is the unit counted or the unit of measurement itself.[56]

9. On the unknown side of an equation, the rank both of the power and of the subordinate terms must be shown as well as the sign or quality of any affection. The same should be given for the coefficients.[57]

10. The first lower-order term is the root that is being sought, the last is that which is one step below the power on the scale and is customarily called the *epanaphora*.

11. Any term lower than the power is the complement[58] of [another] lower term if the product of the two is [of the same rank as] the power. Thus a coefficient is the complement of the term that it supports.

12. Beginning with a length as the root, the steps below the power are those given in the scale.

13. Beginning with a plane as the root, the lower-order terms are—

the square		the plane
the fourth power	or	the square of the plane
the sixth power		the cube of the plane

and so on in regular order.

---

[54]*radix . . . vel potestas.* Viète uses the word *radix* in two senses: In some places he uses it as a synonym for *latus,* the first power; in others (for examples, see paragraphs 13 and 14 of this chapter) he uses it to denote the lowest of a consistent series of powers (e.g., x^3, x^6, x^9, etc), regardless of what this lowest may be.

[55]This and the next paragraph number are reversed in 1591 and 1646.

[56]This is a free translation of a cryptic sentence that has given rise to a number of different readings: *Subgradualis metiens est homogenei adfectionis, gradus ipse mensura.* Vaulezard translates this, "Le subgraduel mesure l'homogene d'affection par un degré parôdique"; Vasset as, "Le degré soubsgraduel servant de mesure en la mesure de l'Homogene de l'affection"; Durret as, "Le sousgraduel mesurant appartient à l'homogene d'affection, le mesme degré en est la mesure"; Ritter as, "Le dégré est la mesure à laquelle on doit rapporter l'homogène de l'affection sous-graduelle"; and Smith as "The measuring subrung is the measure itself of the rung of the element homogeneous in conjunction."

[57]1591 has *magnitudines subgraduales* but in the errata corrects this by substituting *adscititias* for *magnitudines;* 1624 has *magnitudines subgraduales magnitudines;* 1635 has *magnitudines subgraduales;* 1631 and 1646 have *adscititias subgraduales magnitudines.*

[58]*reciprocus*

14. Beginning with a solid as the root, the lower-order terms are—

the cube		the solid
the sixth power	or	the square of the solid
the ninth power		the cube of the solid

15. The square, the fourth power, the eighth power and others that are produced in like manner by squaring a power are powers of the simple mean. The others are powers of a multiple mean.[59]

16. The fixed magnitude with which the other terms are compared is the homogeneous term of comparison.

17. In numerical [equations] the homogeneous terms of comparison are pure numbers.[60]

18. When the unknown is a first power and this is equated to a given homogeneous term, the equation is absolutely simple.

19. When the power of the unknown is free from affection and equated to a given homogeneous term, the equation is simple [but] elevated.[61]

20. When the power of the unknown is affected by the product of a lower-order term and a given coefficient and is equated to a given homogeneous term, the equation is a polynomial in accordance with the number and variety of the affections.

21. A power can have as many affections as there are grades below it. Thus a square may be affected by a first power; a cube by a first power and square; a fourth power by a first power, square and cube; a fifth power by a first power, square, cube [and fourth power]; and so on in an infinite series.

22. Proportions are classified in accordance with, and take their names from, the kinds of equations into which they resolve themselves.

23. The analyst trained in arithmetic exegetics knows how

to add a number to a number
to subtract a number from a number
to multiply a number by a number
to divide a number by a number.

The [analytic] art teaches, in addition, the resolution of [all] powers whatsoever, whether pure or affected, [this last being] something understood by neither the old nor the new mathematicians.

---

[59] *Quadratum, quadrato quadratum, Quadrato-cubo-cubus, & quae continuo eo ordine a se ipsismet fiunt, sunt potestates simplicis medii, reliquae multiplicis.*

[60] *In numeris homogenea comparationum sunt unitates.* Cf. Hume, p. 2f.: "L'unité n'a point de logaryme [exponent]: c'est pourquoy tous les nombres sans logarymes sont unitez, ou nombres absolus."

[61] *simplex Climactica.*

24. [The analyst trained] in geometric exegetics will select and review the standard constructions by which linear and quadratic equations can be completely explained.

25. In order to supply quasi-geometrically a deficiency of geometry in the case of cubic and biquadratic equations, [the analytic art] assumes that

> [It is possible] to draw, from any given point, a straight line intercepting any two given straight lines, the segment included between the two straight lines being prescribed beforehand.

This being conceded—it is, moreover, not a difficult assumption[62]—famous problems that have heretofore been called irrational[63] can be solved artfully:[64] the mesographic problem,[65] that of the trisection of an angle, the discovery of the side of a heptagon, and all others that fall within those formulae for equations in which cubes, either pure or affected, are compared with solids and fourth powers with plano-planes.

26. Since all magnitudes are either lines or surfaces or solids, of what earthly use are proportions above triplicate or, at most, quadruplicate ratio except, perhaps, in sectioning angles so that we may derive the angles of figures from their sides or the sides from their angles?

27. Hence the mystery of sections of angles, perceived by no one up to the present either arithmetically or geometrically, is now clear, and [the analytic art] shows

> how to find the ratio of the sides, given the ratio of the angles;
> how to construct one angle [in the same ratio] to another as one number is to another.

28. A straight line is not comparable to a curve. Since an angle is a something midway[66] between a straight line and a plane figure, this [i.e., such a comparison] would seem to be repugnant to the law of homogeneous terms.

29. Finally, the analytic art, endowed with its three forms of zetetics, poristics and exegetics, claims for itself the greatest problem of all, which is

To solve every problem.

[62] $\alpha\check{\upsilon}\eta\mu\alpha$ *non* $\delta\upsilon\sigma\rho\acute{\eta}\chi\alpha\upsilon\upsilon$
[63] $\check{\alpha}\lambda\upsilon\gamma\alpha$
[64] $\grave{\epsilon}\upsilon\tau\epsilon\chi\upsilon\tilde{\omega}s$
[65] That is, the problem of the duplication of a cube.
[66] *medium quiddam.*

PRELIMINARY NOTES ON SYMBOLIC LOGISTIC[1]

The substance of symbolic logistic rests on the four standard rules[2] which are expounded in the *Introduction*.

PROPOSITION I

To show the fourth proportional to three given magnitudes.

Let the three given magnitudes be shown as the first, the second, and the third. A fourth proportional is to be found. Multiply the second by the third and divide the product by the first. I say that the magnitude arising from the division or, put otherwise, the dividend, is the fourth proportional. For the product of the first and fourth is the same as that of the second and third. Let these, therefore be the magnitudes:

First	*Second*	*Third*		and the fourth proportional will be	
A	B	G			$\dfrac{BG}{A}$
$\dfrac{A^2}{D}$	B	G			$\dfrac{BGD}{A^2}$
$\dfrac{A^3}{D^p}$	$\dfrac{B^2}{Z}$	G			$\dfrac{B^2GD^p}{ZA^3}$

---

[1] The Latin title varies slightly: 1631 has Ad Logisticem Speciosam Notae Priores; 1646 has Ad Logisticen Speciosam Notae Priores.

[2] 1646 adds a footnote at this point as follows: "Namely addition, subtraction, multiplication and division which are treated in the fourth chapter of the *Introduction*, from which the subsequent theorems begin."

PROPOSITION II

To show the third, fourth, fifth and higher-order proportionals *ad infinitum* to two given magnitudes.

Let the two given proportionals be *A* and *B*. The third, fourth, fifth and continued proportionals of higher order *ad infinitum* are to be found. Since, therefore

As	is to	so	is to	therefore	will be the
A	B	B	$\dfrac{B^2}{A}$.	$\dfrac{B^2}{A}$	third
A	B	$\dfrac{B^2}{A}$	$\dfrac{B^3}{A^2}$	$\dfrac{B^3}{A^2}$	fourth proportional.
A	B	$\dfrac{B^3}{A^2}$	$\dfrac{B^4}{A^3}$	$\dfrac{B^4}{A^3}$	fifth

And so one may continue *ad infinitum*.

Corollary

Hence, if there is a series of magnitudes in continued proportion,

As the first is to the third, so the square of the first is to the square of the second.[3]

As the first is to the fourth, so the cube of the first is to the cube of the second.[4]

As the first is to the fifth, so the fourth power of the first is to the fourth power of the second.[5]

And so on in the same order to infinity.

Thus, by the given proposition, these are continued proportionals: First, A; second B; third, B^2/A; fourth, B^3/A^2; fifth, B^4/A^3; and so on.

If the first is A and the third is B^2/A, multiply both by A. The ratio will not be changed by this multiplication, since it is made by a common multiplier. Therefore

$$A : \frac{B^2}{A} = A^2 : B^2.$$

Likewise, if the first is A and the fourth is B^3/A^2, multiply both by A^2. The ratio will not be changed by this multiplication since it is made by a

[3]1631 has "third."
[4]1631 has "fourth."
[5]1631 has "fifth."

common multiplier. Hence

$$A : \frac{B^3}{A^2} = A^3 : B^3.$$

Similarly, if the first is A and the fifth is B^4/A^3, multiply both by A^3. The ratio will not be changed by this multiplication, since it is made by a common multiplier. Hence

$$A : \frac{B^4}{A^3} = A^4 : B^4.$$

There is nothing different in the remaining higher terms. It can be made clear and shown by example that [when] the roots are in simple ratio to each other their powers are in multiple ratio. The power of [the terms in] duplicate ratio is the square, in triplicate ratio the cube, in quadruplicate ratio the fourth power, in quintuplicate ratio the fifth power, and so on to infinity in the same series and by the same method.

Proposition III

To find the mean proportional between two given squares.

Let there be two squares, A^2 and B^2. The mean proportional between them is to be found.

Letting A be the first [proportional] and B the second, the third proportional will be found from the preceding [proposition] and there will be a series like this:

$$\text{First, } A; \text{ second, } B; \text{ third, } \frac{B^2}{A}.$$

Multiply through by A—by that which, in other words, gives rise to the third when B^2 is divided by it. Since, therefore, the three given proportionals are uniformly multiplied by A and a proportion is not changed by common multiplication [of all its terms], the products of A and the proportionals will also be proportionals. These products are A^2, BA and B^2. Therefore the mean proportional between the two given squares has been found.

Proposition IIII

To find the two mean continued proportionals between two given cubes.

Let there be two cubes, A^3 and B^3. Two mean continued proportionals between them are to be found.

Now, letting A be the first [proportional] and B the second, continued proportionals *ad infinitum* can be found by the second proposition. In this case let the system be completed with four.[6] The series of four continued proportionals therefore is

$$\text{First } A; \text{ second, } B; \text{ third } \frac{B^2}{A}; \text{ fourth, } \frac{B^3}{A^2}.$$

Multiply through by the A^2 which gives rise to the fourth when it is divided into B^3. Since, therefore, A^2 is a common multiplier of the four given continued proportionals and a proportion is not changed by common multiplication [of its terms], the products of [A^2 and] the continued proportionals will also be proportionals. These products will be A^3, A^2B, AB^2 and B^3. Hence we have found two mean proportionals between the two given cubes. From this is deduced this general

Corollary

If two roots are raised to equally high powers and if the root of the second is multiplied by the grade next below the power of the first and the square of the second is multiplied by the next highest grade of the first and so on in order, continued proportionals between the powers of the first and second will result.[7] This is evident from the second proposition. Whence, also, [the proposition] could be stated very generally:

Between any two equally high powers, to find as many mean continued proportionals as there are grades lower than the power.

PROPOSITION V

To find any number of continued proportionals between two given roots.

Let there be two roots, A and B. Any number of continued proportionals between them are to be found. Let four be found. Since, therefore, the

---

[6]*Sit hic systema infiniti in quarta*. Ritter translates this "Ce système infini soit composé de quatre termes." I suspect, however, that the *infiniti* of the Latin text is a misprint for *finitum* or something similar and have rendered it accordingly.

[7]E.g., if the roots are a and b, a^n: $a^{n-1} b = a^{n-1} b$: $b^2 = a^{n-2} b^2$: b^3.

root [must be] raised as many steps as there are mean continued proportionals demanded, namely four, the power will necessarily take the fifth place and, since the fifth grade, moreover, is the fifth power,[8] let both A and B be raised to this power. Now between A^5 and B^5 let the four mean continued proportionals be set up in a series like this:

1. A^5 4. A^2B^3
2. A^4B 5. AB^4
3. A^3B^2 6. B^5

[Terms] that are proportionals in a power, however, are also proportionals in the root. Therefore take the fifth roots of the six proportionals that have just been given and the six roots here named will also be in continued proportion, viz.,

1. A 4. $\sqrt[5]{A^2B^3}$
2. $\sqrt[5]{A^4B}$ 5. $\sqrt[5]{AB^4}$
3. $\sqrt[5]{A^3B^2}$ 6. B

Thus there have been shown as many mean continued proportionals between A and B as were demanded.

PROPOSITION VI

To add the difference between two magnitudes to their sum.

Let $A + B$ be added to $A - B$. The sum is $2A$.[9] Wherefore,

Theorem

The sum of two magnitudes plus their difference is equal to twice the greater magnitude.

PROPOSITION VII

To subtract the difference between two magnitudes from their sum.

---

[8] *in quinto autem gradu consistet quadrato-cubus.*
[9] 1631 has 2B.

Let $A - B$ be subtracted from $A + B$. The remainder is 2B. Wherefore,

Theorem

The sum of two magnitudes minus their difference is equal to twice the smaller magnitude.

PROPOSITION VIII

If the same magnitude is diminished by unequal subtrahends, to subtract one [quantity] from the other.

Let $A - E$ be subtracted from $A - B$. The remainder will be $E - B$. Note that this is also the difference between the subtrahends. Wherefore,

Theorem

If a magnitude is diminished by unequal subtrahends, the difference between the remainders is the same as the difference between the subtrahends.

PROPOSITION IX

If the same magnitude is increased by unequal addends, to subtract one [quantity] from the other.

Let $A + B$ be subtracted from $A + G$. The remainder will be $G - B$. Wherefore,

Theorem

If the same magnitude is increased by unequal addends, the difference between the sums is the same as the difference between the addends.

PROPOSITION X

If the same magnitude is increased by an addend and decreased by a subtrahend which are unequal, to subtract one [quantity] from the other.

Let $A - B$ be subtracted from $A + G$. The remainder will be $G + B$. Whence

Theorem

If the same magnitude is increased by an addend and decreased by a subtrahend which are unequal, the difference between the sum and the remainder is equal to the sum of the addend and the subtrahend.

Proposition XI

To construct a pure power from a binomial root.

Let there be a binomial root, $A + B$. A pure power is to be constructed from it.

First, let the square be constructed. Since a root multiplied by itself makes a square, multiply $A + B$ by $A + B$ and collect the individual planes that result. These will be $A^2 + 2AB + B^2$ which are, accordingly, equal to the square of $A + B$.

Second, let the cube be constructed. Since a root multiplied by its square makes a cube, let $A + B$ be multiplied by the square of $A + B$ just set out and collect the individual solids that result. These will be $A^3 + 3A^2B + 3AB^2 + B^3$ which will, therefore, be equal to the cube of $A + B$.

Third, let the fourth power be constructed. Since a root multiplied by its cube makes the fourth power, multiply $A + B$ by the cube of $A + B$ just shown and collect the individual plano-planes that result. These will be $A^4 + 4A^3B + 6A^2B^2 + 4AB^3 + B^4$ which will, accordingly, be equal to the fourth power of $A + B$.

Fourth, let the fifth power be formed. Since a root multiplied by its fourth power makes a fifth power, multiply $A + B$ by the fourth power of $A + B$ just shown and collect the individual plano-solids that result. These will be $A^5 + 5A^4B + 10A^3B^2 + 10A^2B^3 + 5AB^4 + B^5$ which will clearly be equal to the fifth power of $A + B$.

Fifth, let the sixth power be constructed. Since a root multiplied by its fifth power makes a sixth power, multiply $A + B$ by the fifth power of $A + B$ just shown and collect the individual solido-solids that result. These will be $A^6 + 6A^5B^2 + 15A^4B^2 + 20A^3B^3 + 15A^2B^4 + 6AB^5 + B^6$ which will be equal, therefore, to the sixth power of $A + B$.

The construction of any higher power will be no different. From these [examples], therefore, theorems that are worth while for the whole of logistic and useful in zetetics can be derived and comprehended by a uniform method.[10]

---

[10]If the reader is tempted to ask why Viète did not go one step beyond the series of theorems that follow and arrive at a general statement of the binomial formula, since (or so it would seem) it was clearly within his grasp, he must remind himself that the day of numerical

Theorem

On the genesis of the square[11]

If there are two roots, the square of the first plus twice the product of the first and second,[12] plus the square of the second equals the square of the sum of the roots.[13]

Theorem

On the genesis of the cube

If there are two roots, the cube of the first plus the product of the square of the first and three times the second, plus the product of the first and three times the square of the second, plus the cube of the second equals the cube of the sum of the roots.[14]

Theorem

On the genesis of the fourth power[15]

If there are two roots, the fourth power of the first, plus the product of the cube of the first and four times the second, plus the product of the

---

exponents had not yet arrived and that, therefore, the possibility of generalizing to this extent was not nearly so visible as it was to become a little later. We can get more of the contemporary feel of the thing if, though still retaining the modern use of superior elements for exponents, we substitute q (*quadratum*) for 2, c (*cubum*) for 3, qq (*quadrato-quadratum*) for 4, and so on. Viete's five constructions would then read:

$$(A + B)^q = A^q + 2AB + B^q$$
$$(A + B)^c = A^c + 3A^qB + 3AB^q + B^c$$
$$(A + B)^{qq} = A^{qq} + 4A^cB + 6A^qB^q + 4AB^c + B^{qq}$$
$$(A + B)^{qc} = A^{qc} + 5A^{qq}B + 10A^cB^q + 10A^qB^c + 5AB^{qq} + B^{qc}$$
$$(A + B)^{cc} = A^{cc} + 6A^{qc}B + 15A^{qq}B^q + 20A^cB^c + 15A^qB^{qq} + 6AB^{qc} + B^{cc}.$$

[11]*Theorema geneseos quadrati.* Some readers may prefer to substitute "origin," "formation," "development," or "generation" for "genesis" in this and the following titles.

[12]*plus plano a duplo latere primo in latus secundi.* Similarly in the next theorem, substituting *solido* for *plano.*

[13]1646 adds the following example at this point: "Let one root be A, the other B. I say that

$$A^2 + 2AB + B^2 = (A + B)^2$$

from the operation of multiplying $A + B$ by $A + B$."

[14]1646 adds the following example at this point: "Let one root be A, the other B. I say that

$$A^3 + 3A^2B + 3AB^2 + B^3 = (A + B)^3$$

from the operation of multiplying $A^2 + 2AB + B^2$ by $A + B$."

[15]1631 has "square" instead of "fourth power."

square of the first and six times the square of the second, plus the product of the first and four times the cube of the second, plus the fourth power of the second equals the fourth power of the sum of the roots.[16]

Theorem

On the genesis of the fifth power

If there are two roots, the fifth power of the first, plus the product of the fourth power of the first and five times the second, plus the product of the cube of the first and ten times the square of the second, plus the product of the square of the first and five times the fourth power of the second, plus the fifth power of the second equals the fifth power of the sum of the roots.[17]

Theorem

On the genesis of the sixth power

If there are two roots, the sixth power of the first, plus the product of the fifth power of the first and six times the second, plus the product of the fourth power of the first and fifteen times the square of the second, plus the product of the cube of the first and twenty times the cube of the second, plus the product of the square of the first and fifteen times the fourth power of the second, plus the product of the first and six times the fifth power of the second, plus the sixth power of the second equals the sixth power of the sum of the roots.[18]

---

[16]1646 adds the following example at this point: "Let one root be A, the other B. I say that

$$A^4 + 4A^3B + 6A^2B^2 + 4AB^3 + B^4 = (A + B)^4$$

from the operation of multiplying $A^3 + 3A^2B + 3AB^2 + B^3$ by $A + B$."

[17]1646 adds the following example at this point: "Let one root be A, the other B. I say that

$$A^5 + 5A^4B + 10A^3B^2 + 10A^2B^3 + 5AB^4 + B^5 = (A + B)^5$$

from the operation of multiplying

$$A^4 + 4A^3B + 6A^2B^2 + 4AB^3 + B^4 \text{ by } A + B.\text{"}$$

[18]1646 adds the following example at this point: "Let one root be A, the other B. I say that

$$A^6 + 6A^5B + 15A^4B^2 + 20A^3B^3 + 15A^2B^4 + 6AB^5 + B^6 = (A + B)^6$$

from the operation of multiplying $A^5 + 5A^4B + 10A^3B^2 + 10A^2B^3 + 5AB^4 + B^5$ by $A + B$."

If, however, a power is to be constructed from the difference between the roots rather than their sum, all the individual homogeneous terms of the composition will be the same, but they will be alternately positive and negative beginning with the power of the greater root when there is an even number of homogeneous terms, as in the cube, fifth power and every other one thereafter, [while] in the others they will be alternately positive and negative beginning with the power of either the greater or the smaller root, there being no difference since it works out the same in either case.

Corollary

The individual homogeneous terms making up the composition of a power constructed from a binomial root, taken once each in order, are continued proportionals, in accordance with the general corollary to the fourth proposition.

Thus the three planes constructed from the two roots A and B are proportionals: A^2, AB, B^2.

Likewise the four solids: A^3, A^2B, AB^2, B^3.

Similarly the five plano-planes: A^4, A^3B, A^2B^2, AB^3, B^4.[19]

And so on thereafter.

Proposition XII

To add the square of the difference between [two] roots to the square of their sum.

Let one root be A, the other B. The square of $A \sim B$ is to be added to the square of $A + B$. Now the square of $A + B$ is $A^2 + 2AB + B^2$ and the square of $A \sim B$ is $A^2 - 2AB + B^2$. Let these be added. The sum will be $2A^2 + 2B^2$. Hence that has been done that was to be done. Therefore,

Theorem

The square of the sum of [two] roots plus the square of their difference equals twice the sum of their squares.

Proposition XIII

To subtract the square of the difference between two roots from the square of their sum.

[19]1646 adds at this point: "And the six plano-solids are proportionals: A^5, A^4B, A^3B^2, A^2B^3, AB^4, B^5.

"Finally the seven solido-solids are continued proportionals: A^6, A^5B, A^4B^2, A^3B^3, A^2B^4, AB^5, B^6."

Let one root be A, the other B. The square of $A \sim B$ is to be subtracted from the square of $A + B$. Subtract the individual planes of which the square of $A \sim B$ consists from the individual planes of which the square of $A + B$ consists. The difference will be $4AB$. Therefore,

Theorem

The square of the sum of two roots minus the square of their difference equals four times the product of the roots.

Corollary

The product of two roots is less than the square of one-half their sum. Divide both sides of the equation given by the theorem by four. The square of the sum of one-half the roots will exceed the product of the roots by the square of one-half their difference, otherwise the roots will not be different but equal.[20] This is well worth noticing.

Proposition XIIII

To multiply the difference between two roots by their sum.

Let the greater root be A, the smaller B. Multiply $A - B$ by $A + B$ and collect the individual planes. Those will be $A^2 - B^2$. Therefore,

Theorem

The product of the difference between two roots and their sum is equal to the difference between their squares.

Corollary

If the difference between the squares is divided by the difference between the roots, the quotient is the sum of the roots and, on the contrary, if the difference between the squares is divided by the sum of the roots, the quotient is the difference between the roots, since division is a restitution by resolution of the work that multiplication effects by composition.

Proposition XV

To add the cube of the difference between two roots to the cube of their sum.

[20]That is, if the roots are a and b, since $(a + b)^2 - (a - b)^2 = 4ab$, $(a + b)^2/4 - (a - b)^2/4 = ab$, or $[(a + b)/2]^2 = ab + [(a - b)/2]^2$ unless $a = b$.

Let one root be A, the other B. The cube of $A \sim B$ is to be added to the cube of $A + B$. Now the cube of $A + B$ is $A^3 + 3A^2B + 3AB^2 + B^3$ and the cube of $A \sim B$ is $A^3 - 3A^2B + 3AB^2 - B^3$. Let these be added. The sum is $2A^3 + 6AB^2$. Hence arises the

Theorem

The cube of the sum of two roots plus the cube of their difference equals twice the cube of the greater plus six times the product of the greater and the square of the smaller.

PROPOSITION XVI

To subtract the cube of the difference between two roots from the cube of their sum.

Let one root be A, the other B. The cube of $A \sim B$ is to be subtracted from the cube of $A + B$. Let the individual solids making up the cube of $A \sim B$ be subtracted from the individual solids making up the cube of $A + B$. The result is $6A^2B + 2B^3$. Hence

Theorem

The cube of the sum of two roots minus the cube of their difference equals six times the product of the smaller root and the square of the greater plus twice the cube of the smaller.

PROPOSITION XVII

To multiply the difference between two roots by the three individual plano-planes, taken once each, of which the square of the sum of these roots consists.

Let the greater root be A, the smaller B. $A - B$ is to be multiplied by $A^2 + AB + B^2$. Perform each particular multiplication and collect the individual solids. These will be $A^3 - B^3$. Hence

Theorem

The product of the difference between two roots and one each of the three individual planes making up the square of the sum of these roots is equal to the difference between their cubes.

Corollary

The difference between the cubes divided by the difference between the roots is one each of the three individual planes of which the square of the sum of the roots consists. Or, turned about, the difference between the cubes divided by the three individual planes, taken once each, of which the square of the roots consists is the difference between the roots.

PROPOSITION XVIII

To multiply the sum of two roots by the three individual planes, taken once each, of which the square of the difference between these roots consists.

Let one root be A, the other B. $A + B$ is to be multiplied by $A^2 - BA + B^2$. Perform each particular multiplication and collect the individual solids. These will be $A^3 + B^3$. Hence,

Theorem

The product of the sum of two roots and one each of the three individual planes of which the square of the difference between these roots consists is equal to the sum of their cubes.

Corollary

The sum of the cubes divided by the sum of the roots is one each of the individual planes of which the square of their difference consists. And the other way about.

PROPOSITION XIX

To multiply the difference between two roots by the four individual solids, taken once each, of which the cube of the sum of the roots consists.

Let the greater root be A, the smaller B. $A - B$ is to be multiplied by $A^3 + A^2B + AB^2 + B^3$. Perform each particular multiplication and collect the individual plano-planes. These will be $A^4 - B^4$.

Theorem

The product of the difference between two roots and the four individual solids, taken once each, of which the cube of the sum of the roots consists is equal to the difference between their fourth powers.

Corollary

The difference between two fourth powers divided by the difference between their roots is one each of the four individual solids of which the cube of the sum of the roots consists. And the other way around.

PROPOSITION XX

To multiply the sum of two roots by the four individual solids, taken once each, of which the cube of the difference between these roots consists.

$A + B$ is to be multiplied by $A^3 - A^2B + AB^2 - B^3$. Perform each particular multiplication and collect the individual plano-planes. These will be $A^4 - B^4$.

Theorem

The product of the sum of two roots and the four individual solids, taken once each, of which the cube of the difference between the roots consists is equal to the difference between their fourth powers.

Corollary

The difference between the fourth powers divided by the sum of their roots is one each of the four individual solids of which the cube of the difference between the roots consists. And the other way around.[21]

Another Corollary

As the difference between the roots is to their sum, so is [the sum of] the four individual solids, taken once each, of which the cube of the difference between the roots consists to [the sum of] the four individual solids, also taken once each, of which the cube of the sum of these roots consists.[22]

PROPOSITION XXI

To multiply the difference between two roots by the five individual plano-planes, taken once each, of which the fourth power of the sum of these roots consists.

[21]1646 omits this sentence.
[22]I.e., $(a - b)/(a + b) = (a^3 - a^2b + ab^2 - b^3)/(a^3 + a^2b + ab^2 + b^3)$.

Let the greater root be A, the smaller B. $A - B$ is to be multiplied by $A^4 + A^3B + A^2B^2 + AB^3 + B^4$. Perform each particular multiplication and collect the individual plano-solids. These will be $A^5 - B^5$. Hence

Theorem

The product of the difference between two roots and the five individual plano-planes, taken once each, of which the fourth power of the sum of these roots consists is equal to the difference between their fifth powers.

Corollary

The difference between the fifth powers divided by the difference between the roots is one each of the five individual plano-planes of which the fourth power of the sum of these roots consists. And the other way around.

Proposition XXII

To multiply the sum of two roots by the five individual plano-planes, taken once each, of which the fourth power of the difference between the same roots[23] consists.

Let one root be A, the other B. $A + B$ is to be multiplied by $A^4 - A^3B + A^2B^2 - AB^3 + B^4$. Perform each particular multiplication and collect the individual plano-planes. These will be $A^5 + B^5$. Hence

Theorem

The product of the sum of two roots and the five individual plano-planes, taken once each, of which the fourth power of the difference between these roots consists is equal to the sum of the fifth powers.

Corollary

The sum of the fifth powers divided by the sum of the roots gives rise to one each of the five individual plano-planes of which the fourth power of the difference between the same roots[24] consists. And the other way around.

[23]1646 omits the word "roots" here.
[24]1646 omits "roots" here, also.

Proposition XXIII

To multiply the difference between two roots by the six individual plano-solids, taken once each, of which the fifth power of their sum consists.

Let the greater root be A, the smaller B. $A - B$ is to be multiplied by $A^5 + A^4B + A^3B^2 + A^2B^3 + AB^4 + B^5$. Perform each particular multiplication and collect the individual solido-solids. These will be $A^6 - B^6$. Hence

Theorem

The product of the difference between two roots and the six individual plano-solids, taken once each, of which the fifth power of the sum of those roots consists is equal to the difference between their sixth powers.

Corollary

The difference between the sixth powers divided by the difference between the roots is one each of the six individual plano-solids of which the fifth power of the sum of those roots consists.

Proposition XXIIII

To multiply the sum of two roots by the six individual plano-solids, taken once each, of which the fifth power of the difference between those roots consists.

Let one root be A, the other B. $A + B$ is to be multiplied by $A^5 - A^4B + A^3B^2 - A^2B^3 + AB^4 - B^5$. Perform each particular multiplication and collect the individual solido-solids. These will be $A^6 - B^6$. Hence

Theorem

The product of the sum of two roots and one each of the six individual plano-solids of which the fifth power of the difference between those roots consists is equal to the difference between their sixth powers.

Corollary

The difference between the sixth powers divided by the sum of the two roots is one each of the six individual plano-solids of which the fifth power of the difference between those roots consists.

Another Corollary

As the difference between the roots is to their sum, so is [the sum of] the six individual plano-solids, taken once each, of which the fifth power of the difference between these roots consists to [the sum of] the six individual plano-solids, also taken once each, of which the fifth power of the sum of these roots consists.[25] [At this point there is inserted in the text an addition by Beaugrand reading thus in 1631:]

Since universals ought to be enunciated in universal form if we wish to advance learning, the theorems that are deduced from the eight preceding propositions by Francois Viète should not be received too limitedly. I am glad that we, who have not only purged this work of an outstanding man of the innumerable errors in which it abounds and have, moreover, completed more than a quarter of the work that was missing but who have also performed the task of an annotator, as it were—I am glad, I say, to add to the rules of the demonstrations and to collect these general theorems from the propositions and their corollaries.[26]

Theorem I

The product of the difference between two roots and the individual homogeneous terms, taken once each, of which a power of the sum of the roots consists is equal to the difference between the next higher powers [of those roots].[27] Hence

Corollary

The difference between these powers divided by the differences between the roots is one each of the individual homogeneous terms of which the next lower power of the sum of these roots consists. And, contrariwise, the difference between these powers divided by the individual homogeneous terms, taken once each, of which the next lower power of the sum of these roots consists is the difference between the roots.

[25]I.e., $(a - b)/(a + b) = (a^5 - a^4b + a^3b^2 - a^2b^3 + ab^4 - b^5)/(a^5 + a^4b + a^3b^2 + a^2b^3 + ab^4 + b^5)$.

[26]In 1646 this introductory paragraph is replaced by the sentence, "The following general theorems are derived from the preceding propositions."

[27]I.e., $(a - b)(a^n + a^{n-1}b + a^{n-2}b^2 \ldots b^n) = a^{n+1} - b^{n+1}$.

Theorem II

The product of the sum of two roots and the individual homogeneous terms, taken once each, of which a power of the difference between these roots consists is equal to the sum of or the difference between the next higher powers [of these roots]—the sum if the number of individual homogeneous terms is uneven, the difference if the number of individual homogeneous terms is even.[28] Hence

Corollary[29]

The sum of or difference between [two] powers divided by the sum of their roots is one each of the individual homogeneous terms of which the next lower power of the difference between those roots consists.

Another Corollary

If the number of individual homogeneous terms of which a power of the sum of or difference between the roots consists is even, as the difference between the roots is to their sum, so the individual homogeneous terms, taken once each, of which the power of the difference between these roots consists will be to the individual homogeneous terms, taken once each, of which the same power of the sum of these roots consists.[30]

The Genesis of Affected Powers: First [of those] Affected Positively

PROPOSITION XXV

To construct [from a binomial root] a square affected by the addition of a plane based on its first power, the latter being properly supplemented by a linear coefficient.[31]

---

[28]I.e., $(a + b)(a^n - a^{n-1}b + a^{n-2}b^2 \ldots b^n) = a^{n+1} + b^{n+1}$ if $n + 1$ is odd or to $a^{n+1} - b^{n+1}$ if $n + 1$ is even.

[29]This corollary, of course, is true only if the sum of and the difference between the powers are alternated, beginning with $A^2 - B^2$, $A^3 + B^3$, etc.

[30]I.e., if $(a + b)^n$ and $(a - b)^n$ yield an even number of terms, $(a - b)/(a + b) = (a^n - a^{n-1}b + a^{n-2}b^2 \ldots - b^n)/(a^n + a^{n-1}b + a^{n-2}b^2 \ldots + b^n)$

[31]*Quadratum adfectum adiunctione Plani sub latere, adscita congruenter sublaterali coefficiente longutudine, componere.* The titles of the following propositions all observe the pattern of this one with the addition of the *a binomia radico* which is omitted in this one.

Let $A + B$ be a binomial root and let the length D be the coefficient of its first power. The square of $A + B$ affected by the addition of the plane product of D and $A + B$ is to be constructed. Multiply $A + B$ by $A + B + D$ and collect the individual planes that result. These will be $A^2 + 2AB + B^2 + DA + DB$ which will, therefore, be equal to the square of $A + B$ affected by the addition of the product of $A + B$ and the length D. Hence comes the

Theorem[32]

If there are two roots and, in addition, a length as the coefficient of the first power, the square of the first root, plus the plane produced by the first root and twice the second root, plus the square of the second root, plus the plane produced by the first root and the linear coefficient, plus the plane produced by the second root and the same linear coefficient is equal to the square of the sum of the roots affected by the addition of the plane from the coefficient and the aforesaid sum.[33]

PROPOSITION XXVI

To construct, from a binomial root, a cube affected by the addition of a solid based on its first power, the latter being properly supplemented by a plane coefficient.

Let $A + B$ be a binomial root and let D^p be the coefficient of its first power. The cube of $A + B$ affected by the addition of the solid product of D^p and the same $A + B$ is to be constructed. Construct the square of $A + B$ and, having added D^p to this [square], multiply it by $A + B$ and collect the individual solids that result. These will be $A^3 + 3A^2B + 3AB^2 + B^3 +$

[32]In 1646 the title of the theorem is "On the genesis of a square affected positively by a first power."

[33]1646 adds the following at this point: "Let A be one root, B the other, and the length D the coefficient of the first power. I say that

$$A^2 + 2AB + B^2 + DA + DB = (A + B)^2 + D(A + B),$$

from the work of multiplying $A + B$ by $A + B + D$.

Another Theorem

If two squares are constructed from the same binomial root, one pure and the other affected positively by the product of the root and a length adopted for its coefficient, the individual planes that the affected construction adds to the pure construction are

The plane produced by the first root and the coefficient length;

The product of the second root and the same coefficient length. [This comes] from a comparison of the two [cases] supposed."

$D^pA + D^pB$ which equal the cube of $A + B$ affected by the addition of the product of $A + B$ and D^p. Hence is derived the

Theorem

If there are two roots and, furthermore, a plane coefficient for the first power, the cube of the first root, plus the solid produced by the square of the first root and three times the second, plus the solid produced by the first root and three times the square of the second, plus the cube of the second root, plus the solid produced by the first root and the plane coefficient, plus the solid produced by the second root and the same plane coefficient equals the cube of the sum of the roots affected by the addition of the solid produced by the plane coefficient and the aforesaid sum.

PROPOSITION XXVII

To construct, from a binomial root, a cube affected by the addition of a solid based on its square, the latter being properly supplemented by a linear coefficient.

Let $A + B$ be a binomial root and let the length D be the coefficient of its square. The cube of $A + B$ affected[34] by the addition of the solid produced by D and the square of $A + B$ is to be constructed. Let the square of $A + B$ be constructed, multiply it by $A + B + D$, and collect the individual solids that result. These will be $A^3 + 3A^2B + 3AB^2 + B^3 + A^2D + 2ABD + B^2D$ which, therefore, will be equal to the cube of $A + B$ affected by the addition of the solid produced by the square of $A + B$ and the length D. Hence is derived the

Theorem[35]

If there are two roots and, in addition, a length as the coefficient of the square, the cube of the first root, plus the solid produced by the square of the first root and three times the second root, plus the solid produced by the first root and three times the square of the second, plus the cube of the second, plus the solid produced by the square of the first and the linear coefficient, plus the solid produced by twice the plane from the roots times the linear coefficient, plus the solid produced by the square of the second and the linear coefficient is equal to the cube of the sum of the roots

[34]1631 omits this word.
[35]In 1646 the title of the theorem is "On the genesis of a cube with a positive quadratic affection."

affected by the addition of the solid produced by the coefficient and the square of the said sum of the roots.[36]

PROPOSITION XXVIII

To construct, from a binomial root, a fourth power affected by the addition of a plano-plane based on its first power, the latter being properly supplemented by a solid coefficient.

Let $A + B$ be a binomial root and let D^s be the coefficient of its first power. The fourth power of $A + B$ affected by the addition of the plano-plane produced by $A + B$ and D^s is to be constructed. Let the cube of $A + B$ be worked out and, having added D^s to it, multiply by $A + B$ and collect the individual plano-planes that result. These will be $A^4 + 4A^3B + 6A^2B^2 + 4AB^3 + B^4$[37] $+ AD^s + BD^s$ which, therefore, equal the fourth power of $A + B$ affected by the addition of the plano-plane from $A + B$ and D^s. Hence,

Theorem[38]

If there are two roots and, in addition, a solid coefficient, the fourth power of the first root, plus the cube of the first root times four times the second, plus the square of the first times six times the square of the second, plus the first times four times the cube of the second, plus the fourth power of the second, plus the first times the solid coefficient, plus the second times

---

[36]1646 adds the following at this point: "Let A be one root, B the other and D the linear coefficient of the square. I say that

$$A^3 + 3A^2B + 3AB^2 + B^3 + A^2D + 2ABD + B^2D = (A + B)^3 + D(A + B)^2$$

by the process of multiplying $A^2 + 2AB + B^2$ by $A + B + D$.

Another Theorem

If two cubes are formed from the same binomial root, one pure, the other affected positively by the product of the square of this same root and a linear coefficient, the individual solids which the affected construction adds to the pure are:

The solid produced by the square of the first root and the linear coefficient;
The solid produced by the second root and twice the plane which is the product of the first root and the linear coefficient;
The solid produced by the square of the second root and the linear coefficient.

[This comes] from a comparison of the two [cases] supposed."

[37]1631 has B^3.

[38]In 1646, the title of the theorem is "On the genesis of a fourth power with a positive linear affection."

the solid coefficient is equal to the fourth power of the sum of the roots affected by the addition of the plano-plane produced by the aforesaid sum and the solid coefficient.[39]   ·

Proposition XXIX

To construct, from a binomial root, a fourth power affected
by the addition of a plano-plane based on its cube, the latter
being properly supplemented by a linear coefficient.

Let $A + B$ be a binomial root and let the length D be the coefficient [of its cube]. The fourth power of $A + B$ affected by the addition of the plano-plane produced by the cube of $A + B$ and the length D is to be · constructed. Let the cube of $A + B$ be formed, multiply it by $A + B + D$ and collect the individual plano-planes that result. These will be $A^4 + 4A^3B + 6A^2B^2 + 4AB^3 + B^4 + A^3D + 3A^2BD + 3AB^2D + B^3D$ which, therefore, are equal to the fourth power of $A + B$ affected by the addition of the plano-plane produced by the cube of $A + B$ and the length D. Hence the

Theorem[40]

If there are two roots and a length as coefficient, the fourth power of the first root, plus the cube of the first root times four times the second, plus the square of the first times six times the square of the second, plus the first times four times the cube of the second, plus the fourth power of the second, plus the cube of the first times the linear coefficient, plus the solid produced by the square of the first and the product of three times the second and the linear coefficient, plus the solid produced by the first and the product of three times the square of the second and the linear coefficient, plus the cube of the second times the linear coefficient is equal to the fourth power of the sum of the roots affected by the addition of the plano-plane produced by the cube of the aforesaid sum and the linear coefficient.[41]

[39]1646 adds at this point the following: "Let A be one root, B the other and D^s the coefficient of the first power. I say that   ·

$$A^4 + 4A^3B + 6A^2B^2 + 4AB^3 + B^4 + AD^s + BD^s = (A + B)^4 + D^s(A + B),$$

by the process of multiplying $A^3 + 3A^2B + 3AB^2 + B^3 + D^s$ by $A + B$."

[40]In 1646 the title of the theorem is "On the genesis of [a fourth power] with a positive cubic affection." *Plano-plani* appears here, however, instead of *quadrato-quadrati*.

[41]1646 adds at this point the following: "Let one root be A, the other B and let D be the

Proposition XXX

To construct, [from a binomial root,][42] a fourth power affected by the addition of two plano-planes, one based on its first power, the other on its square, they being properly supplemented by solid and plane coefficients.

Let $A + B$ be a binomial root, D^s the coefficient of its first power and G^p the coefficient of its square. The fourth power of $A + B$ affected by the addition of two plano-planes, one of which is from $A + B$ and D^s, the other from the square of $A + B$ and G^p, is to be constructed. Let the square of

---

linear coefficient. I say that

$$A^4 + 4A^3B + 6A^2B^2 + 4AB^3 + B^4 + A^3D + 3A^2BD + 3AB^2D + B^3D$$

$$= (A + B)^4 + D(A + B)^3,$$

by the process of multiplying $A^3 + 3A^2B + 3AB^2 + B^3$ by $A + B + D$.

Another Theorem

If two fourth powers are constructed from the same binomial root, one pure, the other affected by the addition of the plano-plane produced by the cube of this root and a linear coefficient, the individual plano-planes which the affected composition adds to the pure composition are

The plano-plane produced by the cube of the first root and the linear coefficient;

The plano-plane produced by the square of the first root and three times the plane resulting from the second root times the linear coefficient;

The plano-plane produced by the first root and three times the solid resulting from the square of the second root times the linear coefficient;

The plano-plane produced by the cube of the second root and the linear coefficient.

[This comes] from a comparison of the two [cases] supposed:

	Pure		Affected
	A^4		A^4
	$4A^3B$		$4A^3B$
	$6A^2B^2$		$6A^2B^2$
	$4AB^3$		$4AB^3$
	B^4		B^4
I.			A^3D
II.			$3A^2BD$
III.			$3AB^2D$
IV.			$B^3D,$

by the process of multiplying $A^3 + 3A^2B + 3AB^2 + B^3$ by $A + B + D$."

[42]1631 omits the bracketed phrase.

$A + B$ be worked out and, having added to it G^p, let [the sum] be multiplied by $A + B$ and, having added D^s to the resulting solids, let [the sum] again be multiplied by $A + B$ and let the individual plano-planes that result be collected. These will be $A^4 + 4A^3B + 6A^2B^2 + 4AB^3 + B^4 + A^2G^p + 2ABG^p + B^2G^p + AD^s + BD^s$ which plano-planes equal the fourth power of $A + B$ affected by the addition of the plano-planes from the square of $A + B$ and G^p and from $A + B$ and D^s. Hence the

Theorem

If there are two roots and, in addition, two coefficients, one a plane coefficient for the square, the other a solid coefficient for the first power, the fourth power of the first root, plus the cube of the first times four times the second, plus the square of the first times six times the square of the second, plus the first times four times the cube of the second, plus the fourth power of the second, plus the square of the first times the plane coefficient, plus twice the plane produced by the roots times the plane coefficient, plus the square of the second times the plane coefficient, plus the first times the solid coefficient, plus the second times the solid coefficient is equal to the fourth power of the sum of the roots affected by the addition of two plano-planes, one the product of the square of the sum of the roots and the plane coefficient, the other the product of the sum of the roots and the solid coefficient.

PROPOSITION XXXI

To construct, from a binomial root, a fifth power affected by the addition of a plano-solid based on its first power, the latter being properly supplemented by a plano-plane coefficient.

Let $A + B$ be a binomial root and D^{pp} the coefficient of the first power. The fifth power of $A + B$ affected by the addition of the plano-solid derived from $A + B$ and D^{pp} is to be constructed. Let the fourth power of $A + B$ be worked out and, having added D^{pp} to it, multiply by $A + B$ and collect the individual plano-solids that result. They will be $A^5 + 5A^4B + 10A^3B^2 + 10A^2B^3 + 5AB^4 + B^5 + AD^{pp} + BD^{pp}$ which, therefore, will equal the fifth power of $A + B$ affected by the addition of the plano-solid produced by $A + B$ and D^{pp}. Hence is conceived the

Theorem

If there are two roots and, in addition, a plano-plane coefficient for the first power, the fifth power of the first root, plus the product of the fourth power of the first and five times the second, plus the product of the cube of the first and ten times the square of the second, plus the product of the square of the first and ten times the cube of the second, plus the product of the first and five times the fourth power of the second, plus the fifth power of the second, plus the first times the plano-plane coefficient, plus the second times the plano-plane coefficient is equal to the fifth power of the sum of the two roots affected by the addition of the plano-solid produced by the plano-plane coefficient and the sum of the roots.

Proposition XXXII

To construct, from a binomial root, a fifth power affected by the addition of a plano-solid based on its cube, the latter being properly supplemented by a plane coefficient.

Let $A + B$ be a binomial root and D^p the coefficient of the cube. The fifth power of $A + B$ affected by the addition of the plano-solid derived from the cube of $A + B$ and D^p is to be constructed. Take the square of $A + B$ and, having added D^p to it, multiply by the cube of $A + B$ and collect the individual plano-solids that result. These will be $A^5 + 5A^4B + 10A^3B^2 + 10A^2B^3 + 5AB^4 + B^5 + A^3D^p + 3A^2BD^p + 3AB^2D^p + B^3D^p$. Hence arises the

Theorem

If there are two roots and a plane coefficient, the fifth power of the first root, plus the product of the fourth power of the first and five times the second, plus the product of the cube of the first and ten times the square of the second, plus the product of the square of the first and ten times the cube of the second, plus the product of the first and five times the fourth power of the second, plus the fifth power of the second, plus the product of the cube of the first and the plane coefficient, plus the product of the plane coefficient and the solid from the square of the first times three times the second, plus the product of the plane coefficient and the solid from the first times three times the square of the second, plus the product of the cube of the second and the plane coefficient is equal to the fifth power of the sum of the roots affected by the addition of the plano-solid from the plane coefficient and the cube of the sum of the roots.

Proposition XXXIII

To construct, from a binomial root, a sixth power affected by the addition of a solido-solid based on the first power, the latter being properly supplemented by a plano-solid coefficient.

Let $A + B$ be a binomial root and D^{ps} the coefficient of the first power. The sixth power of $A + B$ affected by the addition of the solido-solid from $A + B$ and D^{ps} is to be constructed. Take the fifth power of $A + B$ and, having added D^{ps} to it, multiply by $A + B$ and collect the individual solido-solids that result. These will be $A^6 + 6A^5B + 15A^4B^2 + 20A^3B^3 + 15A^2B^4 + 6AB^5 + B^6 + AD^{ps} + BD^{ps}$. These, therefore, will be equal to the sixth power of $A + B$ plus the solido-solid from $A + B$ and D^{ps}. Hence the

Theorem

If there are two roots along with a plano-solid coefficient for their first power, the sixth power of the first root, plus the product of the fifth power of the first and six times the second, plus the product of the fourth power of the first and fifteen times the square of the second, plus the product of the cube of the first and twenty times the cube of the second, plus the product of the square of the first and fifteen times the fourth power of the second, plus the product of the first and six times the fifth power of the second, plus the sixth power of the second, plus the first times the plano-solid coefficient, plus the second times the plano-solid coefficient is equal to the sixth power of the sum of the roots affected by the addition of the solido-solid produced by the plano-plane coefficient and the sum of the roots.

The Genesis of Powers Affected Negatively

PROPOSITION XXXIIII

To construct, from a binomial root, a square affected by the subtraction of a plane based on the first power, the latter being properly supplemented by a linear coefficient.

Let $A + B$ be a binomial root and the length D the coefficient of its first power. The square of $A + B$ affected by the subtraction of the plane produced by $A + B$ and the length D is to be constructed. Multiply $A + B$ by $A + B - D$. The planes formed will be $A^2 + 2AB + B^2 - AD - BD$, which will therefore be equal to the square of $A + B$ affected by the subtraction of the plane from $A + B$ and the length D. Hence the

Theorem

If there are two roots along with a linear coefficient for the first power, the square of the first root, plus the plane produced by the first root and twice the second, plus the square of the second, minus the plane produced by the first root and the linear coefficient, minus the plane produced by the second root and the linear coefficient is equal to the square of the sum of the roots minus the plane from said sum and the coefficient.

Proposition XXXV

To construct, from a binomial root, a cube affected by the subtraction of a solid based on the first power, the latter being properly supplemented by a plane coefficient

Let $A + B$ be a binomial root and D^p the coefficient of the first power. The cube of $A + B$ affected by the subtraction of the solid produced by $A + B$ and D^p is to be constructed. Form the square of $A + B$ and, having subtracted D^p from it, multiply by $A + B$ and collect the individual solids that result. These will be $A^3 + 3A^2B + 3AB^2 + B^3 - AD^p - BD^p$ which will be equal to the cube of $A + B$ affected by the subtraction of the solid from $A + B$ times D^p. Hence the

Theorem

If there are two roots and, furthermore, a plane for the coefficient of the first power, the cube of the first root, plus the solid from the square of the first and three times the second, plus the solid from the first and three times the square of the second, plus the cube of the second, minus the solid from the first and the plane coefficient, minus the solid from the second and the plane coefficient is equal to the cube of the sum of the roots affected by the subtraction of the solid from the plane coefficient and the sum of the roots.

Proposition XXXVI

To construct, from a binomial root, a cube affected by the subtraction of a solid based on the square, the latter being properly supplemented by a linear coefficient.

Let $A + B$ be a binomial root and the length D the coefficient of the square. The cube of $A + B$ affected by the subtraction of the solid from the square of $A + B$ times D is to be constructed. Work out the square of $A + B$, multiply it by $A + B - D$, and collect the individual solids that result. These will be $A^3 + 3A^2B + 3AB^2 + B^3 - A^2D - 2ABD - B^2D$ which will, therefore, be equal to the cube of $A + B$ affected by the subtraction of the solid from the square of $A + B$ times D. Hence the

Theorem

If there are two roots and, furthermore, a linear coefficient for the square, the cube of the first root, plus the solid from the square of the first and three times the second, plus the solid from the first and three times the square of the second, plus the cube of the second, minus the solid from the square of the first and the linear coefficient, minus the solid from twice the plane produced by the roots times the linear coefficient, minus the solid from the square of the second and the linear coefficient will be equal to the cube of the sum of the roots affected by the subtraction of the solid from the linear coefficient and the square of the sum of the roots.

The Genesis of Powers Affected Both Positively and Negatively

PROPOSITION XXXVII

To construct, from a binomial root, a fourth power[43] affected [both] by the addition of a plano-plane based on the first power [and] the subtraction of a plano-plane based on the cube, they being properly supplemented by a solid coefficient and a linear coefficient.

Let $A + B$ be a binomial root, D^s the coefficient of the first power and the length G the coefficient of the cube. The fourth power[44] of $A + B$ affected by the addition of the plano-plane from $A + B$ and D^s and by the subtraction of the plano-plane from the cube of $A + B$ and the length G is to be constructed. Multiply the square of $A + B$ by $A + B - G$ and, having added D^s to the solids that result, multiply [the sum] by $A + B$ and collect the individual plano-planes that result. These will be $A^4 + 4A^3B + 6A^2B^2 + 4AB^3 + B^4 - A^3G - 3A^2BG - 3AB^2G - B^3G + AD^s + BD^s$. These will clearly be equal to the fourth power of $A + B$ affected by the subtraction of the plano-plane from the cube of $A + B$ times the length G

[43]1631 has "square" here.
[44]1631 has "square" here, also.

and by the addition of the plano-plane from the root $A + B$ and D^s. Hence the

Theorem

If there are two roots and, furthermore, a linear coefficient for their cube as well as a solid coefficient for their first power, the fourth power of the first root, plus the product of the cube of the first and four times the second, plus the product of the square of the first and six times the square of the second, plus the product of the first and four times the cube of the second, plus the fourth power of the second, minus the product of the cube of the first and the linear coefficient, minus the product of the solid derived from the square of the first times the product of three times the second and the linear coefficient, minus the product of the solid derived from the first times the product of three times the square of the second and the linear coefficient, minus the product of the cube of the second and the linear coefficient, plus the product of the first and the solid coefficient, plus the product of the second and the solid coefficient is equal to the fourth power of the sum of the roots affected by the subtraction of the plano-plane from the cube [of the sum of the roots] and the linear coefficient as well as by the addition of the plano-plane [from the same sum][45] and the solid coefficient.

PROPOSITION XXXVIII

To construct, from a binomial root, a fourth power affected [both] by the subtraction of a plano-plane based on the first power [and] by the addition of a plano-plane based on the cube, they being properly supplemented by a solid coefficient and a linear coefficient.

Let $A + B$ be a binomial root, D^s the coefficient of the first power and the length G the coefficient of the cube. The fourth power of $A + B$ affected by the subtraction of the plano-plane produced by $A + B$ and D^s and by the addition of the plano-plane produced by the cube of $A + B$ and the length G is to be constructed. Multiply the square of $A + B$ by $A + B + G$[46] and, having subtracted[47] D^s from the solids that result, multiply [the whole quantity] by $A + B$. The plano-planes that arise therefrom will be $A^4 + 4A^3B + 6A^2B^2 + 4AB^3 + B^4 + A^3G + 3A^2BG + 3AB^2G^{48} + B^3G -$

---

[45]These two bracketed phrases are not in 1631 but are supplied in 1646.
[46]1631 has $A + B - G$.
[47]1631 has "added."
[48]1631 omits this term.

$AD^s - BD^s$. These, therefore, will equal the fourth power of $A + B$ affected by the addition of the plano-plane from the cube of $A + B$ and the length G and by the subtraction of the plano-plane from the root $A + B$ and D^s. Hence is conceived the

Theorem

If there are two roots and, furthermore, a linear coefficient for the cube as well as a solid coefficient for the first power, the fourth power of the first root, plus the product of the cube of the first root and four times the second, plus the product of the square of the first[49] and six times the square of the second, plus the product of the first[50] and four times the cube of the second, plus the fourth power of the second, plus the cube of the first times the linear coefficient, plus the linear coefficient times the solid from the square of the first and three times the second, plus the linear coefficient times the solid from the first and three times the square of the second, plus the cube of the second times the linear coefficient, minus the first times the solid coefficient, minus the second times the solid coefficient is equal to the fourth power of the sum of the roots affected both by the addition of the plano-plane from the cube of the sum of the roots and the linear coefficient and by the subtraction of the plano-plane from the sum of the roots and the solid coefficient.

PROPOSITION XXXIX

To construct, from a binomial root, a fifth power affected [both] by the addition of a plano-solid based on the first power [and] by the subtraction of a plano-solid based on the cube, they being properly supplemented by a plano-plane coefficient and a plane coefficient.

Let $A + B$ be a binomial root, D^{pp} the coefficient of the first power and G^p the coefficient of the cube. The fifth power of $A + B$ affected by the addition of the plano-solid produced by the root $A + B$ and D^{pp} and by the subtraction of the plano-solid produced by the cube of $A + B$ and G^p is to be constructed. Form the square of $A + B$ and, having subtracted G^p from it, multiply by $A + B$. Add D^{pp} to the resulting plano-planes and multiply by $A + B$. These plano-solids will then arise: $A^5 + 5A^4B + 10A^3B^2 + 10A^2B^3 + 5AB^4 + B^5 - A^3G^p - 3A^2BG^p - 3AB^2G^p - B^3G^p + AD^{pp} + BD^{pp}$. Hence the

---

[49]1631 has "second" here.
[50]1631 has "second" here, also.

Theorem

If there are two roots and furthermore a plane coefficient for their cube and a plano-plane coefficient for their first power, the fifth power of the first root, plus the product of the fourth power of the first and five times the second, plus the product of the cube of the first and ten times the square of the second, plus the product of the square of the first and ten times the cube of the second, plus the product of the first and five times the fourth power of the second, plus the fifth power of the second, minus the product of the cube of the first and the plane coefficient, minus the product of the plane coefficient and the solid from the square of the first and three times the second, minus the product of the plane coefficient and the solid from the first and three times the square of the second, minus the product of the cube of the second and the plane coefficient, plus the product of the first and the plano-plane coefficient, plus the product of the second and the plano-plane coefficient is equal to the fifth power of the sum of the roots affected by the subtraction of the plano-solid from the cube of the sum of the roots and the plane coefficient and by the addition of the plano-solid from the sum of the roots and the plano-plane coefficient.

The Genesis of Avulsed Powers[51]

Proposition XL

To construct, from a binomial root, a plane based on its first power [and] affected by the subtraction of its square, the former being properly supplemented by a linear coefficient.

Let $A + B$ be a binomial root and the line D the coefficient of its first power. The plane produced by $A + B$ and the line D, affected by the subtraction of the square of $A + B$, is to be constructed. Multiply $D - A - B$ by $A + B$ and these individual planes will result: $AD + BD - A^2 - 2AB - B^2$. Hence arises the

Theorem

If there are two roots and, in addition, a linear coefficient for their first power, the plane from the first root and the linear coefficient, plus the plane

---

[51]*Genesis potestatum avulsarum.* In some other places Viète uses "inverted" or "inverse" to describe the type of equation in which the power is subtracted (more literally, snatched away from or ripped off) from the lower-order terms. Ritter translates this title as "Formation des puissances retranchées."

from the second root and the linear coefficient, minus the square of the first root, minus twice the plane from the roots, minus the square of the second root equals the plane produced by the sum of the roots and the coefficient, affected negatively by the square of the sum of the roots.

Proposition XLI

To construct, from a binomial root, a solid based on its first power [and] affected by the subtraction of its cube, the former being properly supplemented by a plane coefficient.[52]

Let $A + B$ be a binomial root and D^p the coefficient of its first power. The solid from $A + B$ and D^p, affected by the subtraction of the cube of $A + B$, is to be constructed. Multiply $A + B$ by D^p minus the cube of $A + B$. There then arise these solids: $AD^p + BD^p - A^3 - 3A^2B - 3AB^2 - B^3$. Hence is enunciated the

Theorem

If there are two roots and a plane coefficient for the first power, the solid from the first root and the plane coefficient, plus the solid from the second root and the plane coefficient, minus the cube of the first root, minus the solid from the square of the first root and three times the second, minus the solid from the first root and three times the square of the second, minus the cube of the second is equal to the solid from the square of the sum of the roots and the plane coefficient, affected by the subtraction of the cube of that sum.[53]

Proposition XLII

To construct, from a binomial root, a solid based on its square [and] affected by the subtraction of its cube, the former being properly supplemented by a linear coefficient.[54]

Let $A + B$ be a binomial root and the length D the coefficient of its square. The solid produced by the square of $A + B$ and the length D,

[52]1631 has "linear coefficient."
[53]The translation of this proposition and theorem follows the text of 1646. In 1631 nearly the same language appears under the heading of Proposition XLII.
[54]1631 has "plane coefficient."

affected by the subtraction of the cube of $A + B$ is to be constructed. Multiply the square of $A + B$ by $D - A - B$. There will arise the solids $A^2D + 2ABD + B^2D - A^3 - 3A^2B - 3AB^2 - B^3$. Hence is derived the

Theorem

If there are two roots along with a linear coefficient for [their] square, the solid produced by the square of the first root and the linear coefficient, plus the solid produced by twice the product of the roots times the linear coefficient, plus the solid produced by the square of the second root and the linear coefficient, minus the cube of the first root, minus the solid produced by the square of the first root and three times the second root, minus the solid produced by the first root and three times the square of the second root, minus the cube of the second root is equal to the solid produced by the square of the sum of the roots and the linear coefficient affected by the subtraction of the cube of that sum.[55]

PROPOSITION XLIII

To construct, from a binomial root, a plano-plane based on its first power [and] affected by the subtraction of its fourth power, the former being properly supplemented by a solid coefficient.

Let $A + B$ be a binomial root and D^s the coefficient of its first power. The plano-plane[56] from D^s and $A + B$, affected by the subtraction of the fourth power of $A + B$, is to be constructed. Subtract[57] the cube of $A + B$ from D^s and multiply [the difference] by $A + B$. There will arise the plano-planes $AD^s + BD^s - A^4 - 4A^3B - 6A^2B^2 - 4AB^3 - B^4$. Hence arises the

Theorem

If there are two roots and, furthermore, a solid coefficient, the first root times the solid coefficient, plus the second root times the same, minus the fourth power of the first, minus the cube of the first times four times the second, minus the square of the first times six times the square of the

---

[55]The translation of this proposition and theorem follows the text of 1646. In 1631 the same language appears under the heading of Proposition XLI.

[56]1631 has "solid."

[57]1631 has *augeatur;* 1646 has *auferatur.*

second, minus the first times four times the cube of the second, minus the fourth power of the second equals the plano-plane from the sum of the roots and the solid coefficient, affected by the subtraction of the fourth power of the aforesaid sum.

PROPOSITION XLIIII

To construct, from a binomial root, a plano-plane based on its cube [and] affected by the subtraction of its fourth power, the former being properly supplemented by a linear coefficient.

Let $A + B$ be a binomial root and the line D the coefficient of its cube. The solid from the cube of $A + B$ times D, affected by the subtraction of the fourth power of $A + B$, is to be constructed. Multiply the cube of $A + B$ by $D - A - B$. These individual plano-planes will be formed: $A^3D + 3A^2BD + 3AB^2D + B^3D - A^4 - 4A^3B - 6A^2B^2 - 4AB^3$ [58] $- B^4$. From this, then, will be set up the

Theorem

If there are two roots and, furthermore, a linear coefficient, the cube of the first root times the linear coefficient, plus the product of that length and the solid from the square of the first root and three times the second, plus the product of the length and the solid from the first root and three times the square of the second, plus the cube of the second times the length, minus the fourth power of the first, minus the product of the cube of the first and four times the second, minus six times the product of the square of the first and the square of the second, minus the product of the square of the first and four times the cube of the second, minus the fourth power of the second is equal to [the plano-plane from the linear coefficient and the cube of the sum of the roots] [59] affected by the subtraction of the fourth power of that sum. [60]

[58]1631 has $-AB^3$ without the coefficient.

[59]1631 has "the solid of the sum of the roots" in lieu of the bracketed material.

[60]At this point, the text carries an editorial note by Beaugrand reading: "Furthermore, I would like to point out that every theorem on the origin or derivation of affected powers corresponds in order to the individual problems on the solution of the same power that are solved in that most learned work on *The Numerical Solution of Powers*. This certainly ought to be noted."

. *The Genesis of Triangles*

PROPOSITION XLV

To construct a right triangle from two roots

Let there be two roots, A and B. A right triangle is to be constructed from these.

Now, according to the Pythagorean proposition, the square of the side subtending the right angle is equal to the [sum of the] squares of the sides about the right angle. (It is customary, according to the best [usage], to call the subtending side the hypotenuse[61] and the sides about the right [angle] the perpendicular and the base.) Hence the matter boils down [to this]: that from the two given roots three squares are to be constructed one of which is equal to the [sum of the] other two. The root of the greatest of these is likened to the hypotenuse and the roots of the others to the perpendicular and the base.

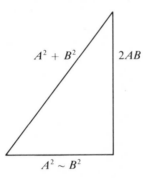

It has already been demonstrated that the square of the sum of two roots is equal to the square of their difference plus four times their product.[62] Hence let a third proportional, B^2/A, be added to the given roots, A and B. The sum of the extremes, the hypotenuse, is $A + B^2/A$. Their difference, the base, is clearly $A \sim B^2/A$. The perpendicular will be $2B$, the square of which is equal to [four times] the product of the extremes. In

---

[61] *Latus autem subtendens solet per excellentiam vocari Hypothenusa.* Ritter translates this as "On a coûtume d'appeler par excellence le côté opposé a l'angle droit 'hypothénuse'." The *per excellentiam* can also be translated as "because of its superiority" but, if this is Viète's meaning, his etymology is clearly deficient.

[62] *et quadruplo sub eisdem lateribus rectangula.* I.e., $(a + b)^2 = (a - b)^2 + 4ab$. Cf. Proposition XIII.

order to reduce all sides to the same type, [multiply] all terms by A:[63] the hypotenuse will be $A^2 + B^2$, the perpendicular $2AB$ and the base $A^2 \sim B^2$.

Hence [one can] construct a right triangle from two roots, for the hypotenuse is analogous[64] to the sum of their squares, the base to the difference between these squares, and the perpendicular to twice the product [of the two roots].

Likewise a right triangle [can be] constructed from three proportionals, for the hypotenuse is analogous to the sum of the extremes, the base to their difference, and the perpendicular to twice the mean.

Corollary

The perpendicular of a right triangle is a mean proportional between the sum of the base and the hypotenuse and their difference.

Proposition XLVI

To construct a third right triangle from two right triangles

Let there be two right triangles [as shown]. Let the hypotenuse of a third be analogous to the product of the hypotenuse of the first and the hypotenuse of the second, namely ZX. [The sum of] the squares of the planes analogous to its base and perpendicular is Z^2X^2, that is, by substitution,[65] the product of $B^2 + D^2$ and $G^2 + F^2$. This product consists of

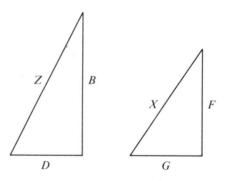

---

[63]*ut ad idem genus adplicationis latera quaeque revocentur.* The word *adplicationis,* Viète's usual term for division, seems to have no place here and has been omitted accordingly. Ritter, however, translates this passage, "On multipliera les trois côtés par A, afin de réduire les côtés au même genre d'application."

[64]*similis.* Ritter translates as "semblable," explaining that *similis* is equivalent to "proportionelle."

[65]*per interpretationem.*

four plano-planes, namely $B^2G^2 + D^2F^2$ and $B^2F^2 + D^2G^2$. Let twice the plano-plane that is the continued [product] of B, D, F and G be added to the first two and subtracted from the last two or, conversely, let it be subtracted from the first two and added to the last two. This adds nothing to and takes nothing away from the [sum of the plano-plane] products, so the resulting plano-planes [are still] equal to the plano-plane Z^2X^2. But, these plano-planes having had added [to them] or subtracted [from them] twice the plano-plane that is the continued product of B, D, F and G, their plane roots can be had. In the first case, one is $BG + DF$, the other $BF \sim DG$; in the second case, one is $BG \sim DF$, the other $BF + DG$. In both cases, the first corresponds to the perpendicular, the second to the base.

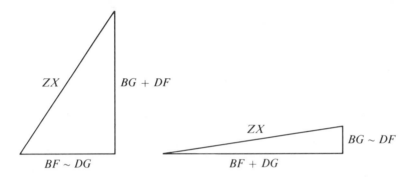

Thus a third right triangle can be constructed from two right triangles by either of these methods. The hypotenuse of the third is analogous to the product of the hypotenuses of the first and second, the perpendicular to the product of the base of the first and the perpendicular of the second plus the reciprocal product of the base of the second and the perpendicular of the first, and the base to the difference between the product of the bases of the first and second and the product of their perpendiculars.

Alternatively, the perpendicular is analogous to the difference between the reciprocal products of the base of one and the perpendicular of the other, and the base to the sum of the product of the bases and the product of the perpendiculars.

Moreover, a right triangle constructed from two other right triangles by the first method is called a synaeresic triangle and [one constructed] by the second method a diaeresic[66] triangle, for reasons set out in the proper

---

[66]Viète borrows these two terms from the language of grammar where synaeresis is defined as the pronunciation of two ordinarily separate vowels as one and diaeresis as the separation of two ordinarily united vowels into two syllables. Ritter points out (p. 273 of his translation) that "la diérèse et la synérèse, dans les proportions, sont les opérations qui

place. Hence the

Theorem

If there are two right triangles, either the square of the plane produced by their hypotenuses is equal to the square of the sum of the reciprocal products of the bases and perpendiculars plus the square of the difference between the product of the bases and the product of the perpendiculars, or it is equal to the square of the difference between the reciprocal products of the bases and perpendiculars plus the square of the sum of the product of the bases and the product of the perpendiculars.

PROPOSITION XLVII

From two similar right triangles, to construct a third such that the square of its hypotenuse is equal to the [sum of the] squares of the hypotenuses of the first and second.

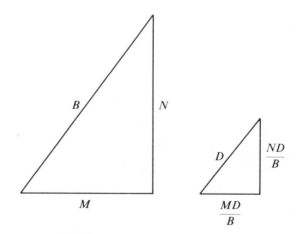

Let there be two similar right triangles, one with the hypotenuse B, perpendicular N and base M, the other with the hypotenuse D, perpendicular consequently ND/B and base MD/B. A third right triangle is to be constructed from these two such that the square of its hypotenuse equals $B^2 + D^2$.

Since, therefore, the square of the hypotenuse [of the third triangle) consists of $B^2 + D^2$, this will be the square of the perpendicular plus the

---

consistent à retrancher les conséquents des antécédents et à ajouter les antécédents aux conséquents."

square of the base of the triangle to be constructed. And if $B^2 + D^2$ is multiplied by $M^2 + N^2$ and divided by B^2, nothing will have been added to or taken away from the square of the constructed hypotenuse, since $M^2 + N^2$ equals B^2 by hypothesis. Perform the multiplication, therefore, and the product will clearly consist of the four plano-planes $B^2M^2 + D^2N^2$ and $B^2N^2 + D^2M^2$. Add twice the plano-plane that is the continued product of B, D, M and N to the first two and subtract it from the last two or, conversely, subtract it from the first two and add it to the last two. This neither adds to nor subtracts from [the sum of] the products that were constructed, and the [sum of the six] plano-planes constructed is equal to the plano-plane product of $B^2 + D^2$ and B^2.[67] Furthermore, each pair of the plano-planes plus or minus twice the common plano-plane, which is the continued product of B, D, M and N, has plane roots. In the first case, one is $BM + DN$, the other $BN \sim DM$. In the second case, one is $BM \sim DN$, the other $BN + DM$. Divide through by B and, in both cases, the first will be analogous to the perpendicular, the second to the base.

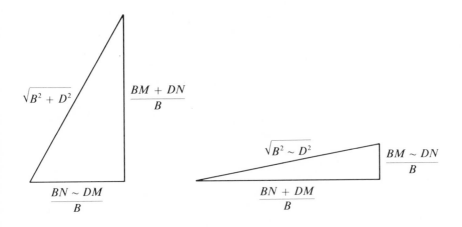

Theorem

If there are two similar right triangles, the sum of the squares of their hypotenuses is equal to the square of the sum of the base of the first and the perpendicular of the second, plus the square of the difference between the perpendicular of the first and the base of the second or, again, is equal to the square of the sum of the perpendicular of the first and the base of the

[67] *Nihil factis accrescit aut deperit quominus facta plano-plana, plano-plano abs B quadrato, et D quadrato in B quadratum aequentur.* I.e., $B^2M^2 + 2BDNM + D^2N^2 + B^2N^2 - 2BDNM + D^2M^2 = B^2(B^2 + D^2)$.

second, plus the square of the difference between the base of the first and the perpendicular of the second.

Proposition XLVIII

From two equal and equiangular right triangles, to construct a third right triangle.

Let there be two right triangles with these common sides: A, the hypotenuse; B, the perpendicular; and D, the base. A third right triangle is to be constructed from these two. Perform the construction as shown in the first case under Proposition XLVI.[68] For this can be constructed only through synaeresis, not diaeresis. This makes the hypotenuse analogous to A^2, the base to $D^2 \sim B^2$ and the perpendicular to $2BD$. For reasons set out in the proper place,[69] the third triangle is called a triangle of the double angle and the first or second is called a triangle of the single angle by way of contrast.

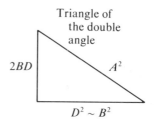

Triangle of
the double
angle

$2BD$ A^2

$D^2 \sim B^2$

Proposition XLIX

From a single-angle right triangle and a double-angle right triangle, to construct a [third] right triangle, which will be called a triangle of the triple angle.

Let there be two right triangles, one of the simple angle with A for its hypotenuse, B for its perpendicular and D for its base, the other of the double angle with its hypotenuse, consequently, analogous to A^2, its base to $D^2 \sim B^2$ and its perpendicular to twice the plane DB. A third right triangle

---

[68]Here and in the following propositions, 1631 refers to "Proposition 36."

[69]The text carries a footnote at this place, presumably by Beaugrand, reading thus: "The reason is that the acute angle of a right triangle derived from two right triangles by synaeresis is equal to the sum of the acute angles of those triangles. Anderson demonstrates the converse of this in the second theorem on angular sections. Moreover, that angle is called acute which the perpendicular subtends."

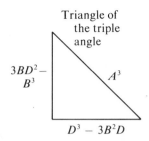

Triangle of the triple angle

$3BD^2 - B^3$

A^3

$D^3 - 3B^2D$

is to be constructed from these two right triangles. Perform the construction as shown in the first case under Proposition XLVI, for this can be constructed only through synaeresis, not through diaeresis. This makes the hypotenuse A^3, the base $D^3 - 3DB^2$ and the perpendicular $3D^2B - B^3$.

PROPOSITION L

From a single-angle right triangle and a triple-angle right triangle, to construct a third right triangle, which will be called a triangle of the quadruple angle.

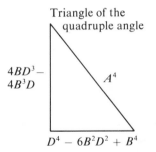

Triangle of the quadruple angle

$4BD^3 - 4B^3D$

A^4

$D^4 - 6B^2D^2 + B^4$

Let there be two right triangles, one of the simple angle, with A as its hypotenuse, B its perpendicular and D its base, the other of the triple angle, with its hypotenuse, consequently, analogous to A^3, its base to $D^3 - 3DB^2$ and its perpendicular to $3D^2B - B^3$. A third right triangle is to be constructed from these. Perform the construction as shown in the first case under Proposition XLVI. This makes the hypotenuse analogous to A^4, the base to $D^4 - 6D^2B^2 + B^4$ and the perpendicular to $4BD^3 - 4B^3D$.

PROPOSITION LI

From a single-angle right triangle and a quadruple-angle right triangle, to construct by synaeresis a third right triangle, which will be called a triangle of the quintruple angle.

Let there be two right triangles, one of the simple angle with A as its hypotenuse, D its base and B its perpendicular, the other of the quadruple angle with its hypotenuse, consequently, analogous to A^4, etc.[70] From these two a third is to be constructed by synaeresis. Perform the construction as shown in the first case under Proposition XLVI. The hypotenuse will be analogous to A^5, the base to $D^5 - 10D^3B^2 + 5DB^4$ and the perpendicular to $5D^4B - 10D^2B^3 + B^5$.

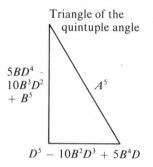

Triangle of the
quintuple angle

$5BD^4 - 10B^3D^2 + B^5$

A^5

$D^5 - 10B^2D^3 + 5B^4D$

[General Corollary]

From the above there follows this general corollary on the construction of right triangles:

If any power of a binomial root is constructed and the individual homogeneous terms that result are separated alternately into two groups in both of which the first [term] is positive, the next negative, [and so on], and the base of a right triangle is assimilated to the first of these and is perpendicular to the second, the hypotenuse will be similar to the power itself. A triangle, moreover, the base of which is similar or equal to one of the roots of the construction and the perpendicular to the other, takes its name from the angle that the perpendicular subtends. Of course, triangles constructed from the same roots will, throughout the whole range of powers, properly be called multiples of the same angle in accordance with the nature of the power: double, that is, when the power is a square; triple, when a cube; quadruple, when a fourth power; quintuple, when a fifth power; and so on in infinite progression.

[70]So in the text.

Proposition LII

From the sum of two roots and their difference to construct a
right triangle.

Let there be two roots, B and D. A right triangle[71] is to be constructed
from $B + D$ for one term and $B \sim D$ for the other. The hypotenuse,
therefore, in accordance with the method already explained, becomes
analogous to the sum of the squares of $B + D$ and $B \sim D$, which two squares
are equal to $2B^2 + 2D^2$. The base will be analogous to the square of $B + D$
minus the square of $B - D$, that is, analogous to $4BD$. Finally the
perpendicular is the product of $B + D$ and twice $B - D$, that is $2B^2 - 2D^2$.

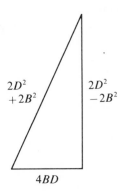

$$2D^2 + 2B^2 \qquad 2D^2 - 2B^2$$

$$4BD$$

This work will turn out the same if [the triangle] is constructed from
the same roots but with the sides which enclose the right angle reversed.

Corollary

If two right triangles are constructed, one from two roots, the other
from their sum and difference, they will be similar, the sides about the right
angle being reversed.[72]

Proposition LIII

From the base of a given right triangle and the sum of its
hypotenuse and perpendicular, to construct a right triangle.

[71]1631 lacks these three words.
[72]I.e., from this Proposition and Proposition XLV, $P'/B'' = B'/P'' = H'/H''$, P', B' and
H' being the components of the triangle constructed from two roots and P'', B'' and H'' being
the components of the triangle constructed from the sum and difference of the same roots.

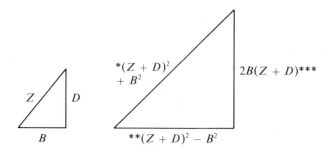

*The figure in the text has $Z + D^2 + B^2$.
** The figure in the text has $Z + D^2 - B^2$.
***The figure in the text has $2BZ + D$.

Let there be a right triangle the hypotenuse of which is Z, the base B and the perpendicular D. A right triangle is to be constructed from B and $Z + D$. Now, by the usual method, the hypotenuse will be analogous to $B^2 + (Z + D)^2$, the base to the difference between these squares,[73] and the perpendicular to twice the plane from B and $Z + D$. If this operation is carefully examined, this triangle will be found to be similar to the first one.[74] So the perpendicular of the first triangle has the same ratio to the base of the second as the base of the first has to the perpendicular of the second.

Corollary I

If a second right triangle is constructed from the base of a given right triangle and the sum of its hypotenuse and perpendicular, the second will be similar to the first, the sides being reversed.

[73]I.e., to $(Z + D)^2 \sim B^2$.
[74]The text carries a note, presumably Beaugrand's, at this point:

"We will demonstrate this, moreover, thus: Since a proportion is not changed by a common multiplication, multiply $2Z + 2D$ both by B and by D. [1631 has $2D$.] Then

$$B:D = (2BZ + 2BD):(2DZ + 2D^2).$$

D^2, however, is equal to $Z^2 - B^2$. Hence if D^2 is subtracted from the fourth term of the proportion and $Z^2 - B^2$ is substituted for it,

$$B:D = (2BZ + 2BD):(Z^2 + 2DZ + D^2 - B^2).$$

But the third proportional is the product of $2B$ and $Z + D$. Likewise $Z^2 + 2ZD + D^2$ is the square of $Z + D$. Hence

$$B:D = (2BZ + D):(Z + D^2 - B^2.$$

Therefore, since the sides of these triangles around the right angle are proportionals, they are equiangular, which is what was to be demonstrated.

Corollary II

In right triangles, the sum of the hypotenuse and the perpendicular is to the base as the sum of the roots from which the triangle is constructed is to their difference. [This follows] from collating the first corollary with the corollary to the preceding proposition.[75]

Corollary III

In right triangles, the sum of the hypotenuse and perpendicular minus the base is to the same sum plus the base as the smaller of the roots is to the greater. (This follows from) diaeresis and synaeresis of the preceding proportion.[76]

Corollary IIII

In a right triangle, the sum of the hypotenuse and the perpendicular minus the base is to the same sum plus the base as the difference between the base and hypotenuse is to the perpendicular.

So the perpendicular of the first has the same ratio to the base of the second as the base of the first has to the perpendicular of the second."

[75]The text carries a note, presumably Beaugrand's, at this point:

"This corollary can also be demonstrated thus: Follow the plan of Proposition XLV in which a right triangle is constructed from the roots A and B. Then, since a ratio is not changed by common multiplication, multiply both $A + B$ and $A \sim B$ by $A + B$. Hence

$$(A^2 + B^2 + 2AB):(A^2 \sim B^2) = (A + B):(A \sim B).$$

But $A^2 + B^2$ is the hypotenuse of the triangle constructed from A and B. [The text has "$A + B$"]. Similarly $2AB$ is the perpendicular of this triangle and $A^2 \sim B^2$ is its base. [1631 gives $2AB$ as the base and $A^2 \sim B^2$ as the perpendicular.] Therefore the sum of the hypotenuse and the perpendicular is to the base as the sum of the roots is to their difference, which is what was to be demonstrated."

[76]The text carries a note, presumably Beaugrand's, at this point:

"Clearly by diaeresis of the proportion in the preceding corollary, the sum of the hypotenuse and perpendicular minus the base is to the base as twice the smaller root is to the difference between the roots.

And by synaeresis of the same proportion, the sum of the hypotenuse, perpendicular and base is to the base as twice the greater root is to the difference between the roots.

Now, inverting the [latter] proportion, the base will be to the sum of the hypotenuse, perpendicular and base as the difference between the roots is to twice the greater root.

Wherefore it follows similarly that the sum of the hypotenuse and perpendicular minus the base is to the sum of the hypotenuse and perpendicular plus the base as the smaller root is to the greater. This in brief is the third corollary, the proof of which was to be adduced although it could have been demonstrated more briefly without the help of the preceding corollary."

The difference between the base and the hypotenuse is to the perpendicular as the smaller of the roots is to the greater. Assuming the two roots are B and D, the former the smaller, the latter the greater, since the hypotenuse is analogous to $B^2 + D^2$ and the base to $D^2 - B^2$, their difference is $2B^2$ and the perpendicular is analogous to $2BD$. Divide both planes by $2B$ and the difference will be to the perpendicular as B is to D.

PROPOSITION LIIII

From a right triangle to construct two right triangles of equal height the union of which results in a triangle of the same height, their hypotenuses forming its legs, the sum of their bases forming its base, and its vertex angle being a right angle.[77]

Given a right triangle with Z as its hypotenuse, B as its base and D as its perpendicular, do that which has been directed.

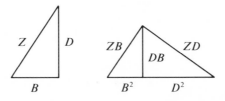

From $Z + D$ as one root and B as the other, another right triangle is to be constructed. Its hypotenuse will be similar to the Z of this one, its base to D and its perpendicular to B. Another triangle similar to this second one is to be constructed, having D as its perpendicular, thus making B to D as D is to its base, which will therefore be D^2/B, and as Z is to its hypotenuse which will be ZD/B. Finally, the sides both of this and of the given [triangle] are multiplied by B. Therefore there are two right triangles: the first, the hypotenuse of which is ZB, the base B^2 and the perpendicular BD; the other, the hypotenuse of which is ZD, the base D^2 and the perpendicular again BD. These two are united into one right triangle, namely [one in which] the hypotenuses become its legs, the sum of the given bases placed end to end its base, the altitude remaining the same and being a proportional between the segments of the base, for BD is the proportional between B^2 and D^2. Likeness of sides in plane figures, moreover, proves

---

[77] At this point in the text appears a note added, presumably, by Beaugrand, to the effect that he had made certain changes in Viète's language to delete an offense against the rules of grammar.

equality of angles, as geometry teaches, so the angle that subtends the perpendicular in the first triangle is equal to the angle that subtends the base in the second. The angle, therefore, resulting from the uniting of the hypotenuses is a right angle.

PROPOSITION LV[78]

From a right triangle, to construct two other triangles of equal height the union of which results in a triangle of the same height, their hypotenuses forming its legs, the sum of their bases forming its base, and its vertex angle being acute.

Given a right triangle the hypotenuse of which is Z, the base B and the perpendicular D, do that which has been ordered.

Assume F to be less than Z and, from $F + D$ as one root and B as the other, construct another right triangle. The hypotenuse will be analogous to $(F + D)^2 + B^2$, the base to $(F + D)^2 - B^2$, the perpendicular to $(F + D)2B$. Construct another triangle similar to this one having D as its perpendicular, thus making $(F + D)2B$ to $(F + D)^2 - B^2$ as D is to the base. This [i.e., the base] will therefore be $\{D[(F + D)^2 - B^2]\}/2B(F + D)$. And as $(F + D)2B$ is to $(F + D)^2 + B^2$, so D is to the hypotenuse which will therefore be $\{D[(F + D)^2 + B^2]\}/(F + D)2B$. Finally multiply the sides both of this and of the given triangle by $(F + D)2B$. There are, therefore, two right triangles, the hypotenuse of one of which is analogous to $Z(F + D)2B$, the base to $B(F + D)2B$ and the perpendicular to $D(F + D)2B$, and the hypotenuse of the other is analogous to $D[(F + D)^2 + B^2]$ and the base to $D[(F + D)^2 - B^2]$ and the perpendicular is the same as that in the first triangle above.

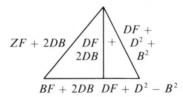

$$ZF + 2DB \quad / \quad DF + 2DB \quad + \quad DF + D^2 + B^2$$

$$BF + 2DB \quad DF + D^2 - B^2$$

These two right triangles are joined into one, their hypotenuses becoming the legs of the new triangle, the sum of their bases placed in a straight line its base, and the altitude therefore remaining the same. Otherwise, as the base of the first is to its altitude, so the altitude is to

---

[78]The diagram accompanying this Proposition appears only in 1646.

something greater than the base of the second. For

$$B(F + D)2B: D(F + D)2B = D(F + D)2B: (2D^3 + 2D^2F).^{79}$$

The base of the second, however, is analogous to $D[(F + D)^2 - B^2]$, that is to $F^2D + 2FD^2 + D^3 - B^2D$. Subtract[80] $2FD^2$ from both and to both add B^2D. Then divide the remaining solids by D. Hence there remains $D^2 + Z^2$ on the one hand[81] and, on the other, $D^2 + F^2$. By hypothesis, however, F^2 is less than Z^2. Hence the altitude is a proportional between the base of the first and something greater than the base of the second. Therefore, the angle that the base of the second subtends is less than that which the perpendicular of the first subtends. So the angle created by the hypotenuses or legs is acute. Therefore there have been created from the [original] right triangle two right triangles of equal height from the union of which a triangle of the same height is constructed, their hypotenuses becoming its legs and the sum of their bases its base, its vertex angle being acute. It is clear, moreover, that F had to be assumed to be such that the square of $F + D$ would be greater than B^2 so that, in setting up the base of the second, B^2 could be subtracted from the square of $F + D$.

PROPOSITION LVI[82]

From a right triangle, to construct two other right triangles
of equal height the union of which results in a triangle of the

[79]At this point the text carries the following footnote, presumably by Beaugrand: "Since

$$B(F + D):D(F + D) = B(F + D):D(F + D),$$

which is clearer than daylight, multiply both the first and second proportional quantities by $2B$ and the third and fourth by $2D$. Then

$$B(F + D)2B:D(F + D)2B = B(F + D)2D:2D^2(F + D).$$

But

$$B(F + D)2D = D(F + D)2B.$$

Similarly, $2D^2(F + D)$ does not differ from $2D^3 + 2FD^2$. Wherefore

$$B(F + D)2B:D(F + D)2B = D(F + D)2B:(2B^3 + 2D^2F),$$

which certainly must have been assumed by the illustrious author."

[80]1631 has *abducatur;* 1646 has *abdicatur.*

[81]The triangle given at the beginning was $Z^2 = B^2 + D^2$. We also have $2D^3 + 2F^2D$ as the third proportional in the proportion set out above and $D[(F + D)^2 - B^2] = F^2D + 2FD^2 + D^3 - B^2D$ as the base of the second triangle. Subtract $2FD^2$ from both and add B^2D to both. Then we have $2D^3 + B^2D$ and $F^2D + D^3$. Divide each by D and the results are $2D^2 + B^2$ and $F^2 + D^2$. But $Z^2 = B^2 + D^2$. Therefore $2D^2 + B^2 = D^2 + Z^2$.

[82]The diagrams do not appear in 1631.

same height, their hypotenuses forming its legs, the sum of their bases forming its base, and its vertex angle being obtuse.

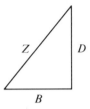

Given a right triangle with hypotenuse Z, base B and perpendicular D, do that which has been directed.

Assume F to be greater than Z, and from $F + D$ as one root and B as the other construct another right triangle. Its hypotenuse will be analogous to $(F + D)^2 + B^2$, its base to $(F + D)^2 - B^2$ and its perpendicular to $(F + D)2B$. Construct another right triangle similar to this second one, with D as its perpendicular, thus making $(F + D)2B$ to $(F + D)^2 - B^2$ as D is to the base, which will therefore be $\{D[(F + D)^2 - B^2]\}/(F + D)2B$. And as $(F + D)2B$ is to $(F + D)^2 + B^2$, so D is to the hypotenuse, which will therefore be $\{D[(F + D)^2 + B^2]\}/(F + D)2B$. Finally multiply the sides both of this and of the given right triangle by $(F + D)2B$. Therefore there are two right triangles, the hypotenuse of the first of which is analogous to $Z(F + D)2B$, the base to $B(F + D)2B$ and the perpendicular to $D(F + D)2B$, and the hypotenuse of the second of which is analogous to $D[(F + D)^2 + B^2]$ and the base to $D[(F + D)^2 - B^2]$, and the perpendicular is the same as that of the preceding right triangle.

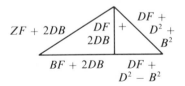

The two right triangles are united, therefore, into one, their hypotenuses becoming the legs of the new one, the sum of their bases in a straight line its base and the altitude, accordingly, remaining the same. Otherwise, as the base of the first is to the altitude, so the altitude is to something less than the base of the second. For as $B(F + D)2B$ is to $D(F + D)2B$, so this magnitude is to $2D^3 + 2FD^2$. And the base of the second is analogous to

$D[(F + D)^2 - B^2]$, that is, to $F^2D + D^3 + 2FD^2 - B^2D$. Subtract[83] $2FD^2$ from both and to both add B^2D. Then divide the remaining solids by D. In one case there remains $D^2 + Z^2$, in the other $D^2 + F^2$. Moreover, F is greater than Z by hypothesis. Therefore the altitude is a proportional between the base of the first and something smaller than the base of the second. Thus, the angle that the base of the second subtends is greater than that which the perpendicular of the first subtends. Hence the angle created by the hypotenuses or legs is obtuse. Which was to be done.

[83] 1631 has *abducatur;* 1646 has *abdicatur.*

FIVE BOOKS OF ZETETICA[1]

FIRST BOOK

Zetetic I[2]

Given the difference between two roots and their sum, to find the roots.

Let *B* be the difference between two roots and let *D* be their sum. The roots are to be found.

Let the smaller root be *A*. The greater will then be $A + B$. So the sum of the roots is $2A + B$. But this has been given as *D*. Hence

$$2A + B = D$$

and, by transposition,

$$2A = D - B.$$

Having divided through by 2,

$$A = \tfrac{1}{2}D - \tfrac{1}{2}B.$$

Or let the greater root be *E*. The smaller will then be $E - B$. Therefore the sum of the roots is $2E - B$. But this has been given as *D*. Hence

$$2E - B = D$$

[1]This title is supplied from the prospectus of the *Opus Restitutae Mathematicae Analyseos, seu Algebra Nova* which appears following the title page of the 1591 edition of the *Isagoge*. In the Latin it is *Zeteticorum Libri Quinque*.

[2]Cf. Diophantus, *Arithmetic*, I, 1. This work is hereafter cited simply as Diophantus. I owe this and most of the subsequent references to Diophantus to Beaugrand's cross-reference table that appears in 1631, p. 70f., and is reprinted practically intact in 1646, p. 4.

and, by transposition,

$$2E = D + B.$$

Dividing through by 2,

$$E = \tfrac{1}{2}D + \tfrac{1}{2}B.$$

Given, therefore, the difference between two roots and their sum, the roots can be found, for

Half the sum of the roots minus half their difference is equal to the smaller root, and [half the sum of the roots] plus [half their difference is equal] to the greater.

It is this that zetetics makes clear.
Let B be 40 and D 100. A is then 30 and E is 70.

Zetetic II [3]

Given the difference between two roots and their ratio, to find the roots.

Let B be the difference between two roots and let the ratio of the smaller to the greater be that of R to S. The roots are to be found.
Let the smaller root be A. The greater will then be $A + B$. Therefore,

$$A:(A + B) = R:S.$$

Resolving this proportion,

$$SA = RA + RB$$

and, by transposition with the contrary sign of affection,

$$SA - RA = RB.$$

Dividing through by $S - R$, $RB/(S - R)$ will equal A. Hence

$$(S - R):R = B:A.$$

Or let the greater root be E. The smaller[4] will be $E - B$. Hence

$$E:(E - B) = S:R.$$

---

[3]Cf. Diophantus, I, 4.

[4]1646 has *Ergo latus—erit E − B*, the elongated minus sign being a misprint for the word *minor*.

Resolving this proportion,

$$RE = SE - SB$$

and, by proper transposition,

$$SE - RE = SB,$$

whence

$$(S - R):S = B:E.$$

Given, therefore, the difference between two roots and their ratio, the roots can be found, for

The difference between [two] true roots is to the larger or smaller true root as the difference between two analogous roots is to the larger or smaller analogous root.[5]

Let B be 12, R 2 and S 3. A is then 24 and E is 36.

Zetetic III[6]

Given the sum of [two] roots and their ratio, to find the roots.

Let the sum of the roots be G and let the ratio of the smaller to the greater be that of R to S. The roots are to be found.

Let the smaller root be A. The larger will then be $G - A$. Hence

$$A:(G - A) = R:S.$$

Resolving this proportion,

$$SA = RG - RA$$

and, transposing in accordance with the art,

$$SA + RA = RG.$$

Hence

$$(S + R):R = G:A.$$

---

[5] *ut differentia similium duorum laterum ad simile latus majus minusve.* That is, as the difference between the two terms of the given ratio is to the larger or smaller term of the ratio.

[6] Cf. Diophantus, I, 2.

Or let the greater root be E. The smaller will then be $G - E$.[7] Hence

$$E:(G - E) = S:R.$$

Resolving this proportion,

$$RE = SG - SE$$

and, transposing in accordance with the art,

$$SE + RE = SG,$$

whence

$$(S + R):S = G:E.$$

Given, therefore, the sum of two roots and their ratio, the roots are given, for

The sum of two true roots is to the greater or smaller true root as the sum of two analogous roots is to the greater or smaller analogous root.

Zetetic IIII[8]

Given two roots that are less than the correct one and the ratio of the deficiencies, to find the correct root.

Let B be the first of two roots that are less than a true one and D the second. And let the ratio of the deficiency in the first to the deficiency in the second be that of R to S. The true root is to be found.

Let the deficiency in the first be A. Then $B + A$ will be the true root. Since, then,

$$R:S = A:\frac{SA}{R},$$

SA/R will be the deficiency in the second. Therefore $D + SA/R$ will also be the true root and,

$$D + \frac{SA}{R} = B + A.$$

Multiply all terms by R.[9] Then

$$DR + SA = BR + AR$$

---

[7]1591 has, *Vel, latus majus esto E latus minus G − E*; 1646 has *Vel, latus majus esto E. Ergo latus minus erit G − E.*

[8]Cf. Diophantus, I, 7.

[9]*Omnia in R.* This is the first of many places in the *Zetetica* where Viète omits any verb

and, setting this up as an equation,[10]

$$DR \sim BR = RA \sim SA.$$

Hence

$$(R \sim S){:}R = (D \sim B){:}A.^{11}$$

Or let the deficiency in the second be E. Then $D + E$ will be the true root. Since, however,

$$S{:}R = E{:}\frac{RE}{S},$$

RE/S will be the deficiency in the first. So $B + RE/S$ will also be the true root and will equal $D + E$. Multiply all terms by S. Then

$$BS + RE = DS^{12} + SE$$

and, setting this up as an equation,

$$DS \sim BS = RE \sim SE.$$

Therefore

$$(R \sim S){:}S = (D \sim B){:}E.^{13}$$

Given, therefore, two roots that are less than the correct ones and the ratio of the deficiencies, the true roots can be found, for

The true difference between [two] deficient roots, which is also [the difference between] the deficiencies [themselves], is to the true deficiency in the first or second root as the difference between the analogous deficiencies is to the analogous deficiency in the first or second root. Properly adding the deficiency [to the deficient root][14] yields the true root.

Let B be 76, D 4, R 1 and S 4. A becomes 24 and E 96.

ALTERNATIVELY

Given two roots that are less than the correct one and the ratio of the deficiencies, to find the correct root.

---

to show that multiplication is called for, relying on the force of the word *in* (see p. 19) to convey the idea by itself.

[10] *Et aequalitate ordinata.* That is, putting all expressions containing the unknown on one side of the equality sign and all others on the other.

[11] 1591 has $(R \sim S) : R = D : (A \sim B)$.

[12] 1591 has *DG*.

[13] 1591 has $(R \sim S) : S = D : (E \sim B)$.

[14] 1591 does not have these words. They were added by the editor in 1646.

As before let B be the first of two roots that are less than the correct one and D the second. Let the ratio of the deficiency in the first to the deficiency in the second be that of R to S. The correct root is to be found.

Let this be A. Therefore $A - B$ will be the deficiency in the first and $A - D$ the deficiency in the second. Hence

$$(A - B){:}(A - D) = R{:}S.$$

Resolving this proportion,

$$RA - RD = SA - SB$$

and, transposing in accordance with the art,

$$SA \sim RA = SB \sim RD.$$

So $(SB \sim RD)/S \sim R$ will equal A.

Given, therefore, two roots that are less than a correct root and the ratio of the deficiencies, the true root can be found, for

If the difference between the product of the first deficient root and the second analogous deficiency and the product of the second deficient root and the first analogous deficiency is divided by the difference between the analogous deficiencies, the true root that is being sought will be produced.

Let B be 76, D 4, R 1 and S 4. A becomes 100.

Zetetic V [15]

Given two roots that are larger than a correct one and the ratio of the surpluses, to find the correct one.

Let B be the first of the two excessive roots and D the second, and let the ratio of the excess in the first to the excess in the second be that of R to S. The true root is to be found.

Let the excess in the first be A. Therefore $B - A$ will be the true root. Since, however,

$$R{:}S = A{:}\frac{SA}{R},$$

SA/R will be the excess in the second. Therefore $D - SA/R$ will also be the true root and will be equal to $B - A$. Multiply all terms by R. Then

$$DR - SA = BR - RA$$

[15]Cf. Diophantus, I, 9.

and, setting this up as an equation,

$$DR \sim BR = SA \sim RA,$$

whence

$$(S \sim R):R = (D \sim B):A.$$

Or let the excess in the second be E. Then $D - E$ will be the true root. Since, however,

$$S:R = E:\frac{RE}{S},$$

RE/S will be the excess in the first. Hence $B - RE/S$ will also be the true root and will be equal to $D - E$. Multiply all terms by S. Then

$$BS - RE = DS - SE.$$

Setting this up as an equation,

$$DS \sim BS = SE \sim RE,$$

whence

$$(S \sim R):S = (D \sim B):E.$$

Given, therefore, two roots larger than a true one and the ratio of the excesses, the true root can be found, for

As the difference between the analogous excesses is to the analogous excess in the first or second root, so is the true difference between the excesses (which is also an excess) to the true excess in the first or second. Having made a proper subtraction [from the excessive root,][16] the true root is found.

Let B be 60, D 40, R 3 and S 1. A is then 30 and E is 10.[17]

ALTERNATIVELY

Given two roots larger than the correct one and the ratio of the surpluses, to find the true root.

Again let B be the first of two roots that exceed a true one and D the second, and let the ratio of the excess of the first to the excess of the second be that of R to S. The true root is to be found.

[16] 1591 does not have the bracketed words. They were added by the editor in 1646.
[17] The text has B 60, D 40, S 3, R 1, A 40 and E 120, but this is impossible.

Let this be A. Hence $B - A$ will be the excess in the first and $D - A$ the excess in the second. Therefore

$$(B - A)^{18}:(D - A) = R{:}S.$$

Resolving this proportion,

$$RD - RA = SB - SA$$

and, transposing in accordance with the art,

$$SA \sim RA = SB \sim RD.^{19}$$

Hence $(SB \sim RD)/S \sim R$ equals A.

Given, therefore, two roots larger than a true one and the ratio of their excesses, the true root can be found, for

If the difference between the product of the first excessive root and the analogous excess in the second and the product of the second excessive and the analogous excess in the first is divided by the difference between the analogous excesses, the true root arises.

Let B be 60, D 140, S 3 and R 1. A becomes 20.

Zetetic VI

Given two roots, one less than the true root, the other greater, along with the ratio of the deficiency to the excess, to find the true root.

Let the two roots be B, which is less than the true root, and D, which is greater, and let the ratio of the deficiency to the excess be that of R to S. The true root is to be found.

Let the deficiency be A. Therefore the true root will be $B + A$. Since, then

$$R{:}S = A{:}\frac{SA}{R},$$

SA/R will be the excess. Hence also $D - SA/R$ will be the true root and will be equal to $B + A.^{20}$ Multiply all terms by R. Then

$$DR - SA = BR + RA$$

[18] 1591 has $(D - A)$.
[19] 1591 has $(SA - RA) = (SB - RD)$.
[20] 1591 has D + A.

and, setting this up as an equation,

$$RA + SA = DR - BR.$$

Hence

$$(S + R):R = (D - B):A.$$

Or let the excess be E. Then the true root will be $D - E$. Since, then,

$$S:R = E:\frac{RE}{S},$$

RE/S will be the deficiency. Thus $B + RE/S$ will also be the true root and will equal $D - E$. Multiply everything by S. Then

$$BS + RE = DS - SE$$

and, setting this up as an equation,

$$RE + SE = DS - BS.$$

Hence

$$(S + R)^{21}:S = (D - B)^{22}:E.$$

Given, therefore, two roots, one smaller than the true root, the other larger, along with the ratio of the deficiency to the excess, the true root can be found, for

The [ratio of the] true difference between the deficient and excessive [roots]—this difference being the sum of the true deficiency and the true excess—to the true deficiency or true excess is that of the sum of the analogous deficiency and the analogous excess to the analogous deficiency or analogous excess. Thus, having added the deficiency [to the deficient root] or having subtracted the excess [from the excessive root,][23] the true root appears.

Let B be 60, D 180, R 1 and S 5. A becomes 20 and E 100.[24]

ALTERNATIVELY

Given two roots, one less than the correct root, the other greater, along with the ratio of the deficiency to the excess, to find the true root.

---

[21]1646 has $(S - R)$.

[22]1591 has $(D + B)$.

[23]Neither bracketed phrase is found in 1591; they were added by the editor of 1646.

[24]1591 has S 3. If this is correct, Van Schooten observes, A should be 30 and E 90. He suggests that S be made 5, as here, in which case, he says E becomes 150, all other terms remaining the same.

Let the roots again be B, which is less than the true one, and D, which is greater, and let the ratio of the deficiency to the excess be that of R to S. The true root is to be found.

Let this be A. So $A - B$ will be the deficiency and $D - A$ will be the excess. Hence

$$(A - B):(D - A) = R:S.$$

Resolving this proportion,

$$RD - RA = SA - SB$$

and, transposing these products in accordance with the art,

$$SA + RA = RD + SB.$$

So $(RD + SB)/(S + R)$ will equal A.

Given, therefore, two roots, one less than the true root, the other greater, and given also the ratio of the deficiency to the excess, the true root can be found, for

The product of the analogous deficiency and the greater root plus the product of the analogous excess and the deficient root divided by the sum of the analogous excess and deficiency gives rise to the true root.

Let B be 60, D 180, R 1 and S 5. A becomes 80.

Zetetic VII[25]

To divide a given root in such fashion that a predefined part of one segment[26] plus a predefined part of the other is equal to a prescribed sum.

Let B be a root that is to be cut into two such segments that the sum of a portion of the first segment with a ratio to the whole (that is, to the first segment itself) of D to B and a portion of the second segment with a ratio to the whole (that is, to the second segment itself) of F to B is H.

Let A be the portion that the first segment is to furnish for H. Therefore the portion that the second segment must contribute will be $H -$

A. And since

$$D:B = A:\frac{BA}{D},$$

---

[25]Cf. Diophantus, I, 5.

[26]*praefinitae unciae unius segmenti.* On the word *uncia,* see n. 6, p. 236 infra.

BA/D will be the whole of the first segment. And since

$$F{:}B = (H - A){:}\frac{BH - BA^{27}}{F},$$

$(BH - BA^{27})/F$ will be the whole of the second segment. These two segments will be equal to the entire root that is to be divided. Hence

$$\frac{BA}{D} + \frac{BH - BA}{F} = B.$$

Having set this up as an equation by multiplying all terms by DF, dividing by B and transposing properly, then [if] D is a greater fraction than F, $(HD - FD)/(D - F)$ will equal A. Therefore,

$$(D - F){:}(H - F) = D{:}A.$$

Or let E be the portion that the second segment must furnish for H. Then the portion that the first must contribute will be $H - E$. And since

$$F{:}B = E{:}\frac{BE}{F},$$

BE/F will be the whole of the second segment. Likewise, since

$$D{:}B = (H - E){:}\frac{BH - BE}{D},$$

$(BH - BE)/D$ will be the whole of the first segment. These two segments are equal to the whole root that is to be divided. Hence

$$\frac{BE}{F} + \frac{BH - BE}{D} = B.$$

Having set this up as an equation by multiplying all terms by FD, dividing by B and transposing properly, $(DF - HF)/(D - F)$ will equal E since, in this case, the fraction of D is known to be greater than that of F. Therefore

$$(D - F){:}(D - H) = F{:}E.$$

Given, therefore, the prescribed portions of the segments,[28] the wholes of the segments themselves are given. That is, BA/D will be the first segment and BE/F will be the second.

Hence a given root can be so cut that a predetermined part of one

---

[27] In these two places, 1646 has $(BH \sim BA)/F$.
[28] The text has "the portions of the preconstituted segments."

segment plus a predetermined part of the other equals a prescribed sum,[29] for

The whole root having been divided in the ratio of the fractions to be contributed by the segments, then [1] as the analogue of the fraction to be contributed by the first segment (if it is greater than that [to be contributed by] the second, minus the analogue of the fraction to be contributed by the second is to the analogue of the fraction to be contributed by the first, so the prescribed sum of the contributions minus the prescribed analogue of the fraction of the second is to the true fraction of the first, or [2] as the analogue of the fraction to be contributed by the first segment minus the analogue of the fraction to be contributed by the second is to the analogue of the fraction to be contributed by the second, so the analogue of the fraction to be contributed by the first minus the prescribed sum of the contributions is to the true fraction to be contributed by the second.[30]

Let B be 60, D 20, F 12 and H (composed of A and E) 14. A is then 5 and E is 9.

It is clear, moreover, that H, the sum of the contributions, should be prescribed as lying between D and F, the former being the smaller and the latter the larger. So, in this case, 14 is less than 20 but greater than 12.

Zetetic VIII[31]

To divide a given root in such fashion that a predefined part of the first segment subtracted from a predefined part of the second is equal to a prescribed difference.

Let B be the root that is to be cut into two such segments that a portion

---

[29]The Latin varies slightly between 1591 and 1646, but with no change in meaning, thanks to Van Schooten's grammatical and clarifying changes.

[30]As translated this passage follows 1591. In 1646 the statement had been revised to read thus: "The [whole] given root having been divided in the ratio of the fractions to be contributed by the segments, then [1] as the analogue of the fraction to be contributed by the first segment (if the fraction to be contributed by it is greater than that [to be contributed by] the second) minus the analogue of the fraction to be contributed by the second is to the prescribed sum of the contributions minus the prescribed analogue of the fraction of the second, so the analogue of the fraction to be contributed by the first is to the true fraction of the first, or [2] as the analogue of the fraction to be contributed by the first segment minus the analogue of the fraction to be contributed by the second is to the analogue of the fraction to be contributed by the first minus the prescribed sum of the contributions, so the analogue of the fraction to be contributed by the second is to the true fraction to be contributed by the second."

[31]Cf. Diophantus, I, 6.

of the first segment is to the whole (that is, to the segment itself) as D is to B. This is to be subtracted from a portion of the second segment that is to the whole (that is, to the second segment itself) as F is to B. The result is H. A different division, of course, would be made if the first segment were called on for the larger fraction, on account of a proposed excess, than when [its fraction is] the smaller. In either case, however, the operation is the same, so D can be either a larger or a smaller fraction than F.[32]

Let the part of the first segment that is called for be A. The part demanded from the second, therefore, will be $A - H$. And since

$$D{:}B = A{:}\frac{BA}{D},$$

BA/D will be the first segment. Likewise, since

$$F{:}B = (A - H){:}\frac{BA - BH}{F},$$

$(BA - BH)/F$ will be the second segment. These two segments will be equal to the whole root that was to be divided. Therefore

$$\frac{BA}{D} + \frac{BA - BH}{F} = B$$

and, setting this up as an equation, $(DF + DH)/(D + F)$ equals A. Therefore

$$(D + F){:}(F + H) = D{:}A.$$

Furthermore, since the part to be contributed by the second is $A - H$, then this is the remainder when H is subtracted from $(DF + DH)/(D + F)$. Let this be E. Therefore $(DF - HF)/(D + F)$[33] will equal E, whence

$$(D + F){:}(D - H) = F{:}E.$$

Given, moreover, the fractions of the prescribed segments, the wholes or the segments themselves are given, namely BA/D for the first and BE/F for the second.

A given root, therefore, can be so divided that a predetermined fraction of the first segment subtracted from a predetermined fraction of the second is equal to a prescribed difference, for

The whole given root having been divided in the ratio of the fractions to be contributed by the segments, then [1] as the analogues of the

---

[32]The text has B.

[33]1591 omits the denominator of this fraction.

fractions to be contributed by the first and second segments are to the prescribed difference between these contributions plus the analogue of the fraction derived from the second, so the analogue of the fraction derived from the first is to the true fraction derived from the first, or [2] as the analogues of the fractions derived from the first and second segments are to the analogue of the fraction derived from the first minus the prescribed difference between the derived [fractions], so the analogue of the fraction derived from the second is to the true fraction derived from the second.

Let *B* be 84, *D* 28, *F* 21 and *H* 7. *A* becomes 16 and *E* 9.

It is apparent, also, that *H*, the difference between the derived [fractions], should be prescribed as less than *D*, the fraction derived from the first segment. As to the remainder that is proposed, [it can be] either larger or smaller than the contribution from the second segment.

Thus, in the last case, 7 is less than 28.[34]

Zetetic IX

To find two roots the difference between which is prescribed and, furthermore, [is such that] a predefined fraction of one root plus a predefined fraction of the other is equal to a prescribed sum.

Let *B* be the difference between two roots, a portion of the first of which is to the whole (that is, to the first root itself) as *D* is to *B*. This plus a smaller portion which is to its whole (that is, to the second root) as *F* is to *B*, makes *H*. The two roots are to be found.

The first root is known to be either the larger or the smaller. Suppose, in the first instance, it is known to be the larger. Therefore let the portion that the first or greater root contributes be *A*. The portion that the second or smaller root contributes will therefore be $H - A$. And, since

$$D{:}B = A{:}\frac{BA}{D},$$

BA/D will be the greater root. Since, also,

$$F{:}B = (H - A){:}\frac{BH - BA}{F},$$

$(BH - BA)/F$ will be the smaller root. Therefore

$$\frac{BA}{D} - \frac{BH - BA}{F} = B$$

[34] The text has 21.

and, setting this up as an equation, $(DF + DH)/(F + D)$ will equal A. Whence

$$(F + D):(F + H) = D:A.$$

Furthermore, since the portion contributed by the second is $H - A$, this is the remainder when $(DF + HD)/(F + D)$ is subtracted from H. Let this be E. Hence $(HF - DF)/(F + D)$ will equal E, and

$$(F + D):(H - D) = F:E.$$

In the second case, let the first segment be known as the smaller. So the second segment will be the larger. Let the portion to be contributed by the second be E again. And, since

$$F:B = E:\frac{BE}{F},$$

BE/F will be the second and greater root. Likewise, since

$$D:B = (H - E):\frac{BH - BE}{D},$$

$(BH - BE)/D$ will be the first and smaller root. Therefore

$$\frac{BE}{F} - \frac{BH - BE}{D} = B$$

and, setting this up as an equation, $(FH + FD)/(D + F)$ will equal E. Hence

$$(D + F):(H + D) = F:E.$$

Furthermore, since the portion contributed by the first is $H - E$, this is what remains when $(FH + FD)/(D + F)$[35] is subtracted from H. Let this be A. Then $(HD - FD)/(F + D)$ will equal A, and

$$(F + D):(H - F) = D:A.$$

Given, moreover, the fractions of the roots, the wholes or the roots themselves are given. That is BA/D will be the first root, BE/F the second.

Two roots can be found, then, the difference between which is prescribed and a predefined fraction of one of which plus a predefined fraction of the other equals a prescribed sum, for

The whole difference between the roots that are to be found having been divided in the ratio of the portions to be contributed by the roots, [1] the [sum of the] analogous portions to be contributed by the greater and

---

[35] 1591 has $(HE + DF)/(F + D)$.

the smaller roots is to the prescribed sum of the contributions plus the analogous part of the smaller root as the analogous part of the greater is to the true part to be contributed by it, or [2] the [sum of the] analogous parts to be contributed by the greater and smaller roots is to the prescribed sum of the contributions minus the analogous part of the greater root as the analogous part of the smaller is to the true part to be contributed by it.

Let B be 38,[36] D 28, F 21 and H 98. A becomes 68 and E 30.

It is clear that the sum of the contributions ought to be so prescribed that it is greater than[37] D, the analogous part derived from the greater segment. Thus 98 is greater than 28.

Zetetic X

To find two roots the difference between which is given and a predefined fraction of the first of which minus a predefined fraction of the second is equal to the given difference.

Let B be the difference between two roots, a portion of the first of which bearing to the whole (that is, to the first root) the ratio of D to B minus a portion of the second bearing to the whole (that is, to the second root) the ratio of F to B makes H. The two roots are to be found.

Let the first root be known as either the greater or the smaller of the two. From it is to be exacted a fraction either greater or smaller than that from the second. The operation is the same [in either case].

Let D, therefore, be the fraction, greater or smaller, furnished by the first root. In the first case let the first root's fractional contribution, which will undergo a loss, be the greater of the two. And let the portion attributable to it be A. Then the portion contributed by the second will be $A - H$, as the difference between the two contributions is H, if an excess exists on account of the first. The first root will be BA/D, the second $(BA - BH)/F$. So

$$\frac{BA}{D} - \frac{BA - BH}{F} = B.$$

Having set this up as an equation, if the F fraction is greater than the D fraction, $(FD - HD)/(F - D)$ will equal A. Hence

$$(F - D):(F - H) = D:A.$$

---

[36] The text has 84.
[37] 1591 has "less than."

Furthermore, since the portion contributed by the second is $A - H$, this is the remainder when H is subtracted from $(FD - HD)/(F - D)$. Let this be E. Therefore $(FD - FH)/(F - D)$[38] will equal E, and

$$(F - D):(D - H) = F:E.^{39}$$

In the second case, let the first root be the smaller of the two and let the portion contributed by it again be A. Hence the portion contributed by the second or greater root will be $A - H$, the first root will be BA/D, and the second root will be $(BA - BH)/F$. Therefore

$$\frac{BA - BH}{F} - \frac{BA}{D} = B.$$

Setting this up as an equation, $(FD + HD)/(D - F)$ will equal A. Hence

$$(D - F):(F + H) = D:A.$$

Furthermore, since the portion contributed by the second or greater root is $A - H$, this is what is left when H is subtracted from $(FD + HD)/(D - F)$. Let this be E. Hence $(DF + HF)/D - F$ will equal E. Whence

$$(D - F):(D + H) = F:E.$$

The course of the work shows that, in this second case, the portion exacted from the first [root] is greater than that exacted from the second. Furthermore, given the fractions of the roots being sought, the wholes or the roots themselves are given. That is, BA/D will be the first root and BE/F will be the second.

Therefore two roots can be found the difference between which is a prescribed amount and a predetermined fraction of the first of which minus a predetermined fraction of the second of which is equal to the given difference, for

Having divided the whole difference between the roots that are being sought in the ratio of the fractions to be contributed by the roots, then if the first of the two roots is the greater and the larger fraction is demanded of it, [1] as the analogous fraction contributed by the first minus the analogous fraction contributed by the second is to the prescribed difference between the contributions minus the analogous fraction contributed by the second, so the analogous fraction contributed by the first is to the true fraction contributed by the first, or [2] as the analogous fraction contributed by the first minus the analogous fraction contributed by the second is to the prescribed difference between these contributions minus

---

[38] 1591 has $(FD \sim DH)/(F \sim D)$ here and in the preceding fraction.
[39] 1591 has $(F \sim D) : (D \sim H) = F : E$.

the analogous fraction contributed by the first, so the analogous fraction contributed by the second is to the true fraction contributed by the second.

But if a smaller part is demanded from the first or greater root than is demanded from the second or smaller root, the same ratios will hold good [but] with the negative [and positive] terms reversed.

If the first root, from a predefined fraction of which the subtraction is to be made, is the smaller of those being sought and the greater fraction is to be exacted from it, the result is that [1] as the analogous fraction contributed by the first root minus the analogous fraction contributed by the second is to the analogous fraction contributed by the second plus the prescribed difference between the contributions, so the analogous fraction contributed by the first is to the true fraction contributed by the first, or [2] as the analogous fraction contributed by the first minus the analogous fraction contributed by the second is to the analogous fraction contributed by the first plus the prescribed difference between the contributions, so the analogous fraction contributed by the second is to the true fraction contributed by the second.

Thus there are three cases:

The first is when the first root—that from a portion of which the subtraction is made—is the greater of the two and the greater fraction is contributed by it.

The second is when the same root remains the greater but the smaller fraction is exacted from it.

The third is when the first root is the smaller of the two and the greater fraction is exacted [from it] and one cannot exact a smaller fraction from it.

In the first case, H must be so prescribed that it is greater than the analogous part of the first segment and, consequently, greater also than F, the analogous fraction of the second segment.

In the second case it must be less than D or F.

In the third case, H may be greater or smaller than D or F. Thus this third case may accord with either the first or the second.

I

Let B (the difference between two roots) be 12, D 4, F 3 and H (the difference by which A exceeds E,[40] 9, since H is greater than either D or F. BA/D is known to be either the greater or smaller root:

[40]The text has F.

1. If it is the greater, A becomes 24 and E 15, and BA/D, the first and greater root, is 72 and BE/F, the second and smaller, is 60. The difference between these is the prescribed B.

2. If, however, it is known that BA/D is the smaller root, A becomes 48 and E 39. And BA/D is 144 and BE/F is 156. The difference between these is the prescribed B.

II

1. Again let B (the difference between two roots) be 48, D 16, F 12 and H (the difference by which A exceeds E^{41}) 10. Since H is less than either D or F and D is greater than F, BA/D is necessarily the smaller root and BE/F the greater root. This makes A 88 and E 78. Then BA/D becomes 264 and BE/F 312. And the difference between these is [what was] prescribed for B.

2. Or let D be 12 and F 16, B remaining 48 and H 10. BA/D is necessarily the greater root. A then becomes 18 and E 8. And BA/D is 72 and BE/F is 24. The difference between these is the prescribed B.

SECOND BOOK
Zetetic I

Given the product of the roots[42] and their ratio, to find the roots.

The plural, without more, is satisfied by the number two. Let, therefore, B^p be a rectangle produced by two roots and let the ratio of the greater of these to the smaller be that of S to R. The roots are to be found.

Let the greater root be A. Since, therefore,

$$S{:}R = A{:}\frac{RA}{S},$$

RA/S will be the smaller root. So the plane produced by the roots will be RA^2/S, which is equal to the given B^p. Multiply all terms by S. RA^2 will then equal SB^p. Reducing the equation to a proportion,

$$R{:}S = B^p{:}A^2.$$

[41] 1646 has D.

[42] *Dato rectangulo sub lateribus.* For simplicity's sake, I have reduced "rectangle on the roots" or "rectangle produced by the roots" to "the product of the roots" here and in many other places hereafter.

Alternatively, let the smaller root be E. Since, therefore,

$$R:S = E:\frac{SE}{R,}$$

SE/R will be the greater root. The rectangle produced by the roots will be SE^2/R which is consequently equal to B^p. Multiply all terms by R, and SE^2 will equal RB^p. Reducing the equation to a proportion,

$$S:R = B^p:E^2.$$

Given, therefore, a plane which is the product of two roots along with the ratio of the roots, the roots can be found, for

As the first analogous root is to the second analogous root, larger or smaller, so the product of the roots is to the square of the second root, larger or smaller.

Let B^p be 20, R 1, S 5 and A x. Then x^2 equals 100. Or let E be x. Then x^2 equals 4.

Zetetic II

Given the product of the roots and the sum of their squares, the roots will be found.

Twice the product of the roots plus the sum of their squares is equal to the square of the sum of the roots, and [twice the product of the roots] subtracted [from the sum of their squares is equal] to the square of the difference [between the roots].

This is clear from the origin of a square. Given, moreover, the difference between, and the sum of, two roots, the roots are given.

Let 20 be the product of the roots, the sum of the squares of which is 104. And let the sum of the roots be x. Then x^2 equals 144. Or let the difference [between the roots] be x. X^2 then equals 64.

Zetetic III[43]

Given the product of the roots and their difference, the roots will be found.

The square of the difference between the roots plus four times their product is equal to the square of the sum of the roots.

[43]Cf. Diophantus, I, 30.

It has already been demonstrated that the square of the sum of the roots minus the square of their difference equals four times the product of the roots. Therefore the only operation [to be performed] is that of transposition. Given, moreover, the difference between, and the sum of, two roots, the roots are given.

Let 20 be the product of two roots the difference between which is 8. Let the sum of the roots be x. Then x^2 equals 144.

Zetetic IIII [44]

Given the product of the roots and their sum, the roots will be found.

The square of the sum of the roots minus four times their product is equal to the square of their difference.

Again, one can arrive at this from the last preceding demonstration by transposition.

Let the product of two roots the sum of which is 12 be 20. And let the difference between the roots be x. X^2 equals 64.

Zetetic V

Given the difference between the roots and the sum of their squares, the roots will be found.

Twice the sum of the squares minus the square of the difference between the roots is equal to the square of the sum of the roots.

It has already been shown that the square of the sum of the roots plus the square of their difference is equal to twice the sum of their squares,[45] so the only operation [required] is that of transposition.

Let the difference between the roots be 8, the sum of their squares 104 and the sum of the roots x. X^2 equals 144.

Zetetic VI [46]

Given the sum of the roots and the sum of their squares, the roots will be found.

[44] Cf. Diophantus, I, 27.
[45] *Preliminary Notes,* Prop. XII.
[46] Cf. Diophantus, I, 28.

Twice the sum of the squares minus the square of the sum of the roots is equal to the square of the difference between the roots.

This may be inferred from the next preceding demonstration by transposition.

Let the sum of the roots be 12, the sum of their squares 104 and the difference between the roots x. X^2 equals 64.

Zetetic VII

Given the difference between the roots and the difference between their squares, the roots will be found.

If the difference between the squares is divided by the difference between the roots, the quotient is the sum of the roots.

It has already been shown that the difference between the roots, when multiplied by the sum of the roots, produces the difference between their squares.[47] Division undoes the work that multiplication effects.

Let the difference between the roots be 8 and between their squares 96. The sum of the roots becomes 12. The greater root is 10 and the smaller 2.

Zetetic VIII[48]

Given the sum of the roots and the difference between their squares, the roots will be found.

If the difference between the squares of the roots is divided by their sum, the quotient is the difference between the roots.

This is clear from the preceding note.

Let the sum of the roots be 12 and the difference between their squares 96. The difference between the roots is 8. Hence the greater root is 10, the smaller 2.

Zetetic IX

Given the product of the roots and the difference between their squares, to find the roots.

[47] *Preliminary Notes,* Prop. XIIII
[48] Cf. Diophantus, I, 29.

Let B^p be the product of the roots and let D^p be the difference between their squares. The roots are to be found.

Let the sum of the squares be A^p. Therefore the square of the sum of the roots will be $A^p + 2B^p$ and the square of the difference $A^p - 2B^p$. The product of the sum of [two] roots and their difference is the difference between their squares. So the square of the sum of the roots times the square of their difference yields the square of the difference between the squares.[49] Hence

$$A^{pp} - 4B^{pp} = D^{pp}$$

and, setting this up as an equation,

$$A^{pp} = D^{pp} + 4B^{pp}.$$

Therefore, given the sum of the squares and their difference or the product of the roots, the roots are given, for

The square of the difference between the squares plus the square of twice their product is equal to the square of the sum of the squares.

Let B^p be 20, D^p 96 and A^p x. X^2 equals 10,816.

Zetetic X

Given a plane consisting of the product of the roots and the squares of the individual roots and given also one of the roots, to find the other root.

Let B^p consist of the [sum of the] product of the roots and the squares of each of them and, furthermore, let D be one of the roots. The second root is to be found.

Let A be the root that is being sought plus one-half the given root. The exact root that is being sought, therefore, will be $A - \frac{1}{2}D$. The square of this is $A^2 - DA + \frac{1}{4}D^2$. The square of the given root, of course, is D^2. These two squares plus the product of the roots are equal to B^p, in accordance with what was proposed. The product of the roots is $DA - \frac{1}{2}D^2$.[50] Hence

$$A^2 + \frac{3}{4}D^2 = B^p$$

and, setting this up as an equation,[51]

$$A^2 = B^p - \frac{3}{4}D^2.$$

[49] I. e., if x and y are the roots, $(x + y)^2(x - y)^2 = (x^2 - y^2)^2$ or, as Viète next makes clear, $(x^2 + y^2)^2 - 4x^2y^2$.

[50] 1591 has $DA - \frac{1}{4}D^2$.

[51] 1591 omits this word.

Given, therefore, a plane that consists of the product of the roots plus the individual squares of the roots and given also one of the roots, the other root is found, for

The plane made up of the product of the roots and the squares of the individual roots minus three-quarters of the square of the given root is equal to the square of a root made up of the sought-for root and one-half the given root.

Let B^p be 124, D 2 and A x. X^2 equals 121. Therefore $\sqrt{121} - 1$ is the root being sought.

Or let B^p be 124, D 10 and A x. X^2 equals 49. Therefore $\sqrt{49} - 5$ is the root being sought.

Zetetic XI

Given a plane which consists of the product of the roots plus the squares of the individual roots and given also the sum of these roots, to determine the roots.

Let B^p consist of the [sum of the] product of the roots and the squares of each of the roots and, furthermore, let G be the sum of the roots. The roots are to be found.

Let A^p be the product of the roots. Since, therefore, the square of the sum of the roots is equal to the squares of the individual roots plus twice their product,

$$G^2 = B^p + A^p$$

and, setting this up as an equation,[52]

$$G^2 - B^p = A^p.$$

Given, then, the sum of the roots and their product, the roots are also given.

Given, therefore, a plane which consists of the product of the roots plus the square of each of them and given, furthermore, the sum of these roots, the roots can be determined, for

The square of the sum [of two roots] minus the composite plane[53] leaves the product of the roots.

Let B^p be 124 and G 12. A^p becomes 20. So the square of the difference between the roots will be 64 and, therefore, $12 + \sqrt{64}$ is twice the greater root and $12 - \sqrt{64}$ is twice the smaller one.

[52]1591 omits this last word.
[53]That is, a plane composed as stated in the title of this zetetic.

Zetetic XII

Given a plane which consists of the product of the roots plus the squares of the individual roots and given also that product itself, the roots can be determined.

This composite plane plus the product will be equal to the square of the sum of the roots.

This is in accord with what was discovered and set out in the preceding zetetic.

Let 124 be a plane consisting of the product of the roots and the squares of the individual roots. Let the product itself be 20 and let the sum of the roots be x. X^2 will equal 144 which, when four times 20 is subtracted from it, leaves 64 the square of the difference. So $\sqrt{144} + \sqrt{64}$ is twice the greater root and $\sqrt{144} - \sqrt{64}$ twice the smaller.

Zetetic XIII

Given the sum of the squares and their difference, to find the roots.

Let D^p be the sum of the squares and B^p their difference. The roots are to be found.

Twice the square of the greater will be $D^p + B^p$, according to the teaching with respect to roots already set out.[54] When twice [the square of the greater] is given, the simple [square is also given], and when the squares are given the roots of the squares are also given.

No new work is involved since what has been noted about roots can be applied to other simple magnitudes. This need hardly be exemplified.

Let D^p be 104, B^p 96 and x the greater root. X^2 equals 100. Or let x be the smaller root. X^2 equals 4.

Zetetic XIIII

Given the difference between the cubes and their sum, to find the roots.

Let the difference between the cubes be B^s and let their sum be D^s. The roots are to be found.

Twice the cube of the greater root will be $D^s + B^s$ and twice the cube

[54] First Book, Zetetic I.

of the smaller will be $D^s - B^s$, according to the teaching already set out with respect to roots and exemplified again with respect to squares where we noted that it could be applied to magnitudes of any sort.[55] Given, therefore, twice [the cube], the simple [cube is also given] and given the cubes their roots are given, so this zetetic is scarcely worthy of the name.

Let B^s be 316, D^s 370 and x the greater root. X^3 will equal 343. Or let x be the smaller root. X^3 will equal 27.

Zetetic XV

Given the difference between the cubes and the product of the roots, the roots will be found

The square of the difference between the cubes plus four times the cube of the product of the roots is equal to the square of the sum of the cubes.

It has already been shown that the square of the sum of the cubes minus the square of their difference is equal to four times the cube of their product,[56] so the only work involved is that of transposition.

Let the difference between the cubes be 316, the product of the roots 21 and the sum of the cubes x. X^2 will equal 136,900. Twice the greater cube, therefore, will be $\sqrt{136,900} + 316$ and twice the smaller $\sqrt{136,900} - 316$.

Zetetic XVI

Given the sum of the cubes and the product of the roots, the roots will be found.

The square of the sum of the cubes minus four times the cube of the product of the roots is equal to the square of the difference between the cubes.

This may be arrived at from the last demonstration by transposition.

Let the sum of the cubes be 370, the product of the roots 21 and the difference between the cubes x. X^2 equals 99,856.[57]

Zetetic XVII

Given the difference between the roots and the difference between their cubes, to find the roots.

---

[55] Preceding Zetetic.
[56] *Preliminary Notes,* Prop. XVI
[57] The text has 99,256.

Let B be the difference between the roots and D^s the difference between the cubes. The roots are to be found.

Let the sum of the roots be E. Therefore $E + B$ will be twice the greater root and $E - B$ twice the smaller. The difference between the cubes of these is $6BE^2 + 2B^3$ which is consequently equal to $8D^s$. Therefore $(4D^s - B^3)/3B$ is equal to E^2. The squares being given, the root is given, and the difference between the roots and their sum being given, the roots are given.

Given, therefore, the difference between the roots and the difference between their cubes, the sum of the roots can be found, for

Four times the difference between the cubes minus the cube of the difference between the roots, if divided by three times the difference between the roots, yields the square of the sum of the roots.

Let B be 6, D^s 504 and x the sum of the roots. X^2 equals 100.

Zetetic XVIII

Given the sum of the roots and the sum of their cubes, to derive the roots.

Let B be the sum of the roots and D^s the sum of the cubes. The roots are to be derived.

Let the difference between the roots be E. So $B + E$ is twice the greater root and $B - E$ twice the smaller. Thus the sum of the cubes is $(2B^3 + 6BE^2)/8$. Consequently $2B^3 + 6BE^2$ [58] is equal to $8D^s$ and $(4D^s - B^3)/3B$ is equal to E^2.

Given, then, a square, its root is given, and given the sum of the roots and their difference, the roots are given.

Hence given the sum of the roots and the sum of their cubes, the roots are given, for

Four times the sum of the cubes minus the cube of the sum of the roots divided by three times the sum of the roots yields the square of the difference between the roots.

Let B be 10, D^s 370 and E x. X^2 equals 16.

Zetetic XIX

Given the difference between the roots and the difference between their cubes, to find the roots.

[58] 1591 has $2B^3 - 6BE^2$.

Let B be the difference between the roots and D^s the difference between the cubes. The roots are to be found.

Let A^p be the product of the roots. It is clear from the origin of a cube that, if the cube of the difference between the roots is subtracted from the difference between the cubes, the remainder is three times the solid which is the product of the difference between the roots and the product of the roots.[59] Hence

$$D^s - B^3 = 3A^pB$$

and, dividing through by $3[B]$, $(D^s - B^3)/3B$ will equal A^p. Given, therefore, the product of the roots and the difference between them the roots are given.

Hence, given the difference between the roots and the difference between the cubes, the roots are known, for

The difference between the cubes of the roots minus the cube of the difference between the roots, if divided by three times the difference between the roots, gives rise to a plane that is the product of the roots.

Let B be 4 and D^s 316. A^p becomes 21, the product of the roots 7 and 3.

But if the difference between the roots is sought from the difference between the cubes and their product, as if it became known that A^p is F^p and the question concerns B, let this be A. So the equation arises

$$A^3 + 3F^pA = D^s.$$

That is,

The cube of the difference between the roots plus three times the product of the rectangle from the roots and the difference between the roots is equal to the difference between the cubes.[60]

This is worth noting.

Zetetic XX

Given once again the sum of the roots and the sum of their cubes, to find the roots.

Let G be the sum of the roots and D^s the sum of the cubes. The roots are to be found.

---

[59]I.e., if the roots are x and y, $(x^3 - y^3) - (x - y)^3 = 3xy(x - y)$.
[60]I.e., if x and y are the roots, $(x - y)^3 + 3xy(x - y) = x^3 - y^3$.

Let A^p be the product of the roots. It is clear from the origin of the cube that, if the sum of the cubes is subtracted from the cube of the sum of the roots, the remainder will be three times the product of the sum of the roots and the rectangle from the roots. So $(G^3 - D^s)/3G$ will equal A^p. Moreover, given the product of the roots and given, also, the sum of the roots, the roots are given.

Given, therefore, the sum of the roots and the sum of the cubes, the roots can be found, for

The cube of the sum of the roots minus the sum of the cubes, if divided by three times the sum of the roots, yields a plane, [viz.,] the product of the roots.

Let G be 10 and D^s 370. A^p becomes 21, the product of the roots 7 and 3.

But if one seeks the sum of the roots from the sum of the cubes and the product [of the roots], as if it becomes known that A^p is B^p and the question concerns G, let this be A. From this arises the equation

$$A^3 - 3B^p A = D^s.$$

That is,

The cube of the sum of the roots minus three times the product of the rectangle from the roots times the sum of the roots is equal to the sum of the cubes.[61]

This is worth noting.

Zetetic XXI

Given two solids, one the product of the difference between the roots and the difference between their squares, the other the product of the sum of the roots and the sum of their squares, to find the roots.

Let the first solid be B^s, the second D^s, and let the sum of the roots be A. Then B^s/A will be the square of the difference between the roots and D^s/A will be the sum of the squares. However, twice the sum of the squares minus the square of the difference between the roots is the square of the sum of the roots. Therefore $(2D^s - B^s)/A$ will equal A^2. Multiply through by A and

$$2D^s - B^s = A^3.$$

[61] I.e., if x and y are the roots, $(x + y)^3 - 3xy(x + y) = x^3 + y^3$.

Given, therefore, the two solids as proposed, the roots can be found,
for

*Twice the product of the sum of the roots and the sum of the squares
minus the product of the difference between the roots and the difference
between the squares is equal to the cube of the sum of the roots.*[62]

Let B^s be 32 and D^s 272, making A^3 512. The sum of the roots,
therefore, is 8, the square of the difference 32/8, that is 4, and the
difference itself is $\sqrt{4}$. So the smaller root is $4 - \frac{1}{2}\sqrt{4}$ and the greater is
$4 + \frac{1}{2}\sqrt{4}$.

Let B^s be 10 and D^s 20, making A^3 30. The sum of the roots, therefore,
is $\sqrt[3]{30}$, the square of the difference is $10/\sqrt[3]{30}$[63] (otherwise $\sqrt[3]{100/3}$) and
therefore the difference is $\sqrt[6]{100/3}$[64] and the smaller root is $\sqrt[3]{30/8} - $
$\sqrt[6]{100/192}$ and the greater root is $\sqrt[3]{30/8} + \sqrt[6]{100/192}$.[65]

Cardano correctly remarks in Chapter 66, Problem 93, of his *Arithmetic*[66] that in this hypothetical case the ratio of the roots, namely that of
the smaller to the larger is $2 - \sqrt{3}$ to 1 or 1 to $2 + \sqrt{3}$, but he unfortunately
omits the roots themselves.

Zetetic XXII

Given the sum of the squares and the ratio of the product of
the roots to the square of the difference between the roots, to
find the roots.

Let B^p be the sum of the squares and let the product of the roots be to
the square of the difference between the roots as R is to S. The roots are to
be found.

Let the product of the roots be A^p. The square of the difference
between the roots will be SA^p/R which, when twice the product is added to
it, makes the sum of the squares. Therefore $(SA^p + 2RA^p)/R$ will equal B^p.
Reducing this equation to a proportion,

$$(S + 2R):R = B^p:A^p.$$

[62]I.e., if x and y are the roots, $2(x + y)(x^2 + y^2) - (x - y)(x^2 - y^2) = (x + y)^3$.
[63]1591 has $^3\sqrt{10/30}$.
[64]1646 has $^5\sqrt{100/3}$.
[65]In this and the preceding phrases, 1646 has $^5\sqrt{100/192}$ ($\sqrt{QC}$ 100/192), perhaps due
to a typographical error in omitting a second radical sign, ($\sqrt{Q}\ \sqrt{C}$) which would make it read
$^6\sqrt{100/192}$.
[66]The reference is to Girolamo Cardano's *Practica Arithmeticae Generalis* (Milan,
1539; reprinted in the author's *Opera Omnia*, vol. IV, which was published in Lyon, 1663 and
reprinted in facsimile Stuttgart, 1966).

Given, therefore, [the terms] that have been set out, the roots are given, for

As the [analogous] square of the difference between the roots[67] plus twice the analogous product of the roots is to the analogous product of the roots, so the true sum of the squares is to their true product.

Let the sum of the squares[68] be 20 and let the product of the roots be to the square of their difference as 2 is to 1.[69] Then

$$(S + 2R):R = 20:8.^{70}$$

So 8 is the product that is being sought. Thus $20 - 16$ (that is, 4) is the square of the difference between the roots and $20 + 16$ is the square of their sum. Whence the difference is $\sqrt{4}$, the sum is $\sqrt{36}$, the smaller root is $\sqrt{9} - \sqrt{1}$, or 2, and the greater is $\sqrt{9} + \sqrt{1}$, or 4.

Allowing the sum of the squares to remain 20, let the product of the roots be to the square of the difference between the roots as 3 to 1.[71] That is, let one be equal to the other. Then as 3 is to 1, so is 20 to 20/3. Wherefore 20/3 is the product of the roots. So $20 - 40/3$—that is 20/3—will be the square of the difference between the roots and $20 + 40/3$—that is 100/3—will be the square of the sum. Wherefore $\sqrt{20/3}$ is the difference and $\sqrt{100/3}$ is the sum. And therefore the smaller is $\sqrt{25/3} - \sqrt{5/3}$ and the larger is $\sqrt{25/3} + \sqrt{5/3}$. Cardano is mistaken with respect to this one[72] in Chapter 66, Problem 94, of his *Arithmetic*.

THIRD BOOK

Zetetic I

Given the mean of three proportional straight lines and the difference between the extremes, to find the extremes.

The extreme proportionals are like roots, and the square of the mean is [equal to] the product of these roots. This has already been shown [in the zetetic entitled] Given the product of the roots and their difference, to find

---

[67] 1591 has *ut quadratum dimidiae differentiae laterum;* 1646 omits the word *dimidiae.* Van Schooten suggests that the inclusion of the word was probably a typographical error for *simile* which, however, he fails to insert.

[68] 1591 has *adgregatum quadratum;* 1646 has *adgregatum quadratorum.*

[69] 1591 has 1 to 2.

[70] 1591 has $S : R = 10 : 8$.

[71] 1591 has 1 to 1.

[72] *Hallucinator itaque Cardanus.*

the roots.[73] So the square of half the difference between the extremes plus the square of the mean is equal to the square of the sum of half the extremes.

Let the difference between the extremes be 10 and the mean 12. The smaller extreme is 8, the greater 18.

Zetetic II

Given the mean of three proportionals and the sum of the extremes, to find the extremes.

This problem, also, has already been set out [in the zetetic entitled] Given the product of the roots and their sum, to find the roots.[74]

Let the mean be 12 and the sum of the extremes 26. The smaller extreme is 8, the greater 18.[75]

Zetetic III

Given the perpendicular of a right triangle and the difference between the base and the hypotenuse, to find the base and the hypotenuse.

This problem, also, has already been explained, for it boils down to, Given the difference between the squares and the difference between the roots, to find the roots.[76] For the square of the perpendicular is the difference between the square of the hypotenuse and the square of the base.

Let the perpendicular of the right triangle be D and let B be the difference between the base and the hypotenuse. The base and the hypotenuse are to be found.

Let A be the sum of the base and the hypotenuse. Therefore BA will equal D^2 and D^2/B will equal A. Given, moreover, the difference between the roots and their sum, the roots are given.

Given, therefore, the perpendicular of a right triangle and the difference between the base and the hypotenuse, the base and the hypote-

[73]Second Book, Zetetic III
[74]Second Book, Zetetic IIII
[75]1591 has 28.
[76]Second Book, Zetetic VII

nuse are given, for

The perpendicular of a right triangle is a proportional between the difference between the base and the hypotenuse and the sum of the same.

Let D be 5 and B 1. The proportionals are 1, 5 and 25. So the hypotenuse of the triangle is 13 and the base 12, the perpendicular being 5.

For which reason, let this be—

Zetetic IIII

Given the perpendicular of a right triangle and the sum of its base and hypotenuse, the base and the hypotenuse are determined.

Let the perpendicular be 5 and the sum of the base and hypotenuse 25. The proportionals are 25, 5 and 1. So the difference between the base and the hypotenuse is 1, the base itself is 12, and the hypotenuse is 13.

Zetetic V

Given the hypotenuse of a right triangle and the difference between the sides around the right angle, to find the sides around the right angle.

This is the same as, Given the difference between the roots and the sum of the squares, to find the roots, a problem that has already been set out.[77]

Let, nevertheless, D be the hypotenuse of the right triangle and B the difference between the sides around the right angle. The sides around the right angle are to be found.

Let the sum of the sides around the right angle be A. Therefore $A + B$ will be twice the greater side adjacent to the right angle and $A - B$ will be twice the smaller side. The squares of these taken individually and added make $2A^2 + 2B^2$ which, then, are equal to $4D^2$. Thus

$$2D^2 - B^2 = A^2.$$

Given, therefore, the hypotenuse of a right triangle and the difference between the sides around the right angle, the sides around the right angle

---

[77]Second Book, Zetetic V

can be found, for

Twice the square of the hypotenuse minus the square of the difference between the sides around the right angle is equal to the square of their sum.

Let D be 13, B 7 and A x. X^2 will then equal 289, which makes x $\sqrt{289}$. Hence the sides around the right angle are $\sqrt{72\frac{1}{4}} + 3\frac{1}{2}$ and $\sqrt{72\frac{1}{4}} - 3\frac{1}{2}$ [or 12 and 5.][78]

Zetetic VI

Given the hypotenuse of a right triangle and the sum of the sides around the right angle, to find the sides around the right angle.

Twice the square of the hypotenuse minus the square of the sum of the sides around the right angle is equal to the square of the difference between the sides around the right angle.

This can be deduced by transposition from the preceding formula.

Let the hypotenuse be 13, the sum of the sides around the right angle 17 and their difference x. X^2 will equal 49. This makes x $\sqrt{49}$. So the sides around the right angle are $8\frac{1}{2} + \sqrt{12\frac{1}{4}}$ and $8\frac{1}{2} - \sqrt{12\frac{1}{4}}$, [or 12 and 5.][79]

Zetetic VII

Three proportional straight lines will be found numerically.

Assuming two roots that are to each other as one number to another, the greater extreme among the proportionals will be analogous to the square of the root assumed to be the greater, the middle one to the product of the roots, and the smaller extreme to the square of the root assumed to be the smaller.

Let B and D be rational roots. If B is set up as the first of the proportionals and D as the second, the third will be D^2/B. Multiply all terms by B and the series of proportionals will be

I	II	III
B^2	BD	D^2

Let B be 2 and D 3. The proportionals become 4, 6 and 9.

---

[78]The bracketed expression does not occur in 1591.

[79]The bracketed expression does not appear in 1591; added by the editor in 1646.

Zetetic VIII

A right triangle will be found numerically

Having set up three proportional quantities numerically, the hypotenuse [of a right triangle] will be analogous to the sum of the extremes, the base to their difference and the perpendicular to twice the mean.

It has already been shown that the perpendicular of a triangle is a proportional between the difference between the base and the hypotenuse and the sum of the same.[80]

Let the proportionals be shown numerically as 4, 6 and 9. From these the hypotenuse of a right triangle may be constructed as 13, its base as 5 and its perpendicular as 12.

Alternatively,

Zetetic IX

A right triangle will be found numerically

Assuming two rational roots, the hypotenuse [of a right triangle] will be analogous to the sum of their squares, the base to the difference between the same, and the perpendicular to twice the product of the roots.

Let the two roots be B and D. There are, therefore, three proportional quantities, B, D and D^2/B. Multiply all of them by B and there are three proportional planes, B^2, BD and D^2. From these proportionals, according to the aforesaid [proposition], the hypotenuse of the triangle is analogous to $B^2 + D^2$, the base to $B^2 \sim D^2$ and the perpendicular to $2BD$. And it has already been shown that the square of the sum of the squares is equal to the square of the difference between the squares plus the square of twice the product of the roots.[81]

Let B be 2 and D 3. The hypotenuse is analogous to 13, the base to 5 and the perpendicular to 12.

Zetetic X

Given the sum of the squares of three individual proportionals and one of the extremes in the series, the other extreme will be found.

[80]*Preliminary Notes*, Prop. XLV, Corollary; *Zetetica*, Third Book, Zetetic III.
[81]Second Book, Zetetic IX.

The sum of the squares minus three-quarters of the square of the given extreme is equal to the square of the sum of one-half the given extreme and the whole of the other [extreme] that is being sought.

This has already been shown and demonstrated, so no new work is involved.[82]

Let the sum of the squares of the three proportionals be 21 and let the greater extreme be 4. Therefore $21 - 12$, that is 9, is the square of the sum of 2 and the minor [extreme], which is being sought. But the root of the square 9 is $\sqrt{9}$, so the minor [extreme] being sought is $\sqrt{9} - 2$, which is 1.

Allowing the sum of the squares to remain 21, let the smaller extreme be 1. Therefore $20\frac{1}{4}$, or $81/4$, is a square made up of $\frac{1}{2}$ and the greater extreme, which is being sought. The root of the square $81/4$ is $\sqrt{81/4}$, so the greater extreme being sought is $\sqrt{81/4} - 1/2$, [which is 4.][83]

Zetetic XI

Given the sum of the squares of three individual proportionals and the sum of the extremes, the extremes will be determined.

The square of the sum of the extremes minus the sum of the squares of the three [individual proportionals] is equal to the square of the mean.

Given, moreover, the sum of the extremes and the mean, the extremes are given. This, also, has already been clearly shown and demonstrated,[84] so the operation involves no new process.

Let the sum of the squares of the three be 21 and the sum of the extremes 5.[85] The square of the mean is $25 - 21$, that is 4. So the mean is $\sqrt{4}$ and the extremes are 1 and 4.

Zetetic XII

Given the sum of the squares of three individual proportionals and their mean, the extremes will be determined.

The sum of the squares of the three plus the square of the mean is equal to the square of the sum of the extremes.

[82]Second Book, Zetetic X.
[83]This expression was added by the editor of 1646.
[84]Third Book, Zetetic II.
[85]1591 omits this figure.

[This follows] from the foregoing formula using the art of transposition. Given, moreover, the sum of the extremes and, in addition, the mean, the extremes are given.

Let the sum of the squares of the three be 21 and let the mean be 2. The square of the sum of the extremes is $21 + 4$, that is 25. Whence the extremes are $\sqrt{25}$ [or] 1 and 4.[86]

Zetetic XIII

Given the difference between the extremes and the difference between the means in a series of four continued proportionals, to find the continued proportionals.

This is also a problem that has already been discussed in two zetetica, for it is really, Given the difference between the roots and the difference between their cubes, to find the roots,[87] as will become clear from the process.

Let the difference between the extremes in a series of four continued proportionals be D, and let B be the difference between the means. The continued proportionals are to be found.

Let the sum of the extremes be A. Therefore $A + D$ will be twice the greater extreme and $A - D$ twice the smaller extreme. So when $A + D$ is multiplied by $A - D$, it yields four times the product of the means or the extremes. Thus $(A^2 - D^2)/4$ is a product which, when it is multiplied by the greater extreme, yields the cube of the greater mean, when multiplied by the smaller extreme yields the cube of the smaller mean[88] and, when multiplied by the difference between the two extremes, yields the difference between the cubes of the means. Hence $(DA^2 - D^3)/4$ is equal to the difference between the cubes of the means.

If, however, the cube of the difference between [any two] roots is subtracted from the difference between the cubes, the remainder is equal to three times the product of the difference between the roots and the rectangle from the roots, as is clear from the development of the cube of the difference between two roots. Hence $(DA^2 - D^3 - 4B^3)/4$ is equal to three times the product of the difference between the means and their rectangle, namely $(3BA^2 - 3BD^2)/4$. Setting this up as an equation, $(D^3 + 4B^3 - 3BD^2)/(D - 3B)$[89] will equal A^2.

---

[86]1591 has $\sqrt{25}$; 1646 has 1 and 4. The change in 1646 was made by the editor.

[87]Second Book, Zetetic XVII.

[88]1591 has *Cum minor Cubus mediae minoris;* 1646 has *Cum minor, fiat cubus mediae minoris.*

[89]1591 omits the signs of addition between D^3 and $4B^3$.

Given, therefore, the difference between the extremes and the difference between the means in a series of four continued proportionals, the continued proportionals are found, for

If the cube of the difference between the extremes plus four times the cube of the difference between the means minus three times the product of the difference between the means and the square of the difference between the extremes[90] *is divided by the difference between the extremes minus three times the difference between the means, the resulting quotient is equal to the square of the sum of the extremes.*

Let D be 7, B 2 and A x. X^2 is equal to 81 and x is $\sqrt{81}$, the sum of the extremes 1 and 8. The means are then 2 and 4 in this series of continued proportionals:

I	II	III	IIII
1	2	4	8

Zetetic XIIII

Given the sum of the extremes and the sum of the means in a series of four continued proportionals, to find the continued proportionals.

This problem has also been discussed before in two zetetica, for it is really, Given the sum of the roots and the sum of their cubes, to find the roots,[91] as will become clear in the process.

Let D be the sum of the extremes and B the sum of the means in a series of four continued proportionals. The continued proportionals are to be found.

Let the difference between the extremes be A. Therefore $D + A$ will be twice the greater extreme and $D - A$ twice the smaller. If $D + A$ is multiplied by $D - A$, it produces four times the product of the means or the extremes. So $(D^2 - A^2)/4$ is a product which, when it is multiplied by the greater extreme, yields the cube of the greater extreme; when multiplied by the smaller extreme yields the cube of the smaller mean; and, when multiplied by the sum of the two extremes, yields the sum of the cubes of the means. Therefore $(D^3 - DA^2)/4$ is equal to the sum of the cubes of the means.

---

[90] The text has "four times the square of the difference between the extremes."
[91] Second Book, Zetetic XVIII.

If, however, the sum of the cubes is subtracted from the cube of the sum of the two roots, the remainder is equal to three times the product of the sum of the roots and the rectangle of the roots, as is clear from the development of the cube of two roots. Therefore $(4B^3 - D^3 + DA^2)/4$ is equal to three times the product of the sum of the means and the rectangle from the means, namely $(3BD^2 - 3BA^2)/4$. Having set this up as an equation, $(3BD^2 + D^3 - 4B^3)/(D + 3B)$ will equal A^2.

Given, therefore, the sum of the extremes and the sum of the means in a series of four continued proportionals, the continued proportionals are given, for

Three times the product of the sum of the means and the square of the sum of the extremes plus the cube of the sum of the extremes minus four times the cube of the sum of the means divided by the sum of the extremes plus three times the sum of the means yields a plane which is equal to the square of the difference between the extremes.

Let D be 9, B 6 and A x. X^2 equals 49, making x equal to $\sqrt{49}$, the difference between the extremes, 1 and 8. The means are 2 and 4 in a series of four continued proportionals:

I	II	III	IIII
1	2	4	8

Zetetic XV

Given once more the difference between the extremes and the difference between the means in a series of four continued proportionals, to find the continued proportionals.

This is [the same as], Given the difference between the roots and the difference between the cubes, to find the roots,[92] as will be evident from the process.

Let D be the difference between the extremes and B the difference between the means in a series of four continued proportionals. The four continued proportionals are to be found.

Let A^p be the product of the means or the extremes. Now the cube of the greater mean is equal to the product of the greater extreme and the rectangle on the extremes. And the cube of the smaller mean is equal to the

---

[92]Second Book, Zetetic XVII.

product of the smaller extreme and the rectangle on the extremes. Therefore DA^p will equal the difference between the cubes of the means. If, however, the cube of the difference between [two] roots is subtracted from the difference between their cubes, the remainder is equal to three times the product of the difference between the roots and the rectangle on the roots, as is clear from the development of the cube of the difference between [two] roots. So

$$DA^p - B^3 = 3BA^p \text{ }^{93}$$

and, having set this up as an equation, $B^3/(D - 3B)$ will equal A^p. Given, then, the product of the roots and their difference, the roots are given.

Given, therefore, the difference between the extremes and the difference between the means in a series of four continued proportionals, the continued proportionals are given, for

As the difference between the extremes minus three times the difference between the means is to the difference between the means, so the square of the difference between the means is to the product of the means or the extremes.

Let D be 7 and B 2. A^p becomes 8, the product of the extremes, 1 and 8, or of the means, 2 and 4, in a series of four continued proportionals:

I	II	III	IIII
1	2	4	8

But if the difference between the means is to be found from the difference between the extremes and their product, as if A^p were known to be F^p and the problem concerns B, let this be A. This will lead to an equality [between] $A^3/(D - 3A)$ and F^p. Setting this up as an equation,[94]

$$A^3 + 3F^pA = F^pD.$$

That is,

The cube of the difference between the means plus three times the product of the rectangle on the roots and the difference between the means is equal to the product of the rectangle on the roots and the difference between the extremes.

This is very worth noting.

[93] 1591 has $DA^p - D^3 = BA^p$.
[94] 1591 has *Ordinata vero;* 1646 has *Ordinata vero aequalitate.*

Zetetic XVI

Given once more the sum of the extremes and the sum of the means in a series of four continued proportionals, to find the continued proportionals.

This is [the same as], Given the sum of the roots and the sum of the cubes, to find the roots,[95] as will become evident from the process.

Let Z be the sum of the extremes and G the sum of the means in a series of four continued proportionals. The continued proportionals are to be found.

Let A^p be the product of the means or the extremes. Now the cube of the greater means is equal to the product of the greater extreme and the rectangle on the extremes, and the cube of the smaller mean is equal to the product of the smaller extreme and the rectangle on the extremes. Therefore ZA^p will be equal to the sum of the cubes of the means. If, however, the sum of the cubes is subtracted from the cube of the sum of the roots, the remainder is equal to three times the product of the sum of the roots and the rectangle from the roots, as is clear from the development of the cube of two roots. Therefore

$$G^3 - ZA^p = 3GA^p.$$

Setting this up as an equation, $G^3/(Z + 3G)$[96] will equal A^p. Given, moreover, the product of the roots and the sum of[97] the roots, the roots are given.

Given, therefore, the sum of the extremes and the sum of the means in a series of four continued proportionals, the proportionals are known, for

As the sum of the extremes plus three times the sum of the means is to the sum of the means, so the square of the sum of the means is to the product of the means or the extremes.

Let Z be 9, G 6 and A^p x. This makes $[A^p]$ 8, the product of the extremes, 1 and 8, or of the means, 2 and 4.

But if the sum of the means is to be found from the sum of the extremes and their product, as if A^p were known to be B^p and G is being sought, let it be A. So the equation becomes

$$A^3 - 3B^pA = B^pZ.$$

[95] First Book, Zetetic XVIII.
[96] 1591 has D^3 for G^3 both here and in the preceding.
[97] 1591 has "the difference between."

That is,

The cube of the sum of the means[98] *minus three times the product of the same sum and the rectangle from the extremes or the means is equal to the product of the sum of the extremes and the rectangle from the means or the extremes.*

This is very worth noting.

FOURTH BOOK

Zetetic I[99]

To find numerically two squares equal to a given square.

Let F^2 be given as a number. Two squares equal to the given F^2 are to be found.

Erect a right triangle numerically and let the hypotenuse be Z, the base B and the perpendicular D. Create a similar triangle having F as its hypotenuse by supposing that as Z is to F so B is to the base of the other, which will therefore be BF/Z, and again that as Z is to F so D is to the perpendicular, which will therefore be DF/Z. Hence the squares of BF/Z and DF/Z will be equal to F^2. This is what was to be done.

It is to this that Diophantus' analysis reduces itself. According to it, B^2 is to be cut into two squares. Let the root of the first square be A and of the second $B - SA/R$. The square of the first root is A^2, of the second $B^2 - 2SAB/R^1 + S^2A^2/R^2$, which two squares are therefore equal to B^2. Setting up an equation, $2SRB/(S^2 + R^2)$ will equal A, the root of the first individual square, and the root of the second will become $(R^2B - S^2B)/(S^2 + R^2)$.[2]

Now a right triangle has been created numerically from the two roots S and R with a hypotenuse analogous to $S^2 + R^2$, a base analogous to $S^2 - R^2$, and a perpendicular analogous to $2SR$. So in order to divide B^2, let $S^2 + R^2$ be to B, the hypotenuse of the analogous triangle, as $S^2 - R^2$ is to its base, the root of one of the individual squares, and as $2SR$ is to its perpendicular, the other root.

Let B be 100, from the square of which are to be found two squares equal to its square.[3] Construct a right triangle numerically from R [which

---

[98] 1591 has "the extremes"; corrected by the editor in 1646.
[99] Cf. Diophantus, II, 8.
[1] 1646 has $2SAD/R$.
[2] 1591 has $(S^2B - R^2B)/(S^2 + R^2)$.
[3] *cujus quadrato invenienda sint duo quadrata aequalia.* Vaulezard and Vasset both translate this as if it required two equal squares to be found.

is] 4 and S [which is] 3.[4] The hypotenuse of the triangle so constructed will be 25, its base 7 and its perpendicular 24. Thus we get

$$25:7 = 100:28$$

and

$$25:24 = 100:96.$$

So the square of 100 will equal the square of 28 plus the square of 96.

Zetetic II[5]

To find numerically two squares equal to two other given squares.

Let B^2 and D^2 be given in numbers. Two other squares are to be found that are equal to these.

Let B be known as the base of a triangle and D as its perpendicular. Hence the square of the hypotenuse will be equal to $B^2 + D^2$. Let Z, a rational or irrational root, be this hypotenuse. Construct another right triangle numerically with the hypotenuse X, base F and perpendicular G. From these two set up a third right triangle either by contraction or by expansion[6] in accordance with what has been set out in the *Notes*.[7] By the first method the hypotenuse will be analogous to ZX, the perpendicular to $BG + DF$ and the base $BF \sim DG$. By the second method, the hypotenuse will be analogous to ZX, the perpendicular to $BG \sim DF$, the base to $BF + DG$. All these planes, which are analogous to the roots of the constructed triangle, are to be divided by X. The hypotenuse remaining Z, the base becomes $(BF \sim DG)/X$ and the perpendicular $(BG + DF)/X$ by the first method. By the second, the base becomes $(BF + DG)/X$ and the perpendicular $(BG \sim DF)/X$. Thus the two squares of the sides that include the right angle will equal the square of the hypotenuse Z, to which also $B^2 + D^2$ was equal by construction. This is what was to be done.

It is to this that Diophantus' analysis leads. According to it, Z^p or Z^2 has already been divided into two squares, namely B^2 and D^2, and it is to be divided into two other squares.

Let $A + B$ be the side of the first square to be created and let $SA/R^8 - D$ be the side of the second. Construct the squares of these and

[4]1591 reverses these values for R and S.
[5]Cf. Diophantus, II, 9.
[6]*synereseos diereseos-ve.*
[7]*Preliminary Notes*, Prop. XLVI.
[8]1646 has SA/M.

compare them with the two given squares. Hence

$$A^2 + 2AB + B^2 + \frac{S^2A^2}{R^2} - \frac{2SDA}{R} + D^2 = B^2 + D^2.$$

Having set this up as an equation, $(2SRD - 2R^2B)/(S^2 + R^2)$ will equal A. So the side of the square first constructed, which was $A + B$, becomes $(2SRD + S^2B \sim R^2B)/(S^2 + R^2)$,[9] and the side of the second square, which was $SA/R - D$, becomes $(S^2D \sim 2SRB \sim R^2D)/(S^2 + R^2)$.[10] Resolving these properly, two triangles have been constituted, the first with its hypotenuse (rational or irrational) Z, its base B and its perpendicular D, the second constructed from the two roots S and R the hypotenuse of which, therefore, will be analogous to $S^2 + R^2$, the base to $S^2 - R^2$ and the perpendicular to $2SR$, and from these can be constructed a third by means of diaeresis. The solids created, which are analogous to roots, will be divided by $S^2 + R^2$. Whence Z becomes the common hypotenuse of the first and third. Therefore [the sum of] the squares of the sides around the right angle of the first is equal to [the sum of] the squares of the sides around the right angle of the third.

But if the side of the first square were given as $A - B$ and of the second as $SA/R - D$, $(2SRD + 2R^2B)/(S^2 + R^2)$ would equal A. Then the side of the square first constituted would be $(2SRD \sim S^2B + R^2B)/S^2 + R^2$[11] and of the second $(2SRB + S^2D \sim R^2D)/(S^2 + R^2)$.[12] This is the creation of a third triangle by synaeresis.

Let B be 15 and D 10, whence Z becomes $\sqrt{325}$. Let [another] right triangle be shown numerically as 5, 3, 4. The one side of [the squares] sought for is 18; the other is 1. Or one is 6 and the other is 17.

Zetetic III[13]

Again to find numerically two squares equal to two given squares.

Let there be two squares, B^2 and D^2. Two other squares equal to these are to be found.

Construct numerically a right triangle with B as its hypotenuse. Construct another similar to it with D as its hypotenuse, and from these two

---

[9]1646 has $(2SRD + S^2B - R^2B)/(S^2 + R^2)$.

[10]1646 has $(S^2D - 2SRB - R^2D)/(S^2 + R^2)$.

[11]1591 has $(2SRD \sim S^2B + R^2B)/(S^2 + R^2)$; 1646 has $(2SRD - S^2B + R^2B)/(S^2 + R^2)$.

[12]1591 has $(2SRB + S^2D \sim R^2D)/(S^2 + R^2)$; 1646 has $(2SRB + S^2D - R^2D)/(S^2 + R^2)$.

[13]Cf. Diophantus, II, 9.

similar triangles construct a third, the square of the hypotenuse of which is equal to [the sum of] the squares of the hypotenuses of the first and second, by the method that has been set out in the *Notes*.[14] Then the square of the hypotenuse of the third will equal $B^2 + D^2$, and to these squares will be equal[15] [the squares of] the sides around the right angle. This method is also derived from the analysis of Diophantus already mentioned.

Let B be 10 and D 15. The sides of the first triangle around the right angle are 8 and 6, and those of the second are 12 and 9. Those around the right angle of the third will be 18 and 1 or 6 and 17, and the squares of these two are equal to the squares of 10 and 15.

Zetetic IIII

To find two similar right triangles having given hypotenuses and the base of a third triangle deduced from them which is the sum of the perpendicular of the first and the base of the second [and] is prescribed beforehand. The predefined base, moreover, must be greater than the hypotenuse of the first.

Let B be the hypotenuse of the first triangle and D of the second, which is similar to the first. From these a third triangle is to be constructed with a base equal to N, the sum of the perpendicular of the first and the base of the second. Let

$$B^2 + D^2 - N^2 = M^2.$$

Therefore the perpendicular of the triangle to be constructed will be M. Let A, moreover, be the base of the first. Then the base of the second will be DA/B, the perpendicular of the first will be $N - DA/B$, the perpendicular of the second either $A + M$ or $A - M$, so that M becomes the difference between the base of the first and the perpendicular of the second.

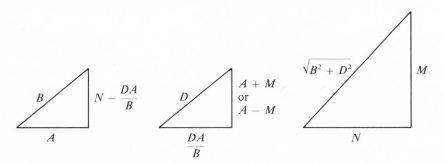

[14] *Preliminary Notes*, Prop. XLVI.
[15] 1591 omits bracketed words; supplied by the editor of 1646.

The two triangles being sought are constituted this way:

First Case

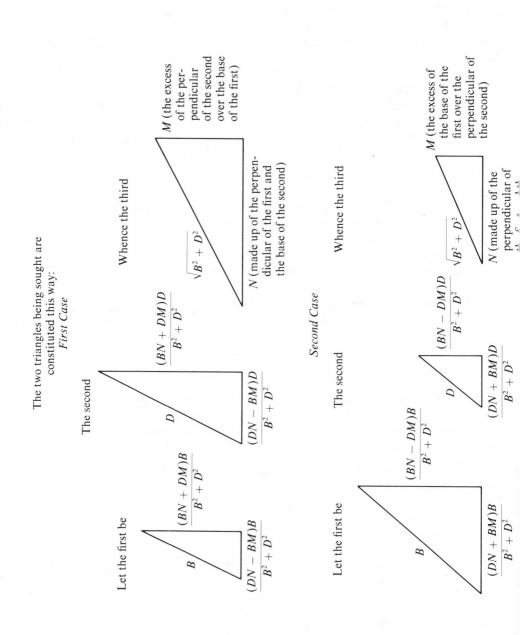

Let the first be

The second

Whence the third

B $\dfrac{(BN + DM)B}{B^2 + D^2}$ $\dfrac{(DN - BM)B}{B^2 + D^2}$

D $\dfrac{(BN + DM)D}{B^2 + D^2}$ $\dfrac{(DN - BM)D}{B^2 + D^2}$

$\sqrt{B^2 + D^2}$ M (the excess of the perpendicular of the second over the base of the first)

N (made up of the perpendicular of the first and the base of the second)

Second Case

Let the first be

The second

Whence the third

B $\dfrac{(BN - DM)B}{B^2 + D^2}$ $\dfrac{(DN + BM)B}{B^2 + D^2}$

D $\dfrac{(BN - DM)D}{B^2 + D^2}$ $\dfrac{(DN + BM)D}{B^2 + D^2}$

$\sqrt{B^2 + D^2}$ M (the excess of the base of the first over the perpendicular of the second)

N (made up of the perpendicular of the first and the base...)

Let it be $A + M$ in the first instance. Therefore,

$$B:D = \left(N - \frac{DA}{B}\right):(A + M).$$

Resolving this proportion and setting all terms in proper order, $(DNB - BMB)/(B^2 + D^2)$ will equal A. Or, returning to a proportion from the equation,

$$(B^2 + D^2):(DN - BM) = B:A.$$

In the second instance, the perpendicular of the second triangle is $A - M$. Hence

$$B:D = \left(N - \frac{DA}{B}\right):(A - M).$$

Resolving this proportion and setting all terms in proper order, $(DNB + BMB)/(B^2 + D^2)$ will equal A. Or, returning to a proportion from the equation,

$$(B^2 + D^2):(DN + BM) = B:A.$$

Thus we have the two triangles that were to be found.

It is clear, finally, that this can happen in the first case only when DN is greater than BM and, in the second, when BN is greater than DM.

Zetetic V

To find numerically two squares equal to two given squares, such that one of those being sought lies within prescribed limits.

Let the given [squares] be B^2 and D^2. Two squares equal to these are to be constructed, one of which is greater than F^p and less than G^p.

Let it be understood that Z^2 or some other plane is equal to $B^2 + D^2$. Therefore Z, rational or irrational, is the hypotenuse of a right triangle the sides around the right angle of which are B and D. What is required is another right triangle the hypotenuse of which is also Z and one of the sides of which around the right angle (say, the base) is greater than N but less than S. The problem reduces itself to this:

Find numerically two similar right triangles having B and D as their hypotenuses and construct from them the base of a third triangle which is the sum of the perpendicular of the first and the base of the second [and which] exists within the prescribed limits. Hence let

$$Z^2 - N^2 = M^2$$

and

$$Z^2 - S^2 = R^2.$$

If, then, N is taken as the base of the third triangle, which is to be divided into two similar triangles having given hypotenuses, the difference between the base and the hypotenuse [of the first of these two triangles] will, in accordance with the first case in the preceding zetetic, be to the perpendicular as $(Z^2 \sim DN) + BM$ is to $BN + DM$, or as X is to $(XBN + XDM)/[(Z^2 \sim DN) + BM]$, which is the first limit.

Or if S is taken as the base of the third triangle, the difference between the base and hypotenuse [of the second triangle] will, in accordance with the same, be to the perpendicular as $(Z^2 \sim DS) + BR$ is to $BS + DR$, or as X is to $(XBS + XDR)/[(Z^2 \sim DS) + BR]$, which is the second limit.

Given, therefore, X as the difference between the base and the hypotenuse in the two similar triangles to be constructed, any other rational [number] may be assumed. Let this be T, lying between $(XBN + XDM)/[(Z^2 \sim DN) + BM]$ and $(XBS + XDR)/[(Z^2 \sim DS) + BR]$. And from these two roots, X and T, a right triangle can be constructed numerically, and two triangles similar to it can [also] be constructed, the first having B for its hypotenuse, the other D, and from these two can be constructed a third such that its base is composed of the perpendicular of the first and the base of the second, and this within [the limits of] N and S, in accordance with the condition of the problem.

Let B be 1, D 3, N 2 and S 3. Z becomes $\sqrt{10}$, M $\sqrt{8}$ and R $\sqrt{7}$. Assuming that X is 1, T can be chosen lying between $\sqrt{98}/(10 - \sqrt{2})$ and $(\sqrt{63} + \sqrt{3})/(10 - \sqrt{27} + \sqrt{7})$. Let the first be 5/4. Therefore a triangle is to be constructed from 1 and 5/4, or from 4 and 5, and two triangles similar to it are to be constructed having 1 and 3 for their hypotenuses. To be deduced from these is the base of a third triangle composed of the perpendicular of the first similar triangle and the base of the second. This makes 67/41, the square of which is 4489/1681, which is greater than 2 but less than 3. The perpendicular will become 111/41, the square of which is 12,321/1,681. The value of these two squares is 10 or the [sum of the] squares of 1 and 3.

Another example: Let B be 2, D 3, N $\sqrt{6}$[16] and S $\sqrt{7}$, making Z $\sqrt{13}$, M $\sqrt{7}$ and R $\sqrt{6}$. Assuming X to be 1, choose a T lying between $(\sqrt{24} + \sqrt{63})/(13 + \sqrt{28} - \sqrt{54})$ and $(\sqrt{28} + \sqrt{54})/(13 + \sqrt{24} - \sqrt{63})$.[17] Let it

---

[16]1591 has $\sqrt{7}$.
[17]1591 has $(28 + \sqrt{54})/(13 + \sqrt{24} - \sqrt{63})$.

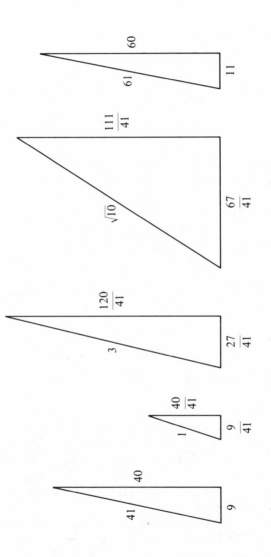

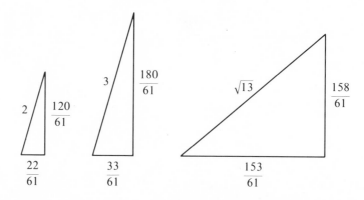

be 5/6. Therefore construct a triangle from 1 and 5/6, or from 5 and 6 and construct two triangles similar to it having 2 and 3 as their hypotenuses and from these deduce the base of the third, making 153/61, composed of the perpendicular of the first and the base of the second. The square of this is 23,409/3,721, which is greater than 6 or 22,326/3,721 but less than 7 or 26,047/3,721. The perpendicular is 158/61, the square of which is 24,964/3,721. These two squares equal 48,373/3,721 or 13, which is [the sum of] the squares of 2 and 3.

Zetetic VI[18]

To find numerically two squares with a given difference between them.

Let B^p be the given difference. Two squares are to be found that differ by B^p.

B^p, therefore, is the square of the base of a right triangle, and rational squares for the hypotenuse and perpendicular are to be found that differ by the given square of the base. But, truly, the base is a proportional between the difference between the perpendicular and the hypotenuse and the sum of these sides.

Assume, therefore, any rational length which, when it is divided into B^p, gives rise to a rational breadth.

The length by which the division is to be made, if it is less[19] than the breadth, will be the difference between the perpendicular and the hypotenuse, and the breadth will be their sum, or the other way around. Therefore you will have the perpendicular and the hypotenuse in numbers.

[18]Cf. Diophantus, II, 10.
[19]1591 has "greater."

Alternatively: Let A^2 be one of the squares being sought, say the square of the perpendicular. Hence $A^2 + B^p$ will be equal to a square, namely [that] of the hypotenuse. Let this be $A + D$. Whence, if[20] D is the difference between the perpendicular and the hypotenuse,

$$A^2 + 2AD + D^2 = A^2 + B^p.$$

Putting this in the form of an equation, $(B^p - D^2)/2D$ will equal A. Whence this

Theorem

If [in a right triangle][21] the square of the first side around the right angle minus the square of the difference between the second side and the hypotenuse is divided by twice this difference, the quotient will be equal to the second side around the right angle.

Alternatively: Let E^2 be one of the squares being sought, say the square of the hypotenuse. Then $E^2 - B^p$ will be equal to the square of the other, namely, the square of the perpendicular. If this is $E - D$, D becomes the difference between the perpendicular and the hypotenuse. Therefore

$$E^2 - 2ED + D^2 = E^2 - B^p$$

and, setting this up as an equation, $(B^p + D^2)/2D$[22] will equal E. Hence this

Theorem

If in a right triangle the square of one side around the right angle plus the square of the difference between the other side around the right angle and the hypotenuse is divided by twice this difference, the breadth that arises will be equal to the hypotenuse.

Likewise, *if the square of one side around the right angle plus the square of the sum of the other side around the right angle and the hypotenuse is divided by twice this sum, the length that arises will be equal to the hypotenuse.*

Whence, *as the sum of the hypotenuse and either side around the right angle is to their difference, so is the square of the sum plus or minus the square of the other side around the right angle to the square of the other side plus or minus the square of the difference.*

Let B^p be 240 and D 6. This makes A $(240 - 36)/12$ or 17 and E

[20]1591 omits this word; inserted by the editor in 1646.
[21]These words are omitted in 1591.
[22]1591 has $(B^p - D^2)/2D$.

(240 + 36)/12 or 23. Therefore the square of the side 23 differs from the square of the side 17 by 240. So the former is 529, the latter 289.

Let there be a 5, 4, 3 triangle. As 9 is to 1, so is 90 to 10 and 72 to 8. So it is true that one may—

Add a small square[23] to a given plane and effect a square.

Let the given plane be known to be the square of one of the sides around the right angle. [The square of][24] the difference between the other side around the right angle and the hypotenuse or of their sum may be assumed to be quite close to the given plane.

Let 17 be the given plane and assume that the difference is 4. Then divide 17 − 16 by 8 and the perpendicular becomes 1/8. So the square of the hypotenuse is $17\frac{1}{64}$, the square root of which is 33/8 or $4\frac{1}{8}$, which is quite close to [the root of] the square, 17.

Let 15 be the given plane and assume that the sum is 4. Therefore 15 − 16 divided by 8 gives rise to $-1/8$[25] for the perpendicular.[26] Whence the square of the hypotenuse is $15\frac{1}{64}$, the square root of which is 31/8 [or $3\frac{7}{8}$][27]

Zetetic VII[28]

To find numerically a plane which, added to either of two given planes, makes a square.

Let the two given planes be B^p and D^p. Another plane is to be found which, added to either B^p or D^p, makes a numerical square.

Let the plane to be added be A^p. Therefore $B^p + A^p$ will equal a square and $D^p + A^p$ will equal a square. A double equation must therefore be set up, Diophantus says. Let B^p, moreover, be greater than D^p. Hence the difference between the squares to be constructed is $B^p - D^p$. Now the square of the sum of two roots is greater than the square of their difference by four times the product of the roots. Therefore $B^p - D^p$ can be called four times the product of [two] roots. Whence $B^p + A^p$ becomes the square of the sum of the roots and $D^p + A^p$ the square of their difference. Therefore A^p [equals] the square of the sum of the roots minus B^p or the square of the difference between the roots minus D^p.

[23]*quadratulum.*
[24]1591 does not have the bracketed words; inserted by the editor in 1646.
[25]1591 omits the minus sign.
[26]1591 omits the words "for the perpendicular"; added by the editor in 1646.
[27]The bracketed words do not appear in 1591; added by the editor in 1646.
[28]Cf. Diophantus, II, 11.

So the problem becomes one of resolving $(B^p - D^p)/4$, that is the product of the roots, into the two roots of which it is the product. Let one be G and let this be greater[29] than the difference between $\sqrt{B^p}$ and $\sqrt{D^p}$ or less[30] than their sum. Let the other be $(B^p - D^p)/4G$. So the root of the greater square will be $[(B^p - D^p) + 4G^2]/4G$ and the root of the smaller square will be $[(B^p - D^p) \sim 4G^2]/4G$.[31]

Let B^p be 192, D^p 128. The difference between these, 64, is four times the product of two roots. The simple [product] is 16, the product of the roots 1 and 16, the sum of which is 17 and the difference [between which] is 15. And when from the square of the sum, 289, is subtracted 192, 97 is left. Therefore $192 + 97$ (that is, 289) is the square of the sum of the roots, and $128 + 97$ (that is, 225) is the square of their difference. Thus you satisfy the problem.

The task can also be performed this way: Since either B^p or D^p must be added to the same plane in order to construct a square, let the first plane be $A^2 - B^p$. When, therefore, B^p is added to this, it makes a square, namely A^2. Hence $D^p + A^2 - B^p$ equals a square. Construct this from $F - A$. Then

$$A^2 + F^2 - 2FA = D^p + A^2 - B^p.$$

Setting this up as an equation, $(F^2 + B^p - D^p)/2F$ will equal A.

Let B^p be 18, D^p 9 and F 9. A then becomes 5, and the plane to be added becomes 7. When added to 18 this makes 25 and when added to 9 it makes 16, the squares of 5 and 4.

Zetetic VIII[32]

To find numerically a plane which, when subtracted from either of two given planes, leaves a square.

Let the two given numerical planes be B^p and D^p. Another plane is to be found numerically that leaves a square when subtracted from either B^p or D^p. Let the sought-for plane that is to be subtracted be $B^p - A^2$. When therefore, $B^p - A^2$ is subtracted from B^p, A^2 is left. And when the same is subtracted from D^p, the remainder is $D^p - B^p + A^2$ which must, therefore, be equal to a square. Let this be [the square of] $A - F$. Hence $(F^2 + B^p - D^p)/2F$[33] will equal A.

[29]1591 has "less."
[30]1591 has "greater."
[31]1591 has $(B^p \sim D^p \sim 4G^2)/4G$
[32]Cf. Diophantus, II, 12.
[33]1591 has $(B^2 + D^p - D^p)/2F$.

The choice of F must be such that the square of the length of the quotient, A, is less than either B^p or D^p. It is best, then, to set up a double equation: Let the plane to be subtracted be A^p. Therefore $B^p - A^p$ is equal to a square and $D^p - A^p$ is equal to a square. Let B^p be greater than D^p, the difference being $B^p - D^p$. Hence $B^p - D^p$ is known to be four times the product of [two] roots, $B^p - A^p$ to be the square of the sum of the roots, and $D^p - A^p$ to be the square of the difference between the roots. Moreover, A^p is the amount by which B^p exceeds the square of the sum or by which D^p exceeds the square of the difference.

Let one root be G and let this be greater than the difference between $\sqrt{B^p}$ and $\sqrt{D^p}$[34] and less than their sum. The other will be $(B^p - D^p)/4G$ and the square of the sum of these, when subtracted from B^p, or the square of the difference between these, when subtracted from D^p, will leave A^p.

Let B^p be 44, D 36 and G (one of the roots) 1. Thus arises 2, the other root, and 3, the sum of the roots. The difference is 1 and the squares are 9 and 1. The plane to be subtracted, therefore, is 35. When it is subtracted from 44, it leaves 9 and when it is subtracted from 36 it leaves 1.

Zetetic IX[35]

To find numerically a plane that yields a square when either
of two other given planes is subtracted from it.

Let the two planes given numerically be B^p and D^p. You are to find a plane which leaves a numerical square when either B^p or D^p is subtracted from it.

Let A^p be the plane of the sort from which the subtraction is to be made. Therefore $A^p - D^p$ equals a square and $A^p - B^p$ equals a square. On this hypothesis a double equation is again to be set up. Assume that B^p is greater than D^p. Therefore the greater square, $A^p - D^p$, is known to be the square of the sum of two roots, and the smaller, $A^p - B^p$, to be the square of their difference. Finally the difference between B^p and D^p will be four times the product of the roots. Let one root be G. The other will be $(B^p - D^p)/4G$ and the square of the sum of these plus D^p[36] or the square of their difference [plus] B^p[37] will be A^p which, when D^p is subtracted from it,

[34] 1591 has "greater than the difference between B^p and D^p."
[35] Cf. Diophantus II, 13.
[36] 1646 has B^p.
[37] 1646 has D^p.

leaves the square of the sum and when B^p is subtracted leaves the square of the difference.

Let B^p be 56, D^p 48 and G (which is one of the roots) 1. This yields 2 for the other root. The sum of these is 3, their difference is 1. Whence A^p becomes 57 and this leaves 9 when D^p is subtracted from it and leaves 1 when B^p is subtracted from it.

Zetetic X[38]

To find numerically two roots the product of which plus the sum of their squares is a square.

Let one root be B, the other A. $A^2 + BA + B^2$ is to be equated to a square. Construct this from $A - D$ and set up an equation. $(D^2 - B^2)/(B + 2D)$ will equal A. Hence the first root will be analogous to $B^2 + 2BD$, the second to $D^2 - B^2$. The product of these added to the two squares is analogous to $D^4 + B^4 + 3B^2D^2 + 2B^3D + 2BD^3$ and the root of this is $B^2 + D^2 + BD$.

Let D be 2 and B 1. One of the roots is 5, the other 3. The root of the square composed of the squares of these two taken individually plus their product is 7, and 49 is the sum of 25, 15 and 9.

Lemma to the Next Zetetic

Three equal solids are produced by two roots:

One from the first root times the square of the second plus the product of the roots;

Another from the second root times the square of the first plus the [same] product;

A third from the sum of the roots times the same product.

Let the two roots be B and D. I say that these roots produce three equal solids:

First, $B(D^2 + BD)$
Second, $D(B^2 + BD)$
Third, $(B + D)BD$

This is clear since each of the three solids is $BD^2 + DB^2$.

[38]Cf. Diophantus, V, first lemma preceding 7.

Zetetic XI[39]

To find numerically three right triangles with equal areas

Let the perpendicular of the first triangle be analogous to $2BA$ and its base to $D^2 + BD$.[40] [Let the perpendicular] of the second [be analogous to] $2DA$ and its base to $B^2 + BD$.[41] [And let the perpendicular] of the third [be analogous to] $(B + D)2A$ and its base to BD.

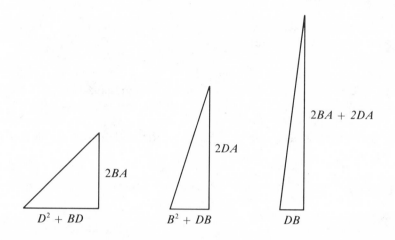

In accordance with the preceding lemma, therefore, the areas will be equal. That is, each will be $BD^2A + DB^2A$. The only remaining question is whether the planes analogous to the hypotenuses are rational.[42] But the planes B and D can be chosen, in accordance with the preceding zetetic, so that $B^2 + D^2 + BD$ equals a square. Let this square be A^2. This, by substitution, makes the base of the first triangle $A^2 - B^2$, of the second $A^2 - D^2$ and of the third $(B + D)^2 - A^2$,[43] [since] bases with roots like these are [analogous to] the difference between their squares and the perpendiculars are analogous to twice their product. The hypotenuses,

---

[39]Cf. Diophantus, V, second lemma preceding 7.

[40]1591 has $B^2 + BD$.

[41]1591 has $D^2 + BD$.

[42]*Superest igitur ut plana hypotenusis similia sint rationalia.* Vasset translates this "il reste donc seullement que les plans semblables aux hypotensuses soient rationaux" and Vaulezard "Il n'est plus question sinon que les plans semblables aux hypotenuses soient rationnaux."

[43]Or, alternatively, $A^2 - (B^2 + D^2)$.

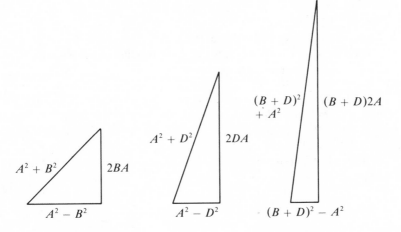

therefore, consist of the sum of the squares of these [terms], in accordance with the regular construction of triangles. Hence the hypotenuse of the first becomes analogous to $A^2 + B^2$, of the second to $A^2 + D^2$ and of the third to $(B + D)^2 + A^2$. So the problem is satisfied.

Let B be 3 and D 5. A becomes 7. And the triangles, in numbers, are these:
The area common to all three is 840.

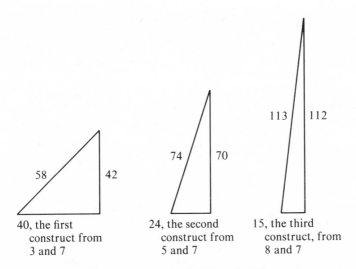

The common area of all three is 840.

Zetetic XII

To find numerically three right triangles such that the product of the perpendiculars is to the product of the bases as one square number is to another.

Set up any right triangle numerically. Let its hypotenuse be Z, its base D and its perpendicular B. And let a second triangle be constructed from Z and D with $2ZD$ as its base. Construct, finally, a third triangle from Z and B with $2ZB$ as its base.

The product of the perpendiculars will be to the product of the bases as B^2 to $4Z^2$.

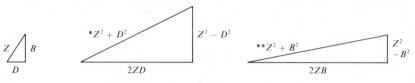

*The text omits $+D^2$. **The text omits $+B^2$.

Let the first triangle be 5, 3, 4. The second will be 34, 30, 16 and the third 41, 40, 9. The product of the perpendiculars, 4, 16 and 9, is to the product of the bases, 3, 30 and 40, as the square of 4 is to the square of 10.

Zetetic XIII

To find numerically two right triangles such that the product of the perpendiculars minus the product of the bases is a square.

Set up numerically any right triangle you wish. Let its hypotenuse be Z, its base D and its perpendicular B, and let twice the perpendicular be

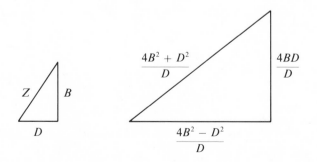

greater than the base D. Then construct another triangle from $2B$ and D or roots similar to these, let $4BD$ be its perpendicular, and let all the planes that are analogous to the sides be divided by D. The product of the perpendiculars minus the product of the bases leaves D^2[44] or something analogous to D^2,[45] inasmuch as the analogizing of the roots to $2B$ and D has changed the operation.[46]

Let the first right triangle be 15, 9, 12. The second will be 73, 55, 48. The product of the perpendiculars, 576, differs from the product of the bases, 495, by the square 81, the root of which is 9.

Zetetic XIIII

To find numerically two right triangles such that the product of their perpendiculars plus the product of their bases is a square.

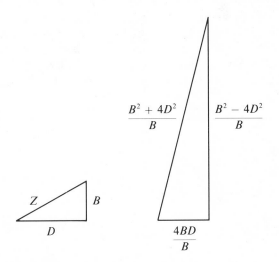

Set up numerically any right triangle you wish. Let its hypotenuse be Z, its base D and its perpendicular B, and let the perpendicular B be greater than twice the base D. Construct another triangle from B and $2D$, let twice $2BD$[47] be assigned to the base and divide all the planes analogous to the

---

[44]1591 has B^2.

[45]The text has B^2.

[46]*prout radicum cum ipsis B dupla & D similitudo opus immutavit.* I find the meaning of this passage obscure.

[47]1591 omits the word "twice."

sides by B. The product of the perpendiculars plus the product of the bases will be B^2.[48]

Let the first triangle be 13, 12, 5.[49] Having constructed [another triangle] from 5 and 6 or their comparables, 10 and 12, the second will be 61, 11, 60.[50] [Multiplied by3,] the product of the perpendiculars is 396, that of the bases 900. The sum, 1296, is a square and its root is 36.

Zetetic XV

To find numerically three right triangles such that the product of the hypotenuses is to the product of the bases as one square number is to another.

Set up numerically any right triangle you choose with Z as its hypotenuse, B its base and D its perpendicular and such also that twice the base B is greater than the perpendicular D. Then construct another triangle from $2B$ and D,[51] assigning $4BD$ to the base. Finally, let the hypotenuse of a third triangle be analogized to the product of the hypotenuses of the first and second and its base to the product of their bases minus the product of their perpendiculars. Consequently its perpendicular will be equal to the reciprocal products of their bases and perpendiculars. The product of the

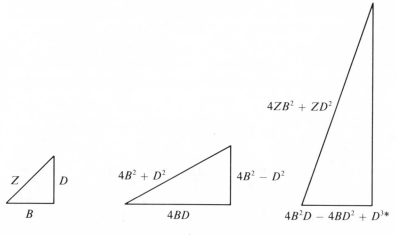

*1646 has $4B^2D - 4DB^2 + D^3$.

[48]1591 has *relinquit B quadratum;* 1646 has *componit B quadratum.*
[49]This is a triangle constructed from the roots 2, 3.
[50]The text has 61, 60, 11.
[51]1591 has "and the base D."

[three] hypotenuses will be to the product of the [three] bases as one square is to another.

Let the first triangle be 5, 3, 4. The second will be 13, 12, 5 and the third will be 65, 16, 63. The product of the hypotenuses will be to the product of the bases as the square of 65 is to the square of 24.

Or set up numerically a right triangle the hypotenuse of which is Z, the base D and the perpendicular B, such that B is greater than twice the base D, and let this be the first. Construct the second from B and $2D$ and assign $4BD$ as its base. Finally, let the hypotenuse of the third be analogous to the product of the hypotenuses of the first and second and its base to the product of the bases plus the product of the perpendiculars. Hence the perpendicular [of the third] is equal to the difference between the reciprocal products of the bases and the perpendiculars [of the other two]. The product of the hypotenuses [of all three] will be to the product of the bases as one square to another.

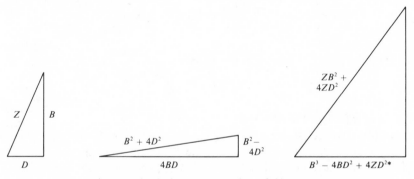

*1646 omits the last two expressions of this term.

Let the first triangle be 13, 5, 12. The second will be 61, 60, 11 and the third 793, 432, 665.[52] The product of the hypotenuses will be to the product of the bases as the square of 793 to the square of 360.

Zetetic XVI

To find numerically a right triangle the area of which is equal to a given [quantity] on stated conditions.

Let the area be given as, say, $(B^4 - X^4)/D^2$. Construct a triangle from B^2 and X^2 and divide the plano-planes that are analogous to the sides by XDB.[53]

[52]These values result from dividing those derived from the formulas by 4.
[53]1591 has $2XDB$.

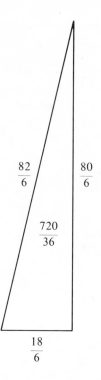

Let B be 3, X 1 and D 2. There are, then, two fourth powers, 81 and 1, and the difference between them is 80. Given 80/4, or 20, as the area, the triangle has been constructed from 9 and 1, making the area 720/36.

So when a number is given for the area, you must see whether what has been proposed, or the same multiplied by a square number, plus 1 or some other fourth power is a fourth power. Thus, if 15 were given, since 15 plus 1 makes 16, the fourth power of 2, a triangle can be made from 4 and 1.

And if the area were given as $(D^3X - X^3D)/X^2$, construct a triangle from D and X and divide the planes, which are analogous to sides, by X.

Let D be 2 and X 1. Therefore the area is given as 6. Construct a triangle from 2 and 1, and the area will become 6. So when a number is prescribed for the area, see whether what has been proposed or the same times a square number is a cube minus its root.

Thus, if 60 were proposed, construct the triangle from 4 and 1.

Zetetic XVII

To find numerically three proportional planes, the middle one of which plus either the first or the last is a square.

Let the second of the planes be E^p. And let the first be $B^2 - E^p$ and the last $G^2 - E^p$. Then when the first plane is added to E^p, it makes a square, namely B^2. Likewise when E^p is added to the last, it makes a square, namely G^2. It follows, therefore, that as the three planes are proportionals and consequently that the square of the mean is equal to the product of the extremes, by a comparison undertaken in accordance with the art, $B^2G^2/(B^2 + G^2)$ will be found to be equal to E^p. So the three proportionals are of this sort:

First	Second	Third
$\dfrac{B^4}{B^2 + G^2}$	$\dfrac{B^2G^2}{B^2 + G^2}$	$\dfrac{G^4}{B^2 + G^2}$

Let B be 1 and G 2. The planes being sought will be: first $1/5$,[54] second $4/5$, third $16/5$. The mean plus the first is 1 and the mean plus the third is 4. The same planes multiplied by any square, say 25, in order to satisfy the conditions given, become 5, 20 and 80, the planes that were ordered by the problem.

Zetetic XVIII

> Given two cubes, to find numerically two other cubes the sum of which is equal to the difference between those that are given.

Let the two given cubes be B^3 and D^3, the first the greater, the second the smaller. Two other cubes are to be found the sum of which is equal to $B^3 - D^3$. Let $B - A$ be the root of the first one that is to be found, and let $B^2A/D^2 - D$ be the root of the second. Forming the cubes and comparing them with $B^3 - D^3$, it will be found that $3D^3B/(B^3 + D^3)$ equals A. The root of the first cube to be found, therefore, is $[B(B^3 - 2D^3)]/(B^3 + D^3)$ and of the second is $[D(2B^3 - D^3)]/(B^3 + D^3)$.[55] And the sum of the cubes of these is equal to $B^3 - D^3$.

One can likewise find four cubes the greatest of which is equal to the other three by taking the two roots B and D, the former the larger, the latter the smaller. The root of the composite cube will be analogous to $B(B^3 + D^3)$, the root of the first individual cube to $D(B^3 + D^3)$, of the second to $B(B^3 - 2D^3)$ and of the third to $D(2B^3 - D^3)$. It is evident from the process

---

[54]1591 has $1/3$.
[55]1591 has $2B^3 - D^3$ for the denominator of this fraction.

that the cube of the largest of the assumed roots must be at least as great as[56] the cube of twice the smallest.

[So it is if] B is 2 and D 1: The cube of the root 6 will equal the individual cubes of 3, 4 and 5.[57] When, therefore, the cubes of $6x$ and $3x$ are given, the cubes of $4x$ and $5x$[58] will appear and the sum of the latter will be equal to the difference between the former.

Zetetic XIX

Given two cubes, to find numerically two other cubes the difference between which is equal to the sum of those given.

Let the given cubes be B^3 and D^3, the former the larger and the latter the smaller. Let $B + A$ be the root of the first cube to be found and $B^2A/D^2 - D$ the root of the second. Form the cubes and compare the difference between them with $B^3 + D^3$. It will be found that $3D^3B/(B^3 - D^3)$ equals A. So the root of the larger cube being sought will be $[B(B^3 + 2D^3)]/(B^3 - D^3)$ and of the second $[D(2B^3 - D^3)]/(B^3 - D^3)$,[59] and the difference between [the cubes of] these is equal to $B^3 + D^3$.

Let B be 2 and D 1. It will be discovered that the cube of 20 is equal to [the sum of] the individual cubes of 17, 14 and 7. So when the cubes of $14x$ and $7x$ are given, the cubes of $20x$ and $17x$ will be shown and their difference will be equal to the sum of the others.

Zetetic XX

Given two cubes, to find numerically two other cubes the difference between which is equal to the difference between those that are given.

Let the two given cubes be B^3 and D^3, the former the greater and the latter the smaller.[60] Let the root of the first cube to be found be $A - D$ and of the second $D^2A/B^2 - B$.[61] Form the cubes and compare their difference with $B^3 - D^3$. It will be found that $3DB^3/(B^3 + D^3)$ equals A. So the root of the first cube is $[D(2B^3 - D^3)]/B^3 + D^3$, of the second $[B(2D^3 - B^3)]/$

---

[56]The text has "greater than."

[57]These are the results of applying the formulae and dividing through by 3.

[58]1591 has $3x$.

[59]1591 omits the denominator of this fraction; supplied by the editor in 1646.

[60]The text has "the latter the greater and the former the smaller."

[61]1591 omits $-B$; supplied by the editor in 1646.

$B^3 + D^3$, and the difference between [the cubes of] these is equal to the difference between B^3 and D^3. The operation would turn out the same if the root of the first cube to be found were assumed to be $B - A$ and of the second $D - B^2A/D^2$.

One can likewise find four cubes such that two are equal to two by assuming that the roots are B and D. the former the larger, the latter the smaller, and that the root of the first cube is analogous to $D(2B^3 - D^3)$, of the second to $D(B^3 + D^3)$, of the third to $B(B^3 + D^3)$ and of the fourth to $B(2D^3 - B^3)$. It is clear from the process that B^3 must be greater than D^3 but less than $2D^3$.

Let B be 5 and D 4. The cubes of 252 and 248 equal the cubes of 5 and 315.[62] When, therefore, the cubes of $315x$ and $252x$ are given, they show the cubes of $248x$ and $5x$, and the difference between the latter will be equal to the difference between the former.

FIFTH BOOK

Zetetic I[63]

To find numerically three planes forming a square, the sum of any two of which also forms a square.

Let the square of $A + B$—namely, $A^2 + 2AB + B^2$—be the sum of three planes. The first plus the second becomes A^2. The third plane, therefore, will be $2AB + B^2$. The second and third are the square of $A - B$—that is, $A^2 - 2AB + B^2$. This, then, leaves the second as $A^2 - 4AB$. Hence the first plane will be $4AB$ which, added to the third, makes $6AB + B^2$. It follows, therefore, that this last plane, made up of the first and third, is equal to a square. Let this be D^2. Thus $(D^2 - B^2)/6B$ will equal A. The first plane, therefore, is analogous to $24D^2B^2 - 24B^4$, the second to $D^4 + 25B^4 - 26B^2D^2$, and the third to $12B^2D^2 + 24B^4$.

Let D be 11 and B 1. The first plane becomes 2880, the second 11, 520 the third 1476, and these satisfy the problem. It can also be satisfied by dividing through by any square, say by 36. This gives rise to the planes 80, 320 and 41.

Let D be 6 and B 1. The first plane becomes 840, the second 385, and the third 456.

[62]These are the figures obtained by applying the formulae given and dividing by 3.
[63]Cf. Diophantus, III, 6.

Zetetic II

To find numerically three squares separated by equal intervals.

Let the first [square] be A^2 and the second $A^2 + 2AB + B^2$. The third will therefore be $A^2 + 4AB + 2B^2$. If the root of the last is assumed to be $D - A$, we have

$$D^2 - 2AD + A^2 = A^2 + 4AB + 2B^2.$$

Hence A will equal $(D^2 - 2B^2)/(4B + 2D)$. So the first root will be analogous to $D^2 - 2B^2$, the second to $D^2 + 2B^2 + 2BD$, and the third to $D^2 + 2B^2 + 4BD$.

Let D be 8 and B 1. This makes the root of the first square 62, of the second 82 and of the third 98, and the squares of these are 3844, 6724 and 9604. Dividing all of these by any square, say 4, [gives us] 961, 1681 and 2401, which are distant from each other by equal intervals—in the former 2880,[64] in the latter 720.

Zetetic III[65]

To find numerically three equidistant planes, the sum of any two of which is a square.

Let three equidistant squares be set out in accordance with the preceding zetetic. Let the first and smallest be B^2, the second $B^2 + D^p$, the third $B^2 + 2D^p$. Then let [the sum of] the first and second of the three equidistant planes that are to be found be B^2, of the first and third $B^2 + D^p$, and of the second and third $B^2 + 2D^p$. Let the sum of all three be A^p. The third will then be $A^p - B^2$, the second $A^p - B^2 - D^p$, and the first $A^p - B^2 - 2D^p$. Thus these three planes are equidistant, for the difference between the first and second is D^p and this is also the difference between the second and third. The conclusion is, therefore, that the sum of these three planes, which is $3A^p - 3B^2 - 3D^p$, is equal to A^p, making $(3B^2 + 3D^p)/2$ equal to A^p. Hence the first plane will be $(B^2 - D^p)/2$, the second $(B^2 + D^p)/2$, and the third $(B^2 + 3D^p)/2$. Multiplying all by 4, the first is analogous to $2B^2 - 2D^p$, the second to $2B^2 + 2D^p$, and the third to $2B^2 + 6D^p$.

[64]The text has 2280.
[65]Cf. Diophantus, III, 7.

The interval between either the first and second or the second and third is $4D^p$. And the first plus the second becomes $4B^2$, the first plus the third $4B^2 + 4D^p$ (a square by hypothesis, since $B^2 + D^p$ was set up as a square), and the second plus the third $4B^2 + 8D^p$ (which is also a square by hypothesis, since $B^2 + 2D^p$ was set up as a square).

Let B^2 be 961 and D^p 720. The first plane will be 482, the second 3362 and the third 6242, the interval being 2880.[66] So the first and second are the square of 62, the first and third the square of 82, and the second and third the square of 98.

Zetetic IIII[67]

To find numerically three planes the sum of any two of which, like the sum of all three, constitutes a square when added to a given plane.

Let Z^p be the given plane and let the sum of the first and second planes that are to be found be $A^2 + 2BA + B^2 - Z^p$, since when Z^p is added to this it makes the square of $A + B$. And let the sum of the second and third be $A^2 + 2DA + D^2 - Z^p$, since when Z^p is added to this it makes the square of $A + D$. And let the sum of all three be $A^2 + 2GA + G^2 - Z^p$,[68] since when Z^p is added to this it makes the square of $A + G$. When, therefore, the sum of the first and second is subtracted from the sum [of all three], there is left for the third plane $2GA + G^2 - 2BA - B^2$. And when from the same sum there is subtracted the sum of the second and third, there is left for the first plane $2GA + G^2 - 2DA - D^2$. So the sum of the first and third supplemented by Z^p will be $4GA + 2G^2 - 2BA - B^2 - 2DA - D^2 + Z^p$, and this must equal a square. Let this be F^2. Therefore $(F^2 + D^2 + B^2 - 2G^2 - Z^p)/(4G - 2B - 2D)$[69] will equal A.

Let Z^p be 3, B 1, D 2, G 3 and F 10, making A 14. The sum of the first and second planes is 222, viz., 3 less than the square of 15. The sum of the second and third planes is 253, viz., 3 less than the square of 16. The sum of the first and third is 97, viz., 3 less than the square of 10.[70] The sum of all three is 286, viz., 3 less than the square of 17. Hence the first of the planes being sought will be 33, the second 189 and the third 64, which is what was directed.

[66] 1691 has 2280.
[67] Cf. Diophantus, III, 8.
[68] 1591 has *G quad Z—plano*, a typographical error that is corrected in 1646.
[69] 1591 omits the minus signs in the denominator of this fraction.
[70] This sentence is lacking in 1591; supplied by the editor in 1646.

Zetetic V[71]

To find numerically three planes the sum of any two of which, like the sum of all three, minus a given plane, constitutes a square.

Let Z^p be the given plane and let $A^2 + Z^p$ be the sum of the first and second so that the remainder, after subtracting Z^p, is the square of A. Let $A^2 + 2BA + B^2 + Z^p$ be the sum of the second and third for the same reason, so that the remainder, after subtracting Z^p, will be the square of $A + B$. And let the sum of all three be $A^2 + 2DA + D^2 + Z^p$ for the same reason, so that the remainder, after subtracting Z^p, will be the square of $A + D$. If, therefore, the sum of the first and second is subtracted from the sum of all three, $2DA + D^2$ is left for the third. And if the sum of the second and third is subtracted from the same [i.e., from the sum of all three], $2DA + D^2 - 2BA - B^2$ is left for the first. Hence the sum of the first and third, after subtracting Z^p, will be $4DA + 2D^2 - 2BA - B^2 - Z^p$. Let this be F^2. Therefore $(F^2 + B^2 + Z^p - 2D^2)/(4D - 2B)$ will equal A.

Let Z^p be 3, B 1, D 2 and F 8, making A 10. The sum of the first and second planes is 103, viz., the square of 10 plus 3. The sum of the second and third is 124, viz., the square of 11 with an added 3. The sum of the three is 147, viz., the square of 12, with 3 in addition. So the sum of the first and third is 67, the square of 8 [increased by 3].[72] Therefore the first plane among those sought will be 23, the second 80 and the third 44, which is what was directed.

Zetetic VI

To find numerically an infinite number of squares each of which plus a given plane makes a square and, on the other hand, an infinite [number of squares each of which] minus the same [makes a square].

Let Z^p be the given plane. Resolve one-fourth of this into the two roots from which it is constructed, as BD and, again, FG. Therefore $4BD$ and likewise $4FG$ will equal Z^p. Hence $(B - D)^2 + Z^p$—that is, [plus] four times the product of the roots—makes a square, namely $(B + D)^2$. And again $(F - G)^2 + Z^{p}$[73] makes a square, namely $(F + G)^2$. The same will be

[71]Cf. Diophantus, III, 9.
[72]1591 omits the bracketed expression.
[73]1591 has 2^p.

true with any two roots, since a division of $Z^p/4$ by one of them gives rise to the other.

Let Z^p be 96. One-fourth of this is 24, which is the product of 1 and 24, 2 and 12, 3 and 8, or 4 and 6, and innumerable other fractions. So the square of 23 plus 96 gives the square of 25, and the square of 10 plus 96 gives the square of 14, and the square of 5 plus 96 gives the square of 11, and the square of 2 plus 96 gives the square of 10, and so on for the rest.

Contrariwise $(B + D)^2 - Z^p$—that is, [minus] four times the product of the roots[74]—leaves $(B - D)^2$, and $(F + G)^2 - Z^p$ leaves $(F - G)^2$.

Subtracting 96 from 625 yields 529, the square of 23. And 196 minus 96 is 100, the square of 10.

Zetetic VII[75]

To find numerically three roots the product of any pair of which is a plane which, when added to a given plane, makes a square.

Let Z^p be the given plane. Assume, moreover, that the product of the first and the second roots is $B^2 - Z^p$, so that adding Z^p to it produces a square, and let the second root be A. The first will then be $(B^2 - Z^p)/A$. The second root remaining A, the third will be $(D^2 - Z^p)/A$. No more is required, therefore, except that the product of the first and third—i.e., the product of $(B^2 - Z^p)/A$ and $(D^2 - Z^p)/A$—be a square after Z^p has been added to it.[76] But if $B^2 - Z^p$ were a square (say F^2) and if $D^2 - Z^p$ were a square (say G^2), an equation could be completed; in this case $(F^2G^2 + Z^pA^2)/A^2$ would be equated to a square. But this causes no trouble since, if this is represented as the square of $(FG \sim HA)/A$, $2HFG/(H^2 \sim Z^p)$ will equal A. In the first supposition, H^2 is greater than Z^p and in the second it is less. So one can discover infinite squares which, when a given plane is subtracted, yield a square and, reciprocally, an infinite number which do the same when a given plane is added. It is not any B^2 and D^2 that can be chosen but only those that fulfill the conditions; that is, roots like F and G must be so chosen that their individual squares, when Z^p is added to them, form squares, as in this case they make B^2 and D^2. Thus the equation we have set out will be created.

Let Z^p be 192, F 8 and G 2. Assume that H is 6. A then becomes 16/13. The first root will be 52, the second 16/13 and the third 13/4. The

---

[74] 1591 omits the words between the dashes; supplied by the editor in 1646.
[75] Cf. Diophantus, III, 10.
[76] *Restat igitur ut quod fit a primo in tertium . . . sit adscito Z plano, quadratum.*

first times the second makes 64. The second times the third produces 4. The first times the third produces 169. The product of the first and second added to 192 is 256, the square of the root 16. The product of the second and third added to 192 is 196, the square of the root 14. Finally the product of the first and third [added to 192][77] is 361, the square of the root 19.

Zetetic VIII[78]

To find numerically three roots the products of which, taken in pairs, minus a given plane yield a square.

Let Z^p be the given plane and let the product of the first and second roots be $B^2 + Z^p$ so that a subtraction of Z^p leaves B^2. Let the second root be A. The first, therefore, will be $(B^2 + Z^p)/A$. The product of the second and third will be $D^2 + Z^p$ for the same reason. The second root being A, the third will be $(D^2 + Z^p)/A$. No more is required, then, except that the product of the first and third—that is, the product of $(B^2 + Z^p)/A$ and $(D^2 + Z^p)/A$—minus Z^p be a square. But if $B^2 + Z^p$ is a square (say F^2) and $D^2 + Z^p$ is also a square (say G^2), an equation can be completed. In this case $(F^2G^2 - Z^pA^2)/A^2$ will be equated to a square. But there will be no trouble if this square is supposed to be the square of $(FG - HA)/A$. In this case $2HFG/(Z^p + H^2)$ will equal A. Thus one can discover infinite squares which, a given plane being added to them, make a square and, on the other hand, an infinite number when it is subtracted. It is not any B^2 and D^2 that can be chosen but only those that meet the conditions; that is, F and G must be so chosen that, when Z^p is subtracted from each of them, they leave a square, as in the present case they leave B^2 and D^2. Thus the equation we have set out will be created.

Let Z^p be 40, F 7 and G 11, thus making B 3 and D 9. Assume that H is 24. This makes A 6, the first root 49/6, the second 6, the third 121/6. The product of the first and second is 49, leaving 9 when 40 is subtracted, a square number [the root of which is 3].[79] The product of the second and third is 121; subtracting 40 leaves 81, a square number, [the root of which is 9].[80] The product of the first and third is 5929/36; subtracting 1440/36 (that is, 40) leaves 4489/36, a square number the root of which is 67/6.

---

[77] The bracketed words were supplied by the editor in 1646.
[78] Cf. Diophantus III, 11.
[79] This expression occurs only in 1646.
[80] This expression occurs only in 1646.

Zetetic IX[81]

To find numerically a right triangle the area of which plus a given plane made up of two squares is a square.

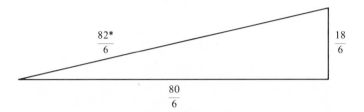

$\dfrac{82^*}{6}$ $\dfrac{18}{6}$

$\dfrac{80}{6}$

*1646 has 16 for the denominator of the fractions shown for this triangle

Let Z^p be a plane composed of B^2 and D^2. Construct a right triangle from the square of the sum of the roots B and D and the square of their difference. The hypotenuse will then be analogous to $2B^4 + 12B^2D^2 + 2D^4$, the base to $8BDZ^{p}$[82] and the perpendicular to the product of $(B + D)^2$ and $2(B - D)^2$. Divide all by the product of $(B + D)$ and $2(B - D)^2$. The area then becomes analogous to $2Z^pBD/(B - D)^2$. Add Z^p. Since

$$(B - D)^2 + 2BD = B^2 + D^2,$$

which is Z^p, the sum will be $Z^{pp}/(B - D)^2$, the square of the root $Z^p/(B - D)$.

Let Z^p be 5, D 1 and B 2. The right triangle will be as shown. Its area will be $720/36$, that is 20. Add 5. The sum is 25, the root of which is 5.

Zetetic X[83]

To find numerically a right triangle the area of which minus a given plane is a square.

Let Z^p, otherwise $2BD$, be the given plane, and let a right triangle be constructed from the square of the sum of the roots B and D and the square of their difference. The hypotenuse will be analogous to $2B^4 + 12B^2D^2 + 2D^4$, the base to $4B^2Z^p + 4D^2Z^p$ and the perpendicular to the

---

[81]Cf. Diophantus, VI, 3, which, however, does not require that the given number be the sum of two squares.

[82]1591 omits the coefficient 8.

[83]Cf. Diophantus, VI, 4.

product of $(B + D)^2$ and $2(B - D)^2$. Divide by the product of $(B + D)$ and $2(B - D)^2$, making the area similar to $(B^2Z^p + D^2Z^p)^{[84]}/(B - D)^2$. Subtract Z^p. Since

$$B^2 + D^2 - (B - D)^2 = Z^p,$$

there is left $Z^{pp}/(B - D)^2$, the square of the root $Z^p/(B - D)$.

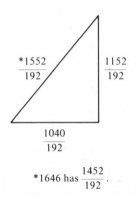

$\dfrac{*1552}{192}$ $\dfrac{1152}{192}$

$\dfrac{1040}{192}$

$*1646$ has $\dfrac{1452}{192}$.

Let D be 1 and B 5. Hence Z^p is 10. The right angle is of the sort shown, with an area of 599,040/36,864. Subtract 10, leaving 230,400/ 36,864, the square of the root 480/192 or 10/4.

Zetetic XI[85]

To find numerically a right triangle the area of which subtracted from a given plane makes a square.

Let Z^p, otherwise $2BD$, be the given plane. Construct a right triangle from the square of the sum of the roots B and D and the square of their difference. The hypotenuse, therefore, will be analogous to $2B^4 + 12B^2D^2 + 2D^4$, the base to $4B^2Z^p + 4D^2Z^p$ and the perpendicular to the product of $(B + D)^2$ and $2(B - D)^2$. Divide through by the product of $B - D$ and $2(B + D)^2$. This makes the area analogous to $(B^2Z^p + D^2Z^p)/(B + D)^2$. Subtract from Z^p. Since

$$(B + D)^2 - B^2 - D^2 = 2BD,$$

$Z^{pp}/(B + D)^2$, the square of the root $Z^p/(B + D)$, is left.

---

[84]1591 has $(B + D)^2$ for the denominator of this fraction and omits the plus sign in the numerator.
[85]Cf. Diophantus, VI, 5.

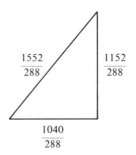

Let D be 1 and B 5. Hence Z^p [will be] 10 [and] the right triangle [will be] as shown, with an area equal to 599,400/82,944. Subtract from 10, leaving 230,400/82,944, the square of the root 480/288 or 5/3.

Zetetic XII

To find numerically three squares such that the plano-plane product of each pair of them plus the product of the sum of the pairs and the square of a given length is a square.

Let X be the length. Let the first square be $A^2 - 2AX + X^2$, the root of which is $A - X$; let the second be A^2, the root of which is A; and let the third be $4A^2 - 4AX + 4X^2$. From the product of the first and second, plus the sum of the first and second times X^2, comes a square with the plane root $A^2 - XA + X^2$.[86] From the product of the second and third, plus the sum of the second and third times X^2, comes a square with the plane root $2A^2 - XA + 2X^2$. Finally, from the product of the first and third, plus the sum of the first and third times X^2, comes a square with the plane root $2A^2 - 3XA + 3X^2$. Let the root of the third be equated to $D - 2A$. Therefore $(D^2 - 4X^2)/(4D - 4X)$ will equal A.

Let X be 3 and D 30. A then becomes 8. So the squares that are being sought are first, 25; second, 64; third, 196, and these satisfy the postulates. For the product of the first and second plus 801 is 2401, the square of 49. Again, the product of the second and third plus 2340 is 14,884, the square of 122. And last, the product of the first and third plus 1989[87] is 6889,[88] the square of 83. Furthermore, when each of these three squares is added to twice the square of the given length, the plano-plane that results from multiplying each of these pairs minus the product of their sum and the square of the given length will be a square. Thus, in the hypothetical case

[86] 1591 has A quadrato X—in $A + X$ quadrato, an error that is corrected in 1646.
[87] 1591 has 1089.
[88] 1591 has 6989.

set out, twice the square of the given length is 18 and this plus each of the three squares makes three planes, the first 43, the second 82, the third 214, which satisfy the requirements. For the product of the first and second minus 1125 is 2401, the product of the second and third minus 2664 is 14,884, and the product of the first and third minus 2313 is 6889.

Zetetic XIII

To divide a given length X so that when B is added to the first segment and D to the second and the parts thus produced are multiplied by each other a square results.

Let the first segment be $A - B$. The other, therefore, will be $X - A + B$. When B is added to the first segment the result is A. And when D is added to the second segment the result is $X - A + B + D$.[89] Hence $A(B + D + X)$[90] $- A^2$ must be equal to a square. Suppose the root [of this square] is SA/X. The square will then be S^2A^2/X^2. Hence $[X^2(B + D + X)]/(S^2 + X^2)$[91] will equal A. In accordance with the assumptions,[92] the first segment will be $[(D + X)X^2 - BS^2]/S^2 + X^2$ and the second will be $[(B + X)S^2 - DX^2]/S^2 + X^2$. For subtraction to take place, S^2 must be less than $[X^2(D + X)]/B$[93] and greater than $X^2D/(B + X)$.

Let X be 4, B 12 and D 20. S^2 must be less than 32 and greater than 20. Let it be 25. Then the first segment is 84/41, the second 80/41. The latter then produces 900/41, the former 576/41. The product of these is 518,400/1681, the square of 720/41.

Let X be 3, B 9 and D 15. S^2 must be less than 18 and greater than 11¼. Let it be 16. The first segment is then 18/25, the second 57/25. The latter produces 432/25, the former 243/25. The product of these is 104,976/625,[94] the square of the root 324/25.

Zetetic XIIII

To equate $A^2 - G^p$ to a single square that is less than DA and greater than BA.

Construct the square of $A - F$. Then

$$A^2 - 2FA + F^2 = A^2 - G^p$$

---

[89] 1591 has $x - A + BD$.
[90] 1591 has $A(BDX)$.
[91] 1591 has $X^2(BDX)$.
[92] *ad positiones.*
[93] 1591 has $X^2(DX)$.
[94] The text has 156,816/625.

and consequently $(F^2 + G^p)/2F$ will equal A. But since

$$A^2 - G^p < DA,$$

therefore

$$A^2 < DA + G^p.$$

Again,

$$A^2 - DA < G^p.$$

Hence

$$A < \sqrt{\tfrac{1}{4}D^2 + G^p} + \tfrac{1}{2}D.$$

Therefore A will be less than S.

Contrariwise, since

$$A^2 - G^p > BA^{95}$$

and

$$A^2 - BA > G^p,$$
$$A > \sqrt{\tfrac{1}{4}B^2 + G^p} + \tfrac{1}{2}B.$$

Suppose, moreover that

$$R \gtreqless \sqrt{\tfrac{1}{4}B^2 + G^p} + \tfrac{1}{2}B.$$

Then A is greater than R.

Therefore $F^2 + G^p$ is less than $2SF$ and greater than $2RF$.[96] Thus F cannot be assumed to be anything you choose but must not wander outside prescribed limits. In accordance with zetetics let it be E. So

$$2SE - E^2 > G^p.{}^{[97]}$$

Then let it be assumed that

$$F < S + \sqrt{S^2 - G^p}{}^{[98]}$$

and, contrariwise, that

$$2RE - E^2 < G^p.{}^{[99]}$$

Assume, furthermore, that

$$F > R + \sqrt{R^2 - G^p}.{}^{[1]}$$

[95] 1591 has $BA + G^p$.

[96] The text has $2RS$.

[97] 1591 has $<$.

[98] 1591 has $\sqrt{S^2 + G^p}$.

[99] 1591 has $> G^p$.

[1] 1591 has $\sqrt{R^2 + G^p}$.

Let G^p be 60, B 5, D 8 and A x. X will then be less than $\sqrt{76} + 4$ and greater than $\sqrt{265/4} + 5/2$. But 12 is less than $\sqrt{76} + 4$ and 11 is greater than $\sqrt{265/4} - 5/2$. Assume therefore that S is 13 and R is 10. F will then be chosen as less than $13 + \sqrt{109}$ but greater than $10 + \sqrt{40}$. But 23 is less than $13 + \sqrt{109}$ and 17 is greater than $10 + \sqrt{40}$. Hence F can be assumed to be 21 or 19 or any rational intermediate number. Assume that it is 20. X then becomes $11\frac{1}{2}$.[2]

This is the solution for the problem proposed by the Greek epigramatist:

,,   Ὀκῶδράχμυς ὧ πινῶδράχμυς χοέας τὶς ἔμιξε,
,,   Τοῖς ωϱϱπολοῖς ποιεῖν χϱησὸν Ἐπιϊάγμϕ Ϙ·
,,   Καὶ τιμϕω̃ ἀπέδωκεν ὑπὲρ πάντων πτϱάγωνον,
,,   Τὰς Ἐπιταχθείσας δεξάμϕϘ μονάδας,
,,   Καὶ ποιοῦντας πάλιν ἱπϱόν σε Φέρϙν πτϱάγωνον
,,   Κτησάμϕον πλϛϱϱὰν σωϑεμά τ̃ χοεῶν.
,,   Ω̃ςε διάςϙλον, τὺς ὀκτϱδράχμυς μίϙσον,
,,   Καὶ πάλι τὺς ἑπέϱυς, παῖ, λέϙε πινταδράχμυς.

σωϑεμα τ̃ χοεῶν	$11\frac{1}{2}$	A
πινταδραχμοι	$6\frac{7}{13}$	
ὀκτϱδραχμοι	$4\frac{11}{13}$	

τιμὴ πινταδραχμῶν	$32\frac{11}{13}$	B in A
τιμὴ ὀκταδραχμῶν	$39\frac{1}{3}$	D in A
τιμὴ συμπᾶσα	$72\frac{1}{4}$ πτϱάγωνϘ A quad. — Z plano.

μονάδες	60	Z planum
ωϱϱϑεσις τιμῆς χ̣ μονάδων $132\frac{1}{4}$ πτϱάγωνϘ κτησάμϕϘ πλϛϱϱὰν		
$11\frac{1}{2}$ A quad.		

Diophantus set out this problem at the end of his Book V, so I place it here at the end of our fifth [book] of zetetics.

[2]This is a translation of the paragraph as it appears in 1646. In 1591 it read thus: Let G^p be 60, B 5, D 8 and A x. X will then be less than $\sqrt{76} + 4$ and greater than $\sqrt{265/4} + 5/2$. But 12 is less than $\sqrt{76} + 4$, for the value of [the square root of] the square of 12 is $\sqrt{64} + 4$. And 11 is greater than $\sqrt{289/4} + \frac{1}{2}$. Assume, therefore, that S is 12 and R is 11. F will then be chosen as less than $12 + \sqrt{84}$ but greater than $11 + \sqrt{61}$. But 21 is less than $12 + \sqrt{84}$, for the value of [the square root of] the square of 21 is $12 + \sqrt{81}$. And 19 is greater than $11 + 161$, for the value of [the square root of] the square of 19 is $11 + \sqrt{64}$. Hence F can properly be assumed to be 21 or 19 or any rational intermediate number. Assume that it is 20. X then becomes $11\frac{1}{2}$.

TWO TREATISES ON THE UNDERSTANDING AND AMENDMENT OF EQUATIONS[1]

FIRST[2] TREATISE: ON UNDERSTANDING EQUATIONS[3]
CHAPTER I

On the Structure of Equations as Shown by Zetetics, Plasmatic Modification[4] and Syncrisis.[5]

This treatise on the understanding of equations fills in and complements the broad principle treated in a general way [in the treatise] on the numerical resolution of powers, for equations frequently stand in need of preparation before they can be solved successfully, especially when powers are subtracted from homogeneous terms, when powers have both positive and negative affections and the negative outweigh the positive, and finally when equations are displayed with fractions or irrationals.

In geometry,[6] to be sure, the accident of a fraction or an irrational does not usually prevent equations from being solved readily.[7] nor does the

---

[1] *De Aequationum Recognitione et Emendatione Tractatus Duo.* 1646 places this work ahead of the preceding though Viète, judging from the order in which he lists the contents of his proposed *Opus Restitutae Mathematicae Analyseos* in the prospectus that appears following the title page of the 1591 edition of the *Isagoge,* intended it to come at this point.

[2] 1615 omits this word.

[3] *De Recognitione Aequationum.* Ritter (biog., p. 57) elaborates on "Recognitione" by adding in parentheses "examen de la nature intime."

[4] *Plasma.* Viète uses this word, which originally meant something formed or molded, more in the sense of the operation of forming or molding. For lack of any simple expression that is both idiomatic and exact, I use the rather cumbersome "plasmatic modification." "Transformation" would be a more congenial term, but Viète reserves this for a wider variety of cases than he allows for under *plasma.*

[5] Viète has borrowed this word from the vocabulary of rhetoric, where it applies to a figure of speech in which opposites are compared. I have frequently rendered it hereafter as "comparison."

[6] Here, as at various other places, Viète uses the broad word "geometry" to refer more specifically to those parts of the *Elements* that deal with ratio and proportion.

[7] ἐυμηχανῶς

imperfection of a negative, for the subject on which the geometer works is always certain. But multiplicity of affections[8] is a hindrance, and the higher the power and the order of an affection, the more likely it is that a fraction or surd[9] will appear in the solution of a problem.

Will an analyst attempt [the solution of] any proposed equation without understanding how it is composed so that he can avoid the rocks and crags? Will he [be able to] transpose, depress, raise and generally work with sureness like an expert anatomist if, by some new discovery of zetetics, an unknown is proposed in terms other than those [originally] given but with a given difference from or ratio to that which was proposed?[10] Above all, the origin of equations and their fundamental structure is worthy of being understood by the analyst who strives for and pursues that expertise by which the way of reduction opens itself to him.

The structure of equations can best be understood through zetetics, plasmatic modification and comparison.

CHAPTER II

On Zetetics

The analyst will not approach zetetics without any forethought or unartfully,[11] since reason will tell him that pure [powers] spring from pure [roots] and affected from affected. Therefore to understand the nature of equations involving [only] pure powers, he will look to the powers of two given roots; to understand the nature of equations of powers with simple affections he will track down one or the other of the roots by means of [the theorems applying to] a stated sum or difference between two roots or their grades and their product or the product of their grades, whether alike or unlike; and to understand the nature of equations involving powers with multiple affections he will connect one affection with another at the various lower grades of the roots.

He will, furthermore, not confine himself to a single formula for [all] problems but will exercise himself in zetetics on any topic, whether already solved or proposed.

---

[8]πολυπάθεία

[9]ἄρρησίς ἤ αλογία

[10]I have followed 1615 rather than 1646 in omitting a question mark after "like a sure anatomist."

[11]ἀτέχνῶς

Being skilled in geometry he will remember that roots are represented by the terminal straight lines in a series of continued proportionals [and] that the products of the roots or their various grades, alike or different, are represented by the powers of one or more of the means.

When, by manipulation, he happens upon a satisfactory solution, he will develop from it a theorem for the construction and explanation of every such equation.[12] We regularly call one equation similar to another when the power is the same or equally high in both and when the affecting or affected terms are of the same order and have the same sign. If, however, any particular [equation] demands special and exceptional [treatment], the similarity is an anomaly.

CHAPTER III

The Constituent Parts of Quadratic Equations According to Zetetics

The structure of affected squares that are equated [to each other] can be classified zetetically quite easily. There are three species of this sort of equation—positive, negative and ambiguous.[13]

Thus the analyst may reflect on their structure in terms of these three theorems:

Theorem I

Positive

If

$$A^2 + AB = Z^2,$$

there are three proportionals the mean of which is Z and the difference between the extremes is B, making A the smaller extreme.

[This follows,] if you please, from the zetetic, Given the mean of three

---

[12] *Et quum incidet in aequationem mechanice suo bene obviam, de illa condet Theorema simile cuiuscunque aequalitatis Systaticum & Exegeticum.* In paraphrasing this, Renaldini (p. 141) uses the words "... *Theorema condet cuisque aequalitatis Systaticum, hoc est constitutivum, & Exegeticum, hoc est expositivum.*"

[13] Καταφατική, Αποφατική, Αμφίβολον

proportional straight lines and the difference between the extremes, to find the smaller extreme,[14] for Campano in the book on proportions[15] shows that comparisons that hold between straight lines can also be applied to [all] roots whatsoever, simple, plane or solid, or to homogeneous terms of a higher order.[16]

Let, therefore, Z be the mean of the three proportionals and let B be the difference between the extremes. The smaller extreme is to be found.

Let this be A. The greater, then, will be $A + B$. Multiply the greater by the smaller, making $A^2 + AB$. Since they are proportionals, the product of the extremes is equal to the square of the mean. Hence

$$A^2 + BA = Z^2,$$

which is what was stated.

[If]

$$x^2 + 10x = 144,$$

144 is the mean between two extremes that differ by 10. Hence x is the smaller extreme in the series of three proportionals, 8, 12 and 18.

Theorem II

Negative

If

$$A^2 - BA = Z^2,$$

there are three proportionals, the mean of which is Z and the difference between the extremes is B, making A the greater extreme.

[This follows] from the zetetic, Given the mean of three proportionals and the difference between the extremes, to find the greater extreme.[17]

[14]Cf. *Zetetica,* Third Book, Zetetic I.

[15]Giovanni Campano da Novara (fl. 1275) translated and commented on Euclid's *Elements.* His work, the first edition of Euclid to be printed, was published in Venice in 1482. I have found no reference to any work of his on proportions and I assume, therefore, that Viète is referring to some note of his attached to Book V of his Euclid which, however, I regret to say, I have not seen. On Campano, see George Sarton, *Introduction to the History of Science* (Baltimore, 1931), vol. II, p. 985f; and T. L. Heath's introduction to his translation of Euclid (2d ed., Cambridge University Press, 1925), vol. I, p. 94f.

[16]As this passage indicates, Viète does not restrict his use of the word *radix* to the first power.

[17]Cf. *Zetetica,* Third Book, Zetetic I.

Let this be A. The smaller, then, will be $A - B$. Multiply the greater by the smaller, making

$$A^2 - BA = Z^2,$$

which is what was stated.

[If]

$$x^2 - 10x = 144,$$

144 is the mean between extremes differing by 10 and x is the greater extreme in the series of three proportionals, 8, 12 and 18.

Theorem III

Ambiguous

If

$$BA - A^2 = Z^2,$$

there are three proportionals the mean of which is Z and the sum of the extremes of which is B, making A the greater or the smaller extreme.

[This follows] from the zetetic, Given the mean of three proportionals and the sum of the extremes, to find either of the extremes.[18]

Let Z be the mean and B the sum of the extremes. The smaller extreme is to be found.

Let this be A. The greater will, therefore, be $B - A$. Hence

$$BA - A^2 = Z^2.$$

Or let A be the greater of the extremes. Then $B - A$ will be the smaller. So again

$$BA - A^2 = Z^2.$$

Therefore A may be said to be either the smaller or the greater of the extremes.

[If]

$$26x - x^2 = 144,$$

144 is the mean between extremes the sum of which is 26. Hence x is either the smaller or the greater of the extremes in the series of three proportionals, 8, 12 and 18.

[18] *Zetetica,* Third Book, Zetetic II.

CHAPTER IIII

The Constituent Parts of Cubic Equations, also According to Zetetics; First, Concerning Those with Linear Affections

The structure of cubic equations involving linear affections is also worth learning from zetetics. The three theorems that follow pertain to this.

Theorem I

Positive

If

$$A^3 + B^2A = B^2Z,$$

there are four continued proportionals the first of which, whether the greater or the smaller of the extremes, is B and the sum of the second and fourth is Z, making A the second.

[This follows] from the zetetic, Given the first and the sum of the second and fourth in a series of four continued proportionals, to find the second.

Let the second be A. The fourth, therefore, will be $Z - A$. The cube of the second, however, equals the product of the fourth and square of the first. Since the square of the first is to the square of the second as the second is to the fourth,

$$A^3 = B^2Z - B^2A$$

and, by transposition,

$$A^3 + B^2A = B^2Z,$$

as was proposed.

    If

$$x^3 + 64x = 2496,$$

there are four continued proportionals, the first of which, the smaller of the extremes, is $\sqrt{64}$, that is 8, and the sum of the second and fourth is $2496/64$, that is 39, making x the second in the series of proportionals 8, 12, 18 and 27.

And if

$$x^3 + 729x = 18,954,$$

the first [of the four proportionals], the greater of the extremes, is $\sqrt{729}$, that is 27, and the sum of the second and fourth is $18,954/729$, that is 26, making x the second of the same series.[19]

Theorem II

Negative

If

$$A^3 - B^2A = B^2D,$$

there are four continued proportionals, the first or smaller of the extremes of which is B and the difference between the second and fourth is D, making A the second.

[This follows] from the zetetic, given the first and smaller of the extremes in a series of four continued proportionals and the difference between the second and fourth, to find the second.

Let B be the first or smaller extreme and D the difference between the second and fourth. The continued proportionals are to be found.

Let A be the second. The fourth, therefore, will be $A + D$. Moreover the cube of the second equals the product of the fourth and the square of the first. Hence

$$A^3 = B^2A + B^2D$$

and, by transposition,

$$A^3 - B^2A = B^2D,$$

as was proposed.

If

$$x^3 - 64x = 960,$$

there are four continued proportionals, the first of which is $\sqrt{64}$, that is 8, and the difference between the second and fourth is $960/64$, that is 15, making x the second in the series of proportionals 8, 12, 18 and 27.

[19] I.e., of the series 27, 18, 12, and 8.

Theorem III

Ambiguous

If

$$B^2A - A^3 = B^2D,$$

there are four continued proportionals the first or greater of the extremes of which is B and the difference between the second and fourth is D, making A the second.

[This follows] from the zetetic, Given the first or greater of the extremes in a series of four continued proportionals and the difference between the second and the fourth, to find the second.

Let B be the first or greater of the extremes and D the difference between the second and fourth. The second is to be found.

Let A be the second. The fourth will therefore be $A - D$. However, the cube of the second equals the product of the fourth and the square of the first. Hence

$$A^3 = B^2A - B^2D$$

and, by transposition,

$$B^2A - A^3 = B^2D.$$

If

$$729x - x^3 = 7290,$$

there are four continued proportionals, the first of which is $\sqrt{729}$ and the difference between the second and fourth is $7290/729$, that is 10, making x the second in the series of proportionals 27, 18, 12 and 8.

The second, however, may have two values, as in these two sets of continued proportionals:

$\sqrt{59,319}$	195	$\sqrt{24,375}$	125[20]
$\sqrt{59,319}$	78	$\sqrt{624}$	8.

Keeping $\sqrt{59,319}$ as the first or greater of the extremes and 70 as the difference between the second and fourth, the second in the latter case is 78, in the former 195.

If 36 were the first in both and the difference between the second and

---

[20] Here, as in various other unnoted places, 1646 labels the terms of proportions I, II, III, etc., to indicate which the author considers first, second, third, etc.

third were 5, there would be two sets of three proportionals:

$$36 \qquad 6 \qquad 1$$
$$36 \qquad 30 \qquad 25.$$

CHAPTER V

The Constituent Parts of Cubic Equations with Quadratic Affections

Cubic equations that involve quadratic affections are composed of almost the same terms as those with linear affections. This is also clear from zetetics. The three theorems about to be given pertain to this:

Theorem I

Negative

If

$$A^3 - BA^2 = BZ^2,$$

there are four continued proportionals of which the first, the greater or smaller of the extremes, is B and the sum of the second and fourth is Z, making A the sum of the first and third.

[This follows] from the zetetic, Given the first and the sum of the second and fourth in a series of four continued proportionals, to find the sum of the first and third.

Let B be the first—that is, the greater or smaller—of the extremes in a series of four continued proportionals [and] let Z be the sum of the second and fourth. The sum of the first and third is to be found.

Let this [sum] be A, and the third will then be $A - B$. However, since the sum of the first and third is to the sum of the second and fourth as the first is to the second,

$$A : Z = B : \frac{BZ}{A},$$

and BZ/A will be the second [of the series]. But the product of the first and third will be equal to the square of the second. Hence

$$BA - B^2 = \frac{B^2 Z^2}{A^2}.$$

Multiply through by A^2 and divide by B. Then

$$A^3 - BA^2 = BZ^2,$$

which is what was stated.

If

$$x^3 - 8x^2 = 12,168,$$

there are four continued proportionals, of which the first among the extremes is 8 and the sum of the second and fourth is $\sqrt{12,168/8}$, that is, 39, making x 26,[21] the sum of the first and third in the series of proportionals 8, 12, 18 and 27.[22]

Theorem II

Positive

If

$$A^3 + BA^2 = BD^2,$$

there are four continued proportionals the first of which, the smaller of the extremes, is B, and the difference between the second and fourth is D, making A the difference between the first and third.

[This follows] from the zetetic, Given the first or smaller of the extremes in a series of four continued proportionals and the difference between the second and fourth, to find the difference between the first and third.

Let B be the first in a series of four continued proportionals and the smaller of the extremes, and let D be the difference between the second and the fourth. The difference between the first and the third is to be found.

Let this [difference] be A. The third, therefore, will be $A + B$. However, since the difference between the first and third is to the difference between the second and fourth as the first is to the second,

$$A : D = B : \frac{BD}{A},$$

[21]1615 omits this figure.
[22]These four terms appear in reverse order in 1615.

and BD/A will be the second. But the product of the first and third equals the square of the second and, therefore,

$$BA + B^2 = \frac{B^2 D^2}{A^2}.$$

Multiply through by A^2 and divide by B, making

$$A^3 + BA^2 = BD^2,$$

which is what was stated.

If

$$x^3 + 8x^2 = 1800,$$

there are four continued proportionals, the first of the extremes of which is 8 and the difference between the second and fourth is $\sqrt{1800/8}$, that is 15, making x 10,[23] the difference between the first and third in the series of proportionals 8, 12, 18 and 27.

Theorem III

Ambiguous

If

$$BA^2 - A^3 = BD^2,$$

there are four continued proportionals of which the first, the greater of the extremes, is B and the difference between the second and fourth is D, making A the difference between the first and third.

[This follows] from the zetetic, Given the first, the greater, of the extremes in a series of four continued proportionals and the difference between the second and fourth, to find the difference between the first and third.[24]

Let B be the first in a series of four continued proportionals and let it also be the greater of the extremes. Let D be the difference between the second and fourth. The difference between the first and third is to be found.

Let this be A. The third, therefore, will be $B - A$. However, since the difference between the first and third is to the difference between the

[23] 1615 omits this figure.
[24] The text has "between the second and third."

second and fourth as the first is to the second,

$$A : D = B : \frac{BD}{A}$$

and BD/A will be the second. But the product of the first and third equals the square of the second, so

$$B^2 - BA = \frac{B^2 D^2}{A^2}.$$

Multiply through by A^2 and divide by B. Then

$$BA^2 - A^3 = BD^2,$$

which is what was said.

If

$$27x^2 - x^3 = 2700,$$

there are four continued proportionals, the first or greater of the extremes of which is 27 and the difference between the second and fourth is $\sqrt{2700/27}$, that is 10, making x the difference between the first and third in the series of proportionals 27, 18, 12 and 8.

CHAPTER VI

Another Construction of Cubic Equations with Linear Affections According to Zetetics

We must not omit a certain special case of the cubic with a linear affection, either positive or negative, that is also derived from zetetics— [the case that occurs,] that is, when four times the cube of one-third the plane coefficient is less than the square of the constant, a case about which you must be forewarned.[25] We offer two theorems concerning it:

Theorem I

If

$$A^3 + 3B^p A = D^s,$$

B^p is the product of roots the cubes of which differ by D^s, making A the difference between these roots.

[25] 1615 has *praemovendus;* 1646 has *praemonendus.*

[This follows] from the zetetic, Given the difference between [two] cubes and the product of their roots, to find the difference between the roots.[26]

If

$$x^3 + 6x = 7,$$

6/3 or 2 is the product of roots the cubes of which differ by 7. This makes x the difference between the roots—[i.e., the difference] between the roots 1 and 2 in the case supposed.[27]

Theorem II

If

$$A^3 - 3B^p A = D^s$$

and if the square of D^s is greater than four times the cube of B^p, B^p is the product of roots the sum of whose cubes is D^s, making A the sum of the roots.

[This follows] from the zetetic, Given the product of [two] roots and the sum of their cubes, to find the roots.[28]

If

$$x^3 - 6x = 9,$$

6/3 or 2 is the product of roots the sum of the cubes of which is 9. This makes x the sum of the roots—[i.e., the sum] of the roots 1 and 2 in the case supposed.

These same theorems, moreover, may be demonstrated geometrically thus:

Alternatively

Theorem I

If

$$A^3 + 3B^p A = B^p D,$$

there are four straight lines in continued proportion. B^p is the product of the means or the extremes and D is the difference between the extremes. A is then the difference between the means.

---

[26] *Zetetica*, Second Book, Zetetic XV.
[27] *& fit 1 N. differentia laterum: ex hypothesi laterum 1 & 2.*
[28] *Zetetica*, Second Book, Zetetic XVI.

[This follows] from the zetetic, Given the difference between the extremes in a series of four proportionals and the product of the means or the extremes, to find the difference between the means.

If

$$x^3 + 24x = 56,$$

there are four continued proportionals and the product of their means or extremes, which is a plane, is equal to 24/3, that is 8, and the difference between the extremes is 56/8, that is 7. Thus x is the difference between the means in the series of continued proportionals 1, 2, 4 and 8.

Alternatively

Theorem II

If

$$A^3 - 3B^p A = B^p D$$

and the square of one-half of D is greater than B^p, there are four straight lines in continued proportion the product of the means or extremes of which is B^p and the sum of the extremes is D, making A the sum of the means.

[This follows from the zetetic,] Given the sum of the extremes and the product of the means or extremes in a series of four continued proportionals, to find the sum of the means.

If

$$x^3 - 24x = 72,$$

there are four continued proportionals and the product of their means or extremes, which is a plane, is equal to 24/3, that is 8, and the sum of the extremes is 72/8, that is 9, making x the sum of the means in the series of continued proportionals 1, 2, 4 and 8

If, however, four times the cube of one-third the plane coefficient is greater than the square of the constant,[29] a solid, the equation has another constitution, one that it shares with the ambiguous or inverse negative [case]. The following theorem pertains to this.

---

[29]This, as will be recognized by the reader, is the irreducible case under Cardano's formula.

Theorem III

If

$$A^3 - 3B^pA = D^s$$

and if the square of D^s is less than four times the cube of B^p, then

$$3B^pE - E^3 = D^s$$

and E may be said [to be either] of two roots, [the sum of] the squares of which plus their product is $[3]B^p$, and D^s to be the product of one of the roots and the sum of the square of the other and the product [of the two roots] or, alternatively, the sum of the roots times their product. A may then be said to be the sum of these roots.[30]

[This follows] from the zetetic, Given a plane consisting of the sum of the squares of two roots and their product and given, furthermore, the solid resulting from the sum of the roots times their product, to find the roots or the sum of the roots.

If

$$x^3 - 21x = 20,$$

since four times the cube of 7 is greater than 400,

$$21y - y^3 = 20$$

and there are two roots the squares of which plus their product make 21. Moreover, the sum of the roots times their product is 20 which, in the inverse negative equation, makes y either of the roots, greater or less, and, in the direct negative, [makes x] the sum of the same roots—[i.e., the sum] of roots which are 1 and 4 in the case supposed.

There would be little difference if this were phrased geometrically, for the geometer would say:

[3]B^p is the sum of the squares of three proportional straight lines and D^s is the product of the sum of the extremes and the square of the mean, or the product of either extreme and the sum of the squares of the others, making A the sum of the extremes and E either the first or third [of the proportionals].

[30] I.e., if the roots are p and q, $E = p$ or q; $3B^p = p^2 + q^2 + pq$; $D^s = p(q^2 + pq)$ or $q(p^2 + pq)$ or $pq(p + q)$; and $A = p + q$.

Thus in the given case, 21 is the sum of the squares of three proportionals and 20, a solid, is the product of the extremes and the square of the mean or is one or the other of the extremes times the [sum of the] squares of the others in the series of proportionals 1, 2 and 4.

The constitution of equations of this sort is more elegantly and clearly brought out by an angular section analysis and is better adapted to easy manipulation[31] in this formula:

Alternatively

Theorem III

If

$$A^3 - 3B^2A = B^2D$$

and if, moreover, B is greater than half of D, then

$$3B^2E - E^3 = B^2D$$

and there are two right triangles of equal hypotenuse, B, such that the acute angle subtended by the perpendicular of the first is three times the acute angle subtended by the perpendicular of the second and twice the base of the first is D, making A twice the base of the second. The base of the second, shortened or extended by a length that, [if] raised to the square, [is] three times the perpendicular of the same,[32] is then E.

Let

$$x^3 - 300\,x = 432$$

or

$$300y - y^3 = 432.$$

There are two right triangles with 10 as their common hypotenuse. The acute angle subtended by the perpendicular of the first is three times the acute angle subtended by the perpendicular of the second. Twice the base of the first, moreover, is $432/100$ and x, in the direct negative equation, is twice the base of the second; in the inverse negative equation y is the simple base of the second plus or minus something which, [if] raised to the square, [is] three times the perpendicular of the second.

[31] ἐυμηχανίαν
[32] *quae potest quadrato triplum perpendiculi eiusdem.*

Let the common hypotenuse be 10 and the base of the second triangle 9, making the perpendicular of the second $\sqrt{19}$. The hypotenuse of the first also being 10, its base is $2^{16}/_{100}$ and thus, in this hypothetical case, it may be said that

$$x^3 - 300\,x = 432$$

making x 18. If it is said that

$$300y - y^3 = 432,$$

y is $9 + \sqrt{57}$ or $9 - \sqrt{57}$.

Now these examples must suffice for an understanding, through zetetics, of equations with affected powers. Although theorems have been given only for equations with a single affection, yet how they may be extended to those with multiple affections will scarcely be unknown, especially if their plasmatic modification is once revealed. The place for discussing this follows. For the zetetic process by which the forementioned constructions have been discovered appears sufficiently in the passages already given, the last theorem being an exception that must be referred back to the special little field of zetetics pertaining to angular sections.

CHAPTER VII

On the General Method of Transforming Equations

The principle of plasmatic modification hinges on the doctrine of transformation of equations generally. This must first be set out and shown.

Transformation by Alteration of the Root

[Discussion of] the transformation of equations begins with the warning that it takes two forms: either the original root that is to be found may be altered or it may be left unaltered. Whatever the change is, there is a given difference or ratio between the original root and the new one. Hence if one is known, the other cannot be unknown.

Now as to the work of transformation: Suppose the altered root that is being sought is equal to the other [i.e., the original] one that is also being sought. On this supposition, it is expressed in terms of a new symbol and the original equation is rearranged and set up anew in these terms.

A root that is being sought may be artfully altered and set up in new terms in a number of ways, but the principle of rearrangement of the first equation in terms of the new symbol remains constant and uniform no matter what the method.

To make this clearer, let an equation with a root A be proposed and let Z be the magnitude to which the other [terms] are equated. This given equation is to be transformed with an altered root [in accordance with] the art.

The root A, then, may be changed and shown under a new symbol—

First, by addition, as, for instance, by supposing and making clear that $A + B$ is E. Then A will be $E - B$.

Second, by subtraction, as, for instance, by supposing and making clear that $A - B$ is E, wherefore $E + B$ will be A. Or, again, that $B - A$ is E, whence A will be $B - E$.

Third, by multiplication, as for instance, by supposing and making clear that BA equals E^p. Then A will be E^p/B.

Fourth, by division, as for instance, by supposing and making clear that A^p/B equals E, wherefore A^p will be BE.

Fifth, by a proportion with an explicit ratio, as, for instance, by saying that

$$A : E = B : G,$$

then resolving the proportion and making clear that BE/G will therefore equal A.

Sixth, by a proportion with an implicit ratio, as, for instance, by saying that

$$A : B = G : E,$$

then resolving the proportion and making clear that BG/E will therefore equal A.

Seventh, by using a substitute for the coefficient[33] in certain kinds of equation, as for instance, in quadratics, by saying that

$$E^2 + AE = D^p$$

---

[33]*per Parabolicam hypostasin.* The standard Greek, Latin and English dictionaries are of little assistance in translating this phrase. But on *hypostasin* as "substitute," cf. the French "hypostase" with its meaning, in the technical language of rhetoric, of using (or substituting) one part of speech for another—for example, using an adjective for a substantive.

(which is a quadratic equation with a positive affection), then making clear that

$$\frac{D^p - E^2}{E} = A.$$

Or by saying that

$$E^2 - EA = D^p$$

(which is a quadratic equation with a negative affection), then making clear that

$$\frac{E^2 - D^p}{E} = A.$$

Or by supposing that

$$EA - E^2 = D^p$$

(which is an equation of a plane based on the root with a negative quadratic affection) and then making clear that

$$\frac{E^2 + D^p}{E} = A.$$

Finally, by composite methods and by skillfully inventing and trying out constructions that best serve to accomplish the object.

However, regardless of what is substituted for A, the equation will be transformed accordingly and a new one will be set up in terms of E, and whatever was said of A in the given equation will be said of the new term substituted for A.

Thus, if A is changed by addition—by supposing $A + B$ to be E, as above, whence $E - B$ becomes A—the same power that A had will be created from $E - B$. Likewise the same lower-order grades of A, with the same constant coefficients, will be created from $E - B$ to form the homogeneous terms of affection. Then all the constructs of this sort will be equated to the given constant term. Hence [the original terms] will have been expunged in accordance with the rules of the art, an equation in E will have been set up, and [the original equation] will have been transformed into a new equation in E—that is, A plus the increment B—which is what was to be done.

It is clear that the same thing takes place in other methods of transformation by which the value of A can be expressed.

Transformation Without Changing the Root

This pertains to the second [branch of the] warning [given above]: To transform an equation without changing its root [calls for] reducing or elevating its degree.

An elevation or reduction[34] may be regular or irregular.

An elevation is regular when both sides of a given equation (they having been arranged well or badly depending on the worker's skill) are squared, cubed or raised to a still higher power. A reduction, on the contrary, is regular when the square, cube or lower root [of both sides] is taken, a supplement, either given or to be found, having been added to it. After the elevation or depression, all [terms] are arranged in proper order.

An elevation is irregular when each individual homogeneous term contained in a given equation is multiplied by the same lower-order term, either pure or with compatible affecting or affected given terms. The products admit of an explanation and arrangement consistent [with the operation].

On the contrary, a reduction [is irregular] when all the individual homogeneous terms are divided either by the root that is being sought or by some grade of the root lower than the power, [the divisor being] either pure or with compatible affected or affecting given terms. The quotients (a supplement, whether given or sought, having been added) admit of an explanation and arrangement consistent [with the operation].

A demonstration of any skillful kind of transformation makes it quite clear that, since things that are equal in the first power are also equal in any other power and vice versa, a common divisor or multiplier does not change an equality or proportion.

Now it is admitted that these [matters] which we have just set out in general terms need particular rules and examples. These are spelled out here and there where it is most convenient, so that examples of skillful ways of transformation may be examined.

CHAPTER VIII
Particulars of Plasmatic Modification

Whenever affected powers are derived from pure ones or from powers of the same degree with a negative affection or whenever higher powers are

---

[34]*Climacticus . . . adscensus, sive descensus.* Cf. Renaldini, p. 151: "Ascensus vero, vel descēsus climacticus, seu scalaris, duplex est regularis, et irregularis."

derived from lower ones, it is to be understood that there has been a plasmatic modification. Such modifications can be carried out by all the methods of transformation except division and reduction in power.

The purpose [of the study] of modification[35] and its principal use is the resolution of equations that are known to have been modified into the simpler ones from which they were derived if, for some weighty reason, this is desirable. When the imagination understands this, it will take careful note of it and will cite it as an indication of the brightness and excellence of the art.

The first [item] especially worthy of consideration is this: Insofar as a power is affected by, or affects, individual lower-order terms, there has been modification by the method of addition or subtraction. The root is known to be affected by an increment or decrement which can be derived from the coefficient of the highest [lower-order] term in accordance with the nature of the power.[36]

Thus in a quadratic equation, the root was affected by one-half the coefficient of the first power, in a cubic by one-third the coefficient of the square, in a biquadratic by one-fourth the coefficient of the cube, in a quintic by one-fifth the coefficient of the fourth power, and so on in continuous progression.

Thus [also] affected squares originate in a pure [square], cubes affected by a square and first power in cubes affected by a first power, biquadratics affected by a cube, square and first power in biquadratics affected by a square, first power or both, and so on in that order.

A second [item to be noted] is this: If a power [has] a plane, a solid or any other homogeneous term of higher order as its root, there has been plasmatic modification by the method of multiplication or implicit proportion.

Thus the origin of a fourth power affected by a square is a square affected by the first power. Since both the individual homogeneous terms in [such a biquadratic] equation are multiples of the square of the coefficient of the linear term, the root of the biquadratic so created is known [to be] the mean proportional between the coefficient of the linear term and the first root that was proposed.[37]

A sixth power affected by a cube likewise originates in a square

---

[35]*plastices.*

[36]*quoniam Radix intelligitur adfecta fuisse cremento, vel decremento, desumpto ex coefficiente sub gradu alteriora, secundum Potestatis conditionem.*

[37]I.e., if $x^2 + ax = N$ and $ax = y^2$ or $x = y^2/a$, then $y^4/a^2 + ay^2/a = N$ and $y^4 + a^2y^2 = a^2N$. In this case $a : y = y : x$. As this indicates, multiplication by the square of the coefficient called for by Viète's statement will be present in the constant, even though it is no longer visible. See Chapter XII, Theorem I.

affected by a first power, whence the root of a sixth power created this way is the second of [four] continued proportionals just as the coefficient of the linear term is the first of these and the root that was first proposed is the fourth.[38]

Similarly, a sixth power affected by a fourth power has its origin in a cube affected by a square, both the homogeneous terms in [such an] equation having been multiplied by the cube of the coefficient of the square. Hence the root of a sixth power so created is a mean proportional between the coefficient of the square and [the root] that was first proposed.[39]

Let [this be noted] in the third place: Every biquadratic affected by a term of lower order, whether one or many, is the result of plasmatic modification.[40] It originates in an elevation of a square affected by a linear term.

Suppose a biquadratic to be affected by a linear term: The individual homogeneous terms of the affected quadratic from which the biquadratic is derived were so distributed that the square[41] formed one side of the equation and a plane based on the linear term formed the other along with the constant. Thus, both sides having been squared, a suitable substitute was found for the homogeneous quadratic term[42] and then all terms were rearranged in the proper order.[43]

Or suppose a biquadratic to be affected by both a square and a first power: The individual homogeneous terms in the affected quadratic equation from which the biquadratic is derived were so distributed that the square plus one-fourth of the plane constant or its product formed one side of the equation and a plane based on the linear term plus the remainder[44] of the plane constant or its product the other. Then, both sides having been squared, everything was put in proper order.[45]

Lastly, suppose a biquadratic to be affected by a cube: The individual terms of the affected quadratic equation from which the biquadratic is derived were so distributed that the square plus a plane based on the linear term was one side of the equation and the plane constant the other. Both sides of the equation having been squared, there was such a substitution

---

[38] I.e., if $x^2 + ax = N$ and $a^2x = y^3$ or $x = y^3/a^2$, then $y^6/a^4 + ay^3/a^2 = N$ or $y^6 + a^3y^3 = a^4N$, and $a : y = ax/y : x$. See Chapter XII, Theorem IIII.

[39] I.e., if $x^3 + ax^2 = N$ and $ax = y^2$ or $x = y^2/a$, then $y^6/a^3 + ay^4/a^2 = N$ and $y^6 + a^2y^4 = a^3N$ and $a : y = y : x$. See Chapter XII, Theorem VII.

[40] *Plasmaticum est.*

[41] *quadrati symbolum.*

[42] *interpretationem congruam acceperit homogeneum sub quadrato.*

[43] See Chapter XIII, Theorem I.

[44] *apotome.* Cf. Renaldini, p. 154, "cum apotome, seu residuo."

[45] See Chapter XIII, Theorems IIII and VII.

that the homogeneous linear and quadratic terms [were eliminated] and then everything was properly ordered.[46]

In the fourth and last place, let [this] be [remembered]: All affected cubics can be derived from quadratics by an irregular elevation[47] [but] the way of reduction to the originals is not evident in such cases except through equations of powers equally high and equally affected. Yet the properties of equations so constituted, when regarded this way, help greatly [in understanding them].[48]

Among the extraordinary features of the process of plasmatic modification, those are especially worthy of note that pertain to homogeneous terms of affection from which powers are subtracted. These derive from a pure quadratic equation, their [original] form, modification by addition or subtraction having been instituted, for when any coefficient greater than a proposed root is assumed for the process of plasmatic modification, whether it is positive or negative by hypothesis, it always results in an equation of a square subtracted from a plane. Whence this porism:

> Whenever any power is subtracted from a homogeneous term of affection, it has a double root, since [the roots of all such] equations, except the double roots of the original itself, flow and are derived from a double-rooted quadratic.

CHAPTER IX

Derivation of Affected Quadratics from Pure

In order that all this may be clearer, as assortment of theorems pertaining to the plasmatic modifications we have mentioned follows:

Theorem I

If A^2 equals Z^p, let

$$A + B = E.$$

---

[46] See Chapter XIII, Theorem X.

[47] Renaldini, p. 155, gives this illustration: $(B^2 + Z^p)A - A^3 = BZ^p$ derives from $A^2 + BA = Z^p$. First multiply through the latter by A, making $A^3 + BA^2 = Z^pA$. Then substitute $Z^p - BA$ for A^2, making $A^3 + BZ^p - B^2A = Z^pA$, whence $A^3 + BZ^p = (B^2 + Z^p)A$ and $(B^2 + Z^p)A - A^3 = BZ^p$, as was said.

[48] *aequationum tamen inde constitutarum spectata proprietas maxime juvat.*

Then

$$E^2 - 2BE = Z^p - B^2.^{49}$$

Since A^2 is given as equal to Z^p and, moreover, $A + B$ is equal to the root E, therefore

$$E - B = A$$

and the square of $E - B$ will equal Z^p. This square, however, consists of the individual planes $E^2 - 2BE + B^2$. Hence, arranging these properly,

$$E^2 - 2BE = Z^p - B^2,$$

as was said.

Theorem II

If A^2 equals Z^p, let

$$A - B = E.$$

Then

$$E^2 + 2BE = Z^p - B^2.$$

Since A^2 equals Z^p and $A - B$ is equal to the root E,[50] then

$$E + B = A$$

and the square of $E + B$ will equal Z^p. This square, however, consists of the individual planes $B^2 + 2BE + B^2$. Hence, arranging these properly,

$$E^2 + 2BE = Z^p - B^2,$$

as was said.

Theorem III

If A^2 equals Z^p, let $B - A$ or $A + B$ equal E. Then

$$2BE - E^2 = E^2 - Z^p.$$

Since A^2 is given as equal to Z^p and $B - A$, moreover, is equal to the root E, therefore

$$B - E = A$$

---

[49] 1615 has $Z^p \sim B^2$.
[50] 1615 repeats this phrase.

and the square of $B - E$ will equal Z^p. This square, however, consists of $B^2 - 2BE + E^2$. Therefore, having arranged all these properly,

$$2BE - E^2 = B^2 - Z^p,$$

as was said.

And if $A + B$ equals E, then

$$E - B = A,$$

wherefore the square of $E - B$ will equal Z^p. This square, however, consists of $E^2 - 2BE + B^2$. Therefore, having arranged all these properly,

$$2BE - E^2 = B^2 - Z^p,$$

as was also said.

CHAPTER X

Derivation of Certain Cubics with a Quadratic Affection from Cubics with a Linear Affection

Theorem I

If

$$A^3 - 3B^2A = Z^s,$$

let

$$A - B = E.$$

Then

$$E^3 + 3BE^2 = Z^s + 2B^3.$$

Since

$$A^3 - 3B^2A = Z^s$$

and, moreover, $A - B$ equals the root E, then

$$E + B = A$$

and the cube of $E + B$ minus the product of $3B^2$ and $E + B$ will equal Z^s. The cube of $E + B$, however, consists of $E^3 + 3BE^2 + 3B^2E + B^3$, and the product of the affection consists of $-3B^2E - 3B^3$. Therefore, having arranged all these terms properly,

$$E^3 + 3BE^2 = Z^s + 2B^3,$$

as was said.

Alternatively

Theorem I

If

$$A^3 - 3B^2A = Z^s,$$

let

$$A + B = E.$$

Then

$$E^3 - 3BE^2 = Z^s - 2B^3.$$

Since

$$A^3 - 3B^2A = Z^s$$

and, moreover, $A + B$ equals the root E, therefore

$$E - B = A$$

and the cube of $E - B$ minus the product of $3B^2$ and $E - B$ will equal Z^s. The cube of $E - B$, however, consists of $E^3 - 3BE^2 + 3B^2E - B^3$ and the product of the affection consists of $-3B^2E + 3B^3$. Wherefore, having arranged all these properly,

$$E^3 - 3BE^2 = Z^s - 2B^3,$$

as was said.

Theorem II

If

$$3B^2A - A^3 = Z^s,$$

let

$$B - A = E.$$

Then

$$3BE^2 - E^3 = 2B^3 - Z^s.$$

Since

$$3B^2A - A^3 = Z^s$$

and $B - A$, moreover, is equal to the root E, therefore

$$B - E = A$$

and the product of $3B^2$ and $B - E$ minus the cube of $B - E$ will equal Z^s. The product of the affected term, however, consists of $3B^3 - 3B^2E$ and the cube to be subtracted from that product consists of $-B^3 + 3B^2E - 3BE^2 + E^3$.[51] Therefore, having arranged all these properly,

$$3BE^2 - E^3 = 2B^3 - Z^s,$$

as was said.

Alternatively

Theorem II

If

$$3B^2A - A^3 = Z^s,$$

let

$$B + A = E.$$

Then

$$3BE^2 - E^3 = 2B^3 + Z^s.$$

Since

$$3B^2A - A^3 = Z^s$$

and, moreover, $B + A$ is equal to the root E, therefore

$$E - B = A$$

and the product of $3B^2$ and $E - B$ minus the cube of $E - B$ will be equal to Z^s. The product of the affected term, however, consists of $3B^2E - 3B^3$ and the cube to be subtracted from that product consists of $-E^3 + 3BE^2 - 3B^2E + B^3$. Therefore, having set all the terms in order,

$$3BE^2 - E^3 = 2B^3 + Z^s,$$

as was said.[52]

---

[51]It will be noticed that here and in many other places Viète anticipates a subtraction that has been ordered and reverses signs accordingly.
[52]1646 omits this phrase.

CHAPTER XI

Derivation of Cubics with Quadratic and Linear Affections from Cubics with a Linear Affection

Theorem I

If

$$A^3 + D^p A = Z^s,$$

let

$$A + B = E.$$

Then

$$E^3 - 3BE^2 + E(3B^2 + D^p) = Z^s + D^p B + B^3.$$

Since it is proposed that

$$A^3 + D^p A = Z^s$$

and, moreover, that $A + B$ is equal to the root E, therefore

$$E - B = A$$

and the cube of $E - B$ plus the product of D^p and $E - B$ will be equal to Z^s. The cube of $E - B$, however, consists of $E^3 - 3BE^2 + 3B^2E - B^3$ and the product of the affection consists of $+D^p E - D^p B$. Wherefore, having arranged all the terms properly,

$$E^3 - 3BE^2 + E(3B^2 + D^p) = Z^s + D^p B + B^3,$$

as was said.

Theorem II

If

$$A^3 + D^p A = Z^s,$$

let

$$A - B = E.$$

Then

$$E^3 + 3BE^2 + E(3B^2 + D^p) = Z^s - D^p B - B^3.$$

Since

$$A^3 + D^pA = Z^s$$

and, moreover, $A - B$ is equal to the root E, therefore

$$E + B = A$$

and the cube of $E + B$ plus the product of D^p and $E + B$ will be equal to Z^s. The cube of $E + B$, however, consists of $E^3 + 3BE^2 + 3B^2E + B^3$ and the product of the affection consists of $+D^pE + D^pB$. Wherefore, having arranged all the terms properly,

$$E^3 + 3BE^2 + E(3B^2 + D^p) = Z^s - D^pB - B^3,{}^{53}$$

as was said.

Theorem III

If

$$A^3 + D^pA = Z^s,$$

let

$$B - A = E.$$

Then

$$E^3 - 3BE^2 + E(3B^2 + D^p) = B^3 + D^pB - Z^s.$$

Since

$$A^3 + D^pA = Z^s$$

and, moreover, $B - A$ is equal to the root E, therefore

$$B - E = A$$

and the cube of $B - E$ plus the product of D^p and $B - E$ will equal Z^s. The cube of $B - E$, however, consists of $B^3 - 3EB^2 + 3E^2B - E^3$ and the product of the affection consists of $+D^pB - D^pE$. Therefore, having arranged all things properly,

$$E^3 - 3BE^2 + E(3B^2 + D^p) = B^3 + D^pB - Z^s,$$

as was said.

[53] 1615 has $D^3 + D^pB - Z^s$.

Theorem IIII

If

$$A^3 - D^p A = Z^s,$$

let

$$A + B = E.$$

Then

$$E^3 - 3BE^2 + E(3B^2 - D^p) = Z^s + B^3 - D^p B.$$

Since

$$A^3 - D^p A = Z^s$$

and $A + B$, moreover, is equal to the root E, therefore

$$E - B = A$$

and the cube of $E - B$ minus the product of D^p and $E - B$ will equal Z^s. The cube of $E - B$, however, consists of $E^3 - 3BE^2 + 3B^2 E - B^3$ and the product of the affection consists of $-D^p E + D^p B$. Therefore, having ordered all things properly,

$$E^3 - 3BE^2 + E(3B^2 - D^p) = Z^s + B^3 - D^p B,$$

as was said.

Theorem V

If

$$A^3 - D^p A = Z^s,$$

let

$$A - B = E.$$

Then

$$E^3 + 3BE^2 + E(3B^2 - D^p) = Z^s + D^p B - B^3.$$

Since

$$A^3 - D^p A = Z^s$$

and, moreover, $A - B$ is equal to the root E, therefore

$$E + B = A$$

and the cube of $E + B$ minus the product of D^p and $E + B$ will equal Z^s. The cube of $E + B$, however, consists of $E^3 + 3BE^2 + 3B^2E + B^{3}$[54] and the product of the affection consists of $-D^pE - D^pB$. Wherefore, having arranged all these properly,

$$E^3 + 3BE^2 + E(3B^2 - D^p) = Z^s + D^pB - B^3,$$

as was said.

Theorem VI

If

$$A^3 - D^pA = Z^s,$$

let

$$B - A = E.$$

Then

$$E^3 - 3BE^2 + E(3B^2 - D^p) = B^3 - D^pB - Z^s.$$

Since

$$A^3 - D^pA = Z^s$$

and $B - A$ is equal to the root E, therefore

$$B - E = A$$

and the cube of $B - E$ minus the product of D^p and $B - E$ will equal Z^s. The cube of $B - E$, however, consists of $B^3 - 3B^2E + 3BE^2 - E^3$ and the product of the affection consists of $-D^pB + D^pE$. Therefore, having arranged all things properly,

$$E^3 - 3BE^2 + E(3B^2 - D^p) = B^3 - D^pB - Z^s,$$

as was said.

Theorem VII

If

$$D^pA - A^3 = Z^s,$$

[54] 1615 has $-B^3$.

let

$$A + B = E.$$

Then

$$E(D^p - 3B^2) + 3BE^2 - E^3 = Z^s + D^pB - B^3.$$

Since

$$D^pA - A^3 = Z^s$$

and $A + B$, moreover, is equal to the root E, therefore

$$E - B = A$$

and the product of D^p and $E - B$ minus the cube of $E - B$ will equal Z^s. The product of D^p and $E - B$, however, consists of $D^pE - D^pB$ and the cube to be subtracted consists of $-E^3 + 3BE^2 - 3B^2E + B^3$. Therefore, having arranged all things properly,

$$E(D^p - 3B^2) + 3BE^{255} - E^3 = Z^s + D^pB - B^3,$$

as was said.

Theorem VIII

If

$$D^pA - A^3 = Z^s,$$

let

$$A - B = E.$$

Then

$$E(D^p - 3B^2) - 3BE^2 - E^3 = Z^s - D^pB + B^3.$$

Since

$$D^pA - A^3 = Z^s$$

and $A - B$, moreover, is equal to the root E, therefore

$$E + B = A$$

and the product of D^p and $E + B$ minus the cube of $E + B$ will equal Z^s. The product of D^p and $E + B$, however, consists of $D^pE + D^pB$ and the cube to be subtracted consists of $-E^3 - 3BE^2 - 3B^2E - B^3$. Hence, having arranged all terms properly,

[55]1615 has $E(D^p + 3B^2) - 3BE^2$.

$$E(D^p - 3B^2) - 3BE^2 - E^3 = Z^s - D^pB + B^3,$$

as was said.

Theorem IX

If

$$D^pA - A^3 = Z^s,$$

let

$$B - A = E.$$

Then

$$E(D^p - 3B^2) + 3BE^2 - E^3 = D^pB - B^3 - Z^s.$$

Since

$$D^pA - A^3 = Z^s$$

and, moreover, $B - A$ is equal to the root E, therefore

$$B - E = A$$

and D^p times $B - E$ minus the cube of $B - E$ will equal Z^s. The product of B^p and $B - E$, however, consists of $D^pB - D^pE$ and the cube to be subtracted consists of $-B^3 + 3B^2E - 3BE^2 + E^3$. Therefore, having arranged all things properly,

$$E(D^p - 3B^2) + 3BE^2 - E^3 = D^pB - B^3 - Z^s,$$

as was said.

CHAPTER XII

Derivation of Certain Powers with Plane or Solid Roots from Powers with Simple Roots

Theorem I

If

$$A^2 + BA = Z^p,$$

let BA be E^2. Then

$$E^4 + B^2E^2 = B^2Z^p.$$

Since

$$A^2 + BA = Z^p$$

and, moreover, BA is equal to E^2, E^2/B will equal A and the square of E^2/B plus the product of B and E^2/B—that is, $E^4/B^2 + E^2$—will equal Z^p. Multiplying all terms by B^2,

$$E^4 + B^2E^2 = B^2Z^p,$$

as was said.

If, however, the root, E^2, were set up as a plane, the statement of the equation would be this:

$$(E^p)^2 + B^2E^p = B^2Z^p.$$

Theorem II

If

$$A^2 - BA = Z^p,$$

let BA be E^2 or E^p. Then

$$E^4 - B^2E^2 = B^2Z^p$$

or

$$(E^p)^2 - B^2E^p = B^2Z^p.$$

The demonstration [of this] is not unlike that given for the preceding theorem.

Theorem III

If

$$BA - A^2 = Z^p,$$

let BA be either E^2 or E^p. Then

$$B^2E^2 - E^4 = B^2Z^p$$

or

$$B^2E^p - (E^p)^2 = B^2Z^p.$$

The demonstration is not unlike that given for the first theorem in this chapter.

Theorem IIII

If

$$A^2 + BA = Z^p,$$

let B^2A be E^3.[56] Then

$$E^6 + B^3E^3 = B^4Z^p.$$

Since

$$A^2 + BA = Z^p$$

and B^2A, moreover, is equal to E^3, therefore E^3/B^2 equals A. Hence the square of E^3/B^2 plus BE^3/B^2—that is, $E^6/B^4 + E^3/B$—equals Z^p. Multiply all terms by B^4 and

$$E^6 + B^3E^3{}^{[57]} = B^4Z^p,$$

as was said.

Theorem V

If

$$A^2 - BA = Z^p,$$

let B^2A equal E^3 or E^s. Then

$$E^6 - B^3E^3 = B^4Z^p.$$

The demonstration is not unlike that given for the preceding theorem.

Theorem VI

If

$$BA = A^2 = Z^p,$$

let B^2A equal E^3 or E^s. Then

$$B^3E^3 - E^6 = B^4Z^p$$

or

$$B^3E^s - (E^s)^2 = B^4Z^p.{}^{[58]}$$

[56] 1646 has E^3 or E^s.
[57] 1615 has B^3E^s.
[58] 1646 has E^4Z^p.

The demonstration is not unlike that given for the fourth theorem of this chapter.

Theorem VII

If

$$A^3 + BA^2 = Z^s,$$

let BA be E^2. Then

$$E^6 + B^2E^4 = B^3Z^s.$$

Since

$$A^3 + BA^2 = Z^s$$

and BA, moreover, is equal to E^2, then E^2/B equals A. Therefore, from what has been proposed,

$$\frac{E^6}{B^3} + \frac{E^4}{B} = Z^s.$$

Multiply all terms by B^3 and

$$E^6 + B^2E^4 = B^3Z^s,$$

as was said. If, however, the root E^2 were set up as a plane, the statement would be this:

$$(E^p)^3 + B^2(E^p)^2 = B^3Z^s.$$

Theorem VIII

If

$$A^3 - BA^2 = Z^s,$$

let BA be E^2 or E^p. Then

$$E^6 - B^2E^4 = B^3Z^s$$

or

$$(E^p)^3 - B^2(E^p)^2 = B^3Z^s.$$

The demonstration is not unlike that given for the preceding theorem.

Theorem IX

If

$$BA^2 - A^3 = Z^s,$$

let BA be E^2 or E^p. Then

$$B^2E^4 - E^6 = B^3Z^s$$

or

$$B^2(E^p)^2 - (E^p)^3 = B^3Z^s.$$

The demonstration is not unlike that given for the seventh theorem of this chapter.

CHAPTER XIII

Derivation of Affected Biquadratics from Affected Quadratics

On Biquadratics with Linear Affections

Theorem I

If

$$A^2 + BA = Z^p,$$

then

$$A^4 + A(B^3 + 2BZ^p) = Z^{pp} + B^2Z^p.$$

Since

$$A^2 + BA = Z^p,$$

by transposition

$$A^2 = Z^p - BA.$$

Therefore

$$A^4 = Z^{pp} - 2BAZ^p + B^2A^2.$$

But the affection B^2A^2 equals $B^2Z^p - B^3A$ by substitution from the given equation.[59] Hence, aided by this substitute and putting all terms in proper order,

$$A^4 + A(B^3 + 2BZ^p) = Z^{pp} + B^2Z^p,$$

as was said.

If

$$x^2 + 8x = 20,$$

then

$$x^4 + 832x = 1,680.$$

Theorem II

If

$$A^2 - BA = Z^p,$$

then

$$A^4 [+] A(-B^3 - 2BZ^p) = Z^{pp} + B^2Z^p.$$

The demonstration is not unlike that given for the preceding theorem.

If

$$x^2 - 8x = 20,$$

then

$$x^4 - 832x = 1,680.$$

Theorem III

If

$$BA - A^2 = Z^p,$$

then

$$A(B^3 - 2BZ^p) - A^4 = B^2Z^p - Z^{pp}.$$

---

[59]*interpretationem ex proposita aequatione accipiens.* I.e., by substituting $Z^p - BA$ for A^2.

The demonstration is not unlike that given for the first theorem of this chapter.

If

$$12x - x^2 = 20,$$

then

$$1,248X - x^4 = 2,480.$$

On Biquadratics with Linear and Quadratic Affections.

Theorem IIII

If

$$A^2 + BA = S^p + D^p,$$

then

$$A^4 \; [+] \; A^2(-2D^p - B^2) + 2BS^pA = S^{pp} - D^{pp}.$$

Since

$$A^2 + BA = S^p + D^p,$$

then, by transposition,

$$A^2 - D^p = S^p - BA.$$

Square both sides of the transposed equation. Then

$$A^4 - 2D^pA^2 + D^{pp} = S^{pp} - 2BAS^p + B^2A^2$$

and, arranging all terms properly,

$$A^4 \; [+] \; A^2(-2D^p - B^2) + 2BS^pA = S^{pp} - D^{pp},$$

as was said.

If

$$x^2 + 8x = 20$$

(20 being composed of 15 and 5),

$$x^4 - 74x^2 + 240x = 200.$$

Theorem V

If

$$A^2 - BA = S^p + D^p,$$

then

$$A^4 \; [+] \; A^2(-2D^p - B^2) - 2BS^pA = S^{pp} - D^{pp},$$

The demonstration is not unlike that given for the preceding theorem.

If

$$x^2 - 8x = 20$$

(20 being composed of 15 and 5),

$$x^4 - 74x^2 - 240x = 200.$$

Theorem VI

If

$$BA - A^2 = S^p + D^p,$$

then

$$A^2(B^2 - 2S^p) - 2BD^pA - A^4 = S^{pp} - D^{pp}.$$

The demonstration is not unlike that given for the fourth theorem of this chapter.

If

$$12x - x^2 = 20,$$

(20 being composed of 15 and 5),

$$114x^2 - 120x - x^4 = 200.$$

Alternates for the Same

Theorem VII

If

$$A^2 + BA = S^p - D^p,$$

then

$$A^4 + A^2(2D^p - B^2) + 2BS^pA = S^{pp} - D^{pp}.$$

Since

$$A^2 + BA = S^p - D^p$$

then, by transposition,

$$A^2 + D^p = S^p - BA.$$

Squaring both sides,

$$A^4 + 2D^p A^2 + D^{pp} = S^{pp} - 2BS^p A + B^2 A^2$$

and, having arranged all terms properly,

$$A^4 + A^2(2D^p - B^2) + 2BS^p A = S^{pp} - D^{pp},$$

as was said.

If

$$x^2 + 8x = 20$$

(20 being the difference between 40 and 60)

$$x^4 + 16x^2 + 960x = 2,000.$$

Theorem VIII

If

$$A^2 - BA = S^p - D^p,$$

then

$$A^4 + A^2(2D^p - B^2) - 2BS^p A = S^{pp} - D^{pp}.$$

The demonstration is not unlike that given for the preceding theorem.
If

$$x^2 - 8x = 20$$

(20 being the difference between 40 and 60),

$$x^4 + 16x^2 - 960x = 2,000$$

Theorem IX

If

$$BA - A^2 = S^p - D^p,$$

then

$$2BD^p A + A^2(B^2 - 2S^p) - A^4 = S^{pp} - D^{pp}.$$

The demonstration is not unlike that given for the seventh theorem of this chapter.

If

$$12x - x^2 = 20$$

(20 being the difference between 40 and 60),

$$960x - 24x^2 - x^4 = 2,000.$$

On Biquadratics with Cubic Affections

Theorem X

If

$$A^2 + BA = Z^p,$$

then

$$A^4 + \frac{A^3(2BZ^p + B^3)}{Z^p + B^2} = \frac{Z^{ppp}{}^{60}}{Z^p + B^2}.$$

Since

$$A^2 + BA = Z^p,$$

then, by transposition,

$$A^2 = Z^p - BA.$$

Multiply all terms by A, and

$$A^3 = Z^pA - BA^2.$$

Then, [substituting] the designated value of A^2,

$$A^3 = Z^pA - BZ^p + B^2A$$

and, [transposing and] dividing both sides of this equation by $Z^p + B^2$, $(A^3 + BZ^p)/(Z^p + B^2)$ will equal A. But it has been said that

$$A^2 = Z^p - BA,$$

so, [substituting] the value of A just given, this may be expressed as

$$A^2 = \frac{Z^{pp} - BA^3}{Z^p + B^2}.$$

I then return to the equation first given,

$$A^2 + BA = Z^p$$

and, squaring both sides,

---

[60] 1615 has Z^{pp}.

$$A^4 + 2BA^3 + B^2A^2 = Z^{pp}.$$

Now the affection B^2A^2, substituting the value of A^2 just developed, will be $(B^2Z^{pp} - B^3A^3)/Z^p + B^2)$. Assisted by this substitution and setting all things straight,

$$A^4 + \frac{A^3(2BZ^p + B^3)}{Z^p + B^2} = \frac{Z^{ppp}}{Z^p + B^2},$$

as was said.

If

$$x^2 + 14x = 147,$$

then

$$x^4 + 20x^3 = 9{,}261.$$

Theorem XI

If

$$A^2 - BA = Z^p,$$

then

$$A^4 \, [+] \, \frac{A^3(-2BZ^p - B^3)}{Z^p + B^2} = \frac{Z^{ppp}}{Z^p + B^2}.$$

The demonstration is not unlike that given for the preceding theorem.

If

$$x^2 - 14x = 147,$$

then

$$x^4 - 20x^3 = 9{,}261.$$

Theorem XII

If

$$BA - A^2 = Z^p,$$

then

$$\frac{A^3(B^3 - 2BZ^p)}{B^2 - Z^p} - A^4 = \frac{Z^{ppp}[61]}{B^2 - Z^p}.$$

[61] 1646 has $(B^3 - 2BZ^p)/(B^2 - Z^p) = Z^{ppp}/(B^2 - Z^p)$.

The demonstration is not unlike that given for the tenth theorem of this chapter.

If

$$21x - x^2 = 98,$$

then

$$15x^3 - x^4 = 2{,}744.$$

CHAPTER XIIII

Derivation of Certain Affected Cubics from Affected Quadratics

Theorem I

If

$$A^2 + BA = Z^p,$$

then

$$A(B^2 + Z^p) - A^3 = BZ^p.$$

When

$$A^2 + BA = Z^p$$

and all terms are multiplied by A, then

$$A^3 + BA^2 = Z^p A.$$

But from what was given,

$$A^2 = Z^p - BA.$$

Hence, aided by this definition [of A^2] to express the value of the solid BA^2 in the cubic equation,

$$A^3 + BZ^p - B^2A = Z^p A$$

and, having arranged all things properly,

$$A(Z^p + B^2) - A^3 = BZ^p,$$

as was said.

If

$$x^2 + 8x = 20,$$

then

$$84x - x^3 = 160.$$

Theorem II

If

$$A^2 - BA = Z^p,$$

then

$$A^3 \,[+]\, A(-B^2 - Z^p) = BZ^p.$$

The demonstration of this is not unlike that given for the preceding theorem.

If

$$x^2 - 8x = 20,$$

then

$$x^3 - 84x = 160.$$

Theorem III

If

$$BA - A^2 = Z^p,$$

then

$$A(B^2 - Z^p) - A^3 = BZ^p.$$

The demonstration of this is not unlike that given for the first theorem of this chapter.

If

$$12x - x^2 = 20,$$

then

$$124x - x^3 = 240.$$

Theorem IIII

If

$$A^2 + BA = BD,$$

then

$$A^3 + A^2(B + D) = BD^2.$$

Since

$$A^2 + BA = BD^{62}$$

multiplying through by A,

$$A^3 + BA^2 = BDA.$$

But from what has been proposed,

$$\frac{BD - A^2}{B} = A.$$

Therefore, assisted by this definition [of A] for the purpose of expressing the value of the solid BDA,

$$A^3 + BA^2 = BD^2 - DA^2$$

and, transposing properly,

$$A^3 + A^2(B + D) = BD^2,$$

as was said.

If

$$x^2 + 16x = 80$$

(80 being the product of 16 and 5), then

$$x^3 + 21x^2 = 400.$$

Theorem V

If

$$A^2 - BA = BD,$$

then

$$A^2(B + D) - A^3 = BD^2.$$

---

[62] 1646 has $A^2 - BA = BD$.

The demonstration of this is not unlike that given for the preceding theorem.

If.

$$x^2 - 16x = 80$$

(80 being the product of 16 and 5), then

$$21x^2 - x^3 = 400.$$

Theorem VI

If

$$BA - A^2 = BD,$$

then

$$A^2(B - D) - A^3 = BD^2.$$

The demonstration of this is not unlike that for the fourth theorem of this chapter.

If

$$9x - x^2 = 18$$

(18 being the product of 9 and 2),

$$7x^2 - x^3 = 36.$$

CHAPTER XV

Demonstration of the Ambiguity of the Roots when Powers Are Subtracted from Homogeneous Terms of Affection in Equations.

Theorem[63]

It is to be shown that when, in equations, powers are subtracted from homogeneous terms of affection, the roots are double.[64]

---

[63] 1615 does not contain this word.
[64] Radices . . . Ancipites.

Let the difference between B and A be equal to S and let B be greater than S. Either B is greater [than A] or A is greater [than B]. In the first case

$$B - A = S$$

and

$$B - S = A.$$

In the second case

$$A - B = S$$

and

$$B + S = A.$$

In the first case, when

$$B - A = S,$$

square both sides of the equation and

$$B^2 - 2BA + A^2 = S^2$$

and, having set the equation in proper order,

$$2BA - A^2 = B^2 - S^2.$$

Likewise, in the second case, when

$$A - B = S,$$

square both sides and

$$B^2 - 2BA + A^2 = S^2$$

and, having set the equation in proper order,

$$2BA - A^2 = B^2 - S^2.$$

Therefore the equation has the same form in both cases and the root is double. The form is that of a plane based on the root and affected by the subtraction of the square [of the root].

Let B be 6, S 4 and A x. Then

$$12x - x^2 = 20,$$

and x is $6 - 4$ or $6 + 4$.

This ambiguity is known to exist in all similar situations. So if it is proposed that

$$DA - A^2 = Z^p,$$

D can be said to be $2B$ and Z^p to be $B^2 - S^2$.[65]

Furthermore, it is clear from the sixth theorem of the preceding chapter that cubes subtracted from solids based on a lower grade are derived from the equation of the ambiguous square and, from the third, sixth and ninth theorems of Chapter XII, that fourth powers subtracted from plano-planes based on a lower grade are derived from the same. It is clear, therefore, that this can be extended to equations of a higher order.

CHAPTER XVI

On Syncrisis

Syncrisis is the comparison of two correlative equations in order to discover their structure.

Two equations are said to be correlatives when they are similar and, in addition, have the same given magnitudes both for the coefficients of their affections and for their homogeneous terms of comparison.[66] Their roots, nevertheless, are different either because their structure is such that they may be solved by two or more roots or because the quality or sign of their affections is different.

In view of the number of those with multiple affections of which one who is expert in plasmatic modification would obviously be able to think, it will suffice [if we confine] our teaching to simple correlatives—that is, those involving only one affection.

There are three different [types] of simple correlative equations:

The first is the ambiguous: in both [equations] the power is subtracted from the homogeneous term of affection.

The second is the contradictory: in one the power is affected positively, in the other negatively.

The third is the inverse: in one the power is affected by a negative homogeneous term and in the other, on the contrary, the power is subtracted from the homogeneous term of affection.

---

[65] 1615 has $S^2 - B^2$.

[66] The text has *sive adfectionum Parabolis sive adfectionum homogeneis,* but the latter *adfectionum* is obviously an error for *comparationum.*

Whether ambiguous, contradictory or inverse, the structure of [such] equations can be well understood by syncrisis. To begin with, the principle of syncrisis is this: Since things equal to the same thing are equal to each other, the two powers, affecting or affected, must always be equated to the same constant term. Furthermore, let the same homogeneous term, affecting or affected, be associated with both powers, be of the same lower order, and have the same coefficient. Therefore one power with its lower-order homogeneous term will be equal to the other power with the [same] lower-order homogeneous term. And, transposing to one side the powers in the equation so set up and to the other the homogeneous terms of affection, there will again be an equality. Whence, if the sum of or the difference between the powers is divided by the difference between or the sum of their roots (the terms will indicate the [correct] operation), there will arise a magnitude equal to the coefficient and from this its composition will be evident.

Then if, after doing this, either of the given equations set up for comparison is no longer exhibited with its own coefficient but,[67] instead, with the value of the coefficient instead, the composition of this [value] having become known, what results will consequently be equal to the given homogeneous term of comparison. Hence the composition [of the latter] cannot be unknown. It arises from dividing the sum of or the difference between the roots or grades times the product of the roots by the same quantity, whether difference or sum, by which the preceding division was made.

It follows that the coefficient of the affections in the ambiguous cases arises from a division of the difference between the powers by the difference between the grades which the coefficient accompanies.

Likewise, the homogeneous term of comparison arises from dividing the difference between the products of the power of one root and the lower grade of the other by the aforesaid difference between the grades by which the other division was made.

This, however, can be quickly demonstrated:

PROBLEM I

To discover by syncrisis the structure of two ambiguous equations.

Let

$$BA^m - A^n = Z$$

---

[67] The text has *seu,* but I take this to be a misprint for *sed.*

and let

$$BE^m - E^n = Z.^{68}$$

From this it is clear that the grades are equal and the powers are equal. The problem is to discover the structure of these equations by syncrisis.

Since things equal to the same thing are equal to each other, it is clear that

$$BA^m - A^n = BE^m - E^n$$

and that by transposition—assuming, if you please, that A is greater than E, which is clearly permissible in view of the postulated ambiguity of the roots[69]—

$$A^n - E^n = BA^m - BE^m.$$

Then dividing through by $A^m - E^m$, $(A^n - E^n)/(A^m - E^m)$ will equal the coefficient B. Hence the coefficient B arises from dividing the difference between the powers by the difference between the grades, as was proposed.

Furthermore, since

$$BA^m - A^n = Z,$$

substitute the now known value of the coefficient B and restate the equation with this substitution. Then $(A^n E^m - E^n A^m)/(A^m - E^m)$ will equal Z, the homogeneous term [of comparison].

The homogeneous term Z, therefore, arises from dividing the difference between the products of the power of one root and the grade of the other by the difference between the grades, as was also said.

In Algebraic Symbols[70]

Let

$$BA - A^2 = Z^p$$

and let

$$BE - E^2 = Z^p.$$

The structure of these equations is to be discovered by syncrisis.
Since things equal to the same thing are equal to each other, it is clear

---

[68] Here and in the discussion that follows I have abbreviated Viète's terms "the power of E" and "the grade of E," etc., to E^n and E^m, etc.

[69] *propter praesuppositam Radicum ἀμφιβολίαλ.*

[70] *In specie.*

that

$$BA - A^2 = BE - E^2$$

and, by transposition—assuming if you please, that A is greater than E, which is certainly permissible because of the assumed ambiguity of the roots—that

$$A^2 - E^2 = BA - BE$$

and, dividing through by $A - E$, that

$$\frac{A^2 - E^2}{A - E} = A + E = B.$$

Therefore B is the sum of the two roots being sought and arises from dividing the difference between their squares by the difference between the roots, as was proposed in general terms.

Furthermore, since

$$BA - A^2 = Z^p,$$

if we substitute for B its now known value, $(A^2 - E^2)/(A - E)$ or $A + E$, [we will have]

$$\frac{A^2 E - E^2 A}{A - E} = EA = Z^p.$$

Z^p, therefore, is the product of the two roots being sought and arises from dividing the difference between the product of the square of one and the root of the other by the difference between the roots, as was also proposed in general terms.

Another

Let

$$B^p A - A^3 = Z^s$$

and let

$$B^p E - E^3 = Z^s.$$

The structure of these equations is to be discovered by syncrisis.

Since, therefore, things equal to the same thing are equal to each other, it is clear that

$$B^p A - A^3 = B^p E - E^3$$

and by transposition—assuming that A is greater than E, which is clearly permissible in view of the assumed ambiguity of the roots—that

$$A^3 - E^3 = B^p A - B^p E$$

and, dividing through by $A - E$, that

$$\frac{A^3 - E^3}{A - E} = A^2 + E^2 + AE = B^p.$$

So B^p is the sum of the squares of the two roots being sought plus their product and arises from dividing the difference between the cubes by the difference between the roots, as has been shown in general terms.

Furthermore, since

$$B^p A - A^3 = Z^s,$$

if the value of B^p—namely $(A^3 - E^3)/(A - E)$ or $A^2 + E^2 + AE$—is now put in its place,

$$\frac{A^3 E - E^3 A}{A - E} = A^2 E + E^2 A = Z^s.$$

So Z^s is the sum of the roots times their product and arises from dividing the difference between the reciprocal products of the cube of one and the root of the other by the difference between these same roots, as has also been proposed.

Hence the structure of the given equations is known by syncrisis, which is what was called for.

Let us illustrate how this formula for an ambiguous quadratic equation is solvable with the roots F or G, the latter the smaller, the former the greater. I will say that

$$A(F + G) - A^2 = FG$$

and that this makes A [equal to] either F or G.

Let F be 10, G 2 and A x. The equation will take the form

$$12x - x^2 = 20$$

and is solvable by 10 or 2.

Let us also illustrate how the formula for an equation of a cube subtracted from its linear homogeneous term of affection is explicable by either of the roots F or G. I will say that

$$A(F^2 + G^2 + FG) - A^3 = FG^2 + GF^2$$

and that this makes A [equal to] either F or G.

Let F be 10, G 2 and A x. The form of the equation will be

$$124x - x^3 = 240,$$

which is solvable by 10 or 2.

In the contradictories, the coefficients of the lower-order terms arise from dividing the difference between the powers by the sum of the lower-order terms which the coefficients support and the constant from dividing the sum of the reciprocal products of the power of one root and the lower grade of the other by the same sum by which the other division was made. This, however, will be quickly demonstrated:

PROBLEM II

To discover by syncrisis the structure of two contradictory equations.

Let

$$A^n + BA^m = Z$$

and let

$$E^n - BE^m = Z.$$

So the grades and powers are the same. The structure of these two equations is to be discovered by syncrisis.

Since things equal to the same thing are equal to each other, it is clear that

$$A^n + BA^m = E^n - BE^m$$

and, by transposition, that

$$E^n - A^n = BE^m + BA^m.$$

Hence, dividing through by $E^m + A^m$, $(E^n - A^n)/(E^m + A^m)$ will equal B. So B, the coefficient of the lower-order terms, arises from dividing the difference between the powers by the sum of the lower terms that the coefficient supports, as was proposed.

Furthermore, since

$$A^n + BA^m = Z,$$

substitute its now known value, viz., $(E^n - A^n)/(E^m + A^m)$, for B and restate the equation with this substitution. Then

$$A^n + \frac{A^m(E^n - A^n)}{E^m + A^m} = Z$$

and this, all terms being put in proper order, is

$$\frac{A^n E^m + E^n A^m}{E^m + A^m} = Z.$$

So Z arises from dividing the sum of the reciprocal products of the power of one root and the grade of the other by the sum of the grades by which the aforesaid division was made, as was said in the second place.

In inverse negative [equations],[71] the coefficients of the lower-order terms arise from dividing the sum of the powers by the sum of the lower-order terms to which the coefficient applies and the constants arise from dividing the difference between the products of the power of one root and the lower-order term of the other by the same sum of the terms having the coefficient by which the other division was made. This can also be quickly demonstrated:

PROBLEM III

To discover by syncrisis the structure of two inverse equations.

Let

$$A^n - BA^m = Z$$

and let

$$BE^m - E^n = Z.$$

From this A and E are known [to have] the same grade and their powers are also the same. The structure of these equations is to be discovered.

Since things equal to the same thing are equal to each other, it is clear from what has been given that

$$A^n - BA^m = BE^m - E^n$$

and, by transposition, that

$$A^n + E^n = BA^m + BE^m.$$

Dividing through by $E^m + A^m$, $(A^n + E^n)/(A^m + E^m)$ will equal B, which is what was said in the first place.

Furthermore, since

$$A^n - BA^m = Z,$$

---

[71] *In inversis plane negatis. Plane* appears to have no place here and has been omitted in the translation.

put the value of B, viz., $(A^n + E^n)/(A^m + E^m)$, in its place and then

$$A^n - \frac{A^n A^m + E^n A^m}{A^m + E^m} = Z$$

and, having arranged all terms correctly, $(A^n E^m - E^n A^m)/(A^m + E^m)$ will equal Z, as was said in the second place.

In the inverse cases, moreover, one [equation] may have a positive affection, the other a negative. The coefficient of the lower-order terms [then] arises from dividing the sum of the powers by the difference between the terms having the coefficient and the constant from dividing the sum of the reciprocal products of the power of one root and the lower-order grade of the other by the same difference between the lower-order grades with coefficients by which the other division was made. This can be shown quickly:

Let

$$A^n + BA^m = Z$$

and let

$$BE^m - E^n = Z.$$

So it is known that the grades and powers of A and E are the same. What is wanted is to discover the structure of these equations.

Since things equal to the same thing are equal to each other, it is clear from what is given that

$$A^n + E^n = BE^m - BA^m.\text{[72]}$$

Then, dividing through by $E^m - A^m$, $(E^n + A^n)/(E^m - A^m)$ will equal B, which is what was said in the first place.

Furthermore, since

$$A^n + BA^m = Z,$$

substituting the value of B, the coefficient of the lower-order term, for it, viz., $(E^n + A^n)/(E^m - A^m)$,

$$A^n + \frac{A^m(E^n + A^n)}{E^m - A^m} = Z$$

[72] In 1646 this sentence reads: Since things equal to the same thing are equal to each other, it is clear from what is given that

$$A^n + BA^m = BE^m - E^n$$

and, by transposition, that

$$A^n + E^n = BE^m - BA^m.$$

and, putting everything in proper order, $(A^nE^m + E^nA^m)/(E^m - A^m)$ will equal Z, and this is what was said in the second place.

We can say that [the formulae for] the double-value cases are fully effective in every order of the powers, since one lesson once learned easily leads to another, as is clear from the zetetics.

But [the formulae for] the contradictory and inverse cases are sometimes helpful, sometimes of little aid,[73] depending on the nature of the power. For example, [the formulae for] a contradictory with a linear term are helpful if [a problem] involves a square or any alternate power beyond that, viz., a fourth power, sixth power, and so on in that order. We rate them slow and unusable, however, for the other powers, viz., the first power and the alternate powers beyond it—the cube, fifth power and so on in that order—since they bring no help or comfort to the analyst, and it will appear to him that there [must be] an easier and happier approach to comparisons.[74]

On the other hand, [the formulae for] the inverse with a linear term, whichever term is subtracted, are helpful when they deal with cubes, fifth powers, etc. The reason is that, when the difference between the powers is divided by the difference between the roots, the quotient is the same as continued proportionals made from the roots themselves, always in a positive series, in the order of the powers, in accordance with what has been expounded in the chapter on the genesis of powers from a binomial root.[75] But when the difference between the powers is divided by the sum of the roots and the powers are cubes, fifth powers, and so on, taking them alternately, the quotient is the same as the continued proportionals with alternate negatives [and positives].[76]

When, however, the sum of the powers is divided by the difference between the roots, terms equivalent to continued proportionals do not arise, whether the powers are even-numbered or odd-numbered.

CHAPTER XVII

A Geometric Expression of Syncritic Teaching

These syncritic conclusions may be embellished and refined by certain proportions. Geometrical operation will be facilitated by them, as will be quite evident and clear.

[73]*interdum efficaces . . . , interdum minime.*
[74]*ad ἀνῦβαλλομέμας facilior foeliciorve aditus.*
[75]See *Preliminary Notes,* Propositions XVII et seq.
[76]1615 has *prosaphaeritice;* 1646 has *prostaphaeritice.*

Proposition I[77]

In a series of three proportionals, the square of the first is to the square of the second as the first is to the third.

In a series of four proportionals, the cube of the first is to the cube of the second as the first is to the fourth.

In a series of five continued proportionals, the fourth power of the first is to the fourth power of the second as the first is to the fifth.

In a series of six continued proportionals, the fifth power of the first is to the fifth power of the second as the first is to the sixth.

In a series of seven continued proportionals, the sixth power of the first is to the sixth power of the second as the first is to the seventh.

[This is so] because the square is the power of duplicate ratio, the cube of triplicate, the fourth power of quadruplicate, and so on, as has been noted elsewhere. Hence a series of proportionals bears the name of the individual powers in accordance with their nature.

Proposition II

In a series of three proportionals, the sum of the squares of the first two is to the sum of the squares of the last two as the first is to the third.

In a series of four proportionals, the sum of the cubes of the first three is to the sum of the cubes of the last three as the first is to the fourth.

In a series of five proportionals, the sum of the fourth powers of the first four is to the sum of the fourth powers of the last four as the first is to the fifth.

In a series of six proportionals, the sum of the fifth powers of the first five is to the sum of the fifth powers of the last five as the first is to the sixth.

In a series of seven proportionals, the sum of the sixth powers of the first six is to the sum of the sixth powers of the last six as the first is to the seventh.

Since the square of the first is to the square of the second as the first is to the third and the square of the second is to the square of the third as the

---

[77]So in 1615; in 1646 these "propositions" are labeled "theorems." This is also the case in the next four chapters.

square of the first is to the square of the second, therefore by synaeresis the square of the first plus the square of the second is to the square of the second plus the square of the third as the first is to the third. The same is true in any other series of proportionals. This can be made clear and explained for any powers agreed upon in accordance with the nature of the extremes.

PROPOSITION III

In a series of three proportionals, the square of the sum of the first two is to the square of the sum of the last two as the first is to the third.

In a series of four proportionals, the cube of the sum of the first three is to the cube of the sum of the last three as the first is to the fourth.

In a series of five proportionals, the fourth power of the sum of the first four is to the fourth power of the sum of the last four as the first is to the fifth.

In a series of six proportionals, the fifth power of the sum of the first five is to the fifth power of the sum of the last five as the first is to the sixth.

In a series of seven proportionals, the sixth power of the sum of the first six is to the sixth power of the sum of the last six as the first is to the seventh.

Merging these, whatever the series of proportionals may be, the sum of all except the last[78] is to the sum of all except the first[79] as the first is to the second. In any series, moreover, the power is fixed—i.e., [it is the same as] the ratio, whatever it may be, that comparison of the extremes prescribes.[80]

PROPOSITION IIII

In a series of three proportionals, the difference between the squares of the first two is to the difference between the squares of the last two as the first is to the third.

In a series of four proportionals, the difference between the cubes of the first three taken alternately is to the

[78]The text has "first."

[79]*altera extrema.*

[80]*In unaquaque autem serie exponitur sua potestas conditionaria: id est tantuplicatae rationis quam extramarum comparatio exigit.* That is, the power is a square, cube, etc., depending on the ratio (duplicate, triplicate, etc.) of the first and last terms.

difference between the cubes of the last three taken alternately as the first is to the fourth.[81]

In a series of five proportionals, the difference between the fourth powers of the first four taken alternately is to the difference between the fourth powers of the last four taken alternately as the first is to the fifth.[82]

In a series of six proportionals, the difference between the fifth powers of the first five taken alternately is to the difference between the fifth powers of the last five taken alternately as the first is to the sixth.[83]

In a series of seven proportionals, the difference between the sixth powers of the first six taken alternately is to the difference between the sixth powers of the last six taken alternately as the first is to the seventh.[84]

PROPOSITION V

In a series of three proportionals, the square of the difference between the first two is to the square of the difference between the last two as the first is to the third.

In a series of four proportionals, the cube of the difference between the first three taken alternately is to the cube of the difference between the last three taken alternately as the first is to the fourth.[85]

In a series of five proportionals, the fourth power of the difference between the first four taken alternately is to the fourth power of the difference between the last four taken alternately as the first is to the fifth.[86]

In a series of six proportionals, the fifth power of the difference between the first five taken alternately is to the fifth power of the difference between the last five taken alternately as the first is to the sixth.[87]

[81] I.e., if the proportionals are p, q, r and s, $(r^3 - q^3 + p^3)/(s^3 - r^3 + q^3) = p/s$.

[82] I.e., if the proportionals are p, q, r, s, and t, $(s^4 - r^4 + q^4 - p^4)/(t^4 - s^4 + r^4 - q^4) = p/t$.

[83] I.e., if the proportionals are p, q, r, s, t and u, $(t^5 - s^5 + r^5 - q^5 + p^5)/(u^5 - t^5 + s^5 - r^5 + q^5) = p/u$.

[84] I.e., if the proportionals are p, q, r, s, t, u and v, $(u^6 - t^6 + s^6 - r^6 + q^6 - p^6)/(v^6 - u^6 + t^6 - s^6 + r^6 - q^6) = p/v$.

[85] I.e., if the proportionals are p, q, r and s, $(r - q + p)^3/(s - r + q)^3 = p/s$.

[86] I.e., if the proportionals are p, q, r, s and t, $(s - r + q - p)^4/(t - s + r - q)^4 = p/t$.

[87] I.e., if the proportionals are p, q, r, s, t and u, $(t - s + r - q + p)^5/(u - t + s - r + q)^5 = p/u$.

In a series of seven proportionals, the sixth power of the difference between the first six taken alternately is to the sixth power of the difference between the last six taken alternately as the first is to the seventh.[88]

PROPOSITION VI

In a series of four continued proportionals the sum of the cube of the fourth and three times the cube of the second differs from the sum of the cube of the first and three times the cube of the third by the cube of the difference between the extremes.

Let there be four continued proportionals, B, D, F and G and let G be the greater extreme. I say that

$$G^3 + 3D^3 - B^3 - 3F^3 = (G - B)^3.$$

The cube of $G - B$ consists of $G^3 - 3BG^2 + 3B^2G - B^3$. Let this be compared with $G^3 + 3D^3 - B^3 - 3F^3$. The result is

$$3B^2G - 3BG^2 = 3D^3 - 3F^3$$

and this is so because B^2G is D^3 and BG^2 is F^3.

PROPOSITION VII

In a series of four continued proportionals the sum of the cube of the fourth and three times the cube of the second plus the sum of the cube of the first and three times the cube of the third is equal to the cube of the sum of the extremes.

The same demonstration holds [here] as in the preceding theorem.

CHAPTER XVIII[89]

The Components of Equations with Two Roots

Equations known by syncrisis, plasmatic modification or zetetics to have two roots are all constituted in this manner:

---

[88]I.e., if the proportionals are p, q, r, s, t, u and v, $(u - t + s - r + q - p)^6/(v - u + t - s + r - q)^6 = p/v$.

[89]1646 has XV instead of XVIII.

Concerning Affections Based on the Lowest Grade or Root

PROPOSITION I

If

$$BA - A^2 = Z^p,$$

B is the sum of two roots the product of which is equal to Z^p, making A either the larger or the smaller root.

Let there be two roots, 2 and 10. It may be said that

$$12x - x^2 = 20,$$

making x 2 or 10.

PROPOSITION II

If

$$B^p A - A^3 = Z^s,$$

B^p is the sum of the squares of three proportionals and Z^s is the product of one of the extremes and the sum of the squares of the other two, making A either the first or the third [of the proportionals].[90]

Let the proportionals be 2, $\sqrt{20}$ and 10. It may be said that

$$124x - x^3 = 240,$$

making x 2 or 10.

PROPOSITION III

If

$$B^s A - A^4 = Z^{pp},$$

B^s is the sum of the cubes of four continued proportionals and Z^{pp} is the product of either of the extremes and the sum of the cubes of the other three, making A either the first or fourth [of the proportionals].[91]

[90] I.e., if $ax - x^3 = N$ and p, q and r are proportionals, then $a = p^2 + q^2 + r^2$; $N = p(q^2 + r^2)$ or $r(p^2 + q^2)$; and $x = p$ or r.

[91] I.e., if $ax - x^4 = N$ and p, q, r and s are proportionals, then $a = p^3 + q^3 + r^3 + s^3$; $N = p(q^3 + r^3 + s^3)$ or $s(p^3 + q^3 + r^3)$; and $x = p$ or s.

Let the continued proportionals be 2, $\sqrt[3]{40}$, $\sqrt[3]{200}$ and 10. Then it may be said that

$$1248x - x^4 = 2480,$$

making x 2 or 10.

Proposition IIII

If

$$B^{pp}A - A^5 = Z^{ps},$$

B^{pp} is the sum of the fourth powers of five continued proportionals and Z^{ps} is the product of either of the extremes and the sum of the fourth powers of the other four, making A either the first or the fifth [of the proportionals].[92]

Let the continued proportionals be 2, $\sqrt[4]{80}$, $\sqrt{20}$, $\sqrt[4]{2000}$ and 10. It may be said that

$$12{,}496x - x^5 = 24{,}960,$$

making x 2 or 10.

Proposition V

If

$$B^{ps}A - A^6 = Z^{ss},[93]$$

B^{ps} is the sum of the fifth powers of six continued proportionals and z^{ss} is the product of either of the extremes and the sum of the fifth powers of the other five, making A either the first or the sixth [of the proportionals].[94]

Let the continued proportionals be 2, $\sqrt[5]{160}$, $\sqrt[5]{800}$, $\sqrt[5]{4{,}000}$, $\sqrt[5]{20{,}000}$ and 10. It may be said that

$$124{,}992x - x^6 = 249{,}920,$$

making x 2 or 10.

---

[92] I.e., if $ax - x^5 = N$ and p, q, r, s and t are proportionals, $a = p^4 + q^4 + r^4 + s^4 + t^4$; $N = p(q^4 + r^4 + s^4 + t^4)$ or $t(p^4 + q^4 + r^4 + s^4)$; and $x = p$ or t.

[93] 1615 omits the minus sign in this equation.

[94] I.e., if $ax + x^6 = N$ and p, q, r, s, t and u are proportionals, then $a = p^5 + q^5 + r^5 + s^5 + t^5 + u^5$; $N = p(q^5 + r^5 + s^5 + t^5 + u^5)$ or $u(p^5 + q^5 + r^5 + s^5 + t^5)$; and $x = p$ or u.

Concerning Affections Based on the Highest Grade or the Complement of the Root

Proposition VI

If

$$BA^2 - A^3 = Z^s,$$

B is the sum of three proportionals and Z^s is the product of either extreme and the square of the sum of the other two, making A the sum of either the first two or the last two [of the proportionals].[95]

Let the proportionals be 1, 2 and 4. It may be said that

$$7x^2 - x^3 = 36,$$

making x 3 or 6.

Proposition VII

If

$$BA^3 - A^4 = Z^{pp},$$

B is the sum of four continued proportionals and Z^{pp} is the product of either extreme and the cube of the sum of the other three, making A the sum of either the first three or the last three.[96]

Let the continued proportionals be 1, 2, 4 and 8. It may be said that

$$15x^3 - x^4 = 2,744,$$

making x 7 or 14.

Proposition VIII

If

$$BA^4 - A^5 = Z^{ps},$$

B is the sum of five continued proportionals and Z^{ps} is the product of either extreme and the fourth power of the sum of

[95] I.e., if $ax^2 - x^3 = N$ and p, q and r are proportionals, then $a = p + q + r$; $N = p(q + r)^2$ or $r(p + q)^2$; and $x = p + q$ or $q + r$.

[96] I.e., if $ax^3 - x^4 = N$ and p, q, r and s are proportionals, then $a = p + q + r + s$; $N = p(q + r + s)^3$ or $s(p + q + r)^3$; and $x = p + q + r$ or $q + r + s$.

the other four, making A the sum of either the first four or the last four.[97]

Let the continued proportionals be 1, 2, 4, 8 and 16. [Then]

$$31x^4 - x^5 = 810,000,$$

making x 15 or 30.

PROPOSITION IX

If

$$BA^5 - A^6 = Z^{ss},$$

B is the sum of six continued proportionals and Z^{ss} is the product of either extreme and the fifth power of the sum of the others, making A the sum of either the first five or the last five.[98]

Let the continued proportionals be 1, 2, 4, 8, 16 and 32. [Then]

$$63x^5 - x^6 = 916,132,832,$$

making x 31 or 62.

Concerning Affections Based on Intermediate Grades Which Can be Reduced by Substitution

PROPOSITION X

If

$$B^pA^2 - A^4 = Z^{pp},$$

B^p is the sum of the squares of the two roots the product of which is Z^{pp}, making A^2 either the greater or the smaller of the two.[99]

---

[97] I.e., if $ax^4 - a^5 = N$ and p, q, r, s and t are proportionals, then $a = p + q + r + s + t$; $N = p(q + r + s + t)^4$ or $t(p + q + r + s)^4$; and $x = p + q + r + s$ or $q + r + s + t$.

[98] I.e., if $ax^5 - a^6 = N$ and p, q, r, s, t and u are proportionals, then $a = p + q + r + s + t + u$; $N = p(q + r + s + t + u)^5$ or $u(p + q + r + s + t)^5$; and $x = p + q + r + s + t$ or $q + r + s + t + u$.

[99] I.e., if $ax^2 - x^4 = N$ and p and q are its roots, then $a = p^2 + q^2$; $N = p^2q^2$; and $x^2 = p^2$ or q^2.

Let the roots be 1 and 4. It may be said that

$$17x^2 - x^4 = 16,$$

making x 1 or 4.

But if x is known to be a square or plane root,

$$17x - x^2 = 16,$$

making x 1 or 16.

PROPOSITION XI

If

$$B^s A^3 - A^6 = Z^{ss},$$

B^s is the sum of two cubes the product of which is Z^{ss}, making A^3 either the greater or the smaller of the two.[1]

Let the roots be 1 and 8. It may be said that

$$513x^3 - x^6 = 512,$$

making x 1 or 8.

But if x is known to be a cube or solid root,

$$513x - x^2 = 512,$$

making x 1 or 512.

PROPOSITION XII

If

$$B^{pp} A^2 - A^6 = Z^{ss},$$

B^{pp2} is the sum of the squares of three plane proportionals and Z^{ss} is the product of one [i.e., the first or last] plane and the sum of the squares of the other two, making A^2 either the greater or the smaller [of the extremes].[3]

Let the three plane proprtionals be 1, 2 and 4. It can be said that

$$21x^2 - x^6 = 20,$$

making x 1 or 2.

[1] I.e., if $ax^3 - x^6 = N$ and p and q are its roots, then $a = p^3 + q^3$; $N = p^3q^3$; and $x^3 = p^3$ or q^3.

[2] The text has B^p.

[3] I.e., if $ax^2 - x^6 = N$ and p^2, q^2 and r^2 are proportionals, then $a = p^4 + q^4 + r^4$; $N = p^2(q^4 + r^4)$ or $r^2(p^4 + q^4)$; and $x^2 = p^2$ or r^2.

But if x is known to be a square or plane root,

$$21x - x^3 = 20,$$

making x 1 or 4.

Proposition XIII

If

$$B^p A^4 - A^6 = Z^{ss},$$

B^p is the sum of three plane proportionals and Z^{ss} is the product of one [i.e., the first or last] plane and the square of the sum of the other two, making A^2 either the greater or the smaller of these two [sums].[4]

Let the three plane proportionals be 5, 20 and 80. It can be said that

$$105x^4 - x^6 = 50,000$$

making x 5 or 10.

The discovery of three plane proportionals, the mean of which plus either the first or last is a square number,[5] is evident from this series:

$$\frac{B^4}{B^2 + G^2} \qquad \frac{B^2 G^2}{B^2 + G^2} \qquad \frac{G^4}{B^2 + G^2}$$

Speaking zetetically, let E^p be the mean of the [three] planes and assume that $B^2 - E^p$ is the first [of them] and $G^2 - E^p$ the last. When, therefore, E^p is added to the first plane, it makes a square, namely B^2 [and when it is added to the last, it makes a square, namely G^2.][6] It follows, therefore, that as these three planes are proportionals and consequently the square of the mean is equal to the product of the extremes, a comparison having been undertaken in accordance with the art, $B^2 G^2/(B^2 + G^2)$ is found to be equal to E^p.

Let B be 1 and G 2. The planes being sought will be $1/5$, $4/5$ and $16/5$. The middle one plus the first makes 1 and plus the last[7] makes 4. The same planes multiplied by a square, say 25, become 5, 20 and 80, the same as that assumed in the example.

---

[4] I.e., if $ax^4 - x^6 = N$ and p^2, q^2 and r^2 are proportionals, then $a = p^2 + q^2 + r^2$; $N = p^2(q^2 + r^2)^2$ or $r^2(p^2 + q^2)^2$; and $x^2 = q^2 + r^2$ or $p^2 + q^2$.

[5] The text has *quadratum numero*, presumably a misprint for *quadratum numerum*.

[6] The bracketed clause does not appear in 1615.

[7] 1615 has *secundo;* 1646 has *postremo.*

Concerning Others

Proposition XIIII[8]

If

$$B^s A^2 - A^5 = Z^{ps},$$

B^s is the cube of the sum of the first two in a series of three
proportionals plus the cube of the sum of the last two plus the
product of either extreme and the square of the sum [of the
other two][9] and Z^{ps} is the product of B^s minus the cube of the
first two and the square of the sum of the first and second or
the cube of the sum of the second and third plus the product
of the third and the square of the sum of the first and second
times the square of the sum of the sum of the first and
second, making A the sum of the first two or of the last
two.[10]

Let the proportionals be 1, 2 and 4. [Then]

$$279x^2 - x^5 = 2,268,$$

and x is 3 or 6.

Proposition XV

If

$$B^p A^3 - A^5 = Z^{ps},$$

B^p consists of the square of the sum of the first three in a
series of four continued proportionals plus the square of the
sum of the last three minus the product of the third and the
sum of the third, second and first or of the second and the
sum of the second, third and fourth and Z^{ps} is the product of
B^p minus the square of the sum of the first three and the cube
of the sum of the last three or the product of B^p minus the
square of the sum of the last three[11] and the cube of the sum

---

[8] 1646 has XIII.
[9] Instead of "the other two," the text has "the second and third."
[10] I.e., if $ax^2 - x^5 = N$ and p, q and r are proportionals, then $a = (p + q)^3 + (q + r)^3 + p(q + r)^2$ or $(p + q)^3 + (q + r)^3 + r(p + q)^2$; $N = [a - (p + q)^3] (p + q)^2$ or $[(q + r)^3 + r(p + q)^2](p + q)^2$; and $x = q + r$ or $p + q$.
[11] 1646 has "the first three."

of the first three, making A the sum of the first three or of the last three.[12]

Let the continued proportionals be 1, 2, 4 and 8. [Then]

$$217x^3 - x^5 = 57{,}624,$$

making x 7 or 14.

CHAPTER XIX

The Components of Contradictory Equations

The structure of the contradictories is like this:

PROPOSITION I

If

$$A^2 + BA = Z^p$$

and

$$E^2 - BE = Z^p,$$

there are two roots the difference between which is B and the product of which is equal to Z^p, making A the smaller root and E[13] the greater.

If the two roots are 1 and 2,

$$x^2 + x = 2,$$

making x 1, and

$$y^2 - y = 2,$$

making y 2.

---

[12] I.e., if $ax^3 - x^5 = N$ and p, q, r and s are proportionals, then $a = (p + q + r)^2 + (q + r + s)^2 - r(p + q + r)$ or $(p + q + r)^2 + (q + r + s)^2 - q(q + r + s)$; $N = [a - (p + q + r)^2]\,(q + r + s)^3$ or $[a - (q + r + s)^2]\,(p + q + r)^3$; and $x = p + q + r$ or $q + r + s$.
[13] 1615 omits this letter.

Proposition II

If

$$A^4 + B^s A = Z^{pp}$$

and

$$E^4 - B^s E = Z^{pp},$$

there are four continued proportionals the cubes of which taken alternately differ by B^s. This makes Z^{pp} the product of one extreme and the difference between the cubes of the others taken alternately, and A becomes the first or smaller of the extremes and E the fourth.[14]

If the continued proportionals are 1, $\sqrt[3]{2}$, $\sqrt[3]{4}$ and 2,

$$x^4 + 5x = 6,$$

making x 1, and

$$y^4 - 5y = 6,$$

making y 2.

Proposition III

If

$$A^6 + B^{ps} A = Z^{ss}$$

and

$$E^6 - B^{ps} E = Z^{ss},$$

there are six continued proportionals the fifth powers of which taken alternately differ by B^{ps}. This makes Z^{ss} the product of either extreme and the difference between the fifth powers of the others taken alternately and A becomes the first or smaller of the extremes and E the sixth.[15]

If the continued proportionals are 1, $\sqrt[5]{2}$, $\sqrt[5]{4}$, $\sqrt[5]{8}$, $\sqrt[5]{16}$ and 2,

$$x^6 + 21x = 22,$$

[14] I.e., if $x^4 + ax = N$ and $y^4 - ay = N$ and p, q, r and s are proportionals, then $a = s^3 - r^3 + q^3 - p^3$; $N = p(s^3 - r^3 + q^3)$ or $s(r^3 - q^3 + p^3)$; $x = p$; and $y = s$.

[15] I.e., if $x^6 + ax = N$ and $y^3 - ay = N$ and p, q, r, s, t and are proportionals, then $a = u^5 - t^5 + s^5 - r^5 + q^5 - p^5$; $N = p(u^5 - t^5 + s^5 - r^5 + q^5)$ or $u(t^5 - s^5 + r^5 - q^5 + p^5)$; and $x = p$ and $u = u$.

making x 1, and

$$y^6 - 21y = 22,$$

making y 2.

Proposition IIII

If

$$A^4 + BA^3 = Z^{pp}$$

and

$$E^4 - BE^3 = Z^{pp},$$

there are four continued proportionals the difference between which, taken alternately, is B. This makes Z^{pp} the product of either extreme and the cube of the difference between the others taken alternately and, if the first is called the smaller of the extremes, A is the difference between the first three taken alternately and E the difference between the last three taken alternately.[16]

If the continued proportionals are 1, 2, 4 and 8,

$$x^4 + 5x^3 = 216,$$

making x 3, and

$$y^4 - 5y^3 = 216,$$

making y 6.

Proposition V

If

$$A^6 + BA^5 = Z^{ss}$$

and

$$E^6 - BE^5 = Z^{ss},$$

there are six continued proportionals the difference between which, taken alternately, is B. This makes Z^{ss} the product of either of the extremes and the fifth power of the difference

---

[16] I.e., if $x^4 + ax^3 = N$ and $y^4 - ay^3 = N$ and p, q, r and s are proportionals, then $a = s - r + q = p$; $N = p(s - r + q)^3$ or $s(r - q + p)^3$; $x = r - q + p$; and $y = s - r + q$.

between the others taken alternately and, if the first is called the smaller of the extremes, A becomes the difference between the first five taken alternately and E the difference between the last five taken alternately.[17]

If the continued proprtionals are 1, 2, 4, 8, 16 and 32,

$$x^6 + 21x^5 = 5{,}153{,}632,$$

making x 11, and

$$y^6 - 21y^5 = 5{,}153{,}632,$$

making y 22.

CHAPTER XX

The Components of Inverse Equations

These are the structures of inverse [equations]:

PROPOSITION I

If

$$B^p A - A^3 = Z^s$$

and

$$E^3 - B^p E = Z^s,$$

there are three proportionals the squares of which taken alternately differ by B^p. This makes Z^s the product of either extreme and the difference between the squares of the others. A is the first or smaller of the extremes and E the third.[18]

If the proportionals are 1, $\sqrt{2}$ and 2:

$$3x - x^3 = 2,$$

[17] I.e., if $x^6 + ax^5 = N$ and $y^6 - ay^5 = N$ and p, q, r, s, t and u are proportionals, then $a = u - t + s - r + q - p$; $N = p(u - t + s - r + q)^5$ or $u(t - s + r - q + p)^5$; $x = u - t + s - r + q$; and $y = t - s + r - q + p$.

[18] I.e., if $ax - x^3 = N$ and $y^3 - ay = N$ and p, q and r are proportionals, then $a = r^2 - q^2 + p^2$; $N = p(r^2 - q^2)$ or $r(q^2 - p^2)$; $x = p$; and $y = r$.

making x 1, and

$$y^3 - 3y = 2,$$

making y 2.

PROPOSITION II

If

$$B^{pp}A - A^5 = Z^{ps}$$

and

$$E^5 - B^{pp}E^{19} = Z^{ps},$$

there are five lengths in continued proportion the fourth powers of which, taken alternately, differ by B^{pp}. This makes Z^{ps} the product of either extreme and the difference between the fourth powers of the others taken alternately, and A is the first or smaller of the extremes and E the fifth.[20]

If the continued proportionals are 1, $\sqrt[4]{2}$, $\sqrt[4]{4}$, $\sqrt[4]{8}$ and 2,

$$11x - x^5 = 10$$

making x 1, and

$$y^5 - 11y = 10,$$

making y 2.

PROPOSITION III

If

$$BA^2 + A^3 = Z^s$$

and

$$BE^2 - E^3 = Z^s,$$

there are three proportionals the difference between which, taken alternately, is B. This makes Z^s the product of either of the extremes and the square of the difference between the others. And if the first is called the smaller of the extremes,

[19]The text has $B^{pp}A$.
[20]I.e., if $ax - x^5 = N$ and $y^5 - ay = N$ and p, q, r, s and t are proportionals, then $a = t^4 - s^4 + r^4 - q^4 + p^4$; $N = p(t^4 - s^4 + r^4 - q^4)$ or $t(s^4 - r^4 + q^4 - p^4)$; $x = p$; and $y = t$.

A will be the difference between the first two[21] and E the difference between the last two.[22]

If the proportionals are 1, 2 and 4,

$$3x^2 + x^3 = 4$$

making x 1, and

$$3y^2 - y^3 = 4,$$

making y 2.

PROPOSITION IIII

If

$$BA^4 + A^5 = Z^{ps}$$

and

$$BE^4 - E^5 = Z^{ps},$$

there are five proportionals the difference between which, taken alternately, is B. This makes Z^{ps} the product of either of the extremes and the fourth power of the difference between the others taken alternately and, if the first is called the smaller of the extremes, A is the difference between the first four taken alternately and E the difference between the last four.[23]

If the proportionals are 1, 2, 4, 8 and 16,

$$11x^4 + x^5 = 10,000$$

making x 5, and

$$11y^4 - y^5 = 10,000,$$

making y 10.

---

[21]The text has a superfluous "taken alternately" here as well as at the end of the preceding sentence.

[22]I.e., if $ax^2 + x^3 = N$ and $ay^2 - y^3 = N$ and p, q and r are proportionals, then $a = r - q + p$; $N = r(q - p)^2$ or $p(r - q)^2$; $x = q - p$; and $y = r - q$.

[23]I.e., if $ax^4 + x^5 = N$ and $ay^4 - y^5 = N$ and p, q, r, s and t are proportionals, then $a = t - s + r - q + p$; $N = t(s - r + q - p)^4$ or $p(t - s + r - q)^4$; $x = s - r + q - p$; and $y = t - s + r - q$.

Proposition V

If

$$B^p A^3 + A^5 = Z^{ps}$$

and

$$B^p E^3 - E^5 = Z^{ps},$$

there are six continued proportionals the product of [the sum of] the extremes of which and the difference between the fourth and first is B^p. This makes Z^{ps} the product of the cube of the difference between the fourth and first and B^p plus the square[24] of the same difference or the product of the cube of the difference between the fifth and second and B^p minus the square[25] of the same difference between the fifth and second and, if the first is called the smaller of the extremes, A becomes the difference between the fourth and first and E the difference between the fifth and second.[26]

If the proportionals are 1, 2, 4, 8, 16 and 32,

$$231x^3 + x^5 = 96,040,$$

making x 7, and

$$231y^3 - y^5 = 96,040,$$

making y 14.

Proposition VI

If

$$B^s A^2 + A^5 = Z^{ps}$$

and

$$B^s E^2 - E^5 = Z^{ps},$$

there are six continued proportionals [the sum of] the extremes of which times the square of the difference between

---

[24] 1646 has "fifth power" here.
[25] 1646 has "fifth power" here.
[26] I.e., if $ax^3 + x^5 = N$ and $ay^3 - y^5 = N$ and p, q, r, s, t and u are continued proportionals, $a = (p + u)(s - p)$; $N = (s - p)^3[a + (s - p)^2]$ or $(t - q)^3[a - (t - q)^2]$; $x = s - p$; and $y = t - q$.

the third and first makes B^s. Z^{ps} is then the product of B^s plus the cube of the difference between the third and first times the square of the same difference or the product of B^s minus the cube of the difference between the second and fourth times the square of the difference between the second and fourth and, if the first is called the smaller of the extremes, A will be the third minus the first and E the fourth minus the second.[27]

If the proportionals are 1, 2, 4, 8, 16 and 32,

$$297x^2 + x^5 = 2,916,$$

making x 3, and

$$297y^2 - y^5 = 2,916,$$

making y 6.

CHAPTER XXI

Another Construction of Inverse Equations

PROPOSITION I

If

$$B^p A - A^3 = Z^s$$

and

$$E^3 - B^p E = Z^s,$$

there are three proportionals the sum of the squares of which is B^p and the sum of the extremes times the square of the mean or either of the extremes times the sum of the squares of the other two is Z^s. This makes A one or the other of the extremes and E their sum.[28]

---

[27] I.e., if $ax^2 + x^5 = N$ and $ay^2 - y^5 = N$ and p, q, r, s, t and u are continued proportionals, $a = (u + p)(r - p)^2$; $N = (r - p)^2[a + (r - p)^3]$ or $(s - q)^2[a - (s - q)^3]$; $x = r - p$; and $y = s - q$.

[28] I.e., if $ax - x^3 = N$ and $y^3 - ay = N$ and p, q and r are proportionals, $a = p^2 + q^2 + r^2$; $N = p(q^2 + r^2)$ or $r(p^2 + q^2)$; $x = p$ or r; and $y = p + r$.

If the proportionals are 1, 2 and 4,

$$21x - x^3 = 20,$$

making x 1 or 4, and

$$y^3 - 21y = 20,$$

making y 5.

PROPOSITION II

If

$$BA^2 - A^3 = Z^s$$

and

$$BE^2 + E^3 = Z^s,$$

there are three proportional roots the sum of which is B. The sum of the first two plus the sum of the last two times the square of the mean, or either of the extremes times the square of the sum of the other two, is Z^s. This makes A either of the aforesaid sums and E the mean between the extremes.[29]

If the proportionals are 1, 2 and 4,

$$7x^2 - x^3 = 36,$$

making x 3 or 6, and

$$7y^2 + y^3 = 36,$$

making y 2.

[29] I.e., if $ax^2 - x^3 = N$ and $ay^2 + y^3 = N$ and p, q and r are proportionals, then $a = p + q + r$; $N = [(p + q) + (q + r)]q^2$ or $p(q + r)^2$ or $r(p + q)^2$; $x = q + r$ or $p + q$; and $y = q$.

SECOND TREATISE: ON THE AMENDMENT OF EQUATIONS[1]
CHAPTER I

On the Five Usual Methods of Preparing Equations Against Difficulties[2] in Numerical Solution, and, First, on Purging by Fractions, the Remedy for a Multiplicity of Affections[3]

Having become acquainted with how equations are constructed, the analyst turns safely toward the preparation of those that would otherwise defy solution or would yield to it only with difficulty. By preparation he achieves ease of solution.[4] The general rule for preparation is that steps taken in setting up a new [equation] through the zetetic, plasmatic or syncritic processes are retraced. There is, in the end, no method of transformation that is not tried. The analyst does not lack particular and limited remedies against defects and impediments in equations in order to solve them either in real terms or numerically.[5] Nearly everything that is useful to the geometer for easy solution is also useful to the arithmetician, and vice versa. Geometrical constructions, however, will be discussed in their own proper place. Here it is more our intent [to deal with] numerical analysis.

There are precisely five usual individual methods of preparation, especially for numerical [solution]:

I. Purging by fractions[6]
II. First-last transformation[7]

[1]*De Emendatione Aequationum Tractatus Secundus.* Ritter (biog., pp. 57, 79) thinks that this work, which is not mentioned in 1591's outline of the contents of the *Opus Restitutae Mathematicae Analyseos,* is the same as the otherwise lost *Ad Logisticem Speciosam Notae Posteriores.*

[2]Δυσμήχανίαν

[3]πολυπάθειαν

[4]ἐυμήχαναƒ

[5]*sive re, sive numero.*

[6]*Expurgatio per uncias.* William Oughtred, in *The Key of the Mathematics New Forged and Filed* (London, 1647), p. 41, speaks of *unciae* as "numerall figures" prefixed to "intermediat species" and John Wallis, in his *Treatise of Algebra, both Historical and Practical* (London, 1675), p. 95, is even more explicit: "The Number prefixed to every one of the intermediate Species or Complements in each Power (which by him [Oughtred] are called Unciae, and serve to show how oft each of those Complements is to be taken). . . ." This, however, was not Viète's use of the term. The word *uncia* (whence the English "ounce" and "inch") originally meant one-twelfth. Viète, it is clear, generalized it to mean any fraction. See also p. 92 supra.

[7]*Transmutatio* πρῶτον ἔσχατον.

III. Anastrophe[8]

IIII. Freeing of fractions[9]

V. Completion of the power[10]

Purging by fractions is by far the most certain and most readily available remedy for a multiplicity of affections. It is a species of transformation by addition or subtraction. By it equations with an affection in the highest parodic grade—[the grade] that has a coefficient homogeneous with the root—can regularly be freed from this affection without destroying the rationality of the numbers.[11] In quadratics it is [a matter of adding or subtracting] half [the coefficient of the affection to or from the root], in cubics one-third, in biquadratics one-fourth, in quintics one-fifth, in sextics one-sixth, and so on in this order to infinity, since affections of this grade [i.e., the highest grade below the power] originate in an increment or decrement known to have affected the root from which or from a power (pure or affected) of which the original equation developed.

The coefficient of the linear term in the quadratics is twice this increment or decrement, the coefficient of the quadratic term in the cubics is three times it, the coefficient of the cubic term in the biquadratics is four times it, the coefficient of the quartic term in the quintics is five times it, the coefficient of the quintic term in the sextics is six times it, and so on in this same order to infinity.

In order to wipe out this plasmatic modification, agreed-upon fractions of the coefficients homogeneous with the root are chosen by the reverse route: In the squares, namely, one-half; in the cubes, one-third; in the biquadratics, one-fourth; in the quintics, one-fifth; in the sextics, one-sixth; and so on in the same order, and the root is affected by these agreed-upon fractions and a transformation made accordingly.

The structure of the whole operation admits of three different cases:

First, suppose a power of A is affected by the addition of a homogeneous term, the product of the coefficient B and the highest grade of A below the power. Since, then, the affection is positive, the root will be affected positively by an agreed-upon fraction of the coefficient B. Call [the root] thus affected E. Hence E minus the agreed-upon fraction of the coefficient B will be equal to A. The original equation is then restated and a new one set up in terms of the new symbol. This will be entirely free from any affection in the highest grade below the power, as carrying out the operation will prove.[12]

---

[8]Viète has borrowed this term from the language of grammar and rhetoric where it is used to mean an inversion of the natural order of two or more terms.

[9]*Isomoeria.*

[10]*Climactica paraplerosis.*

[11]*salva numerorum Symmetria.*

[12]*ut opus comprobabit.*

Second, suppose a power of A is affected by the subtraction of a homogeneous term, the product of the coefficient B and the highest grade of A below the power. Since the affection is negative, [the root] A will be affected negatively by a proper fraction of the coefficient B. Call [the root] thus affected E. Hence E plus the agreed-upon fraction of the coefficient B will be equal to A. The original equation is then restated and a new one set up in terms of the new symbol. This will be entirely free from affection in the highest grade below the power, as carrying out the operation will prove.

Finally, suppose a homogeneous term that is the product of the coefficient B and the highest grade of A below its power is affected by the subtraction of the power of A. Since, therefore, the power affects rather than being affected, seeing that it is subtracted from the homogeneous term of affection, the agreed-upon fraction of B, the coefficient, minus A,[13] will be set up as E, whence the same fraction of B minus the root E will equal A. The original equation is then restated and a new one set up in terms of the new symbol. This will be entirely free from affection in the highest grade below the power, as carrying out the operation will prove.

Quadratic Example

Let

$$A^2 + 2BA = Z^p.$$

Since, then, the root is next below the square on the scale of magnitudes and the given square has a linear affection, the equation has been constructed entirely by plasmatic modification—i.e., from another source. The affection, moreover, is positive and thus the modification occurred by the addition of one-half the coefficient of the linear term, as the nature of the square, a power of duplicate ratio,[14] demands.

To overcome the modification, therefore, purge by one-half [the coefficient]: Let $A + B$ be E, whence $E - B$ will be A. Consequently the square of $E - B$ plus the product of $2B$ and $E - B$ will equal Z^p in accordance with what was given. An equation in E will be set up according to the art and, all steps having been properly taken,

$$E^2 = Z^p + B^2,$$

which new equation is free from the linear affection that burdened the given one. Moreover, when E becomes known, A cannot be unknown, since

---

[13]The text has "the power of A."

[14]1615 has *quae Potestas est rationis duplicitatae;* 1646 has *quae potestas est rationis duplicatae.*

the difference between the two roots is given and E is greater than A by the length B. Therefore that has been done that was to be done.

Cubic Example

Let

$$A^3 + 3BA^2 + D^pA = Z^s.$$

Since, then, the square comes immediately below the cube on the scale of magnitudes, and a cube affected by a square has been proposed, the equation has been constructed entirely by plasmatic modification—i.e., from another source. The affection, moreover, is positive, so the modification has been the addition of one-third the coefficient of B, as the nature of the cube, a power of triplicate ratio, demands. To overcome the modification, therefore, purge by one-third [the coefficient]: Let $A + B$ be E, whence $E - B$ will be A, and consequently the cube of $E - B$ plus the product of $3B$ and the square of $E - B$ plus the product of D^p and $E - B$ will equal Z^s in accordance with what was given. Let an equation in E then be set up according to the art and, all steps having been properly taken,

$$E^3 + E(D^p - 3B^2) = Z^s + D^pB - 2B^3,$$

which new equation is clearly free from the quadratic affection that burdened the original one. When, moreover, E becomes known, A will not be unknown, there being a given difference between the two roots, for E is greater than A by the length B. So that has been done that was to be done.

If a given equation is one of a power affected directly by a negative, as in

$$A^2 - 2BA = Z^p$$

or

$$A^3 - 3BA^2 = Z^s,$$

let $A - B$ be E and set up an equation in E by following the prescribed steps.

If, finally, the equation proposed is one of a power affected by an inverse negative, as in

$$2BA - A^2 = Z^p$$

or

$$3BA^2 - A^3 = Z^s,$$

let $B - A$ be E and, as before, set up an equation in E by following the prescribed steps.

Thus all affected squares can be reduced to pure squares; all affected cubes, without exception, to cubes with only a linear affection; all affected fourth powers, without exception, to fourth powers with only linear and quadratic affections; all affected fifth powers, without exception, to fifth powers with only linear, quadratic and cubic affections; and so on in the same order.

The ancients believed that since quadratic equations could be entirely purged [of affection] by such a reduction as this and easily solved, the higher powers could also be completely purged, and they tried to derive from the standard resolution of pure powers a wholly mechanical operation [for doing so] and were so obstinate about it that they did not inquire into any other method for solving affected equations. Thus they tortured themselves hopelessly and spent many good hours at the expense of the mathematics they were cultivating. In sum this method of solving affected quadratic equations is not universal, although the method of purging equations of a single affection, without destroying the rationality of the numbers, but not of all affections, is universal, so we must not stick to the steadfast opinion of our predecessors.[15]

It is delightful that individual theorems can be derived from the individual formulas for reductions of this sort and put to use. Such are the following:

Three Formulae for the Reduction of Affected Quadratics to Pure

I

If

$$A^2 + 2BA = Z^p,$$

let $A + B$ be E. Then

$$E^2 = Z^p + B^2.$$

Corollary

Hence A, the original unknown, is $\sqrt{Z^p + B^2} - B$. Let B be 1, Z^p 20 and A x:

$$x^2 + 2x = 20,$$

making x equal to $\sqrt{21} - 1$.

---

[15]*ut deinceps veterum pertinaciae non sit inhaerendum.*

II

If

$$A^2 - 2BA = Z^p,$$

let $A - B$ be E. Then

$$E^2 = Z^p + B^2.$$

Corollary

Consequently A, the original unknown, is $\sqrt{Z^p + B^2} + B$. Let B be 1, Z^p 20 and A x:

$$x^2 - 2x = 20,$$

making x equal to $\sqrt{21} + 1$.

III

If

$$2DA - A^2 = Z^p,$$

let $D + E$ or $D - E$ be A. Then

$$E^2 = D^2 - Z^p.$$

Corollary

Consequently A, the original unknown, is $D \pm \sqrt{D^2 - Z^p}$. Let D be 5, Z^p 20 and A x:

$$10x - x^2 = 20,$$

making x equal to $5 - \sqrt{5}$ or $5 + \sqrt{5}$.

Three Formulae for the Reduction of Cubes Affected only by a Square to Cubes Affected only by a First Power.

I

If

$$A^3 + 3BA^2 = Z^s,$$

let $A + B$ be E. Then

$$E^3 - 3B^2E = Z^s - 2B^3.$$

$$x^3 + 6x^2 = 1600 \qquad y^3 - 12y = 1584$$
$$x = 10 \qquad\qquad y = 12$$

Let a sign arithmetically compatible with the terms of the altered root be applied to the difference between the terms of the root first sought.[16]

II

If

$$A^3 - 3BA^2 = Z^s,$$

let $A - B$ be E. Then

$$E^3 - 3B^2E = Z^s + 2B^3.$$

$$x^3 - 6x^2 = 400 \qquad y^3 - 12y = 416$$
$$x = 10 \qquad\qquad y = 8$$

III

If

$$3BA^2 - A^3 = Z^s,$$

let $A - B$ be E. Then

$$3B^2E - E^3 = Z^s - 2B^3.$$

Or let $B - A$ be E. Then

$$3B^2E - E^3 = 2B^3 - Z^s.$$

$$21x^2 - x^3 = 972 \qquad 147y - y^3 = 286$$
$$x = 9 \text{ or } 18 \qquad y = 2 \text{ or } 11$$
$$9x^2 - x^3 = 28 \qquad 27y - y^3 = 26$$
$$x = 2 \qquad\qquad y = 1$$

---

[16] *Ad Arithmetica non incongrue σημεῖον aliquod superimponitur notis alteratae radicis, ad differentiam notarum ejus, de qua primum quaerebatur.* This passage makes little sense either in English or in Latin, and I am far from certain that I have captured Viète's thought accurately.

Seven Formulae for the Reduction of Cubes with both Quadratic and Linear Affections to Cubes with only a Linear Affection

I

If

$$A^3 + 3BA^2 + D^pA = Z^s,$$

let $A + B$ be E. Then

$$E^3 + \mathrm{E}(D^p - 3B^2) = Z^s + D^pB - 2B^3.$$

$x^3 + 30x^2 + 330x = 788$	$y^3 + 30y = 2088$
$x = 2$	$y = 12$
$x^3 + 24x^2 + 132x = 368$	$y^3 - 60y = 400$
$x = 2$	$y = 10$
$x^3 + 30x^2 + 4x = 1320$	$296y - y^3 = 640$
$x = 6$	$y = 16$

II

If

$$A^3 + 3BA^2 - D^pA = Z^s,$$

let $A + B$ be E. Then

$$E^3 \; [+] \; E(-3B^2 - D^p) = Z^s - 2B^3 - D^pB.$$

$x^3 + 6x^2 - 48x = 512$	$y^3 - 60y = 400$
$x = 8$	$y = 10$
$x^3 + 30x^2 - 48x = 32$	$348y - y^3 = 2448$
$x = 2$	$y = 12$

III

If

$$A^3 - 3BA^2 + D^pA = Z^s,{}^{17}$$

<hr>

[17] 1615 has Z^p.

let $A - B$ be E. Then

$$E^3 [+] E(-3B^2 + D^p) = Z^s + 2B^3 - D^pB.$$

$x^3 - 30x^2 + 330x = 1368$	$y^3 + 30y = 68$
$x = 12$	$y = 2.$
$x^3 - 12x^2 + 28x = 80$	$y^3 - 20y = 96$
$x = 10$	$y = 6$
$x^3 - 18x^2 + 88x = 80$	$20y - y^3 = 16$
$x = 10$	$y = 4$

Or let $B - A$ be E. Then

$$E(3B^2 - D^p) - E^3 = Z^s + 2B^3 - D^pB.$$

$x^3 - 30x^2 + 200x = 336$	$100y - y^3 = 336$
$x = 6$	$y = 4$
$x^3 - 30x^2 + 280x = 704$	$y^3 - 20y = 96$
$x = 4$	$y = 6$
$x^3 - 30x^2 + 330x = 1232$	$y^3 + 30y = 68$
$x = 8$	$y = 2$

IIII

If

$$A^3 - 3BA^2 - D^pA = Z^s,$$

let $A - B$ be E. Then

$$E^3 [+] E(-3B^2 - D^p) = Z^s + 2B^3 + D^pB.$$

$x^3 - 6x^2 - 28x = 120$	$y^3 - 40y = 192$
$x = 10$	$y = 8$

V

If

$$D^pA - 3BA^2 - A^3 = Z^s,$$

let $A + B$ be E. Then

$$E(D^p + 3B^2) - E^3 = Z^s + 2B^3 + D^pB.$$

$100x - 30x^2 - x^3 = 72$	$400y - y^3 = 3072$
$x = 2$	$y = 12$

VI

If

$$3BA^2 + D^pA - A^3 = Z^s,$$

let $A - B$ be E. Then

$$E(D^p + 3B^2) - E^3 = Z^s - D^pB - 2B^3.$$

$$18x^2 + 92x - x^3 = 1720 \qquad\qquad 200y - y^3 = 736$$
$$x = 10 \qquad\qquad\qquad y = 4$$

Or let $B - A$ be E. Then

$$E(D^p + 3B^2) - E^3 = 2B^3 + D^pB - Z^s.$$

$$30x^2 + 100x - x^3 = 1464 \qquad\qquad 400y - y^3 = 1536$$
$$x = 6 \qquad\qquad\qquad y = 4$$

VII

If

$$3BA^2 - D^pA - A^3 = Z^s,$$

let $A - B$ be E. Then

$$E(3B^2 - D^p) - E^3 = Z^s + D^pB - 2B^3.$$

$$18x^2 - 78x - x^3 = 20 \qquad\qquad 30y^{18} - y^3 = 56$$
$$x = 10 \qquad\qquad\qquad y = 4$$
$$12x^2 - 18x - x^3 = 20 \qquad\qquad y^3 - 30y = 36$$
$$x = 10 \qquad\qquad\qquad y = 6$$

Or let $B - A$ be E. Then

$$E(3B^2 - D^p) - E^3 = 2B^3 - D^pB - Z^s.$$

$$30x^2 - 100x - x^3 = 264 \qquad\qquad 200y - y^3 = 736$$
$$x = 6 \qquad\qquad\qquad y = 4$$

As equations can be freed from an affection in the grade immediately below the power by purging with these simple fractions, so they can sometimes be freed from lower-order affections by triangular and pyramidal fractions and fractions composed from these, treating the coefficient of

---

[18]1615 has $30y^2$.

the lower-order term as [though it were] a power and taking such a fraction of its root as is required by the rule[19] for the development of pure powers from a binomial root. For just as the coefficients homogeneous to the root that is being sought are determined by simple fractions, so coefficients homogeneous to the square of the root are determined by triangular fractions, those homogeneous to the cube of the root by pyramidal fractions, and so on in this order.

If A^3 is affected by AB^2, this leads to expurgation by one-third of B. If A^4 is affected by A^2B^2, this leads to the expurgation of this affection by one-sixth of B. And if A^5 is affected by A^3B^2, this leads to expurgation by one-tenth of B, for the triangular numbers are 3, 6, 10, 15.

If A^4 is affected by AB^3, this leads to expurgation of this affection by one-fourth of B. And if A^5 is affected by A^2B^3, this leads to expurgation by one-tenth of B, for the pyramidal numbers are 4, 10, 20, 35.

How this can be extended to higher powers is sufficiently clear. Purging by triangular fractions, pyramidal fractions, and others composed from these is worthwhile [for], as long as a proposed equation [has] an affection from which it should be freed, it is burdened down. Individual affections in the remaining grades take the place of the affection that is removed.

CHAPTER II

On First-Last Transformation, the Remedy for the Defect of a Negative

Equations in which the power has a very strong homogeneous term of affection subtracted from it may usefully be amended by a first-last transformation. This is done by means of a proportion with an implicit ratio, [that is] by dividing the homogeneous term of comparison by the unknown root. From this arises another unknown root in terms of which the original equation is restated and a new one set up.

By this means what were negative affections turn into positive affections and vice versa, without destroying the rationality of the numbers. [This method] is also sometimes of benefit in irrational cases.

The name "first-last" comes from the proportion into which the given equation is converted, since under this formula the term that was first

[19]*dicta.*

sought is the first term [of the proportion] and that which is the first after metamorphosis becomes the last term [of the proportion] or contrariwise, all of which will be easily seen from the formula for the operation.

Let

$$A^3 - B^p A = Z^s.$$

This equation is to be solved. Since Z^s is a power with a negative affection, [and] the art is not built on negatives,[20] the original equation should be transformed into one that is explicable, one [that is] that has a positive affection. Therefore let Z^s/A equal E^p. Hence Z^s/E^p equals A and, in accordance with what has been proposed,

$$\frac{Z^{sss}}{E^{ppp}} - \frac{B^p Z^s}{E^p} = Z^s$$

and, multiplying everything by E^{ppp},

$$Z^{sss} - B^p Z^s E^{pp} = Z^s E^{ppp}.$$

Then dividing through by Z^s and performing the proper transposition,

$$E^{ppp} + B^p E^{pp} = Z^{ss}$$

or

$$(E^p)^3 + B^p(E^p)^2 = (Z^s)^2.$$

This equation is entirely explicable by the usual analysis of cubic powers positively affected by [a lower term and] a given coefficient. E^p will therefore be found and, when it is divided into Z^s, will give rise to A, the original unknown.

The proportion disclosed by the equation in A was that A is to $\sqrt[3]{Z^s}$ as $\sqrt[3]{Z^{ss}}$ is to $A^2 - B^p$, that is to E^p, whence comes the name of "first-last."

Let

$$x^3 - 96x = 40$$

and let the construct $40/x$ be y. Then

$$y^3 + 96y^2 = 1600,$$

making y 4. Therefore $40/4$ or 10 is the first unknown.

And if it happens that in a given cubic equation the homogeneous term of comparison is irrational in a solid state but would be rational if squared, its irrationality will vanish in the new equation.

----

[20]*de negatis autem ars non statuitur.*

Let

$$x^3 - 10x = \sqrt{48},$$

and let the construct $\sqrt{48}/x$ be y. Then

$$y^3 + 10y^2 = 48,$$

making y 2. Therefore $\sqrt{48}/2$ or $\sqrt{12}$ is the root first sought.
    Again, let

$$A^4 - BA^3 - D^pA^2 = Z^{pp},$$

and let this be an equation to be solved.

Since, therefore, Z^{pp} is a power affected negatively, and the art is not built on negatives, the original equation should be transformed into one that is explicable, one [that is] that has a positive affection.[21] Therefore let Z^{pp}/A be E^s, wherefore Z^{pp}/E^s will be A. Thus, from what has been proposed

$$\frac{Z^{ppppppp}}{E^{ssss}} - \frac{BZ^{pppppp}}{E^{sss}} - \frac{D^pZ^{pppp}}{E^{ss}} = Z^{pp}.$$

Multiply through by E^{ssss}, and

$$Z^{ppppppp} - BZ^{pppppp}E^s - D^pZ^{pppp}E^{ss} = Z^{pp}E^{ssss}$$

and, dividing through by Z^{pp} and transposing,

$$(E^s)^4 + D^pZ^{pp}(E^s)^{2\ [22]} + BZ^{pppp}E^s = (Z^{pp})^3.$$

Let

$$x^4 - 3x^3 - 8x^2 = 50$$

and let the construct $50/x$ be y. Then

$$y^4 + 400y^2 + 7500y = 125,000,$$

making y 10, wherefore $50/10$ or 5 will be the root first sought.
    And if it happens that in a original biquadratic equation the homogeneous term of comparison is irrational in a plano-plane state but would be rational if cubed, the irrationality will vanish in the new equation.
    Let

$$x^4 - 8x = \sqrt[3]{80}$$

---

[21]"one [that is] . . . affection," which does not appear in 1615, was added in 1646.
[22]1615 has $-D^pZ^{pp}(E^s)^2$.

and let the construct $\sqrt[3]{80}/x$ be y. Then

$$y^4 + 8y^3 = 80,$$

making y equal to 2, wherefore $\sqrt[3]{80}/2$ or $\sqrt[3]{10}$ is the root first sought.

While the operations involved in a first-last transformation are completely set out in these [examples], the [following] observations should be remembered and followed:

I

In affected quadratics, the homogeneous term of comparison remains unchanged, in cubics its square is taken, in biquadratics its cube, in quintics its fourth power, in sextics its fifth power, and so on.

II

Negative affecting homogeneous terms in the [lower] grades are transposed into complementary positive affecting homogeneous terms and, vice versa, positive affections are transformed into negative affections.

III

The coefficient of a linear affection remains unchanged, the coefficient of a quadratic affection is multiplied by the homogeneous term of comparison, the coefficient of a cubic equation is multiplied by the square of the homogeneous term of comparison, the coefficient of a quartic equation is multiplied by the cube of the homogeneous term of comparison, the coefficient of a quintic equation is multiplied by the fourth power of the homogeneous term of comparison, and so on.

IIII

When the homogeneous term of comparison of a given equation is divided by the known root of the newly equated power, it yields the original root that was to be found.

Clearly whatever magnitude is divided by the newly discovered root is such that this division will give rise to the root that was first sought if the given equation has been reconstituted in those terms and transformed in accordance with the art. Affections that were negative always become affirmative without disturbing the rationality of the numbers. But in arithmetic [problems], it is very convenient to divide the homogeneous term of comparison lest the accident of a fraction should require a second reduction, while in geometric [problems] it is better to divide a magnitude homogeneous with the square of the unknown root.

Let

$$A^3 - BA^2 = BZ^2$$

and let BZ/E be A. Then

$$E^3 + B^2E = B^2Z.$$

CHAPTER III

On Anastrophe, or How, as Against the Defect of Ambiguity,[23] Knowledge of a Root Given by One Correlative Equation May Be Had from That of the Other.

Anastrophe is the transformation of inverse negative equations into their correlatives. It is carried out so that the original equation, with the help of its correlative, can be reduced through irregular climactic descent to a lower [power] and, therefore, be more easily solved. It is useful, as we have said, for escaping from ambiguity and difficulty of solution in [certain] equations with inverse negatives—cubics, quintics, and so on in the alternate higher powers. Since anastrophe is not undertaken for the reduction of quadratics, biquadratics and the other alternate higher powers, recourse must be had to completion of the power, of which we will speak in the proper place.

The work of anastrophe is performed this way: First, to the power of the unknown root the equally high power of [another] root is added. The sum of [two] powers in the aforesaid order of powers can easily be divided. Then the homogeneous term of comparison plus the transposed homogeneous terms of affection and the added power is equated to the term [first] created—[i.e., the one] that admits of division. This creates a correlative equation, either positive or directly negative. Knowing the root of the added term, terms arise on one side that can easily be compared with those of the other side, and the equation, otherwise soluble only with difficulty, can be

[23]The text has *adversus vocum* Ἀμφιβολίας, but I think *vocum* is a misprint from *vicium,* the word used at the corresponding place in the captions of the preceding and succeeding chapters.

depressed to one that is easily solved by means of a pretty operation, as is made clear by the examples.

First, on Anastrophe in Cubics

Problem I

Let

$$B^p A - A^3 = Z^s.$$

Since the cube is subtracted from a solid, the equation has two roots and is not fit for resolution. Its ambiguity and difficulty of solution need to be overcome. Hence anastrophe is called for and, to this end, a transposition of the given terms is employed:

$$A^3 = B^p A - Z^s.$$

Add E^3 to both sides. Hence

$$A^3 + E^3 = B^p A + E^3 - Z^s.$$

The first member of the equation can now be easily divided by $A + E$. When the sum of the roots is divided into the sum of the cubes, the result is the sum of the squares minus their product. Therefore this division yields $A^2 - EA + E^2$. It is necessary now that the other member of the equation, when divided by $A + E$, yield a plane that can be compared to the first quotient. This can be accomplished readily. If $B^p E$ is substituted for $E^3 - Z^s$, B^p will be born. [Since the two] are equivalent, let it be substituted.[24] So

$$A^2 - EA + E^2 = B^p.\text{[25]}$$

Since by hypothesis

$$E^3 - Z^s = B^p E,$$

therefore, by transposition,

$$E^3 - B^p E = Z^s.$$

Thus

$$A^2 - EA + E^2 = BP$$

---

[24] *Aequivaleat igitur ut substituatur.*

[25] In the text this sentence occurs after the one that here follows it. I have transposed them for the sake of clarity.

By resolution, then, assisted by proper preparation in accordance with the preceding chapter, E becomes known. Suppose it is D. Then

$$A^2 - AD + D^2 = B^p$$

and, transposing,

$$DA - A^2 = D^2 - B^p.$$

So an inverse negative equation has been transformed into [one] of the same order with a direct negative and, given the root of the new equation, an irregular climactic descent has been made into a lower [power] that is solvable by the root first proposed. This is the work called anastrophe and is what was to be done. Hence we have

Theorem I

If

$$B^p A - A^3 = Z^s,$$

then

$$E^3 - B^{pe} = Z^s.$$

E, however, becomes known to be D and, therefore,

$$DA - A^2 = D^2 - B^p.$$
$$39x - x^3 = 70,$$

wherefore

$$y^3 - 39y = 70,$$

making y 7. So

$$7x - x^2 = 10$$

and the root of this, 2 or 5, is the root that was first sought.

Problem II

Let

$$BA^2 - A^3 = Z^s.$$

An anastrophe is to be performed.

From the given terms, with the help of a proper transposition,

$$A^3 = BA^2 - Z^s$$

and, adding E^3 to both sides,

$$A^3 + E^3 = BA^2 + E^3 - Z^s.$$

But certainly

$$Z^s - E^3 = BE^2$$

or

$$E^3 + BE^2 = Z^s$$

and

$$A^3 + E^3 = BA^2 - BE^2.$$

Consequently a solid affected by the addition of a cube is to be reduced. Dividing, therefore, by $A + E$,

$$A^2 - EA + E^2 = B(A - E).$$

E, however, becomes known to be D by resolution and therefore a quadratic equation is set up. Hence

$$BA + DA - A^2 = D^2 + BD.$$

Therefore an equation with an inverse negative has been transformed into one of the same order that is positive and, given the root of the new equation, an irregular descent has been made into a lower power. This is the operation called anastrophe and is what was to be done. Hence arises

Theorem II

If

$$BA^2 - A^3 = Z^s$$

and

$$E^3 + BE^2 = Z^{s\ \textbf{26}}$$

and it becomes known that E is D, then

$$A(D + B) - A^2 = BD + D^2.$$

[If]

$$7x^2 - x^3 = 36,$$

---

26 1615, as "corrected" in the errata, has $BE^2 - E^3 = Z^s$, a change from $BE^2 + A^3 = Z^s$ on the original page.

then

$$7y^2 + y^3 = 36,$$

making y 2. Therefore

$$9x - x^2 = 18$$

and x, the first unknown, is 3 or 6.

Second, on Anastrophe in Quintics

PROBLEM III

Let

$$B^{pp}A - A^5 = Z^{ps}.$$

An anastrophe is to be performed.

Construct the fourth power of $E - A$. The individual plano-planes, simply stated and taken once each, are $E^4 - AE^3 + A^2E^2 - A^3E + A^4$. Multiplied by $E + A$, you have $E^5 + A^5$.

From the terms proposed,

$$A^5 = B^{pp}A - Z^{ps}.$$

Therefore

$$E^5 + A^5 = E^5 + B^{pp}A - Z^{ps}.$$

Divide both sides by $E + A$. From the first side of the equation there will arise $E^4 - AE^3 + A^2E^2 - A^3E + A^4$, as the rationale of its composition shows.

It does not appear what the quotient on the second side will be, but clearly it was compared to a plano-solid, so it is known that it will be a plano-plane. Therefore let $B^{pp}E + B^{pp}A$ equal the other side, $E^5 + B^{pp}A - Z^{ps}$. Then, deleting the two affections on the grade of A and making the proper transposition,

$$E^5 - B^{pp}E = Z^{ps}.$$

If E becomes known to be D, we will say that

$$D^4 - D^3A + D^2A^2 - DA^3 + A^4 = B^{pp}$$

and, having restated the equation in accordance with the art, that

$$D^3A - D^2A^2 + DA^3 - A^4 = D^4 - B^{pp}$$

Thus an anastrophe has been performed as ordered. Hence arises

Theorem III

If

$$B^{pp}A - A^5 = Z^{ps}$$

and

$$E^5 - B^{pp}E = Z^{ps}$$

and, furthermore, it becomes known that E is D, then

$$D^3A - D^2A^2 + DA^3 - A^4 = D^4 - B^{pp}.$$

[If]

$$11x - x^5 = 10,$$

then

$$y^5 - 11y = 10$$

and y is 2. Hence

$$8x - 4x^2 + 2x^3 - x^4 = 5$$

and x, the root first sought for, is 1.

PROBLEM IIII

Let

$$BA^4 - A^5 = Z^{ps}.$$

An anastrophe has again to be performed.[27]
By a proper transposition and a common addition of E^5,

$$A^5 + E^5 = BA^4 - Z^{ps} + E^5.$$

Divide both sides by $A + E$ and there arises [on one side] $E^4 - AE^3 + A^2E^2 - A^3E + A^4$. If $BA^4 - BE^4$ is equated to the other side, it will also be divisible by $A + E$. The quotient is $BA^3 - BA^2E + BE^2A - BE^3$. Thus let there be such an equation and by it, when it is properly set up,

$$E^5 + BE^4 = Z^{ps}.$$

[If] it becomes known that E is D, then

$$D^4 - D^3A + D^2A^2 - DA^3 + A^4 = BA^3 - BA^2D + BD^2A - BD^3$$

---

[27]This sentence does not occur in 1615.

and, reordering all terms properly,

$$BD^2A + D^3A - BDA^2 - D^2A^2 + BA^3 + DA^3 - A^4 = BD^3 + D^4.$$

Thus an anastrophe has been performed as ordered. Hence arises

Theorem IIII

If

$$BA^4 - A^5 = Z^{ps}$$

and

$$E^5 + BE^4 = Z^{ps}$$

and if, furthermore, it becomes known that E equals D,

$$A(BD^2 + D^3) [+] A^2(-BD - D^2) + A^3(B + D) - A^4$$
$$= BD^3 + D^4$$

$$11x^4 - x^5 = 10,000$$
$$11y^4 + y^5 = 10,000,$$

making y 5. Therefore

$$400x - 80x^2 + 16x^3 - x^4 = 2,000$$

and x, the root that was first sought, is 10.

Anastrophe is also sometimes useful in the reverse way, as when in an ambiguous equation it happens that one out of the two or more roots by which the equation can be solved is given. The steps of the inversion process are retraced in order to find the root of the correlative. Various theorems that flow from this, like these in cubics, are set out:

Theorem V

If

$$A^3 - B^pA = Z^s$$

and again if

$$B^pE - E^3 = Z^s$$

and it becomes known that E is D,

$$A^2 - DA = B^p - D^2.$$

Since

$$A^3 - B^p A = Z^s,$$

and again

$$B^p D - D^3 = Z^s,$$

therefore

$$A^3 - B^p A = B^p D - D^3$$

and, by transposition,

$$A^3 + D^3 = B^p A + B^p D.$$

Divide both sides of the equation by $A + D$, making

$$A^2 + D^2 - DA = B^p$$

and, setting up the equation in accordance with the art,

$$A^2 - DA = B^p - D^2,$$

as was proposed.

If

$$x^3 - 8x = 7,$$

then

$$8y - y^3 = 7$$

and, since y can be 1, x^2/y will equal 7, whence the root first sought will be $\sqrt{29/4} + 1/2$.

Theorem VI

If

$$BA^2 + A^3 = Z^s$$

and if again

$$BE^2 - E^3 = Z^s$$

and it becomes known that E is D, then

$$A^2 + A(B - D) = BD - D^2.$$

Since

$$BA^2 + A^3 = Z^s$$

and again

$$BD^2 - D^3 = Z^s,$$

therefore

$$BA^2 + A^3 = BD^2 - D^3$$

and, by transposition,

$$D^3 + A^3 = B(D^2 - A^2).$$

Divide, therefore, both sides of the equation by $D + A$, making

$$D^2 + A^2 - DA = B(D - A),$$

which equation, properly set up according to the art, [is]

$$A^2 + A(B - D) = BD - D^2,$$

as was prescribed.

If

$$9x^2 + x^3 = 8,$$

therefore

$$9y^2 - y^3 = 8$$

and, since y can be 1,

$$x^2 + 8x = 8,$$

whence the first root sought becomes $\sqrt{24} - 4$.

The following theorems are closely related to these. From them, given one of the ambiguous roots, knowledge of the other may be had, viz.,

Theorem VII

If

$$B^pA - A^3 = Z^s$$

and if again

$$B^pE - E^3 = Z^s$$

and it becomes known that E is D,

$$A^2 + DA = B^p - D^2.$$

Since

$$B^p A - A^3 = Z^s$$

and again

$$B^p D - D^3 = Z^s,$$

therefore

$$B^p A - A^3 = B^p D - D^3$$

and, by transposition,

$$A^3 - D^3 = B^p A - B^p D.$$

Then, dividing both sides of the equation by $A - D$,

$$A^2 + D^2 + DA = B^p.$$

This equation being set up in accordance with the art,

$$A^2 + DA = B^p - D^2.$$

If

$$8x - x^3 = 7,$$

x may be 1. Therefore

$$x^2 + x = 7.$$

X is again $\sqrt{29/4} - 1/2$.

Theorem VIII

If

$$BA^2 - A^3 = Z^s$$

and again if

$$BE^2 - E^3 = Z^s$$

and it becomes known that E is D, then

$$A^2 + A(D - B) = BD - D^2.$$

Since

$$BA^2 - A^3 = Z^s$$

and

$$BD^2 - D^3 = Z^s,$$

therefore

$$BA^2 - A^3 = BD^2 - D^3$$

and, by transposition,

$$A^3 - D^3 = B(A^2 - D^2).$$

Dividing both sides by $A - D$,

$$A^2 + D^2 + DA = BA + BD,$$

Putting this in the form of a proper equation,

$$A^2 + DA - BA = BD - D^2,$$

as was proposed.

If

$$9x^2 - x^3 = 8,$$

x may be 1. Therefore

$$x^2 - 8x = 8.$$

X may also be $\sqrt{24} + 4$.[28]

CHAPTER IIII

On Isomeria [as a Remedy] for the Defect of a Fraction

Isomeria is a species of transformation by multiplication carried out in order to free equations from any fractions by which they may be burdened.

The fractions are [first] reduced to a common denominator by the rules of logistic. Then the given coefficients and constant are multiplied by the common denominator or its various grades—linear coefficients by its first power, plane coefficients and the constant, if it is a plane, by its square, solid coefficients and the constant, if it is a cube, by its cube, and so on in this order. The product of the common denominator and the root of the given equation is the root of the equation thus constructed.

It sometimes happens that what is called for is isomeric division, not

---

[28]1615 has $\sqrt{24} - 4$.

isomeric multiplication. [If so], linear coefficients are divided by the first power [of a common denominator], plane coefficients [by its square], [solid coefficients] and solid constants by its cube, and so on in this order.[29] The quotient arising from dividing the root [of the given equation] by the common denominator is the root of the equation so constructed.

[This process] is founded on and demonstrated by the rule for equations telling us that if equals are multiplied or divided by equals the products or quotients are equal.

In sum, there is nothing to be done in isomeria except to multiply or divide the power of a given equation and its homogeneous terms of affection and comparison by the same term [or one of its powers]. The usefulness of multiplication is clearer than that of division.

Suppose

$$A^3 \frac{B^s A^{30}}{D} = Z^s.$$

The equation is to be cleared of the fraction by which it is burdened. Let DA be E^p. Then E^p/D will be A. Hence

$$\frac{(E^p)^3 + B^s DE^p}{D^3} = Z^s.$$

[Multiply] through by D^3 and

$$(E^p)^3 + B^s DE^p = Z^s D^3.$$

If

$$x^3 + \frac{3}{2}x = 225,$$

then, by isomeria,[31]

$$y^3 + 6y = 1800,$$

and the root of the prepared equation will be to the root of the given equation as 2 is to 1. In the latter equation it will be 12 and in the former 6.

And if

$$A^3 + \frac{B^s A}{D} = \frac{Z^{pp}}{D},$$

[29]*applicantur vidilicet coefficientes longitudines ad radices coefficientis planae, homo-geneaeque datae mensurae solidae ad cubos, & eo constanti ordine.*

[30]1615 has $D^s A/D$.

[31]$\kappa\alpha\tau$ ἰσομοίρίαν. So also in many of the examples that follow.

taking the same steps,

$$(E^p)^3 + B^s DE^p = Z^{pp} D^2.$$

If

$$x^3 + \frac{3}{2}x = \frac{265}{2},$$

then, by isomeria,

$$y^3 + 6y = 1060$$

and, since the root of the latter is 10, it will be 5 in the former.
　　And if

$$A^3 + \frac{B^p A^2}{D} = Z^s,$$

by the same steps,

$$(E^p)^3 + B^p (E^p)^2 = Z^s D^3.$$

If

$$x^3 + \frac{3}{2}x^2 = 270,$$

then, by isomeria,

$$y^3 + 3y^2 = 2160$$

and, since the root in the latter is 12, it will be 6 in the former.
　　And if

$$A^3 + \frac{B^p A^2}{D} = \frac{Z^{pp}}{D},$$

by the same steps

$$(E^p)^3 + B^p (E^p)^2 = Z^{pp} D^2.$$

If

$$x^3 + \frac{3}{2}x^2 = \frac{325}{2},$$

then, by isomeria,

$$y^3 + 3y^2 = 1300$$

and, since the root in the latter is 10, it will be 5 in the former.

But if

$$A^3 + \frac{B^s A}{D} = \frac{Z^{ps}}{H^p},$$

let $DH^p A$ be E^{pp} and E^{pp}/DH^p will equal A. Therefore

$$(E^{pp})^3 = \frac{DH^{pp} B^s E^{pp}}{D^3 H^{ppp}} = \frac{Z^{ps}}{H^p}.$$

[Multiply] through by $D^3 H^{ppp}$ [32] and

$$(E^{pp})^3 + B^s DH^{pp} E^{pp} = Z^{ps} D^3 H^{pp}.$$

If

$$x^3 + \frac{11}{12} x = \frac{19}{4}$$

then, by isomeria,

$$y^3 + 2112y = 525,312$$

and [the ratio of] the root of the prepared equation to that of the given is 48 to 1. Since, then, the root is 72 in the latter, it will be $3/2$ in the former.

This could also have been reduced to the same fraction:

$$x^3 + \frac{11}{12}x = \frac{57}{12},$$

whence, by isomeric operation,

$$y^3 + 132y = 8208$$

and [the ratio of] the root of the prepared [equation] to that of the given would be 12 to 1. Since it is 18 in the latter, it will be $3/2$ in the former. This is arrived at by dividing the first prepared equation isomerically by 4, [for if]

$$x^3 + 2112x = 525,312,$$

then by isomeric division,

$$y^3 + \frac{2112}{16} y = \frac{525,312}{64}$$

which is

$$y^3 + 132y = 8208.$$

[32]1615 has $D^3 H^{pp}$.

Since the root of the first is 72, it will be 18 in the last, the isomeric divisor[33] being 4.

The work of isomeric division can be made evident thus: Suppose

$$(E^p)^3 + GD(E^p)^2 + B^pD^2E^p = Z^sD^3$$

and let E^p/D be A. Therefore E^p will be DA. Hence

$$D^3A^3 + GD(D^2A^2) + B^pD^2 (DA) = Z^sD^3.$$

Dividing all terms by D^3,

$$A^3 + GA^2 + B^pA = Z^s.$$

If

$$x^3 + 12x^2 + 8x = 2280,$$

making x 10, divide all terms isomerically by 2 and the proper powers[34] of this root:

$$y^3 + \frac{12}{2}y^2 + \frac{8}{4}y = \frac{2280}{8}$$

making y 10/2. That is,

$$y^3 + 6y^2 + 2y = 285,$$

making y 5.

So in non-affected powers, if x^3 equals 1728, making x 12, y^3 may equal 1728/216, making y 12/6. That is y^3 equals 8, making y 2.

This operation is sometimes a great time-saver in analysis.

CHAPTER V

On Raising the Power of an Equation Symmetrically [as a Remedy] for the Defect of an Irrational[35]

Symmetrica climactismus is a species of elevation of the power [of an equation]. We have [already] explained generally that an elevation [is]

[33]*radix isomoericae divisionis.*

[34]*congrua . . . scansilia.*

[35]*De Symmetrica Climactismo adversus vicium Asymmetriae.* The Latin title is not free from ambiguity and my translation is, in any event, a free one. I rather suspect, moreover, that Viète is indulging in a play on words: His *symmetrica* may be read either as "symmetrical"—

regular when the degree of both sides of a given equation is raised. It is a quadratic [elevation] when they are squared, cubic when they are cubed, and so on in accordance with the nature of the power. If any terms of a given equation are irrational, they are to be so disposed that one that is seen to be irrational forms one side of the equation, the others the other side. This is repeated, if necessary, until all irrationals disappear. The equation will meanwhile remain unimpaired, since the products of equals are equal. This is the operation that is called symmetrical elevation.

There are, however, various other [remedies] for irrationals, namely isomeria sometimes and sometimes the various formulae for transforming equations that are known and set up from their zetetic construction.

Example of Symmetrical Elevation

Let

$$A^3 - B^p A = \sqrt{Z^{ss}}.$$

The equation is to be purged of its irrational term.

Since the irrational is a square root, square both sides. Hence

$$A^6 + B^{pp}A^2 - 2B^pA^4 = Z^{ss},$$

so that has been doen that was desired.

If

$$x^3 - 2x = \sqrt{1200},$$

then[36]

$$y^3 + 4y - 4y^2 = 1200,$$

making y 12, the square of the unknown root.

[The given equation] could also be reduced to rational terms by the first-last method:

$$x^3 - 2x = \sqrt{1200}$$

$$y^3 + 2y^2 = 1200,$$

making y 10, whence x is $\sqrt{12}$.

Again, let

$$A^3 - A\sqrt[3]{B^{ss}} = Z^s.$$

This equation is to be freed from its irrational term.

---

i.e., alike on both sides of the equation—or, in contrast to the Asymmetriae that follows, as "rational."

[36]As is clear, Viète skips a step here, viz., that represented by $x^6 - 4x^4 + 4x^2 = 1200$.

Since this irrational is cubic, transpose the given terms and divide by A:

$$\frac{A^3 - Z\overline{s}}{A} = \sqrt[3]{B^{ss}}.$$

Therefore cubing everything,

$$\frac{A^9 - 3Z^sA^6 + 3Z^{ss}A^3 - Z^{sss}}{A^3} = B^{ss}.$$

Then multiplying through by A^3 and putting everything in order,

$$A^9 - 3Z^sA^6 + A^3(3Z^{ss} - B^{ss}) = Z^{sss}.$$

So that has been done that was to be done.

If

$$x^3 - x\sqrt[3]{18} = 6,$$

then

$$y^3 - 18y^2 + 90y = 216,$$

making $y12$, the cube of the root that is being sought.

CHAPTER VI

How Biquadratic Equations Are Reduced to Quadratics by Means of Cubes of a Plane Root, or on Completing the Power.

These five methods are entirely sufficient for preparing equations, however affected, so that they can be solved numerically in accordance with the rules of analysis for, even though the roots may be irrational, they can be found by the method of approximation. To show them exactly, however, [is a matter] for geometry rather than arithmetic. Yet quite often when roots are irrational, arithmetic will be assisted [by understanding] how, as has been set out, cubic equations are constructed from the difference between or the sum of the means [in a continued proportion], a given difference between or sum of the extremes, or the product of the means or extremes, or even from the teaching, now about to be set out, of the reduction of biquadratic equations to quadratics by means of the cubes of a plane root. Though a problem can be solved by knowing how biquadratics are constructed by plasmatic modification, a new discovery of zetetics, it can be solved no less easily and, clearly, much more elegantly by that operation that is called completing the power and is exemplified in the next three or four problems.

It has been remarked before that it is entirely by completing the power, not by anastrophe, that quadratic, biquadratic, sextic and other higher equations, taking them two steps at a time, are solved. A supplement having been added—hence the name of *paraplerosis*—this [method involves] also a species of irregular reduction [in power].

PROBLEM I

To reduce to a quadratic a biquadratic equation with a linear affection by means of a cubic with a plane root.

Let

$$A^4 + B^s A = Z^{pp}.$$

What has been ordered is to be done.
From what has been given,

$$A^4 = Z^{pp} - B^s A.$$

Add $A^2 E^2 + 1/4\, E^4$ to both sides of the equation. Then

$$A^4 + A^2 E^2 + \frac{1}{4} E^4 = Z^{pp} - B^s A + A^2 E^2 + \frac{1}{4} E^4.$$

Take the square root of all [the terms on the left-hand side]. This will be $A^2 + 1/2\, E^2$. It was for this reason that there were purposely added to A^4 the two plano-planes in the supplement, $A^2 E^2$ and $1/4\, E^4$, that it lacks to accord with the rule for the development of a square from two plane roots.

If the square root of the other side of the equation could be taken, it would be equal to $A^2 + 1/2\, E^2$. A square on a plane root must therefore be constructed to which the other side of the equation can readily be compared [and] such that $A^2 + 1/2\, E^2$ is equal to this plane root. Let this root be $B^s/2E - EA$, for thus the affections in A and its grades will vanish in the comparison and an equation in terms of E will result. To this we must strive.

The square created [from the plane root], therefore, will be $B^{ss}/4E^2 + E^2 A^2 - B^s A$. This is to be equated to $Z^{pp} - B^s A + E^2 A^2 + 1/4\, E^4$. Striking out the affections $E^2 A^2 - B^s A$ from both and multiplying throughout by $4E^2$,

$$E^6 + 4Z^{pp}E^2 = B^{ss}$$

[Solving this,] it becomes known that E^2 is D^2. Then

$$\frac{B^s}{2D} - DA = A^2 + \frac{1}{2}D^2$$

and, an equation being set up in accordance with the art,

$$A^2 + DA = \frac{B^s}{2D} - \frac{1}{2}D^2.$$

And if it were proposed that

$$A^4 - B^sA = Z^{pp},$$

the plane root of the square that is to be formed would be $B^s/2E + EA$, which must be compared with $A^2 + 1/2\ E^2$.

Converting the same into an inverse negative equation and setting it out with contrary signs of affection,[37] we will have

$$A^4 - B^sA = -Z^{pp}$$

since this is [a matter of] subtracting equals from equals. E^2, however, is less than half of $B^s/2E$ since it is more than that in the direct negative.

From this three theorems on reduction may be formulated:

Theorem I

If

$$A^4 + B^sA = Z^{pp}$$

and

$$(E^2)^3 + 4Z^{pp}E^2 = B^{ss}$$

and if it becomes known that E is D, then

$$A^2 + DA = \frac{B^s}{2D} - \frac{1}{2\ D^2}.$$

Theorem II

If

$$A^4 - B^sA = Z^{pp}$$

[37]I.e., $A^4 - B^sA = Z^{pp}$ becomes $B^SA - A^4 = Z^{PP}$, which becomes $A^4 - B^sA = -Z^{pp}$.

and

$$(E^2)^3 + 4Z^{pp}E^2 = B^{ss}$$

and if it becomes known that E is D, then

$$A^2 - DA = \frac{B^s}{2D} - \frac{1}{2\,D^2}.$$

The structure of both these equations is easily recognized. There are two roots the difference between the fourth powers of which divided by the sum of the roots—that is, twice the product of the rectangle from the roots and their difference plus the cube of the difference—is B^s. The difference between the roots, moreover, is E or D, making Z^{pp} the square of the difference between the roots plus the product of the roots times this same product and A is one root. In the second [theorem] it is the greater, in the first the smaller.[38]

D is the difference between the extremes in a series of four continued proportionals, B^s the difference between the cubes of the individual proportionals taken alternately, and Z^{pp} the product of either of the extremes and the difference between the cubes of the others taken alternately, making A the first, which is the greater of the extremes in the second case, the smaller in the first.[39]

Let the continued proportionals be 2, $\sqrt[3]{40}$, $\sqrt[3]{200}$ and 10. Then

$$x^4 + 832x = 1680$$

then

$$x^2 + 8x = 20,$$

making x 2.

And if

$$x^4 - 832x = 1680,$$

then

$$x^2 - 8x = 20,$$

making x 10.

---

[38]I.e., if the roots are k and h, k being greater than h, then $(k^4 - h^4)/(k + h) = 2kh(k - h) + (k - h)^3 = B^s$; $k - h = E$ or D; $z^{pp} = kh[(k - h)^2 + kh]$; and $A = k$ in Theorem II and h in Theorem I.

[39]I.e., if the proportionals are p, q, r and s, then $D = s - p$; $B^s = s^3 - r^3 + q^3 - p^3$; $Z^{pp} = p(s^3 - r^3 + q^3)$ or $s(r^3 - q^3 + p^3)$; and $A = p$ in Theorem I and s in Theorem II.

Note that the difference between 2 and 10 is 8, since

$$y^3 + 6720y = 692{,}224,$$

making y 64, the square of 8.

Theorem III

If

$$B^s A - A^4 = Z^{pp}$$

and

$$(E^2)^3 - 4Z^{pp}E^2 = B^{ss}$$

and if it becomes known that E is D, then

$$DA - A^2 = \frac{1}{2}D^2 - \frac{B^s}{2D}.$$

The structure of this equation is well known, B^s being the product of the sum of the squares [of two roots] and the sum of the roots or, alternatively, the cube of the sum of the two roots minus twice the product of the rectangle from the roots and the sum of the roots, and Z^{pp} being the product of the square of the sum of the roots minus their product times this rectangle. This makes E or D the sum of these roots and A either the greater or the smaller of them.[40]

B^s is the sum of the cubes of the four individual terms in a series of four continued proportionals, Z^{pp} the product of either of the extremes and the sum of the cubes of the others, and D the sum of the extremes. This makes A either the first or the fourth proportional.[41]

Let the continued proportionals be 2, $\sqrt[3]{40}$, $\sqrt[3]{200}$ and 10. Then

$$1248x - x^4 = 2480$$

and

$$12x - x^2 = 20,$$

making the unknown 2 or 10. Note that 12 is the sum of 2 and 10. If

$$y^3 - 9920y = 1{,}557{,}504,[42]$$

y is 144, the same as the square of 12.

---

[40]I.e., if the roots are k and h, then $B^s = (k^2 + h^2)(k + h)$ or $(k + h)^3 - 2kh(k + h)$; $Z^{pp} = [(k + h)^2 - kh]kh$; E or $D = k + h$; and $A = k$ or h.

[41]I.e., if p, q, r and s are the proportionals, then $B^s = p^3 + q^3 + r^3 + s^3$; $Z^{pp} = p(q^3 + r^3 + s^3)$ or $s(p^3 + q^3 + r^3)$; $D = p + s$; $A = p$ or s.

[42]1615 has 1,557,507.

Problem II

To reduce to a quadratic equation a biquadratic with a cubic affection by means of a cubic with a plane root.

Let

$$A^4 + 2BA^3 = Z^{pp}.$$

That which has been ordered is to be done.

If $A^2 + BA - 1/2\, E^p$ is squared, it will be $A^4 + 2BA^3 + B^2A^2 + 1/4\, E^{pp} - E^pA^2 - E^pBA$. To both sides of this equation add what is missing [on the left-hand side] from the square of this plane root. From this addition of equals to equals,

$$A^4 + 2BA^3 + B^2A^2 + \frac{1}{4}E^{pp} - E^pA^2 - E^pBA = Z^{pp} + B^2A^2$$

$$+ \frac{1}{4}E^{pp} - E^pA^2 - E^pBA.$$

Take the square root of both sides. The left-hand side being recalled by analysis to its origin, $A^2 + BA - 1/2\, E^p$ manifestly arises.

If the square root of the other side could also be taken, it would be equal to these plane roots that have arisen on the first side. A square on a plane root must therefore be created and compared with and equated to the other side of the equation—that is, to Z^{pp} and its affections—so that the roots can be compared and equated to each other. Let this plane root of the square to be created be $E^pB/\sqrt{4B^2 - 4E^p} - \sqrt{A^2(B^2 - E^p)}$,[43] for this way the affections involving A and its grades will vanish in the comparison and it will become an equation in E, which is what is to be striven for. Hence the square created will be $E^{pp}B^2/(4B^2 - 4E^p) + B^2A^2 - E^pA^2 - E^pBA$. This is equated to Z^{pp} and the other plano-planes that accompany and affect it. Deleting from both sides the affections both in A and in A^2,

$$\frac{E^{pp}B^2}{4B^2 - 4E^p} = Z^{pp} + \frac{1}{4}E^{pp}.$$

Multiplying through by $4B^2 - 4E^p$,

$$E^{pp}B^2 = 4Z^{pp}B^2 + E^{pp}B^2 - 4Z^{pp}E^p - E^{ppp}.$$

Then, having deleted $E^{pp}B^2$ from both sides and putting everything in

---

[43]In 1615 this last expression is written $Lv\ \{B\ quadrato/E\ plano\}\ in\ A\ quadratum$, L standing for *latus* and v for *universalis*. In 1646 it is written $\sqrt{B\ quad - E\ plano}\ in\ A$. This difference in form occurs time and again in the following paragraphs.

proper order,

$$(E^p)^3 + 4Z^{pp}E^p = 4Z^{pp}B^2.$$

E^p, however, it becomes known, is D^p. Therefore

$$A^2 + BA - \frac{1}{2}D^p = \frac{D^pB}{\sqrt{4B^2 - 4D^p}} - \sqrt{A^2(B^2 - D^p)}$$

and, arranging the equation in accordance with the art,

$$A^2 + BA + \sqrt{A^2(B^2 - D^p)} = \frac{1}{2}D^p + \frac{D^pB}{\sqrt{4B^2 - 4D^p}}.$$

If it were proposed that

$$A^4 - 2BA^3 = Z^{pp},$$

the plane root of the square to be constructed would be $E^pB/\sqrt{4B^2 - 4E^p}$ $+ \sqrt{A^2(B^2 - E^p)}$,[44] which is to be compared with $A^2 - BA - 1/2\,E^p$.[45]

And if it were proposed that

$$2BA^3 - A^4 = Z^{pp},$$

it could be shown that

$$A^4 - 2BA^3\text{ [46] } = -Z^{pp}$$

because there would be a subtraction of equals from equals. The plane root of the square to be created would be $E^pB/\sqrt{4B^2 - 4E^p} - \sqrt{A^2(B^2 + E^p)}$ which is to be compared with $BA + 1/2\,E^p - A^2$.

Thus in all these cases that has been done that was ordered. From them are derived three theorems on reduction:

Theorem I

If

$$A^4 + 2BA^3\text{ [47] } = Z^{pp}$$

and

$$(E^p)^3 + 4Z^{pp}E^p\text{ [48] } = 4Z^{pp}B^2$$

---

[44]1615 has $- \sqrt{A^2(B^2 - E^p)}$.
[45]The text has $A^2 + BA - 1/2E^p$.
[46]1646 omits the minus sign.
[47]1615 omits the coefficient 2.
[48]1646 has $-4Z^{pp}E^p$.

and, if it becomes known that E^p is D^p, then

$$A^2 + BA + \sqrt{A^2(B^2 - D^p)} = \frac{D^p B}{\sqrt{4B^2 - 4D^p}} + \frac{1}{2} D^{p}.^{49}$$

Theorem II

If

$$A^4 - 2BA^3 = Z^{pp}$$

and

$$(E^p)^3 + 4Z^{pp}E^{p\ 50} = 4Z^{pp}B^2$$

and, if it becomes known that E^p is D^p, then

$$A^2 - AB - \sqrt{A^2(B^2 - D^p)} = \frac{D^p B}{\sqrt{4B^2 - 4D^p}} + \frac{1}{2} D^{p}.^{51}$$

The structure of both the preceding equations is well known. There are two roots, the difference between the fourth powers of which divided by the sum of their cubes yields 2B. The square of the difference between the roots minus B when subtracted from B^2 leaves D^p or E^p. This makes Z^{pp} arise from dividing $(D^p)^3$ by $4(D^2 \sim B^2)^{52}$ and A is one of the roots—in the second case the greater, in the first the smaller.[53]

The difference between four continued proportionals taken alternately is 2B; Z^{pp} is the product of either of the extremes and the cube of the difference between the other three taken alternately; and E^p or D^p is one-fourth of the difference between the square of the difference between the proportionals taken alternately and the square of the difference between the extremes minus three times the difference between the means. Hence $\sqrt{4B^2 - 4D^p}$ is the difference between the extremes minus three times the difference between the means. And since the first is known to be the smaller of the extremes, A becomes the difference between the first

[49] 1615 omits 1/2.

[50] The text has $-4Z^{pp}E^p$.

[51] 1615 has $A^2 + AB + \sqrt{A^2(B^2 - D^p)} = D^p B/\sqrt{4B^2 - 4D^p} + 1/2D^p$; 1646 has $A^2 - AB - \sqrt{A^2(B^2 - D^p)} = D^p B/\sqrt{4B^2 - 4D^p} + 1/2D^p$.

[52] This is Anderson's wording in 1615, which is carried over into 1646. In inserting it in the text, he replaced Viete's formula which, he tells us, was *quadrati aggregati laterum, minus triplo rectangulo sub lateribus, ad rectangulum sub lateribus,* and which does not work.

[53] I.e., if the roots are k and h, k being the greater, then $2B = (k^4 - h^4)/(k^3 - h^3)$; D^p or $E^p = B^2 - [(k - h) - B]^2$; $Z^{pp} = (D^p)^3/[4(D^2 \sim B^2)]$; and $A = k$ in the second case or h in the first.

three taken alternately in the first case and the difference between the last three taken alternately in the second case.[54]

Let the continued proportionals be 1, 2, 4 and 8. If

$$x^4 + 5x^3 = 216,$$

then

$$x^2 + 3x = 18,$$

making x 3.

And if

$$x^4 - 5x^3 = 216,$$

then

$$x^2 - 3x = 18,$$

making x 6.

Moreover, 3 is known. Since

$$y^3 + 864y = 5400,$$

y is 6, one-fourth the difference between the square of the given length 5 [55] and the square of 1, whence it is discerned that this is the length that makes 6, twice this 3, when it is added to the length 5, twice this 3.

Theorem III

If

$$2BA^3 - A^4 = Z^{pp}$$

and

$$(E^p)^3 - 4Z^{pp}E^p = 4Z^{pp}B^2$$

and if it becomes known that E^p is D^p, then

$$BA + \sqrt{A^2(B^2 + D^p)} - A^2 = \frac{D^p B}{\sqrt{4B^2 + 4D^p}} + \frac{1}{2}D^p.$$

[54]I.e., if the proportionals are p, q, r and s, then $2B = s - r + q - p$; $Z^{pp} = \dfrac{p(s - r + q)^3}{}$ or $s(r - q + p)^3$; E^p or $D^p = \{(s - r + q - p)^2 - [(s - p) - 3(r - q)]^2\}/4$; $\sqrt{4B^2 - 4D^p} = (s - p) - 3(r - q)$; and $A = (s - r + q)$ in the negative case or $(r - q + p)$ in the positive case.

[55]The text has *quadratum abs dato latere 5,* but the *latere* makes little sense. I have, therefore, assumed that it is an error and have substituted *longitudine* for it in preparing this translation.

The structure of this equation is well known. There are two roots the difference between the fourth powers of which divided by the difference between their cubes makes $2B$. The difference between the square of the sum of the roots minus B and the square of this same B is D^p. And Z^{pp} results from dividing the cube of D^p by the sum of four times the squares of B and D. A is then either the greater or the smaller root.[56]

In a series of four continued proportionals, $2B$ is the sum of all of them and Z^{pp} is the product of either of the extremes and the cube of the sum of the other three. This makes E^p or D^p one-fourth of the difference between the square of the sum of the extremes plus three times the sum of the means and the square of the sum of all of them. Hence $\sqrt{4B^2 + 4D^p}$ is the sum of the extremes plus three times the sum of the means and A is the sum of the first three or the last three.[57]

Let the continued proportionals be 1, 2, 4 and 8. Then

$$15x^3 - x^4 = 2744,$$

whence

$$21x - x^2 = 98,$$

making x 7 or 14.

Moreover, 21 is known. Since

$$y^3 - 10{,}976\,y = 617{,}400,$$

making y 126, one-fourth of the difference between 225 and 729, it is understood that it is $\sqrt{729}$ (that is, the length 27), which makes 42, twice this 21, when it is added to the length 15.

PROBLEM III

To reduce a biquadratic equation with both a linear and a quadratic affection to a quadratic by means of a cubic with a plane root.

Let

$$A^4 + 2G^p A^2 + B^s A = Z^{pp}.$$

That is to be done which has been ordered.

It is clear that if a square is constructed from $A^2 + G^p + 1/2E^2$, it will

---

[56] I.e., if k and h are the roots and k is greater than h, then $2B = (k^4 - h^4)/(k^3 - h^3)$; $D^p = [(k + h)^2 - B] - B^2$; $Z^{pp} = (D^p)^3/(4B^2 + 4D^2)$; and $A = k$ or h.

[57] I.e., if the proportionals are p, q, r and s, then $2B = p + q + r + s$; $Z^{pp} = p(q + r + s)^3$ or $s(p + q + r)^3$; E^p or $D^p = \{[(p + s) + 3(q + r)]^2 - (p + q + r + s)^2\}/4$; $\sqrt{4B^2 + 4D^p} = (p + s) + 3(q + r)$; and $A = p + q + r$ or $q + r + s$.

be $A^4 + G^{pp} + 2G^pA^2 + 1/4E^4 + E^2A^2 + G^pE^2$. Since, therefore, what has been proposed is, with the help of transposition,

$$A^4 + 2G^pA^2 = Z^{pp} - B^sA,$$

add to both sides of this equation what [its left-hand side] lacks from the square created from the given plane root. By this addition of equals to equals, one side will [again be] equal to the other.

Now take the square root of both sides. On the left-hand side, its development being recalled from analysis, there manifestly arises $A^2 + G^p + 1/2E^2$. If the square root of the other side of the equation could also be had, what would arise would be equal to the plane roots arising on the first side.

A square based on a plane root must therefore be constructed and this must be compared with and equated to the other side of the equation—that is, to Z^{pp} and its affections—so that their roots can also be compared with and equated to each other. Let the plane root of the square that is to be constructed be $B^s/2E - EA$, for thus in the comparison the affections in A and its grades will vanish and it will turn into an equation in E, which is what is to be striven for.

The square thus constructed will be $B^{ss}/4E^2 + E^2A^2 - B^sA$ and this will be equal to $Z^{pp} - B^sA + G^{pp} + 1/4E^4 + E^2A^2 + G^pE^2$. Then, removing the affections on A and A^2 from both,

$$\frac{B^{ss}}{4E^2} = Z^{pp} + G^{pp} + \frac{1}{4}E^4 + G^pE^2.$$

Multiplying all terms by $4E^2$ and setting out the product properly,

$$(E^2)^3 + 4G^p(E^2)^2 + E^2(4Z^{pp} + 4G^{pp}) = B^{ss}.$$

If it becomes known that E equals D, then

$$A^2 + DA = \frac{B^s}{2D} - G^p - \frac{1}{2}D^2.\text{[58]}$$

And if it were proposed that

$$A^4 + 2G^pA^2 - B^sA = Z^{pp},$$

the root of the square to be constructed would be assumed to be $B^s/2E + EA$,[59] which is to be compared with $A^2 + G^p$ [60] $+ 1/2E^2$.

---

[58] The text has $+ 1/2D^2$.
[59] The text has $- EA$.
[60] 1615 has E^p.

And if it were proposed that

$$A^4 - 2G^pA^2 - B^sA = Z^{pp},$$

the root of the square to be constructed would be assumed to be $B^s/2E + EA$, which is to be compared with $A^2 - G^p + 1/2E^2$.

And if it were proposed that

$$2G^pA^2 + B^sA - A^4 = Z^{pp},$$

then, having altered the signs of the affections,[61] let the plane root of the square to be constructed be $B^s/2E + EA$, which is to be compared with $A^2 - G^p + 1/2E^2$.

And if it were proposed that

$$2G^pA^2 - B^sA - A^4 = Z^{pp},$$

then, having altered the signs of the affections, let the plane root of the square that is to be constructed be $EA + B^s/2E$, which is to be compared with $A^2 - G^p + 1/2E^2$.[62]

Finally, if it were proposed that

$$B^sA - 2G^pA^2 - A^4 = Z^{pp},$$

then, having altered the signs of the affections, let $EA + B^s/2E$ be the plane root of the square to be constructed and let it be compared with $A^2 + G^p + 1/2E^2$.

Thus the reduction that was ordered has been carried out in all these cases.[63]

ALTERNATIVE [PROBLEM III]

To reduce a biquadratic equation with both a linear and a quadratic affection to a quadratic by means of a cubic having a plane root.

Let

$$A^4 + G^pA + B^sA = Z^{pp}.$$

That is to be done which has been ordered.

[61]So in the text, but the actual process requires, of course, alteration of the signs of all terms.

[62]The text has $A^2 - G^p - 1/2E^2$.

[63]It will be noted that Viète omits the case of $A^4 - 2G^pA^2 + B^sA = Z^{pp}$, in which the root of the square to be constructed is $B^s/2E - EA$, which is to be compared with $A^2 - G^p + 1/2E^2$. See Theorem III.

By transposing what has been proposed,

$$A^4 = Z^{pp} - G^p A - B^s A.$$

Add $E^p A^2 + 1/4 E^{pp}$ to both sides. One will still be equal to the other. Take the square root of the left-hand side. The result is $A^2 + 1/2 E^p$. Let the square root of the other side also be taken and, in order to do this, construct the square of a suitable root and compare it with and equate it to the other part. If this root is set up as $B^s / \sqrt{4E^p - 4B^p} - \sqrt{A^2(E^p - G^p)}$, then

$$\frac{B^{ss}}{4E^p - 4G^p} + A^2(E^p - G^p) - B^s A$$

$$= Z^{pp} - G^p A^2 - B^s A + E^p A^2 + \frac{1}{4} E^{pp}.$$

Hence

$$(E^p)^3 - G^p(E^p)^2 + 4Z^{pp} E^p = B^{ss} + 4Z^{pp} G^p.$$

If it becomes known, however, that E^p is F^p, then

$$\frac{B^s}{\sqrt{4F^p - 4G^p}} - \sqrt{A^2(F^p - G^p)} = A^2 + \frac{1}{2} F^p.$$

And if it were proposed that

$$A^4 + G^p A^2 - B^s A = Z^{pp},$$

the plane root of the square to be constructed would be set up as $\sqrt{A^2(E^p - G^p)} + B^s / \sqrt{4E^p - 4G^p}$ [64] which is to be compared with $1/2 E^p + A^2$.

Finally, if it were proposed that

$$B^s A - G^p A^2 - A^4 = Z^{pp},$$

the plane root of the square to be constructed would be $\sqrt{A^2(E^p - G^p)} + B^s / \sqrt{4E^p - 4G^p}$, which is to be compared with $1/2 E^p + A^2$.

In all these cases, the reduction that was ordered has been carried out.

The following theorems are now set up in accordance with the first formula:

[64] The text has $\sqrt{A^2(E^p + G^p)} - B^s / 4E^p - 4G^p$.

Theorem I

According to the First Formula

If,

$$A^4 + 2G^p A^2 + B^s A = Z^{pp},$$

then

$$(E^2)^3 + 4G^p(E^2)^2 + E^2(4Z^{pp} + 4G^{pp}) = B^{ss}$$

and if it becomes known, moreover, that E is D, then

$$A^2 + DA = \frac{B^s}{2D} - \frac{1}{2}D^{2\,[65]} - G^p.$$

$$x^4 + 6x^2 + 880x = 1800,$$

making x 2.

$$y^3 + 12y^2 + 7236y = 774{,}400,$$

making y 64, the square of the root 8.

$$x^2 + 8x = 20,$$

making x 2.

Theorem II

If

$$A^4 + 2G^p A^2 - B^s A = Z^{pp},$$

then

$$(E^2)^3 + 4G^p(E^2)^{2\,[66]} + E^2(4Z^{pp} + 4G^{pp}) = B^{ss}$$

and if it becomes known that E equals D, then

$$A^2 - DA = \frac{B^s}{2D} - \frac{1}{2}D^{2\,[67]} - G^p.$$

$$x^4 + 6x^2 - 880x = 1800,$$

making x 10.

$$y^3 + 12y^2 + 7236y = 774{,}400,$$

[65] 1615 has $+ 1/2D^2$.
[66] 1615 has $4G^{pp}(E^2)^2$.
[67] 1615 omits the coefficient $1/2$.

making y 64, the square of 8.

$$x^2 - 8x = 20,$$

making x 10.

Theorem III

If

$$A^4 - 2G^p A^2 + B^s A = Z^{pp},$$

then

$$(E^2)^3 - 4G^p(E^2)^2 + E^2(4Z^{pp} + 4G^{pp}) = B^{ss}$$

and if it becomes known that E equals D, then

$$A^2 + DA = \frac{B^s}{2D} - \frac{1}{2}D^2 + G^p.$$

$$x^4 - 4x^2 + 800x = 1600,$$

making x 2.

$$y^3 - 8y^2 + 6416y = 640,000,$$

making y 64, the square of 8.

$$x^2 + 8x = 20,$$

making x 2.

Theorem IIII

If

$$A^4 - 2G^p A^2 - B^s A = Z^{pp},$$

then

$$(E^2)^3 - 4G^p(E^2)^2 + E^2(4Z^{pp} + 4G^{pp}) = B^{ss}$$

and if it becomes known that E is D, then

$$A^2 - DA = \frac{B^s}{2D} - \frac{1}{2}D^2 + G^p.$$

$$x^4 - 4x^2 - 800x = 1600,$$

making x 10.

$$y^3 - 8y^2 + 6416y = 640,000,$$

making y 64, the square of 8.

$$x^2 - 8x = 20,$$

making x 10.

Theorem V

If

$$2G^p A^2 + B^s A - A^4 = Z^{pp},$$

then

$$(E^2)^3 - 4G^p(E^2)^2 + E^2(4G^{pp} - 4Z^{pp}) = B^{ss}$$

and if it becomes known that E is D, then

$$DA - A^2 = \frac{1}{2}D^2 - G^p - \frac{B^s}{2D}.$$

$$44x^2 + 720x - x^4 = 1600,$$

making x 10 or 2.

$$y^3 - 88y^2 - 4464y = 518{,}400,$$

making y 144, the square of 12.

$$12x - x^2 = 20,$$

making x 10 or 2.

Theorem VI

If

$$2G^p A^{2\,68} - B^s A - A^4 = Z^{pp},$$

then

$$(E^2)^3 - 4G^p(E^2)^2 + E^2(4G^{pp} - 4Z^{pp})^{69} = B^{ss},$$

and if it becomes known that E is D, then

$$DA - A^2 = \frac{1}{2}D^2 - G^p - \frac{B^s}{2D}.\ ^{70}$$

$$114x^2 - 120x - x^4 = 200,$$

---

[68] 1615 has $2G^p A$.
[69] The text has $E^2(4Z^{pp} - 4G^{pp})$.
[70] 1646 has $+ B^s/2D$.

making x 2 or 10.

$$y^3 - 228y^2 + 12,196y = 14,400,$$

making x 144, the square of 12.

$$12x - x^2 = 20,$$

making x 10 or 2.

Theorem VII

If

$$B^s A - 2G^p A^2 - A^4 = Z^{pp},$$

then

$$(E^2)^3 + 4G^p(E^2)^2 [+] E^2(-4Z^{pp} + 4G^{pp}) = B^{ss}$$

and if it becomes known that E is D, then

$$DA - A^2 = \frac{1}{2}D^2 + G^p - \frac{B^s}{2D}.$$

$$1440x - 16x^2 - x^4 = 2800,$$

making x 10 or 2.

$$y^3 + 32y^2 - 10,944y = 2,073,600,$$

making y 144, the square of 12.

$$12x - x^2 = 20,$$

making x 10 or 2.

The following [theorems] pertain to the second formula:

Theorem I

According to the Second Formula

If

$$A^4 + G^p A^2 + B^s A = Z^{pp}$$

then

$$(E^p)^3 - G^p(E^p)^2 + 4Z^p E^{p71} = B^{ss} + 4Z^{pp}G^{p72}$$

[71] The text has $4Z^p E^p$.
[72] 1615 omits the coefficient 4.

and if it becomes known that E^p equals F^p,

$$A^2 + \sqrt{A^2(F^p - G^p)} = \frac{B^s}{\sqrt{4F^p - 4G^p}} - \frac{1}{2}F^p.$$

$$x^4 + 6x^2 + 880x = 1800,$$

making x 2.

$$y^3 - 6y^2 + 7200y = 817,600,$$

making y 70 and $70 - 6$ is the square of 8.

$$x^2 + 8x = 20,$$

making x 2.

Theorem II

If

$$A^4 + G^p A^2 - B^s A = Z^{pp},$$

then

$$(E^p)^3 - G^p(E^p)^2 + 4Z^{pp}E^p = B^{ss} + 4Z^{pp}G^p$$

and if it becomes known that E^p equals F^p, then

$$A^2 - \sqrt{A^2(F^p - G^p)} = \frac{B^s}{\sqrt{4E^p - 4G^p}} - \frac{1}{2}F^p$$

$$x^4 + 6x^2 - 880x^{73} = 1800,$$

making x 10.

$$y^3 - 6y^2 + 7200y = 817,600,$$

making y 70, and $70 - 6$ is the square of 8.

$$x^2 - 8x = 20.$$

making x 10.

Theorem III

If

$$A^4 - G^p A^2 + B^s A = Z^{pp},$$

[73] 1615 has 800x.

then

$$(E^p)^3 + G^p(E^p)^2 + 4Z^{pp}E^p = B^{ss} - 4Z^{pp}G^p$$

and if it becomes known that E^p equals F^p, then

$$A^2 + \sqrt{A^2(F^p + G^p)}^{74} = \frac{B^s}{\sqrt{4F^p + 4G^p}} - \frac{1}{2}F^p.$$

$$x^4 - 4x^2 + 800x = 1600,$$

making x 2.

$$y^3 + 4y^2 + 6400y = 614,400,$$

making y 60, and 60 + 4 is the square of 8.

$$x^2 + 8x = 20,$$

making x 2.

Theorem IIII

If

$$A^4 - G^p A^2 - B^s A = Z^{pp},$$

then

$$(E^p)^3 + G^p(E^p)^2 + 4Z^{pp}E^p = B^{ss} - 4Z^{pp}G^{p\,75}$$

and if it becomes known that E^p is F^p, then

$$A^2 - \sqrt{A^2(F^p + G^p)} = \frac{B^s}{\sqrt{4F^p + 4G^p}} - \frac{1}{2}F^p.$$

$$x^4 - 4x^2 - 800x = 1600,$$

making x 10.

$$y^3 + 4y^2 + 6400y^{76} = 614,400,$$

making y 60, and 60 + 4 is the square of 8.

$$x^2 - 8x = 20,$$

making x 10.

---

[74] 1615 has $\sqrt{A^2(F^2 - G^p)}$.
[75] 1615 has $+ 4Z^{pp}G^p$.
[76] 1615 has 64y.

Theorem V

If

$$G^p A^2 + B^s A - A^4 = Z^{pp},$$

then

$$(E^p)^3 + G^p(E^p)^2 - 4Z^{pp}E^p = B^{ss} + 4Z^{pp}G^p$$

and if it becomes known that E^p is F^p, then

$$\sqrt{A^2(F^p + G^p)} - A^2 = \frac{1}{2}F^p - \frac{B^s}{\sqrt{4F^p + 4G^p}}.$$

$$44x^2 + 720x - x^4 = 1600,$$

making x 10 or 2.

$$y^3 + 44y^2 - 6400y = 800{,}000,$$

making y 100, and 100 + 44 is the square of 12.

$$12x - x^2 = 20,$$

making x 10 or 2.

Theorem VI

If

$$G^p A^2 - B^s A - A^4 = Z^{pp},$$

then

$$(E^p)^{3\,[77]} + G^p(E^p)^2 - 4Z^{pp}E^p = B^{ss} + 4Z^{pp}G^p$$

and if it becomes known that E^p is F^p, then

$$\sqrt{A^2(F^p + G^p)} - A^2 = \frac{1}{2}F^p + \frac{B^s}{\sqrt{4F^p + 4G^p}}.$$

$$114x^2 - 120x - x^4 = 200,$$

making x 2 or 10.

$$y^3 + 114y^{2\,[78]} - 800y = 105{,}600,$$

[77] 1615 has $(E^2)^3$.
[78] 1615 has 144y.

making y 30, and $30 + 114$ is the square of 12.

$$12x - x^2 = 20,$$

making x 2 or 10.

Theorem VII

If

$$B^s A - G^p A^2 - A^4 = Z^{pp},$$

then

$$(E^p)^3 - G^p (E^p)^2 - 4Z^{pp} E^p = B^{ss} - 4Z^{pp} G^p$$

and if it becomes known that E^p is F^p, then

$$\sqrt{A^2 (F^p - G^p)} - A^2 = \frac{1}{2} F^p - \frac{B^s}{\sqrt{4F^p - 4G^p}}.$$

$$1440x - 16x^2 - x^4 = 2800,$$

making x 2 or 10.

$$y^3 - 16y^2 - 11,200y = 1,894,400,$$

making y 160, and $160 - 16$ is the square of 12.

$$12x - x^2 = 20,$$

making x 2 or 10.

What remains is to achieve other transformations in which cubic affections vanish by expurgation by one-fourth [the coefficient]. The foregoing, however, are enough and more than enough.

CHAPTER VII

How to Reduce Cubic Equations to Quadratics with a Solid Root, or on Double Substitution[79]

What is called double substitution is a no less elegant method of transformation [than the one just set out]. It is very helpful in finding irrationals in the roots of certain cubics with linear affections. Thanks to a

[79] *De Duplicata Hypostasis.*

discovery of the new zetetics, [it derives] from the known special structure of those cubics of which we spoke at the beginning of the preceding chapter.

It will assist to subjoin the following problems:

PROBLEM I

To reduce a cube with a positive linear affection to a square based on a solid root that is similarly affected

Let

$$A^3 + 3B^p A = 2Z^s.$$

That is to be done that has been proposed.
[Let]

$$E^2 + AE = B^p.$$

From the way in which this sort of equation is constructed, B^p is known to be the product of two roots the smaller of which is E, which differs from the greater by A. Therefore $(B^p - E^2)/E$ will be A. Hence

$$\frac{B^{ppp} - 3E^2 B^{pp} + 3E^4 B^p - E^6}{E^3} + \frac{3B^{pp} - 3B^p E^2}{E} = 2Z^s.$$

Multiplying through by E^3 and arranging everything artfully,

$$(E^3)^2 + 2Z^s E^3 = (B^p)^3,$$

which is an equation of a positively affected square on a solid root. Thus the reduction which was ordered has been made.

Corollary

So, if

$$A^3 + 3B^p A^{80} = 2Z^s$$

and

$$\sqrt{B^{ppp} + Z^{ss}} - Z^s = D^3,$$

A, the unknown, is $(B^p - D^2)/D$.
    If

$$x^3 + 81x = 702,$$

---

[80]The text omits the letter A.

since $\sqrt{19{,}683 + 123{,}201}$ or $\sqrt{142{,}884}$ or 378 minus the solid 351 is 27, the cube of the root 3, therefore x is $(27 - 9)/3$ or 6.

Alternatively and Secondly

[If]

$$E^2 - AE = B^p,$$

then, from the structure of this type of equation, B^p is known to be the product of two roots the greater of which is E, which exceeds the smaller by A. Hence $(E^2 - B^p)/E$ will equal A. Therefore from what has been given and arranging everything in accordance with the art

$$(E^3)^2 - 2Z^s E^3 = (B^p)^3,$$

which is an equation of a negatively affected square on a solid root. So again the reduction that was ordered has been made.

Second Corollary

So if

$$A^3 + 3B^p A = 2Z^s$$

and

$$\sqrt{B^{ppp} + Z^{ss}} + Z^s = G^3,$$

then $(G^2 - B^p)/G$ will equal A.
    If

$$x^3 + 81x = 702,$$

since $378 + 351$ is 729, the cube of the root 9, therefore x is $(81 - 27)/9$ or 6.

Corollary to the Two Preceding Corollaries

Finally there are two roots, the smaller of which is D, the greater is the other, G, and the difference between them is A, the unknown. So $\sqrt[3]{\sqrt{B^{ppp} + Z^{ss}} + Z^s} - \sqrt[3]{\sqrt{B^{ppp} + Z^{ss}} - Z^s}$ is the A that is being sought.
    If

$$x^3 + 6x = 2,$$

x is $\sqrt[3]{4} - \sqrt[3]{2}$.

PROBLEM II

To reduce a cube with a negative linear affection to a square on a solid root minus a square.

The cube of one-third the coefficient of the affection in the proposed equation must be less than one-fourth the square of the constant.

Let

$$A^3 - 3B^p A = 2Z^s.$$

What was proposed is to be done.

[If]

$$AE - E^2 = B^p,$$

B^p is known, from the structure of this sort of equation, to be the product of two roots the greater or smaller of which is E and the sum of the greater and smaller of which is A. Hence $(B^p + E^2)/E$ will equal A. Therefore

$$\frac{B^{ppp} + 3E^2 B^{pp} + 3E^4 B^p + E^6}{E^3} \, [+] \, \frac{-3B^{pp} - 3B^p E^2}{E} = 2Z^s.$$

Multiplying all terms by E^3 and arranging them according to the art,

$$2Z^s E^3 - (E^3)^2 = (B^p)^3,$$

which is an equation of an inverse negative square having a solid root. Thus the reduction that was ordered has been made.

It is apparent, moreover, from the properties of the reduced equation that the square of Z^s must be greater than the cube of B^p. It is to this that the stipulation prefixed to the problem refers.

Corollary

So, if

$$A^3 - 3B^p A = 2Z^s,$$

the A that is being sought is $\sqrt[3]{Z^s + \sqrt{Z^{ss} - B^{ppp}}} + \sqrt[3]{Z^s - \sqrt{Z^{ss} - B^{ppp}}}.$

If

$$x^3 - 81x = 756,$$

since $378 + 351$ is 729, the cube of the root 9, and $378 - 351$ is 27, the cube of the root 3, x is $9 + 3$ or 12.

CHAPTER VIII

On the Standard Transformation of Equations so that the Coefficients of Their Lower Terms Are as Prescribed

Logistic also resorts to reduction[81] to prepare equations so that their coefficients and homogeneous terms of comparison will be whatever is prescribed. This is clearly permissible under the established teaching on transformation. [If] a coefficient of 1 is given, reduction[82] [is not] useful, for it is clear that powers affected by a product of 1 and any of the lower grades (provided the root is a [rational] number) are resolved the same way as if they were pure powers. Nor is the operation otherwise disturbed by having coefficients the ratio of which [to each other] is unity, but this is omitted from this work.[83] If the root found [for the derived equation] is not a [rational] number, it is certain that the original root is not a [rational] number.

If

$$x^3 + x = 10,$$

the root being sought is 2, since the cube nearest [to 10] is 8 and its root is 2, and this multiplied by 1 and added to 8 makes 10.

Likewise, if

$$x^3 - x = 24,$$

the root sought is 3, since the nearest lower cube is 8, the cube root of which is 2, which differs from 3 by 1, and the product of 3 and 1 is a solid which, when subtracted from the cube of 3, leaves 24.

However, suppose

$$x^3 + x = 9.$$

Since the nearest cube is 8, the root of which is 2, and this, multiplied by 1 and added to 8, makes 10, not 9, the root x is irrational.

---

[81]*ad impendia.* Viète's use of the word *impendium* here makes little sense when the definitions of classical times are applied to it. It appears to have taken on something approaching the meanings of *compendium* and is so translated.

[82]*impendii vel ex eo.* It is not clear what force *vel ex eo* has in this context and I have, accordingly, omitted the expression in translation.

[83]*neque enim negotium conturbat habenda alioqui (sed quae ex isthoc opere, salva fit) parabolarum quarum quaeque unitas est, ratio.* Viète's meaning is quite obscure, and I am far from certain that my translation is correct.

Again, [suppose]

$$x^3 - x = 25.$$

Since the nearest lower cube is 8, the root of which is 2, which differs from 3 by 1, and the product of this and 1 is a solid which, when subtracted from the cube of 3, leaves 24, not 25, x is irrational.

In order to carry out a transformation of this sort, the coefficient that is demanded must be of the same nature as the coefficient in the given equation. If, then, the root of the given equation is also of this nature, it will be admitted that the root that is being sought is to the newly created root as the coefficient in the given equation is to the coefficient that is demanded.

But if the coefficient of a term is next above the root in nature,[84] it will be admitted that as the coefficient in the given equation is to the coefficient demanded, so the equally high grade of the root that is being sought will be to the equally high grade of the newly created root. By solution of the admitted proportion, the value of the root being sought will be shown in its new form and the given equation will be restated and set up anew.

This becomes clear from one or another of these examples:
Let

$$A^3 + BA^2 = Z^s.$$

This equation is to be so transformed that the positive quadratic affection remains such but with X as its coefficient, not B. Let

$$B : X = A : E,$$

wherefore A will be BE/X. Hence, from what has been given,

$$\frac{B^3E^3}{X^3} + \frac{B^3E^2}{X^2} = Z^s$$

and, multiplying through by X^3 and dividing by B^3,

$$E^3 + XE^2 = \frac{X^3Z^s}{B^3}.$$

Hence what was to be done has been done.
Let

$$x^3 + 20x^2 = 96,000.$$

Then

$$y^3 + y^2 = 12,$$

making y 2. So the root originally sought is 40.

[84] *Sin coefficiens gradui Radicis genere communicet.*

Again, let

$$A^3 - B^2 A = Z^s.$$

This equation is also to be so transformed that the negative linear affection remains such but its coefficient becomes X^2, not B^2. Let

$$B^2 : X^2 = A^2 : E^2.$$

Consequently

$$B : X = A : E.$$

Therefore BE/X will be A. Hence, in accordance with what has been given

$$\frac{B^3 E^3}{X^3} - \frac{B^3 E}{X} = Z^s$$

and, multiplying through by X^3 and dividing by B^3,

$$E^3 - X^2 E = \frac{X^3 Z^s}{B^3}.$$

Hence what was to be done has been done.

Let

$$x^3 - 144x = 10{,}368.$$

Then

$$y^3 - y = 6,$$

and y is 2. Whence the root originally sought is 24.

Nor is the operation any different for prescribed homogeneous terms of comparison. There is no doubt that as one term equal to an affected power is to an equally high homogeneous term that is called for, so the power of the root being sought is to the power of the newly created root and that, by the resolution of this admitted proportion, the value of the root being sought is shown in new terms and the given equation is restated and set up anew. For example, let

$$A^3 + B^p A = Z^3.$$

This equation is to be transformed in such fashion that the power affected positively by a linear term with a plane coefficient is compared to D^3. Let it be conceded that

$$Z : D = A : E.$$

Therefore ZE/D will be A. Hence

$$\frac{Z^3E^3}{D^3} + \frac{B^pZE}{D} = Z^3.$$

Multiplying through by D^3 and dividing by Z^3,

$$E^3 + \frac{B^pD^2E}{Z^2} = D^3.$$

Hence that has been done that was to be done.

Let

$$x^3 + 860x = 1728.$$

Then

$$y^3 + 215y = 216$$

and y is 1. So the root first sought is 2.

CHAPTER IX

Anomalous Reductions of Certain Cubic Equations to Quadratic or Simple Equations

These, then, are the standard methods for the preparation of equations. No rules can be set up for irregular cases, since their peculiarities are no more limited than the force and skill of the artificer in investigating them. Yet in order to stimulate his force and skill, it is proper that certain individual constitutive and reductive theorems about such equations which exhibit any especially outstanding significance or elegance be noted. Such are the following:

PROPOSITION[85] I

If

$$A^3 - 2B^2A = B^3$$

then

$$A^2 - BA = B^2.$$

[85] In 1646 this and the following are given as "Theorems," not "Propositions."

From what has been given, it is clear that, by transposition,

$$A^3 = B^3 + 2B^2A.$$

Then adding B^3 to both sides

$$A^3 + B^3 = 2B^3 + 2B^2A.$$

Dividing through by $A + B$, the left-hand side becomes $A^2 - BA + B^2$, the right-hand $2B^2$. Consequently, subtracting B^2 from both,

$$A^2 - BA = B^2.$$

If

$$x^3 - 18x = 27,$$

then

$$x^2 - 3x = 9.$$

Proposition II

If

$$2B^2A - A^3 = B^3,$$

then

$$A^2 + BA = B^2.$$

From what is given, it is clear that, by transposition,

$$A^3 = 2B^2A - B^3.$$

Then, subtracting B^3 from both sides,

$$A^3 - B^3 = 2B^2A - 2B^3.$$

Dividing through by $A - B$, the left-hand member becomes $A^2 + BA + B^2$, the right-hand $2B^2$. Consequently, subtracting B^2 from both,

$$A^2 + BA = B^2.$$

If

$$18x - x^3 = 27,$$

then

$$x^2 + 3x = 9.$$

PROPOSITION III

If

$$A^3 - 3B^2A = 2B^3,$$

$2B$ is the A that is to be found.

Since $2B$ is the A that is to be found, therefore from what is given

$$8B^3 - (B^2 \times 6B) = 2B^3.$$

These, indeed, are the same.

[If]

$$x^3 - 12x = 16,$$

then x is 4.

PROPOSITION IIII

If

$$3B^2A - A^3 = 2B^3,$$

B is the A that is to be found.

Since B is the A that is to be found, therefore from what is given

$$(B^2 \times 3B) - B^3 = 2B^3.$$

These, indeed, are the same.

[If]

$$6x - x^3 = \sqrt{32},$$

x is $\overline{2}$.[86]

PROPOSITION V

If

$$A^3 - BA^2 + D^pA = BD^p,$$

B is the A that is to be found.

[86] 1615 omits the radical sign.

Since B is the A that is to be found, therefore, from what is given,

$$B^3 - (B \times B^2) + D^p B = BD^p.$$

These are clearly the same.

$$x^3 - 4x^2 + 5x = 20,$$

[20 being] the product of 4 and 5. Therefore x is 4.

PROPOSITION VI

If

$$A^3 + BA^2 - D^2 A = BD^2,$$

D is the A that is to be found.

Since D is the A that is to be found, therefore, from what has been given,

$$D^3 + BD^2 - (D^2 \times D) = BD^2.$$

These are clearly the same.

$$x^3 + 5x^2 - 4x = 20,$$

[20 being] the product of 5 and 4. Therefore x is $\sqrt{4}$.[87]

PROPOSITION VII

If

$$BA^2 + D^2 A - A^3 = D^2 B,$$

either B or D is the A that is to be found.

Since B is the A that is to be found, therefore, from what has been given,

$$B^3 + D^2 B - B^3 = BD^2.$$

This is manifestly so.

Again, since D is the A that is to be found, therefore, from what has been given,

$$BD^2 + D^3 - D^3 = D^2 B.$$

[87] 1646 adds "or 2."

This is manifestly so.

$$6x^2 + 4x - x^3 = 24,$$

making x 6 or 2.

PROPOSITION VIII

If

$$DA^2 + BDA - A^3 = B^3,$$

then

$$DA + BA - A^2 = B^2.$$

From what is given, it is clear that, by transposition,

$$B^3 + A^3 = DA^2 + DBA.$$

Dividing both sides by $A + B$, then,

$$A^2 - BA + B^2 = DA$$

and, by transposition,

$$DA + BA - A^2 = B^2.$$

If,

$$10x^2 + 20x - x^3 = 8,$$

since the cube root of 8 multiplied by 10 is 20,

$$12x - x^2 = 4,$$

making x $6 - \sqrt{32}$ or $6 + \sqrt{32}$.

PROPOSITION IX

If

$$A^3 - DA^2 + DBA = B^3,$$

then

$$DA - BA - A^2 = B^2.$$

From what has been given, it is clear that, by transposition, assuming A is known to be greater than B,

$$A^3 - B^3 = DA^2 - DAB.$$

Divide both sides by $A - B$. Then

$$A^2 + BA + B^2 = DA$$

and, by transposition,

$$DA - BA - A^2 = B^2.$$

But, assuming that B is known to be greater than A,

$$B^3 - A^3 = DAB - DA^2.$$

Divide both sides of the equation by $B - A$. Then

$$B^2 + A^2 + BA = DA,$$

as before.

If

$$x^3 - 10x^2 + 20x = 8,$$

since $\sqrt[3]{8}$ times 10 is 20,

$$8x - x^2 = 4,$$

making x 4 $- \sqrt{12}$ or 4 $+ \sqrt{12}$.

Proposition X

If

$$A^3 - 3B^pA = \sqrt{2B^{ppp}},$$

then $(\sqrt{3B^p} + \sqrt{B^p})/\sqrt{2}$ is the A that is being sought.

Since $(\sqrt{3B^p} + \sqrt{B^p})/\sqrt{2}$ is the A that is to be found, therefore, from what is given

$$\frac{\sqrt{27B^{ppp}} + \sqrt{81B^{ppp}} + \sqrt{27B^{ppp}} + \sqrt{B^{ppp}}}{\sqrt{8}}\ [+] - \frac{\sqrt{27B^{ppp}} - \sqrt{9B^{ppp}}}{\sqrt{2}}$$
$$= 2\sqrt{B^{ppp}},$$

which can clearly be had by subtracting likes from likes in the first part.

[If]

$$x^3 - 6x = 4,$$

x is $\sqrt{3} + 1$.

Proposition XI

If

$$3B^pA - A^3 = \sqrt{2B^{ppp}},$$

then the A that is being sought will be $(\sqrt{3B^p} - \sqrt{B^p})/\sqrt{2}$.

This will be apparent if the path taken in the preceding demonstration is followed.

$$6x - x^3 = 4.$$

Hence x is $\sqrt{3} - 1$, which is the smaller [root]. The other is 2.

CHAPTER X

Continuation of Similar Reductions

Proposition I

If

$$A^3 + 3BA^2 + D^PA^{88} = 2B^3 - D^pB,$$

then

$$A^2 + 2AB = 2B^2 - D^p.$$

Since

$$A^2 + 2AB = 2B^2 - D^p,$$

multiplying through by A,

$$A^3 + 2A^2B = 2B^2A - D^pA.$$

And multiplying the same by B,

$$BA^2 + 2B^2A = 2B^3 - D^pB.$$

Add the equal products to the equal products, and

$$A^3 + 3BA^2 + 2B^2A = 2B^2A - D^PA + 2B^3 - D^pB.$$

Subtracting the affection $2B^2A$ from both sides and transposing the

---

[88] 1615 has B^pA.

affection D^pA in order to set up the equation properly,

$$A^3 + 3BA^2 + D^pA = 2B^3 - D^pB,$$

which is clearly so.

If

$$x^3 + 30x^2 + 44x = 1560,$$

then

$$x^2 + 20x = 156,$$

making x 6.

PROPOSITION II

If

$$A^3 + 3BA^2 - D^pA = 2B^3 + D^pB,$$

then

$$A^2 + 2AB = 2B^2 + D^p.$$

Since

$$A^2 + 2AB = 2B^2 + D^p,$$

multiplying through by A,

$$A^3 + 2A^2B = 2B^2A + D^pA.$$

And if the same terms are multiplied by B,

$$BA^2 + 2B^2A = 2B^3 + D^pB.$$

Add the equal products to the equal products, and

$$A^3 + 3BA^2 + 2B^2A = 2B^2A + D^pA + 2B^3 + D^pB.$$

Then, deleting the affection $2B^2A$ from both sides and transposing the affection D^pA in order to set up the equation properly,

$$A^3 + 3BA^2 - D^pA = 2B^3 + D^pB,$$

which is clearly so.

If

$$x^3 + 30x^2 - 24x = 2240,$$

then

$$x^2 + 20x = 224,$$

making x 8.

Proposition III

If

$$A^3 - 3BA^2 + D^pA = D^pB - 2B^3,$$

and if $3B^2$ is greater than D^p, then

$$2BA - A^2 = D^p - 2B^2.$$

Since

$$2BA - A^2 = D^p - 2B^2,$$

then, multiplying through by $B - A$,

$$2B^2A - BA^2 - 2BA^2 + A^{3\ 89} = 2B^2A - D^pA + D^pB - 2B^3$$

and, arranging the equation properly,

$$A^3 - 3BA^2 + D^pA = D^pB - 2B^3,$$

which is clearly so.

If

$$x^3 - 30x^2 + 236x = 360,$$

then

$$20x - x^2 = 36,$$

making x 2 or 18.

Given the same, A can also equal B, whether $3B^2$ is greater or less than D^p.[90] For, since it is proposed that

$$A^3 - 3BA^2 + D^pA = D^pB - 2B^3,$$

and A is equal to B, then

$$B^3 - 3B^3 + D^pB = D^pB - 2B^3,$$

which is clearly so.

[89] 1646 has $2A^3$.
[90] 1615 has B^p.

If

$$x^3 - 30x^2 + 236x = 360,$$

x has been shown to be 2 or 18. It is also 10.

$$x^3 - 30x^2 + 264x = 640,$$

making x 4 or 16, for

$$20x - x^2 = 64,$$

making x 4 or 16.

PROPOSITION IIII

If

$$3BA^2 + D^pA - A^3 = 2B^3 + D^pB,$$

then

$$A^2 - 2BA = 2B^2 + D^p.$$

Since

$$A^2 - 2BA = 2B^2 + D^p,$$

multiply through by $B - A$, and

$$BA^2 - 2B^2A - A^3 + 2BA^2 = 2B^3 + BD^p - 2B^2A - D^pA$$

and, setting up the equation properly,

$$3B^2A \ ^{91} + D^pA - A^3 = 2B^3 + D^pB,$$

which is clearly so.

If

$$30x^2 + 24x - x^3 = 2240,$$

then

$$x^2 - 20x = 224,$$

making x 28.

Using the same terms that have been given, A also becomes B for, if it is proposed that

$$3BA^2 + D^pA - A^3 = 2B^3 + D^pB$$

[91]1615 has $3BA^2$.

and that A is B, then

$$3B^3 + D^pB - B^3 = 2B^3 + D^pB,$$

which is clearly so.
　If

$$30x^2 + 24x - x^3 = 2240,$$

x is 10.

PROPOSITION V

　If

$$3BA^2 - D^pA - A^3 = 2B^3 - D^pB,$$

　then

$$A^2 - 2BA = 2B^2 - D^p.$$

Since

$$A^2 - 2BA = 2B^2 - D^p,$$

multiplying through by $B - A$,

$$BA^2 - 2B^2A - A^3 + 2BA^2 = 2B^3 - D^pB - 2B^2A + D^pA$$

and, setting the equation straight,

$$3BA^2 - D^pA - A^3 = 2B^3 - D^pB,$$

which is clearly so.

$$30x^2 - 156x - x^3 = 440,$$

therefore

$$x^2 - 20x = 44,$$

making x 22.
　Using the same terms as those given, A can also be B. For if it is proposed that

$$3BA^2 - D^pA - A^3 = 2B^3 - D^pB$$

and that A is B, then

$$3B^3 - D^pB - B^3 = 2B^3 - D^pB,$$

which is clearly so.

$$30x^2 - 156x - x^3 = 440,$$

making x 10.

PROPOSITION VI

Pertaining to the Biquadratic

If

$$A^4 - 2XA^3 + 4X^3A = 2X^4,$$

then

$$2X^2A^2 - A^4 = 4X^4 - 2X^3\sqrt{3X^2}.$$

[For, when

$$2X^2A^2 - A^4 = 4X^4 - 2X^3\sqrt{3X^2},$$

then, by transposition and dividing by $2X^3$,

$$\frac{4X^4 + A^4 - 2X^2A^2}{2X^3} = \sqrt{3X^2}.]^{92}$$

Squaring both sides, multiplying by $4X^6$ and making the proper transposition,

$$16X^6A^2 + 4X^2A^6 - A^8 - 12X^4A^4 = 4X^8$$

which is clearly so, for, when both sides of the first equation,

$$4X^3A - 2XA^3 = 2X^4 - A^4,$$

are squared and everything is set straight, it becomes the equation of the eighth power[93] already set out. So A^2 becomes X^2 plus or minus the root of the residual or negative binomial $\sqrt{12X^4 - 3X^2}$.[94]

Let X be 1 and let A be x. Then

$$x^4 - 2x^3 + 4x = 2,$$

whence

$$2x^2 - x^4 = 4 - \sqrt{12},$$

making x^2 1 plus or minus the root of the negative binomial $\sqrt{12} - 3$.

[92]The bracketed material does not appear in 1615.

[93]1615 has "fifth power."

[94]I.e., $A^2 = X^2 \pm \sqrt{\sqrt{12X^4} - 3X^2}$.

CHAPTER XI

A Collection of Certain Special Equations with Multiple Affections

PROPOSITION I

If

$$A^2 + BA = B^2,$$

$2B$ is a length divided into three proportional segments, the first and greatest of which is B and the second is A. In this operation it may be said that B is to be divided between the mean and the [smaller] extreme in simple ratio.

PROPOSITION II

If

$$A^3 + BA^2 + B^2A = B^3,$$

$2B$ is a length cut into four segments in continued proportion, the first and greatest of which is B and the second is A. In this operation, B may be said to be divided between the mean and the [smaller] extreme in duplicate ratio.

PROPOSITION III

If

$$A^4 + BA^3 + B^2A^2 + B^3A = B^4,$$

$2B$ is a length cut into five segments in continued proportion, the first and greatest of which is B and the second is A. In this operation, B may be said to be divided between the mean and the [smaller] extreme in triplicate ratio.

PROPOSITION IIII

If

$$A^5 + BA^4 + B^2A^3 + B^3A^2 + B^4A = B^5,$$

$2B$ is a length cut into six segments in continued proportion, the first and greatest of which is B and the second is A. In this operation, B may be said to be divided between the mean and the [smaller] extreme in quadruplicate ratio.

PROPOSITION V

If

$$A^6 + BA^5 + B^2A^{4\ 95} + B^3A^3 + B^4A^2 + B^5A = B^6,$$

$2B$ is a length cut into seven segments in continued proportion, the first and the greatest of which is B and the second is A. In this operation, B may be said to be divided between the mean and the [smaller] extreme in quintuplicate ratio.

CHAPTER XII

Another Collection of the Same

PROPOSITION I

If

$$A^2 + BA = BZ,$$

B is the first or smaller of the extremes in a series of three proportionals and Z is the sum of the other two, making A the second.

PROPOSITION II

If

$$A^3 + BA^2 + B^2A = B^2Z,$$

B is the first in a series of four continued proportionals and Z is the sum of the other three, making A the second.

PROPOSITION III

If

$$A^4 + BA^3 + B^2A^2 + B^3A = B^3Z,$$

B is the first in a series of five continued proportionals and Z is the sum of the other four, making A the second.

[95] 1615 has BA^4.

PROPOSITION IIII

If

$$A^5 + BA^4 + B^2A^3 + B^3A^2 + B^4A = B^4Z,$$

B is the first in a series of six continued proportionals and Z is the sum of the other five, making A the second.

PROPOSITION V

If

$$A^6 + BA^5 + B^2A^4 + B^3A^3 + B^4A^2 + B^5A = B^5Z,$$

B is the first in a series of seven continued proportionals and Z is the sum of the other six, making A the second.

CHAPTER XIII

A Third Collection of the Same

PROPOSITION I

If

$$BA - A^2 = BZ,$$

B is the first or greater of the extremes in a series of three proportionals and Z is the difference between the other two, making A the second. It is possible, moreover, for there to be two [values for A], for it is also the difference between the first and second terms.

But if

$$A^2 - BA = BZ,$$

B is the first or smaller of the extremes and the difference between the other two is Z, making A the second, as before.

Let the proportionals be 4, 6, 9:

$$9x - x^2 = 18,$$

making x 6 and also 3, But if

$$x^2 - 4x = 12,$$

x is 6.

PROPOSITION II

If

$$A^3 - BA^2 + B^2A = B^2Z,$$

B is the first in a series of four continued proportionals and Z is the difference between the other three taken alternately, making A the second.

Let the continued proportionals be 1, 2, 4, 8:

$$x^3 - 8x^2 + 64x = 192,$$

making x 4. Or

$$x^3 - x^2 + x = 6,$$

making x 2.

PROPOSITION III

If

$$B^3A - B^2A^2 + BA^3 - A^4 = B^3Z,$$

B is the first or greatest in a series of five continued proportionals and the difference between the other four taken alternately is Z, making A the second or greatest of the means. There can also be two [values for A].

But if

$$A^4 - BA^3 + B^2A^2 - B^3A = B^3Z,$$

B is the first or smaller of the extremes and the difference between the other four taken alternately is Z, making A the smallest of the means.

Let the continued proportionals be 1, 2, 4, 8, 16:

$$4096x - 256x^2 + 16x^3 - x^4 = 20,480,$$

making x 8. Or

$$x^4 - x^3 + x^2 - x = 10,$$

making x 2.

PROPOSITION IIII

If

$$A^5 - BA^4 + B^2A^3 - B^3A^2 + B^4A = B^4Z,$$

B is the first and greatest in a series of six continued proportionals and Z is the difference between the remaining five taken alternately, making A the second.

Let the continued proportionals be 1, 2, 4, 8, 16, 32:

$$x^5 - 32x^4 + 1024x^3 - 32{,}768x^2 + 1{,}048{,}576x = 11{,}534{,}336,$$

making x 16. Or

$$x^5 - x^4 + x^3 - x^2 + x = 22,$$

making x 2.

Each of these [theorems] is demonstrable by zetetics. The collection that now follows leaves the given theorems free for examination in their own terms. It pertains to equations which, marvelously, are solvable by multiple roots.

CHAPTER XIIII

A Fourth Collection

PROPOSITION I

If

$$A(B + D) - A^2 = BD,$$

A is explicable by either B or D.

$$3x - x^2 = 2,$$

making x 1 or 2.

Proposition II

If

$$A^3 - A^2(B + D + G) + A(BD + BG + DG) = BDG,$$

A is explicable by any of the three, *B, D* or *G*.

$$x^3 - 6x^2 + 11x = 6,$$

making *x* 1, 2 or 3.

Proposition III

If

$$A(BDG + BDH + BGH + DGH) - A^2(BD + BG + BH$$
$$+ DG + DH + GH) + A^3(B + D + G + H) - A^4$$
$$= BDGH,$$

A is explicable by any of the four, *B, D, G* or *H*.

$$50x - 35x^2 + 10x^3 - x^4 = 24,$$

making *x* 1, 2, 3, or 4.

Proposition IIII

If

$$A^5 - A^4(B + D + G + H + K) + A^3(BD + BG + BH +$$
$$BK + DG + DH + DK + GH + GK + HK) - A^2(BDG$$
$$+ BDH + BDK + BGH + BGK + BHK + DGH + DGK$$
$$+ DHK + GHK) + A(BDGH + BDGK + BDHK + BG$$
$$HK + DGHK) = BDGHK,$$

A is explicable by any of the five, *B, D, G, H* or *K*.

$$x^5 - 15x^4 + 85x^3 - 225x^2 + 274x = 120,$$

making *x* 1, 2, 3, 4 or 5.

I have treated [elsewhere] at length and in other respects with the elegant reasoning behind this beautiful observation, [so] this must be the end and crown [of this work].

ON THE NUMERICAL
RESOLUTION OF POWERS BY
EXEGETICS[1]

[Excerpts]

ON THE NUMERICAL RESOLUTION OF PURE POWERS

There is nothing more natural, according to all the philosophers, than for anything to resolve itself into the stuff from whence it sprang. So a pure square, a pure cube, or any [other] pure power, whatever its position among the proportionally ascending terms, is clearly made up, by arithmetic operation, of as many individual roots as the whole root had digits in the beginning. These must be separated [from each other] and extracted in order [to find] the value of the individual parts.

[If] the root of a number is contained [, for example,] in the single digit 7, from which a power is to be developed, it is 7 that is squared or raised to the degree that the nature of the power demands.

Suppose a root consists of two digits, say 12. Its power is derived from 10 and 2.

If a root consists of three digits, say 124, its power will derive from 100, 20 and 4. And if [the root consists] of more [digits], then [the power derives] from more [individual terms].

So the resolution of any power begins by distributing it among and extracting as many individual roots as the whole root had digits to begin with in order [to find] the value of the individual [roots].

But resolution cannot be accomplished in one step, since the route of the most simple composition, one [involving] only two [terms], is a broken one. So it proceeds by stages. That is, the first resolution of the whole is into two roots, the greatest and the next-to-greatest. Then the greatest and next-to-greatest are added together and treated as one root. What follows is treated as another root, and so on in that order.

---

[1]This is the title in 1600: *De Numerosa Potestatum ad Exegesim Resolutione.* 1646's is more complete: *De Numerosa Potestatum Purarum, atque Adfectarum ad Exegesin Resolutione Tractatus.*

The whole art [of doing this] is set out in the following precepts:

1

First, let the last digit of the power to be resolved—that is, the first digit moving from right to left—be the seat of the unit making up the power[2] of the last and least of the individual roots and note it by placing a dot underneath it.

2

Let the next digit, proceeding from right to left, be the seat of the first step parodic to the power and designate it by the sign N or R ("R" standing for the simple [root]).[3]

3

Let the following digit be named for the second parodic step and let it be designated by the sign S [for square], and so on in this way until you arrive at the power.

4

When [in this designating process] you have arrived at the power, again place a dot to mark the last column among those making up the power of the next-to-last root and again, moving forward beyond the dot, let symbols be placed in the order of the parodic steps. Continue this way until you have arrived at the power of the first and greatest of the individual [roots].

5

Then, in resolving the number, say that the root that is being sought consists of as many digits as, in the [whole] power, there are dots for the individual powers.

[2] *sedes . . . unitatum metientium potestatem.* That is, the last column among those in which the digits comprising the power are found.

[3] In the Latin the designators are N (presumably for *nomen*) and S (for *simplex*). In the next paragraph the designator is Q (for *quadratum*). I have changed S to R in order to have S available for square.

6

Extract the first, which is also the greatest, root from the units making up the first—that is, the greatest—individual power either by common knowledge or from the table set out below, since the art does not cover the solution of powers the roots of which are one-digit numbers.

7

Multiply the lower-order grades of the first individual root as many times as the nature of the power [requires][4] seat the individual results at the proper place, [add them] and divide[5] [the sum] into the term to be resolved, after having subtracted the first individual power from the latter. Then assume that what results from the division is the second root. I point out, [however,] that the division many not be completely exact, for it must be understood that such a root arises from this division that the [sum of the] homogeneous terms derived from the second individual root itself and from the products of its lower-order grades and the first root and the reciprocal grades of the first root may equal the term to be resolved or may fall short of it.

8

If they are equal, call the work complete. If they are less and another dot is left over, let the two roots that have already been elicited be worked with [together] as though they were one and let this now be the first and greater [root] and, in exactly the same way as before, proceed to the discovery of the next, the second and smaller, [root] and continue thus in proper order.

9

But if, although they are less, there is no dot for a power left over, it is clear that the root of the term to be resolved is irrational. To the collective

---

[4]*secundum Potestatis conditionem, tantuplantor. Tantuplico* is not a dictionary word. It is constructed, presumably, by analogy to *duplico, triplico,* and the like. In effect, what Viète is saying is that in, for instance, the case of a pure fourth power, the first root is to be cubed and multiplied by 4, then squared and multiplied by 6, and finally taken by itself and multiplied by 4, these being the "parodic" (lower-order) grades and their coefficients in the usual binomial expansion of the fourth degree.

[5]*subjiciuntor,* an unusual term for this operation.

root, therefore, add a fraction the numerator of which is the remainder of the term to be solved and [the denominator of which is] the same as what the divisors would be if another point were added to the term to be resolved.[6] This fraction, added to the sum of the individual roots, makes a root for the power to be resolved larger than the true root. If, in the second power, the denominator is increased by 1, it makes a root smaller than the true one. The root lies implicitly between these divisors.[7] It may be elicited as closely as you wish by, say, adding zeros[8] to that which is to be solved and continuing the work. And this is necessarily within the limits of the tenth,[9] otherwise the operation has not been carried out correctly.

To illustrate [these rules] more particularly, first let a table be set out for the extraction of one-digit roots:

x	1	2	3	4	5	6	7	8	9
x^2	1	4	9	16	25	36	49	64	81
x^3	1	8	27	64	125	216	343	512	729
x^4	1	16	81	256	625	1,296	2,401	4,096	6,561
x^5	1	32	243	1,024	3,125	7,776	16,807	32,768	59,049
x^6	1	64	729	4,096	15,625	46,656	117,649	262,144	531,441
x^7	1	128	2,187	16,384	78,125	279,936	823,543	2,097,152	4,782,969
x^8	1	256	6,561	65,536	390,625	1,679,616	5,764,801	16,777,216	43,046,721
x^9	1	512	19,683	262,144	1,953,125	10,077,696	40,353,607	134,217,728	387,420,489

Following this, let us construct individual problems for each of the powers.

PROBLEM I

To extract analytically the root of a pure square given numerically.

Let x^2 equal 29, 16.[10] How much is x, the root of the given pure square?

The given square is known to be composed of as many individual roots as, at the outset or at the time the square was constructed, there were digits in the whole root that is to be found. To show this number of digits clearly, the last digit of the given square, reading from left to right, is marked with a dot and [likewise] every second digit moving towards the front, since one

[6]*fragmentus cuius numerator est numerus a magnitudine resoluta reliquus. Divisores iidem, qui essent si aliquod punctum Potestati addictum superesset resolvendum.*

[7]*In divisiboribus . . . inest implicite latus.*

[8]*numerales circulos.*

[9]*intra denarii metam.*

[10]So printed in 1600; 1646 has 2916.

arrives at the square in one ascending step. Thus if there are two dots the whole square will be said to be made up of that many individual squares and the whole root to be made up of that many individual roots, since the way of resolution is the same as that of composition.

When, moreover, a square is constructed from two individual roots, the square of the first root, plus the plane produced by twice the first root and the second, plus the square of the second is equal to the composite square. Therefore let the resolution be commenced in accordance with the synthetic theorem [already] set out. Thus the digit marked by the first dot on the left is said to be the seat of the units making up the square of the first or greater root, the next place to be the seat of the plane based on the first power, and the last the seat of the units making up the square of the second root. If there were more dots, the resolution would nevertheless be commenced [this way], since the square would be understood from the beginning to be composed of only two roots which, when extracted, are joined together as one, and after that it would be treated as if composed of that sum for the first root and of the [next] following for the second, and so on in this order.

In accordance with the given theorem, the root of the first square is to be extracted from 29, which is clearly not a square number. But since it is greater than 25, the nearest square number, let us say that the first root is 5, if this accords with everything else—a matter that the outcome of the work will indicate shortly—and let it be shown by one digit which, it is understood, is followed by as many zeroes as there are quadratic dots left over. When, then, 25 is subtracted from 29, the remainder is 4. So the whole remainder—4, 16—is made up of the plane derived from the first root times the second, plus the square of the second.

Twice the root of the first square constitutes, as it were, a divisor having its seat under the plane digit indicated by "N" and extending forward from there if doubling it so requires. Twice 5 is 10. When this is divided into 41, the result is the breadth 4. If it [i.e., the trial division] did not yield a breadth less than 10, it would be clear that 5, the root first extracted, was too small and that the work should be commenced again by extracting a root closer to the greater square and then [proceeding] by the same method.

Therefore when 4 is multiplied by 10, it makes 40, twice the plane derived from the first and second roots. Then the square of the second root, 4, is 16, and when this is placed below the dot assigned to it, and the plane [is placed] under its seat, as appear to be proper seeing that the first root is known, as has been noted, to be accompanied by zeros, the two added together make 4, 16, a number equal to the remainder of the given square. Thus it is concluded that 54 is the root of the square 29, 16.

Model for the Resolution of a Pure Square

I Extraction of the First Individual Root

		0	0	As many zeros as there are quad-
	r	5	4	ratic points or
	r^2	25	16	individual roots

Square to be resolved	2 9	1 6
	·	N · Seats of individual squares and
	S'	S'' of planes based on the roots
Plane to be subtracted	2 5	Square of the first root
Remainder of square to be resolved	4	1 6

II Extraction of the Second Individual Root

	4	1 6 ·
Divisor: twice the first root	1	0
Planes to be subtracted	4	0 Second root times twice the first
		1 6 Square of the second root
Sum of planes to be subtracted equal to remainder of square to be resolved.	4	1 6

So if x^2 is 2916, x is 54 from the reverse of the way of composition which, it will be seen, has been strictly observed.

But if the sum of the planes were not equal to the remainder, but were less than it, it would be clear that the root is irrational. Therefore it cannot be shown except by using a radical sign.[11] If x^2 is 2 and x is to be found, it will be said to be $\sqrt{2}$.

But if you are looking for the approximate root of 2, extract the nearest root, which is 1, and divide the remainder by twice the root just discovered and add this as a fraction to the root discovered. Thus the root of the number 2 can be said to be $1\frac{1}{2}$, but this is more than the true root. Or add 1 to the denominator and the root will be said to be $1\frac{1}{3}$, which is less than the true root. Midway between the two is $1\frac{5}{12}$, which is very close to the true root.

Alternatively, pairs of zeros may be added to the given square up to

---

[11] *notam asymmetriae exhibendo.* In 1600 the symbol used in the next sentence is L; in 1646 it is $\sqrt{}$.

infinity and the root may be extracted from [a number] extended this way as from an exact square number. Thus if you are seeking the root of 2, a square, extract, if you wish, the root of 2 0̇0 0̇0 0̇0 0̇0 0̇0 0̇0 0̇0 0̇0 0̇0 0̇0 0̇0 0̇0 0̇0, [which is] 141,421,356,237,309,505. So the root of 2 is said to be approximately

$$\frac{141,421,356,237,309,505}{100,000,000,000,000,000}.$$

Likewise the root of 3 equals approximately

$$\frac{173,205,080,756,887,730}{100,000,000,000,000,000}.$$

PROBLEM II

To extract analytically the root of a pure cube given numerically.

Let x^3 equal 157,464. How much is x, the root of the given pure cube?

The cube given in numbers is known to be composed of as many individual roots as the whole root that is being sought had digits in the beginning or at the time the cube was formed. To find the number of digits of the given numerical cube, mark with a dot the last digit, progressing from left to right, and every third one thereafter, moving towards the front, the two remaining intermediate ones (since there are two steps above the units) [being marked] N and S. Since there are two dots, it may be said that the whole cube consists of that many individual cubes or the [whole] root of that many individual roots. And since the way of resolution is the same as that of composition—when a cube is constructed from two individual roots, the cube of the first root, plus the solid from three times the first and the square of the second, plus the solid from the second and three times the square of the first, plus the cube of the second equals the composite cube—begin the resolution in accordance with the synthetic theorem already set out. So the first digit marked by a dot occurring on the left may be called the seat of the digits making up the cube of the first and greater root, and next digit the seat of three times the solid based on the square of the same, the next the seat of three times the solid based on the root itself, and the last the seat of the digits making up the cube of the second root. But if there were more dots, the resolution would nevertheless be instituted [thus], since the cube would be understood at the beginning to be composed of only those two roots which, when extracted, are treated as if they were one and afterwards would be understood to be composed of that sum as if it were the first root and what follows as the second, and so on in order to infinity.

The root of the first cube in the problem that has been proposed is to be extracted from 157, which is clearly not a cubic number. Since it is greater than 125, the nearest cubic number, we say that the first root is 5, if everything else agrees. This the outcome of the work will indicate shortly. Only one figure is extracted but it is followed, as must be understood, by as many zeros as there are additional cubic dots.

Now when 125 is subtracted from 157, it leaves 32. So the whole residual number, 32,464, is made up of the solid from the square of the second root and three times the first, plus the solid from the second and three times the square of the first,[12] plus the cube of the second. Hence three times the square of the first is placed at the seat indicated for the second grade—that is, [at the spot] nearest the dot for the first cube—and three times the second [at the spot] under the next succeeding grade, although the divisors of the number may, if necessary, be carried forward from this. Three times the square of 5 is 75 which, if divided into 324, gives the length 4. So 4 will be the second root, if the other divisors agree, which is something the outcome of the operation will indicate shortly. But if the division of 324 could not be made with a number or length less than 10, it would be clear that 5, the first root extracted, was too small and the work would be done all over again and the root of the next greater cube would be extracted following the same process.

Furthermore, when 4 is multiplied by 75, it makes 300, three times the solid from the second root and the square of the first. The square of 4 is 16 which, when it is multiplied by 15, three times the first root, is 240, to be allocated to the next seat, three times the solid from the first root and the square of the second root.[13] Finally the cube of 4 is[14] 64. And when this cube of the second root is placed under the dot assigned to it, the solid from three times[15] the first root and the square of the second under the symbol for the first step, and three times[16] the solid from the second root and the square of the first under the symbol for the second step, as is obviously proper, especially since the first root is known, as has been noted, to be accompanied by a zero, their sum is 32,464, a number equal to the remainder of the proposed cube. So it is concluded that 54 is the root of the cube 157,464.

[12] 1600 has "plus the solid from three times the first and the square of the second."
[13] 1600 has "three times the solid from the second root and the square of the first."
[14] 1600 has *ex*, a misprint for *est*.
[15] 1600 omits these two words.
[16] 1600 omits these two words.

Model for the Resolution of a Pure Cube

I   Extraction of the First Individual Root

			0	0	As many zeros as there are cubic dots or individual roots
r			5	4
r^2			25	16
r^3			125	64

Cube to be resolved	1 5 7	4 6 4
	.	$S\,N$.	Seats of individual cubes and of solids based on the lower terms
	C'	C''
	— — —	— — —
Solid to be subtracted	1 2 5		Cube of the first root
	— — —	— — —
Remainder of the cube to be resolved	3 2	4 6 4
	— — —	— — —

II   Extraction of the Second Individual Root

Remainder of the cube to be resolved	3 2	4 6 4 .
	— — —	— — —
Divisors $\left\{\vphantom{\begin{array}{c}a\\b\end{array}}\right.$	7	5	Three times the square of the first root
	— — —	1 5	Three times the first root
		— — —
Sum of the divisors	7	6 5
	— — —	— — —
Solids to be subtracted $\left\{\vphantom{\begin{array}{c}a\\b\\c\end{array}}\right.$	3 0	0	Product of the second root and three times the square of the first
	2	4 0	Product of the square of the second root and three times the first
		6 4	Cube of the second root
	— — —	— — —
Sum of the solids to be subtracted equal to the remainder of the cube to be resolved	3 2	4 6 4
	— — —	— — —

So if x^3 equals 157,464, x is 54 from the reverse of the way of composition which, it will be seen, has been strictly observed.

If the sum of the solids were not equal to the remainder [of the cube] but were less than it, it would indicate that the cube root is irrational. Therefore it cannot be shown except by using a radical sign. When x^3 equals 2 and x is to be found, it is said to be $\sqrt[3]{2}$.

But if you are looking for the approximate [cube] root of 2, add to the given cube [as many] groups of three zeros [as you wish] up to infinity and extract the root from this [more nearly] accurate cube number as so extended. Thus if the cube root of 2 is being sought. From the cube 2,000,000,000,000,000,000,000,000,000,000 there comes the root

125,992,104,989. So the cube [root] of 2 is said to be approximately

$$1\,\frac{25,992,104,989}{100,000,000,000}+.$$

So also the cube [root] of 4 equals

$$1\,\frac{58,340,105,196}{100,000,000,000}+.$$

[Problems III and IIII, here omitted, deal with the extraction of the roots of pure fourth and fifth powers.]

PROBLEM V

To extract the root of a pure sixth power given numerically.

Let x^6 equal 191,102,976. How much is x, the root of the given pure sixth power?

Place a cubo-cubic dot under 6, the last digit, to mark the units making up the last [individual] sixth power. Then, since there are five grades between the units and the sixth power—x, x^2, x^3, x^4 and x^5—skip five intermediate digits—7, 9, 2, 0 and 1—and mark the next one with a dot again. This is 1. Next consider carefully the theorem on the development [of a pure sixth power]. According to it the sixth power of the first root, plus the second root times six times the fifth power of the first, plus the square of the second times 15 times the fourth power of the first, plus the cube of the second times 20 times the cube of the first, plus the fourth power of the second times 15 times the square of the first, plus the fifth power of the second times six times the first, plus the sixth power of the second is equal to the sixth power of the sum of all the roots. Carry out the resolution in accordance with this theorem, as in the model:

Model for the Resolution of a Pure Sixth Power

I   Extraction of the First Individual Root

Sixth power to be resolved	1 9 1	1 0 2 9 7 6	Seats of the indi-		0	0 As many
	·	SC SS C S N ·	vidual powers	r	2	4 zeros as
			and of the	r^2	4	16 there are
			solido-solids	r^3	8	64 cubo-cubic
			based on its	r^4	16	256 dots or
	CC'	CC''	[lower-order]	r^5	32	1024 individual
			grades.	r^6	64	4096 roots
Solido-solid to be subtracted	6 4		Sixth power of first root			
Remainder of the sixth power to be resolved	1 2 7	1 0 2 9 7 6				

II   Extraction of the Second Individual Root

Remainder of the sixth power to be resolved	1 2 7	1 0 2 9 7 6	

	1 9	2		Six times fifth power of first root
	2	4 0		Fifteen times fourth power of same
Divisors		1 6 0		Twenty times cube of same
		6 0		Fifteen times square of same
		1 2		Six times first root

Sum of the divisors	2 1	7 6 6 1 2

	7 6	8	Second root times six times fifth power of first
	3 8	4 0	Square of second root times 15 times fourth power of first
Solido-solids to be subtracted	1 0	2 4 0	Cube of second root times 20 times cube of first
	1	5 3 6 0	Fourth power of second root times 15 times square of first[17]
		1 2 2 8 8	Fifth power of second root times six times first
		4 0 9 6	Sixth power of second root

Sum of the solido-solids equal to remainder of sixth power to be resolved	1 2 7	1 0 2 9 7 6

So if x^6 equals 191,102,976, x is 24. By the reverse of the way of composition which, it will be seen, has been strictly observed.

And if x^6 equals 2,000,000, since 2,000,000 is not an exact cubo-cubic number, the approximate root can be extracted by adding zeroes in sixes:

$$11 \frac{224,175}{1,000,000}$$

will be less than the true root and

$$11 \frac{224,176}{1,000,000}$$

will be greater than the true root. The mean of these,

$$11 \frac{448,351}{2,000,000}$$

will be very near it.[18]

[17] 1600 has "Fourth power of first root times 15 times the square of second."

[18] These values are given as they appear in 1646 and in the errata to 1600. In the original text of 1600 they are given as

$$11 \frac{228,439}{1,254,423}, \quad 11 \frac{228,439}{1,254,422} \quad \text{and} \quad 11 \frac{456,878}{2,508,845},$$

respectively.

ON THE NUMERICAL RESOLUTION OF AFFECTED POWERS

The resolution of affected powers follows closely that of pure powers, especially when the affected powers have been suitably prepared. They are understood, moreover, to be suitably prepared when they are burdened with the fewest possible affections, all of which are either positive or negative; thus, indeed, the power should be positive and should not be subtracted from a homogeneous term or terms and there should be no ambiguity [arising from] mixed positive and negative terms.[19]

Affected powers of this sort, though deceptive, are composed and resolved like pure powers, merely having additional given terms which, with specified grade, make up the homogeneous terms of affection and for this reason are properly called "coefficients."[20]

It is understood, in other words, that affected powers are derived from two roots plus one or more coefficients and that they are resolved in the same way—that is, the reverse of the way of composition—[as pure powers] by observing the proper location, order, law and progression of the coefficients as well as of the power and the lower-order terms.

As in the case of pure powers, theory shows, and a review[21] of the work accomplished by symbolic logistic demonstrates, the plan of composition and, from this, theorems firmly rooted in the art and the rule of multiplication associated with it.

The root of a given affected power is the sum of the [individual] roots resulting from the resolution.

A multiplicity of affections[22] does not lead to a complete impossibility of solution but it creates difficulty and anxiety, especially in the higher parodic grades.

It is known that any power can be freed from an affection in the highest grade; that an affected fourth power can be reduced to a second power by means of cubes on a plane root; and that the powers of a plane root or any other higher term can be transformed to powers of a simple root.

When a power is subtracted from a lower-order homogeneous term, there are two roots. There is also ambiguity when powers have affections

---

[19]The clarity of this sentence in the Latin leaves a great deal to be desired: *Tunc autem decenter praeparari intelliguntur, cum parcissime fuerint adfectionibus obrutae, iisque omnino adfirmatis, aut negatis omnino, ita tamen ut Potestas adfirmata sit, non etiam ab Homogenea vel Homogeneis gradu insignitis avellatur, ac denique mixtim ita negatis & adfirmatis, ut non insit ambiguitas.* As will be seen, Viète carries numerical resolution into fields that the injunction of this sentence warns against.

[20]*subgraduales.*

[21]ἀνακεφαλαίωσις

[22]πολυπαθεία

partly negative and partly positive if a higher grade times its coefficient [produces] a negative homogeneous term that outweighs the positive homogeneous products [of other terms and their] coefficients.[23]

Every doubt must first be resolved, lest the role of conjecture[24] be stronger than that of art, for an exact art cannot be erected on doubtful [foundations].

Furthermore, as in the case of pure powers, so also in that of affected powers, we require rational integral numbers to be used, not fractions or irrationals.

Let [problems] that are less amenable to the resolving process be reduced by art to those that are more amenable, so that the resolution of the former becomes clear from that of the latter through a known difference or ratio between the roots of the two. How such reductions, whether arithmetic or geometric, are made will be shown more conveniently in a treatise specially devoted to this subject.[25]

Having set out these cautions, I go on to the matter at hand and first to the analysis of powers affected positively.

PROBLEM I

To extract analytically the root of a given numerical square affected by the plane derived from its root and a given linear coefficient.

Let

$$x^2 + 7x = 60,750.$$

What is to be found is x, the root of the given affected square.

That is, a certain number multiplied by itself and by 7 makes 60,750. What is that number?

The square, 60,750, is not pure but is affected by the product of its root and 7, the given length.

It may be noted that every affected square can be reduced to a pure square. But a general art must be expounded generally, lest it fall into the error of the old analysts.

---

[23]*quando coefficientes sub gradu elatiore homogeneas negatas coefficientibus adfirmatas praepollent.*

[24]*divinationi locus.*

[25]The reference is to the *Two Treatises on the Understanding and Amendment of Equations.*

The development of a square affected positively adds to the development of a pure square only the product of the individual root that is first extracted and the linear coefficient plus the second root times the same. In order to extract the roots of the affected square, therefore, mark the seats of the units making up the individual squares at each alternate digit as in the analysis of a pure square, properly placing dots underneath from right to left. And, since the coefficient of the first power is a length, set up as many places for the simple roots as there are places or dots for the squares. Set these up above the individual digits and mark them with dots placed there, and let the linear coefficient rest at the last seat of the roots—that is, at the first, moving from left to right. If this [i.e., the coefficient] consists of more than one digit, the others are placed towards the front.

Having done all this, the individual roots are extracted in the same way as in the analysis of a pure square except that the coefficient is included among the divisors and the individual roots, [as they are] extracted, are multiplied by it, the resulting plane being placed under the seat of the coefficient and subtracted from the given affected square. Then, when the other divisors are moved, the coefficient is subjoined to the following places in orderly fashion, as in this model:

Model for the Resolution of a Square with a Positive Affection on the First Power

I   Extraction of the First Individual Root

			0	0	0
		r	2	4	
		r^2	4	16	

As many zeros as there are dots for the squares or individual roots

Linear coefficient of the first power		7		
			·	· ·
	—	— —	— —	
	6	0 7	5 0	
	·	R ·	R ·	
	S'	S''	S'''	
	—	— —	— —	

As many linear dots as there are quadratic

Quadratic dots

Planes to be subtracted	{	4		
			1 4	

Square of the first root
Plane derived from the first root and coefficient

		—	— —	— —
Sum of the planes to be subtracted		4	1 4	
		—	— —	— —
Remainder of the affected square to be subtracted		1	9 3	5 0

II   Extraction of the Second Individual Root

Upper part of the divisors				7	Linear coefficient
Remainder of the affected square to be subtracted	1	9 3	5 0		
Lower part of the divisors		4			Twice the first root
Sum of the divisors		4 0	7		
Planes to be subtracted $\left\{\vphantom{\begin{array}{c}1\\1\\1\end{array}}\right.$	1	6			Second root times twice the first
		1 6			Square of the second root
		2	8		Second root times the coefficient
Sum of the planes to be subtracted	1	7 8	8		
Remainder of the affected square to be resolved		1 4	7 0		

Now let the two roots that have been extracted be treated as one, the first, and proceed to

III   Extraction of the Third Individual Root as if it were the Second

Upper part of the divisors			7	Linear coefficient	
Remainder of the affected square to be resolved	1 4	7 0			
Lower part of the divisors		4 8	Twice the root extracted		
Sum of the divisors		4 8 7			
Planes to be subtracted $\left\{\vphantom{\begin{array}{c}1\\1\\1\end{array}}\right.$	1 4	4	Second root times the first		
		9	Square of the second root		
		2 1	Second root times the coefficient		
Sum of the planes to be subtracted equal to the remainder of the affected square to be resolved	1 4	7 0			

	00	0
r	24	3
r^2	576	9

So if

$$x^2 + 7x = 60{,}750,$$

x is 243, from the reverse of the way of composition which, it will be seen, has been strictly observed.

It sometimes happens that the coefficient extends forward beyond the affected square or is so great that, even in its own place, it cannot be subtracted from it. This indicates that the square affects rather than being affected, since it is less than the affecting plane.

In this case the coefficient must be moved to the succeeding places, one after another, until it is at a point where division [is possible]. The work is then ready to start, and as many quadratic places and dots must be erased as [the number of] places [by which] the coefficient retreated from where it was at the beginning of the operation, as in this problem:

A certain number multiplied by itself and by 954 makes 18,487. In symbols,

$$954x + x^2 = 18,487.$$

What is x?

18,487 is a square plus the product of its first power and the coefficient, 954. The plane is greater than the square, however, as is indicated by the seat of the coefficient, so that, with it among the divisors, there can be no subtraction from the dividend. So, since the coefficient, rather than the root of the square, is the principal divisor, move it [i.e., the coefficient] back into the following place, erase the first quadratic dot on the left and proceed to the work of divison from the beginning, as seen in the model:

Model when the Plane of Affection Is Greater than the Square

I   Fruitless Extraction of the First Root Before Transfer

Linear coefficient of the first power	9	5 4		
		•	• •	As many linear dots as quadratic
	—	— —	— —	
Affecting square to be resolved	1	8 4	8 7	
	•	R •	R •	Quadratic dots
	S	S	S	
	—	— —	— —	

Since 9 is greater than 1, make a transfer:

II   Extraction of the First Root After Transfer

Linear coefficient of the first power		9 5	4		0	0	As many zeros
			•	•	r	1	9	as there are
		— —	— —	r^2	1	81	quadratic dots
	1	8 4	8 7				or roots
		•	R •				
		S′	S″				
	—	— —	— —				
Planes to be subtracted		9 5	4	First root times linear coefficient			
		1		Square of first root			
	—	— —	— —				
Sum of the planes to be subtracted		9 6	4				
	—	— —	— —				
Remainder of the affecting square to be resolved		8 8	4 7				
	—	— —	— —				

III[26] Extraction of the Second Individual Root

	9	5 4	Linear coefficient
Upper part of the divisors	9	5 4	Linear coefficient
		·	
	— —	— —	
Remainder of the affecting square to be resolved	8 8	4 7	
		·	
	— —	— —	
Lower part of the divisors		2	Twice the first root
	— —	— —	
Sum of the divisors	9	7 4	
	— —	— —	
	8 5	8 6	Second root times the coefficient
Planes to be subtracted	1	8	Second root times twice the first
		8 1	Square of the second root
	— —	— —	
Sum of the planes to be subtracted equal to the remainder of the affecting square to be resolved	8 8	4 7	

So, if

$$954x + x^2 = 18,487,$$

x is 19, from the reverse of the way of composition which, it will be seen, has been strictly observed.

[Problem II deals with the extraction of the root of a cube affected by the addition of a solid based on the first power. The examples used are $x^3 + 30x = 14,356,197$ and $x^3 + 95,400x = 1,819,459$.]

PROBLEM III

To extract analytically the root of a given numerical cube affected by the addition of a solid derived from the square of its root and a given linear coefficient.

Let

$$x^3 + 30x^2 = 86,220,288.$$

How much is x, the root of the given affected cube?

That is, the square of a certain number multiplied by its root and by 30 makes 86,220,288. The question is what that number is.

The cube, 86,220,288, is not pure but is affected by the addition of the solid produced by the square of the root and 30, the given linear coefficient. The regular development of a cube affected this way adds to the develop-

---

[26]The text has II.

ment of a pure cube only the product of the square of the first individual root and the linear coefficient, the product of the second root and twice the rectangle formed by the first root and the linear coefficient and, finally, the product of the square of the same second root and the linear coefficient.

To extract the roots of a cube so affected, let the seats of the units making up the individual cubes be constituted in the usual fashion, marking them with dots underneath. Then, since the coefficient belongs to the square, locate as many places for the squares above, taking the digits two at a time, as there are dots or seats for the cubes. And let this [i.e., the coefficient] occupy the last quadratic seat, otherwise the first reading from left to right. If it consists of more than one digit, let the others be placed ahead.

Having done all this, the roots are extracted in the same way as in the analysis of a pure cube with this addition, that the coefficient is [one] of the divisors and, moreover, after the extraction of the first individual root, the plane derived from the coefficient and twice the first individual root occupies the place that is next ahead of the dot for the coefficient. This, moreover, is called the complementary plane[27] or the *congruens scansorium*.

The squares of the roots, as they are extracted, are multiplied by the coefficient and the roots by the complementary plane. The solids thus produced are placed under the appropriate sites as shown by an understanding of the multiplication and, along with the remaining solids, are subtracted from the given affected cube.

Then the coefficient is moved to the next place for the squares, the complementary planes aways preceding it, and the lower divisors are also moved. This is clear in the example:

[27] *Planum expletionis.*

Model for the Resolution of a Cube Affected by the Addition of a Solid Derived from a Linear Coefficient and the Square of the Root

I Extraction of the First Individual Root

			As many zeros
r	4	3	as there are
r^2	16	9	cubic dots
r^3	64	27	

Linear coefficient of the quadratic term	3 0[28]		
	·	· ·	As many seats or dots for the squares as for the cubes
Affected cube to be resolved	8 6	2 2 0	2 8 8
	·	S R ·	S R ·
	C′	C″	C‴
Solids to be subtracted	6 4		Cube of the first root
	4	8 0	Solid from the square of the first root times the linear coefficient
Sum of the solids to be subtracted	6 8	8 0	
Remainder of the affected cube to be resolved	1 7	4 2 0	2 8 8

II Extraction of the Second Individual Root

Upper part of the divisors	2 4 0		Complementary plane from the coefficient times twice the first root
	3	0	Linear coefficient
Remainder of the affected cube to be resolved	1 7	4 2 0	2 8 8
Lower part of the divisors	4 8		Three times the square of the first root
	1 2		Three times the first root
Sum of the divisors	5	1 6 3	
Solid products to be subtracted — From the lower and more important divisors	1 4 4		Second root times three times the square of the first
	1 0 8		Square of the second root times three times the first
	2 7		Cube of the second root
From the upper divisors	7 2 0		Solid from the second root times the complementary plane
	2 7		Square of the second root times the linear coefficient
Sum of the solids to be subtracted	1 6	2 5 4	0
Remainder of the affected cube to be resolved	1	1 6 6	2 8 8

[28]1600 has 9 3 0.

Two roots having now been extracted, they are treated as one, or the first, leading to—

III   Extraction of the Third Individual Root as [if it Were] the Second

| Upper part of the divisors | 2 5 | 8 0 | Complementary plane from the coefficient times twice the first root | r r^2 r^3 | 00 43 1849 | 0 2 4 8 |
| | | 3 0 | Linear coefficient | | | |

| Remainder of the affected cube to be resolved | 1 | 1 6 6 | 2 8 8 | | |

| Lower part of the divisors | 5 5 4 | 7 | Three times the square of the first root |
| | 1 | 2 9 | Three times the first root |

| Sum of the divisors | 5 8 1 | 8 2 0 |

Solid products to be subtracted	From the lower divisors	1 1 0 9	4	Second root times three times the square of the first
		5 1 6	Square of the second root times three times the first
		8	Cube of the second root
	From the upper divisors	5 1 6 0	Second root times the complementary plane
		1 2 0	Square of the second root times the linear coefficient

| Sum of the solids to be subtracted equal to the remainder of the affected cube to be resolved | 1 | 1 6 6 | 2 8 8 |

So if

$$x^3 + 30^2 = 86{,}220{,}288,[29]$$

x is 432, from the reverse of the way of composition which, it will be seen, has been strictly observed.

It sometimes happens, however, that the coefficient carries forward beyond the affected cube or that, even in its own place, [it is such] that when it becomes a divisor it cannot be subtracted from the affected cube. This indicates that the cube affects rather than being affected, since it is less than the affecting solid. In this case, the coefficient is moved back to the next succeeding place for the squares or the next quadratic dot marked

[29] 1600 has 86,200,288.

above [the digits] until divison can take place. The work is then ready to start anew, observing fully the law of homogeneous terms. And as many cubic dots underneath are deleted as the number of places the coefficient retreated from where it was at the beginning of the operation. As in this problem:

The square of a certain number multiplied by its root and by 10,000 is 5,773,824.[30] In symbols,

$$10,000x^2 + x^3 = 5,773,824.[31]$$

The question is what that number is.

The number 5,773,824 is a cube plus the solid derived from the square of the root and 10,000, the given length. The solid, however, is greater than the cube, as the location of the linear coefficient, which clearly carries forward, indicates. So it must be moved back to the next following quadratic point. The first cubic dot that occurs on the left will also be erased and the work will proceed by beginning with a division rather than with the extraction of a root. Thus since the solid is divided by a length, it will be noted that the quotient is not the root itself but the square of the root. This takes heed of the law of homogeneous terms. [All this] is seen in the model:

Model when the Solid of Affection Based on the Square Is Greater than the Cube

I   Fruitless Extraction of the First Individual Root Before Transfer

Linear coefficient of the square	1 0 0	0 0			
		·	·	·	Quadratic dots
	---	---	---		
Affecting cube to be resolved	5	7 7 3	8 2 4		
	·	$S\,R$ ·	$S\,R$ ·	Cubic dots	
	C'	C''	C'''		

Since the coefficient of the quadratic term runs ahead of the digits for the affecting cube, transfer it to the next quadratic dot, deleting also a cubic dot.

[30]The text has 57,732,824 here and in next paragraph.
[31]The text has $10,000x + x^3 = 57,732,824$.

II Extraction of the First Individual Root After Transfer

Linear coefficient	1	0 0 0	0	
			. .	
—	—	— — —	— — —	
Affecting cube to be resolved	5	7 7 3	8 2 4	
		.	S R ·	
		C'	C''	
Solids to be subtracted	4	0 0 0	0	Square of first root times linear coefficient
			8	Cube of first root
Sum of solids to be subtracted	4	0 0 8	0	
Remainder of affecting cube to be resolved	1	7 6 5	8 2 4	

	0	0
r	2	4
r^2	4*	16
r^3	8	64

*Quotient

III Extraction of the Second Individual Root

Upper and chief part of the divisors		4 0 0	0 0	Complementary plane: coefficient times twice the first root
		1 0	0 0 0	Linear coefficient
			.	
—	—	— — —	— — —	
Remainder of cube to be resolved	1	7 6 5	8 2 4	
			.	
Lower part of the divisors		1	2	Three times the square of first root
			6	Three times first root
Sum of the divisors		4 1 1	2 6 0	
Solids to be subtracted derived from — Upper divisors	1	6 0 0	0 0	Second root times complementary plane
		1 6 0	0 0 0	Square of second root times linear coefficient
— Lower divisors		4	8	Second root times three times square of the first
			9 6	Square of second root times three times the first
			6 4	Cube of second root
Sum of solids to be subtracted equal to remainder of cube to be resolved	1	7 6 5	8 2 4	

So if

$$10,000x^2 + x^3 = 5,773,824,$$

x is 24, from the reverse of the way of composition which, it will be seen, has been strictly observed.

[Problems IIII and V, here omitted, deal with the extraction of the root of a fourth power affected by the addition of a linear term and of a fourth power affected by the addition of a cubic term. The examples used are $x^4 + 1000x = 355,776$, $x^4 + 100,000x = 2,731,776$, and $x^4 + 10x^3 = 470,016$.]

Problem VI

To extract analytically the root of a given numerical fourth power affected by the addition of two plano-planes, one derived from the root and a given solid coefficient, the other from the square of the root and a given plane coefficient.

The square of a certain number multiplied by itself and by 200 is 446,976. What is that number?
In symbols,

$$x^4 + 200x^2 = 446,976.$$

What is x?
This problem needs no special explanation, for if

$$x^4 + 200x^2 = 446,976,$$

then

$$y^2 + 200y = 446,976^{32}$$

and y is known to be the square of the root that is sought first.
But if the affecting plano-plane from the square of the root and a given plane coefficient is combined with an affecting plano-plane from the root and a given solid coefficient, there is need for special analysis, as in this proposition:

A certain number multiplied by its cube and by 100, plus the product of 200 and its square, is 449,376. What is the number?
In symbols,

$$x^4 + 200x^2 + 100x = 449,376.$$

How much is x?
The fourth power, 449,376, is one that is affected by two plano-planes, one derived from the root of this same fourth power and 100, the given

---

[32]Needless to say, Viète does not switch from x to y as we do here.

solid, the other from the square of the same root and 200, the given plane. The regular development of a fourth power affected this way adds to the development of a pure fourth power only the product of the individual root that is first extracted and the solid coefficient, the product of the square of the same root and the plane coefficient, the product of the second root and the solid derived from twice the first root and the plane coefficient, the product of the square of the second root and the same plane coefficient, and the product of the same second root and the solid coefficient.

In order to extract the roots of a fourth power affected in this way, mark off the seats of the individual fourth powers by placing dots underneath in the usual fashion and set up above, digit by digit, as many places for the simple roots as there are seats or dots for the fourth powers. Then set up the places for the squares by taking the digits two at a time. Place the solid coefficient of the first power at the last seat of the roots and place the plane coefficient of the square at the last place for the squares.

The roots are extracted just as they are in the analysis of a pure fourth power, except that the coefficients are numbered among the divisors. Moreover, after the first root has been extracted, the complementary solid—namely, the product of the plane coefficient and twice the first individual root—occupies the place immediately ahead of the dot at which the plane coefficient rests.

The squares of the roots as they are extracted are multiplied by the plane coefficient and the lengths by the solid coefficient and, in addition, by the complementary solid, the plano-planes that result then being put under the spot compatible with the rationale of the multiplication, and are subtracted, along with the other plano-planes, from the given affected fourth power. Then the plane coefficient (that is, the coefficient of the second power) is moved to the next location for the squares, the complementary solid always preceding it, and the solid coefficient (that is, the coefficient of the first power) is moved to the next succeeding place for the simple [roots], and the lower divisors are also moved, as is seen in the model:

Model for the Resolution of a Fourth Power Affected both by a Linear and by a Quadratic Term

I   Extraction of the First Individual Root

			As many zeros
r	2	4	as there are
r^2	4	16	biquadratic
r^3	8	64	dots
r^4	16	256	

Plane coefficient of quadratic term   2 | 0 0

· ·   As many quadratic dots as there are biquadratic

Solid coefficient of the linear term | 1 0 0

· ·   As many dots for the simple roots as there are biquadratic

Affected fourth power to be resolved   4 4 | 9 3 7 6
                                        · | C S R ·   Biquadratic dots
                                      SS' | SS"

Plano-planes to be subtracted
 ⎧ 1 6   Fourth power of first root
 ⎨   8 | 0 0   Square of first root times plane coefficient
 ⎩ | 2 0 0 First root times solid coefficient

Sum of [plano-] planes to be subtracted   2 4 | 2 0 0

Remainder of affected fourth power to be resolved   2 0 | 7 3 7 6

II Extraction of the Second Individual Root

Upper part of divisors	⎧	8 0 0		Complementary solid (plane coefficient times twice first root)
	⎨	2 0 0		Plane coefficient
		·		
	⎩	1 0 0		Solid coefficient
		·		
Remainder of affected fourth power to be resolved		2 0 | 7 3 7 6		
		·		
Lower part of divisors	⎧	3 | 2		Four times cube of first root
	⎨	2 4		Six times square of same
	⎩	8		Four times first root
Sum of all divisors		4 | 2 7 8 0		
Plano-plane products of divisors — Lower	⎧	1 2 | 8		Second root times four times cube of first root
	⎨	3 | 8 4		Square of second root times six times square of first root
		5 1 2		Cube of second root times four times first root
	⎩	2 5 6		Fourth power of second root
Plano-plane products of divisors — Upper	⎧	3 | 2 0 0		Second root times complementary solid
	⎨	3 2 0 0		Square of second root times plane coefficient
	⎩	4 0 0		Second root times solid coefficient
Sum of plano-planes to be subtracted equal to remainder of affected fourth power to be resolved		2 0 | 7 3 7 6		

So if

$$x^4 + 200x^2 + 100x = 449{,}376,$$

x is 24, from the reverse of the way of composition which, it will be seen, has been strictly observed.

But if it happens that the affecting plano-planes are greater than the fourth power, the coefficients will be the principal divisors and the same procedure is followed that has already been explained for the other powers. There is no need here to set out and illustrate this very wordy [operation].

Furthermore it is now clear why the direct resolution of a pure fourth power was set out. This is something that the arithmeticians usually neglected, since they resolved it as if it were a square and then extracted the root of the root as from a square. But this method of resolution is not adapted to the affected fourth power. So also in the sixth power and others beyond it, ascending by even numbers in the order of the powers, one should always shoot for the most direct resolution when the powers are affected.

The rules for a fourth power affected by a cubic term, moreover, need not be set out since this affection can be done away with.[33]

[Problems VII and VIII, here omitted, deal respectively with the extraction of the root of a fifth power affected by the addition of a linear term and of a fifth power affected by the addition of a cubic term. The examples used are $x^5 + 500x = 254,832$ and $x^5 + 5x^3 = 257,452$.]

Problem IX

To extract analytically the root of a given numerical sixth power affected by the addition of the solido-solid derived from its root and a given plano-solid coefficient.

A certain number multiplied by its fifth power and by 6000 makes 191,246,976. The question is what that number is.

In symbols,

$$x^6 + 6000\, x = 191,246,976.$$

How much is x?

The sixth power, 191,246,976, is one affected by the addition of the solido-solid from its root and 6000, the given plano-solid. The regular development of a sixth power affected this way adds to the development of a pure sixth power only as much as the product of the individual root that is first extracted and the plano-coefficient and the product of the second root and the same.

To extract the roots of a sixth power so affected, place the dots underneath as in the analysis of a pure sixth power and count off the same number of places for the simple roots by the same method that was expounded for the lower powers [and] as seen in the model:

[33]See p. 350.

Model for the Resolution of a Sixth Power Affected by a Linear Term

I   Extraction of the First Individual Root

Plano-solid coefficient of the linear term		6 0 0 0		0 0 As many

As many	r	2	4	zeros as
linear or	r^2	4	16	there are
simple	r^3	8	64	cubo-cubic
dots as	r^4	16	256	dots
cubo-cubic	r^5	32	1024	
	r^6	64	4096	

```
              1 9 1 | 2 4 6 9 7 6
                  . | SC SS C S R ·   Cubo-cubic dots
                CC' |   CC''
```

Plano-solids to be subtracted $\{$	6 4		Sixth power of first root
		1 2 0 0 0	First root times plano-solid coefficient
Sum of plano-solids to be subtracted	6 4	1 2 0 0 0	
Remainder of affected sixth power to be resolved	1 2 7	1 2 6 9 7 6	

II   Extraction of the Second Individual Root

Upper part of divisors		6 0 0 0	Plano-solid coefficient
Remainder of affected sixth power to be resolved	1 2 7	1 2 6 9 7 6	

Lower part of divisors $\{$	1 9	2	Six times fifth power of first root
		2 4 0	Fifteen times fourth power of same
		1 6 0	Twenty times cube of same
		6 0	Fifteen times square of same
		1 2	Six times first root
Sum of divisors	2 1	7 7 2 1 2 0	

Solido-solid products to be subtracted $\{$	Lower	7 6	8	Second root times six times fifth power of first
		3 8	4 0	Square of second root times fifteen times fourth power of first
		1 0	2 4 0	Cube of second root times twenty times cube of first
		1	5 3 6 0	Fourth power of second root times fifteen times square of first
	Upper		1 2 2 8 8	Fifth power of second root times six times first
			4 0 9 6	Sixth power of second root
			2 4 0 0 0	Second root times plano-solid coefficient
Sum of solido-solids to be subtracted equal to remainder of affected sixth power to be resolved		1 2 7	1 2 6 9 7 6	

So if

$$x^6 + 6000x = 191,246,976,$$

x is 24 from the reverse of the way of composition which, it will be seen, has been strictly observed.

Analysis of Powers Affected Negatively

PROBLEM X

To extract analytically the root of a given numerical square affected by the subtraction of the plane derived from its root and a given linear coefficient.

Let

$$x^2 - 7x = 60,750.$$

The question is how much x, the root of the given affected square, is.

To extract the roots of 60,750, a square with a negative affection, the process will be entirely the same, the development [of such a square] being clear, as in the resolution of a square affected positively, except that it is not the sum (as it would be for a square affected positively) but the difference between the regular divisors of a pure square and the coefficient that one pays attention to when dividing. The lower divisors, moreover, are greater [than the upper].

When the individual roots, as they are extracted, are multiplied by the coefficient, the plane that results is placed under the seat of the coefficient but, instead of being subtracted, is added to the given negatively affected square, as in this model:

Model for the Resolution of a Square Affected Negatively by a Linear Term

I   Extraction of the First Individual Root

Linear coefficient of the first power	7	.	. .	As many linear dots as quadratic	As many zeros as there are quadratic dots or individual roots

		0	0 0
	r	2	5 0
	r^2	4	25

	–	– –	– –	
Affected square to be resolved	6	0 7	5 0	
	.	R .	R .	Quadratic dots
	S'	S''	S'''	
	–	– –	– –	
Restorative planes[34] { To be subtracted	4			Square of first root
To be added		1 4		First root times coefficient
	–	– –	– –	
Excess of planes to be subtracted	3	8 6		
	–	– –	– –	
Remainder of square to be resolved	2	2 1	5 0	
	–	– –	– –	

II   Extraction of Second Individual Root

Upper part of divisors			7		Linear coefficient
			. .		
	–	– –	– –		
Remainder of square to be resolved	2	2 1	5 0		
		.	.		
	–	– –	– –		
Lower part of divisors		4			Twice the first root
	–	– –	– –		
Excess of lower divisors		3 9	3 0		
	–	– –	– –		
Planes to be subtracted {	2	0			Second root times twice the first
		2 5			Square of second root
	–	– –	– –		
Sum of planes to be subtracted	2	2 5			
	–	– –	– –		
Plane to be added		3 5			Second root times coefficient
	–	– –	– –		
Excess of planes to be subtracted	2	2 1 5			
	–	– –	– –		
Remainder of affected square to be resolved		0			
	–	– –	– –		

[34] *Plana prostaphaeretica.*

Although this [i.e., the remainder of the affected square to be resolved] is zero, one quadratic dot still remains. Hence the two [individual] roots that have been extracted are treated as one and the remaining one, which is being sought, will be 0. So if

$$x^2 - 7x = 60,750,$$

x is 250, from the reverse of the way of composition which, it will be seen, has been strictly observed.

It sometimes happens that the linear coefficient has more digits taken singly than the negatively affected square has digits taken in pairs. This indicates that the affecting plane is greater than the negatively affected square that is to be resolved [and it is then] rightly called an acephalic square. To effect a resolution, place a number of zeros ahead of the given mutilated square so that there are as many quadratic dots as the linear coefficient has simple digits. Then let the first digit of the linear coefficient, reading from left to right, be the first individual root of the negatively affected square that is to be resolved, everything else remaining as it was in the preceding method, as in this problem:

A certain number multiplied by itself minus 240 yields 484. The question is what this number is.

The square 484 is one lacking the plane derived from its root and 240. The plane, 240x, moreover, is greater than 484, the term to be resolved, since the linear coefficient, 240, has three digits while the plane, 484, has only two quadratic points. So two zeros must be placed ahead of the plane, 484, and only then is the coefficient admitted to its seat. Its first digit, if compatible with everything else, or the next greater figure, is then assumed to be the first root of the mutilated square.

Model for the Resolution of an Acephalic Square

I Extraction of the First Root

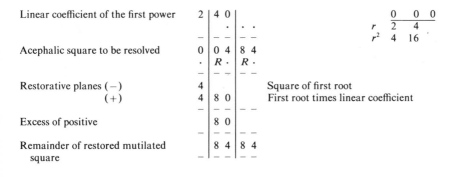

II Extraction of the Second Root

Upper part of divisors		2 4	0		Coefficient
Remainder of restored mutilated square to be resolved		8 4	8 4		
Lower part of divisors		4			Twice the first root
Excess of lower divisors		1 6			
Planes to be subtracted	{ 1	6			Second root times twice first
		1 6			Square of second root
Sum of planes to be subtracted	1	7 6			
Planes to be added		9 6			Second root times linear coefficient
Excess to be subtracted		8 0			
Remainder of affected square to be resolved		4	8 4		

Now the two roots that have been extracted are treated as one, leading to—

III Extraction of the Third Root as [if it were] the Second

Upper part of divisors	2	4 0	Coefficient			00	0
					r	24	2
Remainder of affected square to be resolved	4	8 4			r^2	576	4
Lower part of divisors	4	8	Twice first root				
Excess of lower divisors	2	4 0					
Planes to be subtracted	{ 9	6	Second root times twice the first				
		4	Square of second root				
Sum of planes to be subtracted	9	6 4					
Plane to be added	4	8 0	Second root times coefficient				
Excess of addend equal to remainder of square to be resolved	4	8 4					

So if

$$x^2 - 240x = 484,$$

x is 242 from the reserve of the way of composition which, it will be seen, has been strictly observed.

But, even though a negatively affected square the resolution of which is being undertaken consists of as many pairs of digits as the linear coefficient has individual digits, the coefficient may nevertheless sometimes extend beyond its place so that, unless the analyst understands the meaning of this, he will not infrequently go astray in extracting the root. Hence it is important to understand that, in this case, the given negatively affected square must be added to the square of the linear coefficient and that the root extracted from it, increased in this way, will be either the proper one or one just a little less than the proper one.

As if it were said,

$$x^2 - 60x = 1600.$$

Having lined up the digits as the art requires, [they are] doubtless

```
      6 0
        . .
    _ _ _ _
    1 6 0 0
        .   .
```

Since the square of 6 added to 16 makes 52 and since the nearest root greater than the square, 52, is 8, I assume the root to be 8. A continuation of the work would show that this is correct. But the quotient would have been only 2 or at most 3. Thus if the logists used this corrective device[35] for a quotient, a device that is [equally applicable] to positively affected squares especially when the coefficients carry forward, they would for the most part work to greater advantage and their divisions would not be erroneous. In this case, however, it is the difference, not the sum, of the products that is taken.

Let

$$x^2 + 8x = 128.$$

The digits being set up after devolution as the art requires, [they are] undoubtedly

```
          8
      _ _ _
      1 2 8
          .
      _ _ _
```

Since the difference between the plane, 128, and the square of the coefficient, 8, is 64, the root is taken to be 8.

---

[35]*artificium . . . epanorthicum.*

Problem XI

To extract analytically the root of a given numerical cube affected by the subtraction of the solid derived from its root and a given plane coefficient.

Let

$$x^3 - 10x = 13,584.$$

The question is how much x, the root of the given affected cube, is.

Zetetics makes clear that, in order to extract the root of 13,584, a cube with a negative affection based on its root, the process is entirely the same as that for the resolution of a cube affected positively except that, when dividing, it is the difference between the plane coefficient and the usual divisors for a pure cube to which one pays attention, not their sum as in the case of a cube affected positively, and that, when the individual roots are extracted and have been multiplied by this same plane coefficient, the solid that results, placed beneath the seat of the coefficient, which would be subtracted in the case of a positively affected cube, is added to the negatively affected cube or subtracted from the solids that are to be subtracted, as in this model:

Model for the Resolution of a Cube Affected by the Subtraction of a Solid Derived from a Plane Coefficient and the Root

I   Extraction of the First Individual Root

Plane coefficient term of the linear		1 0						As many zeros
		· ·	As many		0	0		as there are
			linear	r	2	4		cubic dots or
			dots as	r^2	4	16		individual
	− −	− − −	cubic	r^3	8	64		roots
Affected cube to be resolved	1 3	5 8 4						
	·	$S\ R$ ·	Cubic dots					
	C'	C''						
	− −	− − −						
Restorative solids $\begin{cases}(-)\\(+)\end{cases}$	8		Cube of the first root					
		2 0	First root times plane coefficient					
		− − −						
Excess of solid to be subtracted	7	8 0						
	− −	− − −						
Remainder of affected cube to be resolved	5	7 8 4						
	− −	− − −						

II Extraction of Second Individual Root

Upper part of divisors	1 0	Plane coefficient
Remainder of affected cube to be resolved	5	7 8 4
Lower part of divisors	{ 1	2	Three times square of first root
	6	Three times first root
Difference between divisors	1	2 5 0
Solids to be subtracted	{ 4	8	Second root times three times square of first
	9 6	Square of second root times three times first
	6 4	Cube of second root
Sum of subtrahends	5	8 2 4
Solid to be added	4 0	Second root times plane coefficient
Excess of subtrahends equal to remainder of affected cube to be resolved	5	7 8 4

So if

$$x^3 - 10x = 13,584,$$

x is 24, from the reverse of the way of composition which, it will be seen, has been strictly observed.

It sometimes happens that the plane coefficient has more pairs of digits than the negatively affected cube has triplets of digits. This indicates that the affecting solid is greater than the negatively affected cube that is to be resolved. It is properly called acephalic. So, in order to permit a resolution, set up a number of zeros ahead of the given mutilated cube, so that there are as many cubic dots for it as there are quadratic dots for the plane coefficient. Then, other things being compatible, let the root of the plane coefficient be extracted as if it were a square or, if this yields too little, let the next greater [root] be the first individual root of the negatively affected cube that is to be resolvd, the method heretofore set out not being changed in other respects. As in this problem:

A certain number multiplied by its square minus 116,620, makes 352,947. In symbols,

$$x^3 - 116,620x = 352,947.$$

The question is what this number is.

The cube, 352,947, is one lacking the solid derived from its root and the plane, 116,620. This solid, 116,620x, however, is greater than 352,947, the solid to be resolved, since the plane coefficient, 116,620, has three quadratic dots while the solid, 352,947, has only two cubic dots. So three zeros are prefixed to 352,947, the solid that is to be resolved, and then, the coefficient having been assigned to its seat, the work begins by extracting a square root that harmonizes with the root of the cube to be resolved, as is seen in this model:

Model for the Resolution of an Acephalic Cube with a Linear Affection
I   Extraction of the First Individual Root

Plane coefficient	1 1	6 6 2	0			0	0 0
			. . .		r	3	4
	— —	— — —	— — —		r^2	9	16
Mutilated affected cube to be resolved	0	3 5 2	9 4 7		r^3	27	64
	.	S R .	S R .				
	C'	C''	C'''				
	— —	— — —	— — —				
Restorative solids { (+)	3 4	9 8 6		First root times plane coefficient			
(−)	2 7			Cube of first root			
	— —	— — —	— — —				
Excess of positive	7	9 8 6					
	— —	— — —	— — —				
Remainder of restored mutilated cube to be resolved	8	3 3 8	9 4 7				

II   Extraction of Second Individual Root

Upper part of divisors	1	1 6 6	2 0	Plane coefficient
			. .	
	— —	— — —	— — —	
Remainder of affected cube to be resolved	8	3 3 8	9 4 7	
		.	.	
	— —	— — —	— — —	
Lower part of divisors {	2	7		Three times square of first root
		9		Three times first root
	— —	— — —	— — —	
Excess of lower divisors	1	6 2 3	8 0[36]	
	— —	— — —	— — —	
Solids to be subtracted {	1 0	8		Second root times three times square of first
	1	4 4		Square of second root times three times first
		6 4		Cube of second root
	— —	— — —	— — —	
Sum of subtrahends	1 2	3 0 4		
	— —	— — —	— — —	
Solid to be added	4	6 6 4	8 0	Second root times plane coefficient
	— —	— — —	— — —	
Excess of subtrahends	7	6 3 9	2 0	
	— —	— — —	— — —	
Remainder of affected cube to be resolved		6 9 9	7 4 7	

[36] 1600 has 163,620.

Now, having extracted two roots, they are treated as one, leading to—

III   Extraction of Third Individual Root as [if it were] the Second

Upper part of divisors	1 1 6	6 2 0	Plane coefficient	00 0
		.	r $\overline{34\quad 3}$	
			r^2 1156 9	
Remainder of affected cube to be resolved	6 9 9	7 4 7	r^3 27	
Lower part of divisors {	3 4 6	8	Three times square of first root	
	1	0 2	Three times first root	
Excess of lower divisors	2 3 1	2 0 0		
Solids to be subtracted {	1 0 4 0	4	Second root times three times square of first	
	9	1 8	Square of second root times three times first	
		2 7	Cube of second root	
Sum of subtrahends	1 0 4 9	6 0 7		
Solid to be added	3 4 9	8 6 0	Second root times plane coefficient	
Excess of subtrahends equal to remainder of affected cube to be resolved	6 9 9	7 4 7		

So if

$$x^3 - 116{,}620x = 352{,}947,$$

x is 343, from the reverse of the way of composition which, it will be seen, has been strictly observed.

But although a negatively affected cube the resolution of which is in question may consist of as many three-digit groups as the plane coefficient has two-digit groups, [the latter] may yet sometimes extend beyond its place. So unless the analyst understands the meaning of this, he may go astray in extracting the root. This is why it is better, in this case, that the root of the plane coefficient that is under the appropriate dot be extracted as if it were a square. The cube of this [root], it is understood, is to be added to the given cube and the root of the sum to be extracted. This will either be correct or just a little less[37] than the correct [amount].

Thus if one says

$$x^3 - 6400\,x = 153{,}000,$$

[37]1600 has "more."

set up the digits for the operation as the art requires, namely

Since the square root of the number 64 is 8 and the cube of the same is 512 which, when added to 153, makes 665, and the next greater root of the cube 665 is 9, we assume 9 to be the root. A continuation of the work will show this to be right, [whereas] the length that would have resulted from division would have been only 2 or at most 3. If logists use this corrective device of a quotient by which [to solve] cubes affected positively by a root, especially when the plane coefficient extends forward, they will for the most part do very well and their divisions will not be frustrated. In that case it is not the sum of the products that is taken, but the difference.

Let

$$x^3 + 64x = 1024.$$

The digits being set up as the art demands after devolution,

$$
\begin{array}{cc}
6 & 4 \\
& \cdot \\
\hline
\end{array}
$$
$$
\begin{array}{cccc}
1 & 0 & 2 & 4 \\
& & & \cdot
\end{array}
$$

Since the root of 64, the plane treated as a square, is 8 and its cube, 512, subtracted from 1024, leaves 512, the cube root of which is 8, let 8 be taken as the root.

> [Problem XII, here omitted, deals with the case of a cube affected by the subtraction of a quadratic term. The illustrations used are $x^3 - 7x^2 = 14,580$, $x^3 - 10x^2 = 288$, and $x^3 - 7x^2 = 720$.]

Analysis of Powers with Mixed Positive and Negative Affections

PROBLEM XIII

> To extract analytically the root of a given numerical fourth power affected by the addition of the plano-plane derived from the root and a given solid coefficient and by the subtraction of the plano-plane derived from the cube and a given linear coefficient.

Let

$$x^4 - 68x^3 + 202{,}752x = 5{,}308{,}416.$$

How much is x, the root of the given [fourth power] that is affected negatively by a cubic term and positively by a linear term?

In order to extract the roots of the given magnitude, 5,308,416, it is clear from the development of an affected fourth power that the process of resolving it is entirely the same as that for resolving a pure fourth power, with the addition that the individual root that is first extracted is multiplied by a solid coefficient, that the second root is multiplied by the same coefficient, that the second root is multiplied by a complementary solid (namely, that that is derived from the linear coefficient and three times the square of the first root), that the square of the same root is multiplied by a complementary plane (namely, that that is derived from the linear coefficient and three times the first root), and finally that the cube of the second root is multiplied by the linear coefficient. The homogeneous products of the solid coefficient are to be subtracted just as the regular products that derive from the linear coefficient are to be added.

Let the first root be extracted after the coefficients have been sited and marked in the usual way. The lower divisors remain the same as in the resolution of a pure fourth power, the upper ones the same as those shown in the resolution of a fourth power affected positively by a linear term and of a fourth power affected positively[38] by a cubic term. And the second root is found by taking the difference between the upper divisors that are to be subtracted and those that are to be added and dividing by this [difference], all as in this model:

---

[38]So in the text, presumably because the author does not analyze separately the case of $x^4 - cx^3 = N$ but trusts that the reader will supply the necessary minus signs.

Model for the Resolution of a Fourth Power with Two Affections, One a Positive Linear Affection and One a Negative Cubic Affection

I Extraction of the First Individual Root

Linear coefficient of the cubic term $(-)$	6	8			r	$\begin{array}{cc} 0 & 0 \\ \hline 3 & 2 \end{array}$
	$\cdot$	$\cdot\quad\cdot$		r^2	9	4
Solid coefficient of the linear term $(+)$	2 0 2	7 5 2		r^3	27	8
		$\cdot\quad\cdot$		r^4	81	16
Affected fourth power to be resolved	5 3 0	8 4 1 6				
	$\cdot$	$C\ S\ R\ \cdot$				
	SS'	SS''				
Plano-planes to be subtracted $\Big\{$	8 1		Fourth power of first root			
	6 0 8	2 5 6	First root times solid coefficient			
Sum of subtrahends	6 8 9	2 5 6				
Plano-plane to be added	1 8 3	6	Cube of first root times linear coefficient			
Excess of subtrahends	5 0 5	6 5 6				
Remainder of affected fourth power to be resolved	2 5	1 8 5 6				

II Extraction of Second Individual Root

Label		L1	L2	‖	R1	R2	R3	R4	Description
Upper part of divisors	Complementary solid (−)	1	8	‖	3	6			Linear coefficient times three times square of first root
	Complementary plane (−)			‖		6	1	2	[Linear] coefficient times three times first root
	Linear coefficient (−)			‖			6	8 ·	
	Solid coefficient (+)	2	0	‖	2	7	5	2 ·	
Remainder of affected fourth power to be resolved		2	5	‖	1	8	5	6 ·	
Lower part of divisors		1	0	‖	8				Four times cube of first root
				‖		5	4		Six times square of same
				‖			1	2	Four times first root
Sum of divisors, positive affection		3	1	‖	6	2	7	2	
Sum of divisors, negative affection		1	8	‖	9	7	8	8	
Excess of divisors from positive affection		1	2	‖	6	4	8	4	
Plano-planes to be subtracted derived from	Lower divisors	2	1	‖	6				Second root times four times cube of first
			2	‖		1	6		Square of second root times six times square of first
				‖			9	6	Cube of second root times four times first
				‖				1 6	Fourth power of second root
	Upper divisors	4	0	‖	5	5	0	4	Second root times solid coefficient
Sum of plano-planes to be subtracted		6	4	‖	4	0	8	0	
Plano-planes to be added		3	6	‖	7	2			Second root times complementary solid
			2	‖		4	4	8	Square of second root times complementary plane
				‖		5	4	4	Cube of second root times coefficient
Sum of plano-planes to be added		3	9	‖	2	2	2	4	
Excess of [plano-planes to be] subtracted equal to remainder of affected fourth power to be resolved		2	5	‖	1	8	5	6	

So if

$$x^4 - 68x^3 + 202,752x^{39} = 5,308,416,$$

x is 32, from the reverse of the way of composition which, it will be seen, has been strictly followed.

[Problems XIIII and XV, here omitted, deal respectively with the resolution of a fourth power affected by a negative linear term and a positive cubic term and of a fifth power affected by a positive linear term and a negative cubic term. The examples used are $x^4 + 10x^3 - 200x = 1,369,856$ and $x^5 - 5x^3 + 500\ x = 7,905,504.$]

Preliminary Note on the Resolution of Avulsed Powers

Among avulsed powers, which we have already pointed out are ambiguous, the art defines the limits within which the roots that are being sought exist. For this reason, the structure of these powers must first be understood. The first individual root, whether the greater or the smaller, comes either from dividing the term to be resolved by the coefficient, if division is possible, or from extracting the [first] root of the coefficient in accordance with its nature.[40] This gives us our predefined limits. The first method is always in order when it is the smaller [whole] root that is being sought, the first or the second when it is the larger.

Adding the power of the first individual root to the given term to be resolved restores the avulsed power. This is then subtracted from the homogeneous lower-order term from which it [i.e., the power] is avulsed or, contrariwise, the homogeneous lower term is subtracted from the restored power. The latter is always the case when the problem is that of finding the smaller root, either the first or the second when it is the larger that is to be found. If there is any doubt about the choice for the greater [first individual] root, the art teaches us to raise the coefficient to the nature of the term to be resolved, to subtract the term to be resolved from the term so raised, and to extract the root of the remainder. This will [give us] the greater [first individual] root the power of which restores the avulsed power.[41]

[39]1600 has simply 202,752.

[40]That is, a square root if the coefficient is a plane, a cube root if it is a solid, and so forth.

[41]*At cum aliqua dubitatio accideret in electione radicis majoris, ex arte est, ut coefficiens reducatur ad genus magnitudinis resolvendae, & ex reducta auferatur magnitudo resolvenda, ac demum ex residua eliciatur radix illa major, cujus potestas avulsae sit restitutoria.*

In the extraction of the second individual root, pay attention to the difference between the divisors as in powers affected by direct subtraction. The upper divisors, however, are the greater.[42]

But the division must, in most cases, be by a power. What is "division by a power"?[43]

In resolving powers, either pure or affected, lengths, planes, solids, plano-planes, plano-solids and terms of other sorts [are] mixed together promiscuously in the sum of the lower divisors. Hence the [nature of the] *parabola* (for so Diophantus calls the term that arises from a divison) is often not easily understood. Likewise the upper divisors are a mixture of linear coefficients and assisting complementary terms—planes, solids and others of higher nature.

Suppose a solid is to be divided by the difference between divisors of this sort. Since the divisors of the affection are diverse, it sometimes happens that the difference between the affection to be subtracted and the complementary plane of affection to be added and three times the square of the extracted root is zero or negligible. Or the lengths by which a solid is divided yield a plane, not a linear, quotient. When, therefore, the quotient from this sort of division [consists of] two digits, it is rated as a plane and the appropriate root will be extracted from it, as from a square. If compatible with everything else, this will be the second root. So also if a plano-plane divided by the difference produces a three-digit quotient, it is rated a solid and from it, as from a cube, the approximate root will be extracted. If compatible with everything else, this will be the second root. And so forth for all the other sorts of magnitudes in accordance with this art and method.

Analysis of Avulsed Powers

PROBLEM XVI

To extract analytically the root of a given numerical plane derived from the root and a given linear coefficient affected by the subtraction of the square.

Let

$$370x - x^2 = 9261.$$

How much is x, the root of the given avulsed square?

---

[42]So, judging from the examples, if it is the smaller root that is being extracted; not so if it is the greater.

[43]*At divisio ut plurium climactice instituenda est. Quid vero est climactice dividere?*

The plane 9261 derives from a root and the given linear coefficient, 370, affected by the subtraction of a square. When a power is subtracted from a lower homogeneous term, its roots are double. So the given equation can be solved by two roots, one of which is greater than half the coefficient, the other less. Put otherwise, one is less than the square root of 9261, the other greater. Likewise if twice the plane, 9261, is divided by 370, the length that results is greater than the smaller root and less than the greater root. Either root can be found thus:

First Model for the Resolution of an Avulsed Square— To Find the Smaller Root

I   Extraction of the First Individual Root

Linear coefficient of first power	3 7	0		0	0
		· ·	r	2	7
	— —	— —	r^2	4	49
Plane based on root minus square of root to be resolved	9 2	6 1			
	·	R ·			
	S'	S''			
	— —	— —			
Restorative plane	4		Square of first root		
	— —	— —			
Restored plane	9 6	6 1			
	— —	— —			
Principal plane to be subtracted	7 4	0	First root times linear coefficient		
	— —	— —			
Excess of restored plane or remainder of avulsed square to be resolved	2 2	6 1			
	— —	— —			

II   Extraction of the Second Individual Root

Upper part of divisors	3	7 0	Linear coefficient
		·	
	— —	— —	
Remainder of avulsed square to be resolved	2 2	6 1	
		·	
	— —	— —	
Lower part of divisors		4	Twice first root
	— —	— —	
Excess of upper divisors	3	3 0	
	— —	— —	
Planes to be added	2	8	Second root times twice the first
		4 9	Square of second root
	— —	— —	
Sum of planes to be added	3	2 9	
	— —	— —	
Plane to be diminished	2 5	9 0	Second root times linear coefficient
	— —	— —	
Excess of plane to be diminished equal to remainder of avulsed square to be resolved	2 2	6 1	
	— —	— —	

So if

$$370x - x^2 = 9{,}261,$$

x is 27, one and, as the predefinition of limits indicates, the smaller of the two roots by which the equation can be solved. If the plane 9,261 is divided by the length 27, the result is 343, or if the length 27 is subtracted from 370, the remainder is 343. Hence the greater root will be 343.

Second Model for the Resolution of an Avulsed Square—to Find the Greater Root

I Extraction of the First Individual Root

Since the root being sought is greater than 185 and therefore consists of more than two digits, it is clear that the plane based on the greater root minus the square is acephalic and the first digit of the coefficient will be the root, everything else agreeing.

Linear coefficient of first power	3	7 0				
		·	· ·			
	— —	— —	— —			
Plane based on root minus square to be resolved	0	9 2	6 1			
	·	R ·	R ·			
	S'	S''	S'''			
	— —	— —	— —			
Restorative plane	9			Square of first root		
	— —	— —	— —			
Restored plane	9	9 2	6 1			
	— —	— —	— —			
Principal plane to be diminished	1 1	1 0		First root times linear coefficient		
	— —	— —	— —			
Excess of principal plane or remainder of avulsed square to be resolved	1	1 7	3 9			

	0	0	0
r	3	4	
r^2	9	16	

II   Extraction of the Second Individual Root

Upper part of divisors		3 7	0	Linear coefficient
		·	·	
Remainder of avulsed square to be resolved	1	1 7	3 9	
		·	·	
Lower part of divisors		6		Twice first root
Excess of lower divisors		2 3	0	
Planes to be subtracted	{ 2	4		Second root times twice first
		1 6		Square of second root
Sum of planes to be subtracted	2	5 6		
Plane to be added	1	4 8		Second root times linear coefficient
Excess of subtrahends	1	0 8		
Remainder of avulsed square to be resolved		9	3 9	

Now the two roots are treated as one, leading to—

III   Extraction of Third Individual Root as [if it were] the Second

Upper part of divisors	3	7 0	Linear coefficient		00	0
		·		r	34	3
Remainder of avulsed square to be resolved	9	3 9		r^2		9
		·				
Lower part of divisors	6	8	Twice the first root			
Excess of lower divisors	3	1 0				
Planes to be subtracted	{ 2 0	4	Second root times twice the first			
		9	Square of second root			
Sum of planes to be subtracted	2 0	4 9				
Plane to be added	1 1	1 0	Second root times coefficient			
Excess of addend equal to remainder of avulsed square to be resolved	9	3 9				

So if

$$370x - x^2 = 9,261$$

x is 343, one and, as the predefinition of the limits indicates, the greater of the two roots by which the equation can be solved. If this length, 343, is divided into the plane, 9,261, there arises 27 or if the length 343 is subtracted from 370 it leaves 27. So the smaller root will be 27.

[Problem XVII, here omitted, deals with the extraction of the root of a linear term minus a cube. The example used is $13,104x - x^3 = 155,520$.]

PROBLEM XVIII

To extract analytically the root of a given numerical solid derived from the square and a given linear coefficient affected by the subtraction of the cube.

Let

$$57x^2 - x^3 = 24,300.$$

How much is x, the root of the given avulsed cube?

The solid 24,300 is one based on a square and affected by the subtraction of a cube. When a power is subtracted from a lower homogeneous term, the root is double, so the given equation can be solved by [either of] two roots, one of which is less than two-thirds of 57, the other greater, and either can be found thus:

First Model for the Resolution of a Cube Subtracted from a Solid Based on the Square—to Find the Smaller Root

I   Extraction of the First Individual Root

Linear coefficient of quadratic term	5	7			0 0
		. .		r	3 0
	— —	— — —		r^2	9
Solid minus the cube	2 4	3 0 0		r^3	27
	.	$S\,R\,\cdot$			
	C'	C''			
	— —	— — —			
Restorative solid	2 7		Cube of first root		
	— —	— — —			
Restored solid	5 1	3 0 0			
	— —	— — —			
Principal solid to be subtracted	5 1	3	Square of first root times linear coefficient		
	— —	— — —			
Excess of restored [solid]	0				
	— —	— — —			

So if

$$57x^2 - x^3 = 24,300,$$

x is equal to 30, one of the two roots by which the equation can be solved and, as the predefinition of the limits indicates, the smaller of the two. The square of this is 900 which, when it is divided into 24,300, the solid, yields 27, the same as the remainder when 30 is subtracted from 57. But it must be understood that there are three proportional lengths, the third of which is 27 and the sum of the first and second of which is 30. The other root by which the double-rooted equation can be solved is the sum of the second and third. Therefore let the other root be y and

$$y^2 - 27y = 810,$$

the plane derived from 27 times 30. This makes y equal to 45, the greater root.

Second Model for the Resolution of a Cube Subtracted from a Solid Based on the Square—to Find the Greater Root

I Extraction of the First Individual Root

Linear coefficient of quadratic term	5	7

	0	0
r	4	5
r^2	16	25
r^3	64	125

Label	C'	C''	Description
Solid on quadratic term minus cube of root	2 4	3 0 0 *S R* ·	
Restorative solid	6 4		Cube of first root
Restored solid	8 8	3 0 0	
Principal solid to be diminished	9 1	2	Square of first root times linear coefficient
Excess of principal solid; remainder of cube to be resolved	2	9 0 0	

II Extraction of Second Individual Root

Upper part of divisors	4	5 6	Complementary plane—twice first root times coefficient
		5 7	Linear coefficient
Remainder of cube to be resolved	2	9 0 0	
Lower part of divisors	4	8	Three times square of first root
		1 2	Three times first root
Difference between divisors		3 0 3	
Solids to be subtracted	2 4	0	Second root times three times square of first
	3	0 0	Square of second root times three times first
		1 2 5	Cube of second [root]
Sum of solids to be subtracted	2 7	1 2 5	
Solids to be added	2 2	8 0	Second root times complementary plane
	1	4 2 5	Square of second [root] times coefficient
Sum of solids to be added	2 4	2 2 5	
Excess of addends equal to remaining cube to be resolved	2	9 0 0	

So if

$$57x^2 - x^3 = 24{,}300,^{44}$$

x is 45, one and, as the predefinition of the limits indicates, the greater of the two roots by which the equation can be solved. The square of this is 2025. When this is divided into 24,300, the quotient is 12 which is also the remainder when 45 is subtracted from 57. Let it be understood that there are three proportional lengths, the first of which is 12 and the sum of the second and third of which is 45. The other root by which the equation can be solved is the sum of the first and second. Call it y. Then

$$y^2 - 12y = 540^{45}$$

and y, the smaller root, is 30.

On Ambiguity in a Cube with Multiple Affections

A cube affected negatively by a quadratic term and positively by a linear term is ambiguous when three times the square of one-third the linear coefficient [of the square] is greater than the plane coefficient [of the first power].

Let

$$x^3 - 6x^2 + 11x = 6.$$

Since 12, which is three times the square of one-third of 6, is greater than 11, the plane coefficient, x can be solved by three roots, the sum of which is 6, the three rectangles from which [add up to] 11, and the solid produced by which is 6.[46] Since, however, 6, a solid, plus 16, twice the cube of one-third the linear coefficient, is equal to 22, a solid that is the product of the plane coefficient and one-third the linear coefficient, the three roots being sought differ from each other by equal amounts. Let y equal the excess of the greatest over 2, one-third the linear coefficient. Then y^2 will equal 1, the amount by which three times the square of one-third the linear coefficient exceeds 11, the plane coefficient. So the three roots are 3, 2 and 1.

Again, let

$$x^3 - 12x^2 + 29x = 18.$$

Since 48, three times the square of one-third of 12, is greater than 29, the plane coefficient, x can be explained by three roots, the sum of which is 12,

---

[44]1600 has $57x - x^3 = 24{,}300$.

[45]1600 has 5400.

[46]I.e., if the three roots are p, q and $r, p + q + r = 6, pq + pr + qr = 11$, and $pqr = 6$.

the three rectangles from which [add up to] 29, and the solid produced by which is 18. Since, however, the solid 18 plus 128, twice the cube of one-third of 12, is greater than the solid 116, the product of 4, one-third the linear coefficient, and 29, the plane coefficient, the three roots being sought will differ from each other by unequal amounts and the middle and lowest of them will be less than 4, one-third the linear coefficient. Let the excess of the greatest over 4 be y. Since 48 is greater than 29 by 19 and the solid 18 plus 128 is greater than the solid 116 by 30,

$$y^3 - 19y = 30$$

and y is 5. So the greatest root will be 9, the middle one 2, and the smallest 1.

Again, let

$$x^3 - 18x^2 + 95x = 126.$$

Since 108, three times the square of one-third of 18, is greater than 95, the plane coefficient, x can be explained by [any one of] three roots, the sum of which is 18, the three rectangles from which are 95, and the solid product of which is 126.

Since, however, the solid, 126, plus 432, twice the cube of one-third the linear coefficient, is less than the solid 570, which is the product of 6, one-third the linear coefficient, and 95, the plane coefficient, the three roots being sought will differ by unequal amounts and either the largest or the middle one will be greater than 6, one-third the linear coefficient. Let the excess of one or the other be y. Since 108 is greater than 95 by 13 and the solid 126 plus 432 is less than the solid 570 by 12, therefore

$$13y - y^3 = 12$$

and y is 1 or 3. So 3 will be the excess of the greatest one over 6 and 1 will be the excess of the middle one [over the same]. So the three roots are 9, 7 and 2.

And if it were said that

$$x^3 - 9x^2 + 24x = 20,$$

the three roots would be 2, 2 and 5, two of the three being equal to each other.

When three times the square of one-third the linear coefficient is equal to the plane coefficient, the three individual roots are equal. So if

$$x^3 - 6x^2 + 12x = 8$$

the three roots are 2, 2 and 2.

If three times the square of [one-third] the linear coefficient is less than the plane coefficient, the root is unambiguous and the cube is solved with its double affection or is freed from one of its affections in accordance with the art.

Clearly when the product of a linear coefficient and a plane coefficient is equal to the term to be resolved, it needs neither resolution nor expurgation, for the linear coefficient will be the root that is being sought. Let

$$x^3 - 6x^2 + 40x = 240.$$

Since 240 is the product of 6 and 40, x will be 6. This is worth noting.

Problem XIX

To extract analytically the root of a given numerical plano-plane derived from a root and a given solid coefficient and affected by the subtraction of the fourth power.

Let

$$27,755x - x^4 = 217,944.$$

How much is x, the root of the given avulsed fourth power?

The plano-plane 217,944 is one derived from a root and 27,755, the given solid coefficient, [minus the fourth power of the root]. When a power is subtracted from a lower-order homogeneous term, it has two roots, so the equation that has been proposed can be solved by [either of] two roots, the cube of the smaller of which is less than 6,938¾,[47] one-fourth the solid coefficient, and the cube of the greater is more than this. And, if four times the plano-plane 217,944, is divided by [three times] the solid 27,755, the quotient is a length that is greater than the smaller root and less than the greater. So it can be solved either way thus:

First Model for the Resolution of a Fourth Power Subtracted from a Plano-Plane Based on Its Root—To Find the Smaller Root

I   Futile Extraction of the First Individual Root Before Transfer

Solid coefficient of first power	2 7	7 5 5
		· ·
	— —	— — —
Plano-plane based on first power	2 1	7 9 4 4
minus fourth power of root	·	C S R ·
	SS'	SS''
	— —	— — —

[47] 1600 has 6893¾.

Since the smaller root that is to be found is less than the cube root of the solid 6938,[48] the first digit cannot be 2. If 1 is assumed to be the principal plano-plane, which would be to diminish rather than to be diminished, it would be greater than the restored plano-plane. So perform a devolution—

Extraction of the First Individual Root After Transfer

Solid coefficient	2	7 7 5 5 ·	r 8
			r^2 64
	— —	— — — —	r^3 512
Plano-plane based on first power minus fourth power of root	2 1	7 9 4 4 ·	r^4 4096
	— —	— — — —	
Restorative plano-plane		4 0 9 6	Fourth power of first root
	— —	— — — —	
Restored plano-plane	2 2	2 0 4 0	
	— —	— — — —	
Principal plano-plane to be diminished equal to restored plano-plane	2 2	2 0 4 0	First root times solid coefficient

So if

$$27,755x - x^4 = 217,944,$$

8 is one and, as the predefinition of the limits indicates, the smaller root. If, moreover, the plano-plane 217, 944 is divided by 8, the result is a solid, 27,243, the same as the remainder if the cube of 8 is subtracted from 27,755, a solid. It must be understood that there are four cubes in continued proportion, the smaller extreme of which is 512 and the sum of the other three of which is 27,243. Let the cube that is the greater[49] extreme be y^3. Then

$$y^3 + 8y^2 + 64y = 27,243,$$

and y is 27, the other and greater root of the given avulsed fourth power.

[48] 1600 has 6893.
[49] 1600 has "smaller."

Second Model for the Resolution of a Fourth Power Subtracted
from a Plano-Plane Based on the Root—to Find the Greater Root

I   Extraction of the First Individual Root

Solid coefficient of first power	2 7	7 5 5	
		· ·	
	— —	— — —	
Plano-plane minus fourth power to be resolved	2 1	7 9 4 4	
	·	C S R ·	
	SS′	SS″	
	— —		
Restorative plano-plane	1 6		Fourth power of first root
	— —	— — — —	
Restored plano-plane	3 7	7 9 4 4	
	— —	— — — —	
Principal plano-plane—minuend	5 5	5 1 0	First root times solid coefficient
	— —	— — — —	
Excess of principal plano-plane—remainder of fourth power to be resolved	1 7	7 1 5 6	

	0	0
r	2	7
r^2	4	49
r^3	8	343
r^4	16	2401

II   Extraction of Second Individual Root

Upper part of divisors	2	7 7 5 5	Solid coefficient
		·	
	— —	— — —	
Remainder of fourth power to be resolved	1 7	7 1 5 6	
		·	
	— —	— — —	
Lower part of divisors	3	2	Four times cube of first root
		2 4	Six times square of first root
		8	Four times first root
	— —	— — —	
Sum of lower divisors	3	4 4 8	
	— —	— — —	
Excess of lower divisors		6 7 2 5	
	— —	— — —	
Plano-planes to be subtracted[50]	2 2	4	Second root times four times cube of first
	1 1	7 6	Square of second root times six times square of first
	2	7 4 4	Cube of second root times four times first
		2 4 0 1	Fourth power of second root
	— —	— — —	
Sum of plano-planes to be subtracted	3 7	1 4 4 1	
	— —	— — —	
Plano-plane to be added	1 9	4 2 8 5	Second root times solid coefficient
	— —	— — —	
Excess of subtrahends equal to remainder of avulsed fourth power to be resolved	1 7	7 1 5 6	
	— —	— — —	

[50] 1600 has "added."

So if

$$27,755x - x^4 = 217,944,$$

x is 27, one and, as the predefinition of the limits indicates, the greater of the roots. If 27 is divided into the plano-plane 217,944, there arises the solid 8,072, the same as the remainder when the cube of the root 27, namely 19,683, [is subtracted from the solid 27,755.][51] It must be understood, moreover, that there are four cubes in continued proportion, the greater extreme of which is 19,683 and the sum of the others of which is 8,072. Let the smaller extreme be y^3. Hence

$$y^3 + 27y^2 + 729y = 8,072,$$

making y equal to 8, the other and smaller root of the given avulsed fourth power.

Problem XX

To extract analytically the root of a given numerical plano-plane derived from the cube and a given linear coefficient and affected by the subtraction of the fourth power.

Let

$$65x^3 - x^4 = 1,481,544.$$

How much is x, the root of the given avulsed fourth power?

The plano-plane 1,481,544 is the product of a cube and 65, the given linear coefficient, [minus a fourth power]. Since a power subtracted from a lower term has a double root, the proposed equation can be solved with [either of] two roots, one of which is less than three-fourths of 65 and the other greater. And when four times the plano-plane 1,481,544 is divided by three times 65, a length, there arises a solid that is greater than the cube of the smaller root, less than the cube of the greater root. Therefore both cubes can be found thus:

[51]1600 lacks these bracketed words.

Finding the Smaller Root—First Model for the Resolution of a Fourth Power Subtracted from a Plano-Plane Based on the Cube

I   Extraction of the First Individual Root

		0	0
r		3	8
r^2		9	64
r^3		27*	512
r^4		81	4096

*Quotient

	SS′	SS″	
Linear coefficient of the cubic term	6	5	
Plano-plane minus fourth power to be resolved	1 4 8	1 5 4 4	
	·	$C\ S\ R$ ·	
Restorative plano-plane	8 1		Fourth power of first root
Restored plano-plane	2 2 9	1 5 4 4	
Principal plano-plane—minuend	1 7 5	5	Cube of first root times linear coefficient
Excess of restored plano-plane—remainder of avulsed fourth power to be resolved	5 3	6 5 4 4	

II Extraction of Second Individual Root

Upper part of divisors	⎧	1 7	5 5	Complementary solid: coefficient times three times square of first root
	⎨		5 8 5	Complementary plane: coefficient times three times first root
	⎩		6 5 ·	Linear coefficient

Remainder of avulsed fourth power to be resolved	5 3	6 5 4 4	
Lower part of divisors	⎧ 1 0	8	Four times cube of first root
	⎨	5 4 ·	Six times square of first root
	⎩	1 2	Four times first root
Excess of upper divisors	6	8 0 0 3[52]	

Plano-planes to be added	⎧	8 6	4	Second root times four times cube of first
	⎨	3 4	5 6	Square of second root times six times square of first
		6	1 4 4	Cube of second root times four times the first
	⎩		4 0 9 6	Fourth power of second root
Sum of plano-planes to be added		1 2 7	5 1 3 6	

Plano-planes to be subtracted	⎧	1 4 0	4 0	Second root times complementary solid
	⎨	3 7	4 4 0	Square of second root times complementary plane
	⎩	3	3 2 8 0	Cube of second root times linear coefficient
Sum of plano-planes to be subtracted		1 8 1	1 6 8 0	
Excess of minuends equal to remainder of avulsed fourth power		5 3	6 5 4 4	

So if

$$65x^3 - x^4 = 1,481,544,$$

x is 38, one and, as the predefinition of limits indicates, the smaller of the two roots by which the equation can be solved. The cube of this is 54,872 which, when it is divided into 1,481,544, gives rise to 27, a length, as much as remains when the length 38 is subtracted from 65. It should be noted that there are four continued proportionals, the first, second and third of

[52]1646 has 67,895.

which add up to 38, and the fourth of which is 27. Their sum is 65, the same as the coefficient. The other root is composed of the fourth, second and third. Let the third be y. Then

$$y^3 + 27y^2 + 729y = 27,652,$$

the product of the given 38 and 729, the square of the fourth. So the third will be 18 and the second 12. Hence the greater root is 57.

Finding the Greater Root—Second Model for the Resolution of a Fourth Power Subtracted from a Plano-Plane Based on the Cube

I Extraction of the First Individual Root

Linear coefficient of cubic term		6	5					0	0
			.	.			r	5	7
		– – –	– – – –				r^2	25	49
Plano-plane[53] minus fourth power	1 4 8	1 5 4 4				r^3	125	343
to be resolved		.	$C\ S\ R$.				r^4	625	2401
	SS'	SS''							
		– – –	– – – –						
Restorative plano-plane	6 2 5				Fourth power of first root				
		– – –							
Restored plano-plane	7 7 3	1 5 4 4							
		– – –	– – – –						
Principal plano-plane—minuend	8 1 2	5			Linear coefficient times cube of				
					first root				
		– – –	– – – –						
Excess of principal plano-plane—		3 9	3 4 5 6						
remainder of avulsed fourth		– – –	– – – –						
power to be resolved									

[53] 1600 has "plane."

II Extraction of Second Individual Root

Upper part of divisors	4 8 | 7 5	Complementary solid—coefficient times three times square of first root
	9 7 5	Complementary plane—coefficient times three times first root
	6 5	Linear coefficient
Remainder of avulsed fourth power to be resolved	3 9 | 3 4 5 6	
Lower part of divisors	5 0 | 0	Four times cube of first root
	1 | 5 0	Six times square of first root
	2 0	Four times first root
Sum of lower divisors	5 1 | 5 2 0	
Sum of upper divisors	4 9 | 7 3 1 5	
Excess of lower divisors	1 | 7 8 8 5	
Plano-planes to be subtracted	3 5 0	Second root times four times cube of first
	7 3 | 5 0	Square of second root times six times square of first
	6 | 8 6 0	Cube of second root times four times first
	2 4 0 1	Fourth power of second root
Sum of plano-planes to be subtracted	4 3 0 | 6 0 0 1	
Plano-planes to be added	3 4 1 | 2 5	Second root times complementary solid
	4 7 | 7 7 5	Square of second root times complementary plane
	2 | 2 2 9 5	Cube of second root times linear coefficient
Sum of plano-planes to be added	3 9 1 | 2 5 4 5	
Excess of subtrahends equal to remainder of avulsed fourth power to be resolved	3 9 | 3 4 5 6	

So if

$$65x^3 - x^4 = 1,481,544,$$

x is 57, one and, as the predefinition of limits indicates, the greater of the two roots by which the equation can be solved. The cube of this is 185,193 which, when it is divided into 1,481,544, yields 8, a length, the same as the remainder when 57 is subtracted from 65. It should be noted that there are four continued proportionals, the first, second and third of which make up

57, and the fourth of which is 8. Hence the sum of all of them is 65, the coefficient. The other root is the sum of the fourth and third. Let the third be y. Hence

$$y^3 + 8y^2 + 64y = 3,648,$$

the product of the given 57 and 64, the square of the fourth. So the third will be 12 and the second 18. Therefore the smaller[54] root is 38.

[The text follows with a "general corollary" consisting of a summary of the procedure to be followed in the extraction of roots, all as set out in more detail in the examples above.]

[54]1600 has "greater."

A CANONICAL SURVEY OF GEOMETRIC CONSTRUCTIONS[1]

This is a review of the rules of geometric construction by which all equations not exceeding the quadratic can be readily solved.

PROPOSITION I

To add one given straight line to another

$$A \text{ ——————+———— } C$$
$$B$$

The operation is that of addition. Let the two given straight lines be *AB* and *BC*. One is to be added to the other. Extend *AB* by the length *BC*. I say that that has been done that was ordered, for *AC* is the sum of *AB* and *BC*.

PROPOSITION II

To subtract one given straight line from another longer one

$$A \text{ ——————+——— } B$$
$$C$$

The operation is that of subtraction. Let the two unequal straight lines be *AB* and *BC*. The shorter is to be subtracted from *AB*, the longer. Cut off *BC* from *AB*. I say that that has been done that was ordered, for *AC* is the difference between *AB* and *BC*.

---

[1] *Effectionum Geometricarum Canonica Recensio.*

Proposition III

To draw three proportional straight lines

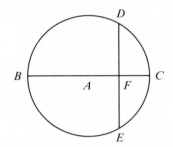

Describe a circle around a center, *A*, at any distance you choose and draw the diameter *BAC*. Assume that the arcs *CD* and *CE* in opposite parts of the circumference are equal. Let the connecting line *DE* cut *BC* at *F*. I say that that has been done that was to be done, for *BF*, *FD* and *FC*² are proportionals.

Proposition IIII

To draw a right triangle

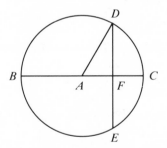

After repeating the preceding construction, draw the connecting line *AD*. I say that that has been done that was ordered, for *AFD* is a triangle and it is a right triangle since the angle *AFD* is a right angle, as is demonstrated in the *Elements*.

Proposition V

Given two straight lines, to find the mean proportional between them

² 1593 has *FG*.

The operation is that of multiplication. This is [the same as], Given [two] sides, to find a plane or to exhibit the square equal to this plane.[3] It has been shown, moreover,[4] that the product of the extremes is equal to the square of the mean.

Let *BF* and *FC* be the two given straight lines. The mean proportional between them is to be found. Extend *BF* by the length *FC* and let *BC* be cut in half at *A*. Describe a circle around the center, *A*, at the distance *AB* or *AC* and at the point *F* erect a perpendicular cutting the circumference at *D*. I say that that has been done that was to be done, for *DF* is the mean being sought as in clear from the canonical definition of three proportionals. So, given the plane, the square equal [to it] is also given.

PROPOSITION VI

Given two straight lines, to find a third proportional.

The operation is that of division. This is [the same as], To divide a given plane or square equal to a plane by a straight line and to exhibit the quotient. In other words, divide the square of a mean by the first [proportional] and the third results.

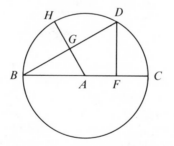

Let *BF* and *FD* be the two given straight lines. A third proportional is to be found. Let *BF* and *FD* form a right angle and draw the connecting line *BD* which cuts the straight line *AH* in half at a right angle, intercepting it at *G* and *BF* at *A*. Describe a circle around the center *A* at the distance *AB* or *AD*. Extend *BF* to its circumference at *C*. I say that that has been done that was to be done, for *FC* is a third proportional to the givens *BF* and *FD*, as is clear from the canonical definition of three proportionals.

[3]"This is . . . to this plane" is not in 1593 but does appear in 1646.
[4]1593 has *enim*; 1646 has *autem*.

These are certain minor canonical constructions:

1. Given three straight lines, to find their fourth proportional.
2. To construct one straight line in the same ratio to another as one number is to another. The second straight line is to be found, the other items being given.
3. To construct one straight line is the same ratio to another as one square is to another. The second straight line is to be found, the other items being given.
4. To construct one square in the same ratio to another as one straight line is to another. The side of the second square is to be found, the other items being given.

These can be had from the *Elements* if assistance is needed. The following operations are not wholly standard. They are recommended because of their importance and the frequency of their use.

PROPOSITION VII

Given the two sides of a right triangle around the right angle,
to find the third side

The operation is that of the addition of planes, for Pythagoras showed that the squares of the sides around a right angle are equal to the square of the remaining side. The principles of analysis also make this clear from the definition of a triangle.

It has been shown by analysis that the sum of two lines times their difference yields the difference between their squares. The sum of *AD* or *BA* and *AF* is *BF* and the difference between *AD* or *AC* and *AF* is *FC*. The product of *BF* and *FC*, moreover, is the square of *DF*. So the square of *DF* is the difference between the square of *AD* and the square of *AF*. By transposition, which is called *antithesis,* the square of *AD* is the sum of the squares of *AF* and *DF*.

Let the two sides of a right triangle lying around its right angle be *AF* and *FD*. The third side—that which subtends the right angle—is to be found. Let *AF* and *FD* stand at right angles and draw the connecting line *AD*. I say that that has been done that was to be done, for the side being sought is *AD*, the subtend of the triangle's right angle, *DFA*, constructed from the givens *AF* and *FD*.

PROPOSITION VIII

Given the side subtending the right angle of a triangle and
one of the other sides, to find the third side.

The operation is that of subtracting planes. Let the two given sides of a right triangle be *AC*, which subtends the right angle, and *AF*, which lies at the right angle. The remaining side is to be found.

Describe a circle around the center *A* at the distance *AC*. Cut off *AF* from *AC* and at the point *F* erect a line perpendicular to *AC* cutting the circumference at *D*. Draw the connecting line *AD*. I say that that has been done that was to be done, for the side *DF* is that which was sought, lying at the right angle in the triangle *AFD*, the remaining sides of which are *AF* and *AD*, that is *AC*.

PROPOSITION IX

If there are three proportional straight lines, the square of the smaller extreme plus the rectangle produced by the difference between the extremes and the smaller extreme is equal to the square of the mean.

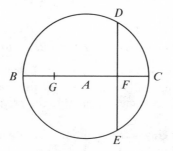

Set up the standard diagram of three proportional straight lines and call *FC* the smaller extreme. Assume that *BG* is equal to it, whence *FG* is the difference between *BF*, the greater extreme, and *BG* (that is, *FC*) the smaller. I say that

$$CF^2 + (CF \times FG) = DF^2,$$

for CF^2 is also the product of *CF* and *GB*. Thus the two products, $CF \times GB$ and $CF \times FG$, are equal to $CF \times FB$. Consequently DF^2, *DF* being the mean between the extremes, is equal to this product of the extremes.

Corollary on the Geometric Solution[5] of a Square Affected by the Addition of a Plane Based on the First Power

If it is proposed that

$$A^2 + BA = D^2,$$

---

[5]*Consectarium ad Mechanicem.* As is apparent, I have translated the word *mechanicem* (1593's spelling; 1646's is *mechanicen*) in accordance with the process Viète uses it to describe rather than in accordance with its dictionary definitions.

D is known to be the mean between [two] extremes and B to be their difference. The extremes are to be found from the mean and the difference between the extremes. The smaller of these will be A, the unknown.

Thus in this case the proportionals BF, FD and FC are constructed from the given terms GF and FD, and FC is the smaller unknown. We were able to show this in the Zetetica[6] and it is now demonstrated by synthesis from a geometric figure.

Proposition X

If there are three proportional straight lines, the square of the greater extreme minus the product of the difference between the extremes and the greater extreme is equal to the square of the mean.

Repeat the preceding construction. I say that

$$BF^2 - (BF \times GF) = DF^2.$$

Since

$$BF^2 = (BF \times GF) + (BF \times BG),$$

if $BF \times BG$ is subtracted from BF^2, the remainder is $BF \times BG$, that is, the product, by construction, of [BF and] FC. Consequently, the square of DF, the mean between the extremes, is equal to the product of the extremes.

Corollary on the Geometric Solution of a Square Affected by the Subtraction of a Plane Based on the First Power

Thus if it is proposed that

$$A^2 - BA = D^2,$$

D is known to be the mean between [two] extremes and B their difference. The extremes are to be found from the mean and the difference between the extremes. The greater extreme will be A, the unknown.

In this case the proportionals BF, FD and FC are constructed from the given terms GF and FD, and BF will be the greater unknown. We were able to show this in the Zetetica and it is now demonstrated by synthesis from a geometric figure.

Proposition XI

If there are three proportional straight lines, the product of the sum of the extremes and either the greater or smaller of

[6]Third Book, Zetetic I.

these minus the square of the same is equal to the square of the mean.[7]

Set up the standard diagram for three proportionals. I say that

$$(BC \times FC) - FC^2 = DF^2$$

and again that

$$(BC \times BF) - BF^2 = DF^2.$$

Since BC is the sum of BF and FC,

$$BC \times FC = (BF \times FC) + (FC \times FC),$$

the latter being FC^2. So when FC^2 is subtracted from $BC \times FC$, the product of BF and FC is left. To this product of the extremes, consequently, is equal the square of DF, the mean between the extremes. Let this be the first [demonstration].

Likewise, since BC is composed of CF and FB,

$$BC \times BF = (CF \times BF) + (BF \times BF),$$

the latter being BF^2. So when BF^2 is subtracted from $BC \times BF$, the product of CF and BF is left. Consequently, the square of BF, the mean between the extremes, is equal to the product of the extremes, as was to be demonstrated in the second place.

Corollary on the Geometrical Solution of a Plane Based on a Root from Which a Square Is Subtracted

Thus when it is proposed that

$$BA - A^2 - D^2,$$

D is known to be the mean between [two] extremes and B is their sum. The extremes are to be found from the mean and the sum of the extremes, either of which is A, the unknown.

We were able to show this in the Zetetica[8] and it is now demonstrated synthetically from a geometric figure.

PROPOSITION XII

Given the mean of three proportionals and the difference between the extremes, to find the extremes.

[7] 1593 has "to the product of the extremes."
[8] Third Book, Zetetic II.

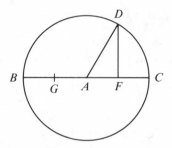

[This involves] the geometrical solution of a square affected by a [plane based on a] root.

Let *FD* be the mean of three proportionals and let *GF* be the difference between the extremes. The extremes are to be found.

Let *GF* and *FD* stand at right angles and let *GF* be cut in half at *A*. Describe a circle around the center *A* at the distance *AD* and extend *AG* and *AF* to the circumference at the points *B* and *C*.

I say that that has been done that was to be done, for the extremes are found to be *BF* and *FC* between which *FD* is the mean proportional. Moreover, *BF* and *FC* differ by *FG*, since *AF* and *AG* are equal by construction and *AC* and *AB* are also equal by construction. Thus subtracting the equals *AG* and *AF* from the equals *AB* and *AC*, there remain the equals *BG* and *FC*. *GF*, moreover, is the difference between *BF* and *BG* or *FC*, as was to be demonstrated.

PROPOSITION XIII

Given the mean of three proportionals and the sum of the extremes, to find the extremes.

[This involves] the geometrical solution of a plane based on a root minus its square.

Let *E* be the mean of three proportionals and *BC* the sum of the extremes. The extremes are to be found.

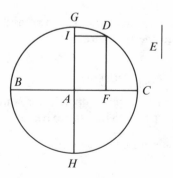

Let *BC* be cut in half at *A* and describe a circle around the center *A* at the distance *AB* or *AC*. But the diameter *BAC* is also cut at right angles by another diameter, *GAH*. From *AG* cut off *AI* equal to *E* and through *I* draw a straight line parallel to *BC* and intercepting the circumference at the point *D*. From this point drop *DF*, a perpendicular, to *BC* equal and parallel to *IA*. I say that that has been done that was to be done, for the extremes being sought are *BF* and *FC*, the sum of which is the given *BC*. This makes the mean proportional between them *DF* or *IA*, that is, the given *E*.

PROPOSITION XIIII

The square of the mean proportional between the hypotenuse of a right triangle and its perpendicular is the proportional between the square of the perpendicular and the square of the same perpendicular plus the square of the base.

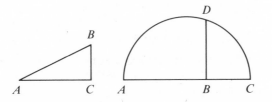

Let *ABC* be a right triangle, thus making *BD* the mean between its hypotenuse, *AB*, and its perpendicular, *BC*. I say that BD^2 is the proportional between BC^2 and the same $BC^2 + AC^2$.

Since *BA*, *DB* and *BC* are proportionals, their squares are also proportionals, namely AB^2, DB^2 and BC^2. Furthermore, AB^2 is, by substitution, $BC^2 + AC^2$.

Likewise, the square of the mean proportional between the hypotenuse of a right triangle and its perpendicular is the proportional between the square of the hypotenuse and the square of the same hypotenuse minus the square of the base.

It has already been noted that AB^2, BD^2 and BC^2 are proportionals. Furthermore, BC^2 is, by substitution, $AB^2 - AC^2$.

Corollary on the Geometrical Solution of a Fourth Power Affected by [a Plano-Plane Based on] the Square

If

$$A^4 + B^2 A^2 = D^4,$$

B is known to be the base of a right triangle and D the mean between its perpendicular and hypotenuse. Find A, the perpendicular, from the mean and the base.

In this case, BC is to be found from the givens, AC and BD. Then by resolution of the proportion first set out,

$$BC^4 + (AC^2 \times BC^2) = BD^4.$$

And if

$$A^4 - B^2A^2 = D^4,$$

B is again known to be the base of a right triangle and D the mean between its perpendicular and hypotenuse. The hypotenuse, A, is to be found from the mean and the base.

In this case AB is to be found from the givens, AC and BD. Then by resolution of the second proportion set out

$$AB^4 - (AC^2 \times AB^2) = BD^4.$$

PROPOSITION XV

The square of the mean proportional between the base of a right triangle and its perpendicular is the proportional between the square of the base and the square of the hypotenuse minus the square of the perpendicular or between the square of the perpendicular and the square of the hypotenuse minus the square of the perpendicular.

Let the right triangle be ABC. CD is then the mean [proportional] between AC and BC, the sides around the right angle. I say that CD^2 is the proportional between AC^2 and $AB^2 - AC^2$.

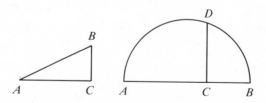

Since AC, CD and BC are proportionals, their squares—namely AC^2, CD^2, and BC^2—are proportionals. Moreover, BC^2 is, by substitution, $AB^2 - AC^2$.

Or again, I say that CD^2 is the proportional between BC^2 and $AB^2 - BC^2$.

[This follows] since, as has just been said, AC^2, CD^2 and BC^2 are proportionals and AC^2, moreover, is $AB^2 - BC^2$, by substitution.

Corollary on the Geometrical Solution of a Plano-Plane Based on a Square Minus a Fourth Power

If

$$B^2 A^2 - A^4 = D^4,$$

B is known to be the hypotenuse of a right triangle and D to be the mean between its perpendicular and base. A, the base or perpendicular, is to be found from the mean and the hypotenuse.

In this case, AC or BC is to be found from the givens, AB and DC. By resolution of the first proportion set out above,

$$(AB^2 \times AC^2) - AC^4 = CD^4.^9$$

Or, by resolution of the second proportion set out above,

$$(AB^2 \times BC^2) - BC^4 = DC^4.$$

PROPOSITION XVI

Given the first of three proportionals and something the square of which is equal to the sum of the squares of the second and third, the second and third are given.

These, truly, are proportionals:

    I. The third plus the first.
    II. [The square root of the sum of the squares of the second and third].[10]
    III. The third.[11]

In this series, the first and the difference between the extremes are given. Then from Proposition XII of this book, when the mean and the difference between the extremes are given, the extremes are given.

The proportion being set out, what is otherwise confirmed by zetetics is clear from the equation into which it resolves. For [the product of] the extremes is equal to the square of the third plus the product of the first and third—that is, plus the square of the second. These two squares equal the square of the mean.

[9] 1593 has CE^4.

[10] Viète's language is *Potens illas quadrato,* a phrase that Durret translates "celle qui les peut par son quarré"; I find the Latin so enigmatic that I cannot cope with it in direct translation. The same or similar expressions occur elsewhere in this proposition and in later ones.

[11] I.e., if $p : q = q : r$, then $(p + r) : \sqrt{q^2 + r^2} = \sqrt{q^2 + r^2} : r$.

This proposition is inscribed among the canonicals since it is prepara-
tory to the geometrical solution of a fourth power affected by [a plano-
plane based on] a square. So that this will be clearer, the whole operation is
set out visually. Let it be proposed, therefore

> Given the first of three proportionals and something the
> square of which is equal to the sum of the squares of the
> second and third, to find the proportionals.

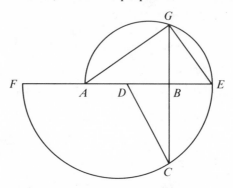

Let the first of the three given proportionals be *AB* and let *BC* be the
square root of the sum of the squares of the other individual proportionals.[12] The second and third are to be found.

Let *AB* and *BC* form a right angle and let *AB* be cut in half at *D*. From
the center *D* at the distance *DC* describe a circle cutting an extension of *AB*
at the points *E* and *F*, *E* being opposite *B* and *F* opposite *A*, making *AE* the
diameter of another circle to which *BG* is produced. I say that the
proportionals being sought are *GB*, the second, and *BE*, the third.

To begin with, it is clear from the standard diagram of three
proportionals that *AB*, *BG* and *BE* are proportionals. Moreover, it follows
that the subtend *GE* is equal to the given *BC*. Since *FD* and *DE* are equal
by construction, for either is a radius of the circle first described, and *AD*
and *DB* are also equal by construction, therefore *FA* and *BE* become equal.
FB and *AE* are also equal by the subtraction of equals from equals and the
addition of equals to equals. *BC*, however, is the mean proportional between
EB and *BF* from the same standard diagram. The mean between *EB* and
AE or *BF* is *GE*. Hence *GE* is the same as *BC*, which is what was to be
shown.

From *AB*, the first given, and *BC*, the square root of the sum of the
squares of the other two proportionals,[13] have been discovered the three
proportionals *AB*, *BG* and *BE*, as was to be done.

---

[12]*Quae vero potest quadrata singulas reliquas BC*. Cf. n. 8 supra.
[13]See n. 6 supra.

Proposition XVII

If the square of the mean proportional between the perpendicular of a right triangle and its hypotenuse is divided by the base, the perpendicular is a proportional between the base and something the square of which is equal to the difference between the square of the length arising from the division and the square of the perpendicular.

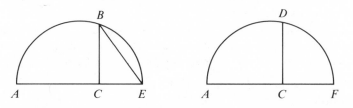

Let AB be the hypotenuse of a right triangle, AC its base and BC its perpendicular and let the mean proportional between AB and BC be CD, the square of which divided by AC makes the length CF. The square of BC divided by AC likewise makes the length CE, the square of which plus the square of BC is equal to the square of BE. I say that BE is equal to CF. So CE is that the square of which is equal to the difference between the square of CF or BE and the square of BC. Consequently BC is the proportional between it and AC, as the proposition states.

By construction,

$$AC : CD = CD : CF.$$

Likewise, because the triangles ACB and ABE are similar,

$$AC : BC = AB : BE.$$

By hypothesis, the square of CD is equal to the product of BC and AB. Therefore the mean between AC and CF and between AC and BE is the same. So BE and CF are equals and the proposition is demonstrated.[14]

---

[14] An alternative demonstration that BE and CF are equal would be this: First, find BE in terms of AB, BC and AC by these steps: (1) $AC : BC = BC : CE$; (2) $CE = BC^2/AC$; (3) $BE^2 = BC^2 + BC^4/AC^2$; (4) $BE = \sqrt{BC^2 + BC^4/AC^2}$. Second, find CF in terms of AB, BC and AC: (1) $AC : DC = DC : CF$. (2) $AB : DC = DC : BC$; (3) $DC^2 = AB \times BC$; (4) $AC : \sqrt{AB \times BC} = \sqrt{AB \times BC} : CF$; (5) $CF = (AB \times BC)/AC$. Finally, test the assumption that $BE = CF$: (1) $(AB \times BC)/AC = \sqrt{BC^2 + BC^4/AC^2}$; (2) $(AB^2 \times BC^2)/AC^2 = BC^2 + BC^4/AC^2$; (3) $AB^2 \times BC^2) = (AC^2 \times BC^2) = (AC^2 \times BC^2) + BC^4$; (4) $AB^2 = AC^2 + BC^2$, which is clearly true.

Proposition XVIII

Given the base of a right triangle and the mean proportional between its hypotenuse and perpendicular, the triangle is given.

According to the preceding proposition, these are proportionals:

I. The base

II. The perpendicular

III. The root of a square that is equal to the difference between the square of the perpendicular and the square of the length that arises from dividing the square of the mean by the base.

In this series the first and the root of a square equal to the sum of the squares of the other two are given. So the other two are given by Proposition XVI.[15]

This, moreover, is the geometrical solution for a fourth power affected by a quadratic term. Hence it is inscribed among the number of canonical [propositions]. For this reason it is fitting that the whole operation be set out. Let the proposition be—

Given the base of a right triangle and the mean between its hypotenuse and perpendicular, to show the triangle itself.

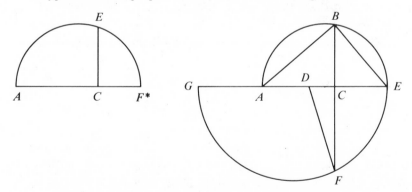

*This follows the lettering in 1646; in 1593, A and F are reversed.

Let AC be the base of a right triangle and let CE be the mean between its hypotenuse and its perpendicular. The triangle is to be exhibited.

Divide the square of CE by AC, resulting in the length CF. Then draw CF perpendicularly to AC cutting AE[16] in two parts at D. The proportion-

---

[15] 1593 has XV.

[16] The text has AC.

als *CE*, *CF* and *CG* are thus constructed. Let *AE* be the diameter of a circle from the circumference of which the perpendicular *BC* falls. I say that *ACB*[17] is the triangle being sought, viz., one the base of which is the given *AC*. Since, moreover, *AC* is to *AB* as *BC* is to *BE*, that is, to *CF*, as the operation shows and the preceding [proposition] demonstrates, *CE* is truly the mean between *AC* and *CF*. Consequently *CE* is also the mean between *AB* and *BC*. Hence what was required has been done.

The same problem may be stated thus:

> Given the mean of three proportionals and something the square of which is equal to the difference between the squares of the extremes, to find the extremes.

In this case *AB* and *BC* are discovered from the givens *AC* and *CE*.

Proposition XIX

If the square of the mean between the base and the perpendicular of a right triangle is divided by the hypotenuse, the length that results will be a proportional between two segments of the hypotenuse, the square of the first of which plus the square of the length is equal to the square of the base and the square of the second of which plus the square of the length is equal to the square of the perpendicular.

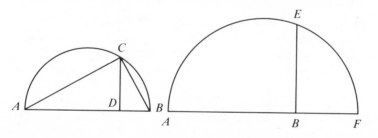

Let *AB* be the hypotenuse of a right triangle, *AC* its base, *BC* its perpendicular, and *BE* the mean between the base and the perpendicular, the square of which divided by *AB* results in the length *BF*. Let *CD* drop perpendicularly from the point *C* to *AB*. These, then, are proportionals: *AD*, the first segment of the hypotenuse; *CD*, as drawn; and *DB*, the other segment of the hypotenuse. I say that *DC* is equal to *BF* and that, therefore, *BF*[18] is a proportional between *AD*, the square of which added to the square

---

[17] 1593 has ACD.

[18] 1593 has *BE* in both these places.

of *CD* is equal to the square of *AC*, the base, and *DB*, the square of which added to the square of *CD* is equal to the square of *CB*, the perpendicular, as the theorem says.

By construction

$$AB : BE = BE : BF.$$

And by the similarity of the triangles *ACB* and *ADC*,

$$AB : CB = AC : CD.$$

The square of *BE*, moreover, is equal to the product of *CB* and *AC*. Therefore the mean between *AB* and *BF* is the same as that between *AB* and *CD*. So *BF* and *CD* are equal. Therefore the proposition is confirmed.

PROPOSITION XX

Given the hypotenuse of a right triangle and the mean proportional between its base and perpendicular, the triangle is given.

From the preceding proposition, the following are proportionals:

  I. One segment of the hypotenuse
 II. The length that results from dividing the square of the mean by the hypotenuse
III. The other segment of the hypotenuse.

In this series, the mean and the sum of the extremes are given and the square of the aforesaid length added to the square of one segment of the hypotenuse forms the square of one of the sides around the right angle and added to the square of the other segment forms the square of the other side.

This is the geometrical solution of a plano-plane based on a square from which is subtracted the fourth power. Hence it is inscribed among the canonicals. For this reason it is worth setting out the whole operation. Let this be the proposition:

Given the hypotenuse of a [right] triangle and the mean proportional between the sides around its right angle, to exhibit the triangle itself.

Let *AB* be the hypotenuse of a right triangle and *AC* the mean proportional between the sides around the right angle. The triangle is to be exhibited.

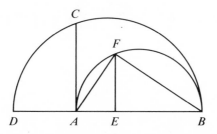

Find the third proportional, *AD*, to the given terms, *AB* and *AC*, and let *AB* be the diameter of a circle to which *FE*, which is equal to *AD*, is dropped at right angles from the circumference and let *AF* and *FB* subtend it. I say that *AF* and *FB* are the sides around the right angle that are being sought and that, therefore, the triangle being sought is *AFB*, the hypotenuse of which is the given *AB*. The right triangles *AFE* and *AFB* are similar, so

$$FE : AF = FB : AB.$$

But by construction *FE*—that is, *AD*—is to *AC* as *AC* is to *AB*. Hence *AC* is the proportional between *AF* and *FB*.

Thus from the given *AB*, the hypotenuse, and *AC*, the given proportional between the sides around the right angle, there has been shown the triangle *AFB*, as was to be done.

This problem may also be conceived of thus:

> Given the mean of three proportionals and something the square of which is equal to the sum of the squares of the extremes, to find the extremes.

In this case from *AC*, the mean, and *AB*, [the square root of the sum of the squares of the extremes],[19] have been found the extremes *AF* and *FB*.

[19]See n. 8 supra.

A SUPPLEMENT TO GEOMETRY[1]

POSTULATE

In order to make up for a deficiency in geometry, let it be agreed that

[One can] draw a straight line from any point to any two
given straight lines, the intercept between these being any
possible predefined distance.

Since in drawing straight lines two points are regularly fixed ahead of time,
the predefined distance between the two lines determines the location of the
second point. This being conceded, let it [also] be agreed that

[One can] draw another straight line from any given point to
two convergent and indefinitely extended straight lines, it
being intercepted by them with any length you choose.
 Likewise, [one can] draw another straight line from any
designated point within a circle or on its circumference to
any indefinitely continued straight line that converges on the
circumference, the intercept being any length you choose.[2]

 The first of these operations seems to have been solved by Nicomedes
with his first conchoid, the latter, with his second conchoid.[3] Moreover, the

---

[1]*Supplementum Geometriae*

[2]*Item. A quovis puncto in area circuli vel circumferentia signato, ad quamvis lineam rectam cum circulari concurrentem & indefinite continuatam, aliam insuper lineam rectam ducere, interceptam longitudine quacumque.* Ritter (biog., p. 86) translates thus: "Par un point quelconque pris dans l'aire ou sur la circonférence d'un cercle coupé nar une droite indéfinie, mener une droite telle que le segment intercepté entre cette droite et le cercle ait une longueur donnée."

[3]See Ivor Thomas, *Selections Illustrating the History of Greek Mathematics* Cambridge, Mass.: Loeb Classical Library, 1939), vol. I, p. 297ff.

postulate is completely admitted by Archimedes who undertook the construction of parabolas, spirals and even spiral tangents.

But, from the definition of a spiral, one angle is to another as one straight line to another. So any polygon whatsoever may be constructed within or around a circle. This does not mean that one knows the ratio between the diameter and the sides that are subtended by the arcs or the ratio of the sides to each other. However, from the principles of analysis it has become known that a given magnitude, when it is shown as a thing, can become known as somehow affected by homogeneous terms.

It does not follow that Archimedes intended to demonstrate, from the tangent of a spiral, that a straight line is equal to the circumference of a circle. It can be shown that there is a straight line greater than the ambit of any polygon inscribed in a circle and less than the ambit of any circumscribed polygon. Is it therefore equal to the circumference? It can [also] be shown that there is an angle less than obtuse, greater than acute. Is it therefore a right angle?[4] If Archimedes is right, Euclid is wrong. But these matters can be decided more readily after studying angular sections analytically.

PROPOSITION I

If two straight lines drawn from the same point outside a circle cut the same, one through the center, the other elsewhere, [and if] the exterior part of the one that passes through the center is less than the proportional between the interior and exterior parts of the other, a proportional can be drawn from the same point that intercepts the circle and an extension of it beyond this also cuts the circle.

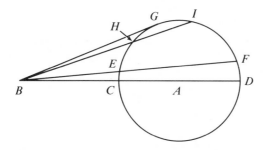

Given a circle with A as its center and assuming there are two straight lines from the same point B outside the circle that cut the circle, one BCD passing through the center A, the other BEF, let the exterior parts of the secants be *BC* and *BE* and the interior parts *CD* and *EF*. Let, moreover, *BC* be less than the mean proportional between *BE* and *EF*. This always happens when *EF* is greater than *BE*. Since *BC* is the shortest of the lines cutting the circle from point *B*, the mean proportional between *BE* and *EF* will be greater than *BE*.

I say that a mean proportional can be drawn from *B* such that it intercepts the circle and that its extension beyond this will also cut the circle. For *BG* is tangent to the circle and will, therefore, be greater than the proportional between *BE* and *EF*, since it is a proportional between BE and the whole of *BF*. Hence the line to be drawn will lie between the points *C* and *G*. It may well lie at *H*. A further extension of *BH* will cut the circle, perhaps at *I*. So the proposition stands.

PROPOSITION II

If two straight lines drawn from the same point outside a circle cut the same,[5] the first secant is to the second as the exterior part of the second is to the exterior part of the first.

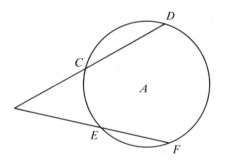

Let a circle be described with *A* as its center and let it be cut by two straight lines drawn from the point *B* outside the circle. One is *BCD*, the other *BEF*. Hence the exterior parts of the secants are *BC* and *BE*. I say that

$$BD : BF = BE : BC.$$

It is shown in the *Elements*[6] that the product of *BD* and *BC* is equal to the product of *BF* and *BE*. Therefore the proposition stands.

---

[5] At this point the text qualifies the preceding by saying "one through the center, the other elsewhere." I have omitted these words because the statement of the problem does not include them and the accompanying diagram is inconsistent with them.

[6] The reference is presumably to III, 36 of the *Elements* or the corollary thereto proposed by Clavius and others. See Heath's edition of Euclid, vol. II, p. 73f.

PROPOSITION III

If two straight lines drawn from a point outside a circle cut it and the exterior part of the first is a proportional between the exterior and interior parts of the second, the exterior part of the second will also be a proportional between the exterior and interior parts of the first.

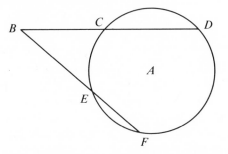

Let two straight lines drawn from the same point, B, exterior to a circle described around A, its center, cut it, one at the points C and D, the other at the points E and F. Hence the exterior parts of the secants are BC and BE and the interior parts are CD and EF. Let, moreover, BE be a proportional between BC and CD. I say that BC is also a proportional between BE and EF.

Since BCD and BEF [drawn] from the same point B cut the circle, therefore

$$BE : BC = BD : BF.$$

By hypothesis, however,

$$CD : BE = BE : BC.$$

Hence

$$CD : BE = BD : BF$$

and, by subtraction,

$$CD : BE = BC : EF.^7$$

Consequently,

$$CD : BE = BE : BC = BC : EF.$$

So BC is a proportional between BE and EF,[8] as was to be shown.

---

[7] I.e., $CD : BE = (BD - CD) : (BF - BE)$.
[8] The text has BF.

Proposition IIII

If two straight lines drawn from a point outside a circle cut it and the product of the exterior parts of the lines is equal to the product of the interior parts, the exterior parts taken alternately will be continued proportionals between the interior parts.

Let two straight lines drawn from the same point, B, assumed to be outside a circle described around A, its center, cut this circle, one at the points C and D, the other at the points E and F. So the exterior parts of the secants are BC and BE, the interior parts CD and EF. Let, moreover, the product of BC and BE be equal to the product of DC and EF. I say that BC and BE are continued proportionals between DC and EF, taking them alternately—that is, the exterior part of the second secant following the interior part of the first or the exterior part of the first following the interior part of the second. Stated otherwise,

$$DC : BE = BE : BC = BC : EF.$$

Since by hypothesis the product of CD and EF is equal to the product of BC and BE, therefore

$$CD : BE = BC : EF.$$

By synaeresis,[9]

$$CD : BE = BD : BF.$$

But by construction,

$$BE : BC = BD : BF.$$

Therefore CD is to BE as BE is to BC and, consequently, as BC is to EF, which was to be demonstrated.

Proposition V

Given two straight lines, to find two mean continued proportionals between them.

Let Z and X be the given straight lines. Two mean continued proportionals are to be found between Z and X. Let Z be the greater and X the smaller.

Describe a circle [around] A, its center, at the distance AB, which is equal to one-half of Z. Within it draw BC equal to X. Extend BC to D, making BD double BC and join D [and] A. Parallel to this [i.e., to DA]

[9]I.e., by taking $CD + BC$ and $BE + EF$.

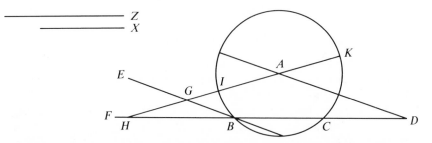

construct *BE* of indefinite [length]. Extend *DB* indefinitely to *F* and from the point *A* draw the straight line *KAIGH* [intercepting] *BE* and *BF*. This will cut *BE* and *BF* at the points *G* and *H*, so that *GH* is equal to *AB*, and the circle at the points *I* and *K*. Let *I* be closer to *H* [than *K*]. I say that *IK*, *HB*, *HI* and *BC* are continued proportionals.

Since *DA* and *BG* were constructed as parallels, therefore

$$HG : HB = GA : BD.^{10}$$

and

$$HG : IK = BC : BD,$$

or as single to double. Therefore

$$IK : HB = GA : BC.^{11}$$

[10] I.e., since *HGB* and *HAD* are similar triangles,

$$HG : HB = HA : HD$$

and therefore,

$$HG : HB = (HA - HG) : (HD - HB) = GA : BD.$$

[11] I.e., since

$$HG : HB = GA : BD$$

and

$$HG : IK = BC : BD,$$

therefore

$$HG \times BD = HB \times GA$$

and

$$HG \times BD = IK \times BC.$$

Whence

$$IK \times BC = HB \times GA$$

and

$$IK : GA = HB : BC.$$

Since *GH* and *AI* are equals, *HI* and *GA* will also be equals. Hence

$$IK : HB = HI : BC.$$

From the assumed point *H* outside the circle have been drawn two straight lines cutting the same and the product of their exterior parts (viz., *HB* and *HI*) is equal to the product of their interior parts (viz., *IK* and *BC*). Therefore the exterior parts taken alternately are continued proportionals between the interior parts. That is, *IK*, *HB*, *HI* and *BC* are continued proportionals. Given, therefore, the two straight lines *Z* and *X*, that is *IK* and *BC*, the continued proportionals *HB* and *HI* have been found between them, as was to be done.

PROPOSITION VI

Given a right triangle, to find another and larger right triangle equally high, such that the product of the difference between their bases and the difference between their hypotenuses is equal to a given rectangle.

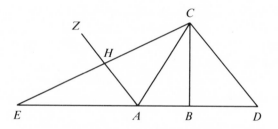

Let the given right triangle be *ABC*, with *AB* as its base, *AC* as its hypotenuse and *BC* as its perpendicular. Another larger right triangle with the same perpendicular is to be found such that the product of the difference between *AB* and the base of the triangle to be found and the difference between *AC* and the hypotenuse of the triangle to be found is equal to a given rectangle. Let the rectangle be the product of *AC* and any *AD* whatsoever and if it is not given in this form (i.e., in the form of a rectangle] let it be converted to it. If necessary, let *AB* be assumed to be continued to *AD*. Connect *DC* and construct *AZ* parallel to it. From *C* draw a straight line that will cut *DA* continued at *E* and *AZ* at *H*, so that the segment *HE* is equal to *CA*. I say that the triangle *CBE* is what is being sought.

EA is the difference by which the base *EB* exceeds the base *AB* and *CH* is the difference by which the hypotenuse *CE* exceeds the hypotenuse *CA* or *HE*, which has been constructed equal to it. The product of *EA* and

CH, moreover, is equal to the product of *AD* and *HE*. Since *CD* and *HA* have been constructed as parallels,

$$AD : CH = AE : HE.$$

Furthermore, the perpendicular of the triangle CBE is the same as that of the triangle *CBA*, namely *BC*. Given, therefore, the right triangle *ABC*, there has been discovered another right triangle greater than it and of equal height such that the product of *AE*, the difference between the bases, and *CH*, the difference between the hypotenuses, is equal to the product of *AD* and *HE*, the given rectangle or its equivalent, which is what was to be done.

From this the discovery of two mean continued proportionals between two given ones is clear. This is shown clearly by poristics.[12] The square of the fourth or greater of the extremes differs from the square of the first as the square of the sum of the fourth and twice the second differs from the square of the first and twice the third. So if two right triangles are constructed, one with its base equal to the first or smaller of the extremes and its hypotenuse equal to the fourth, the other with its base equal to the sum of the first and twice the third and its hypotenuse equal to the sum of the fourth and twice the second, the triangles will be equally high. The mesographic operation, therefore, reduces to this: Having constructed a triangle the base of which is equal to a first [proportional] and the hypotenuse to a fourth, there is to be found another triangle of equal height the base of which is equal to the sum of the first and twice the third and the hypotenuse to the sum of the fourth and twice the third. The triangle being sought may then be found by this proposition since the difference[13] between the hypotenuses is twice the second and between the bases twice the third. The product of these differences, whatever it is, is equal to four times the product of the first and fourth. Thus everything is given that the law of the proposition requires.

PROPOSITION VII

Given the first of three proposed proportional straight lines and [another line] the square of which is equal to the difference between the square of the sum of the second and third and the square of the sum of the second and first, to find the second and third proportionals.

[12] *Ostensum enim est in Poristicis,* which might also be translated, "This has been shown in the Poristics." If so, it must refer to a lost work of Viète's. Perhaps the subject was covered in the *Later Notes to Symbolic Logistic,* a work that apparently once existed but is no longer extant.

[13] *excessus.*

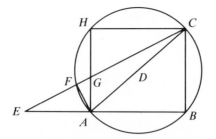

Let *AB* be given as the first of the three proposed proportional straight lines and let the straight line *BC* also be given such that its square is equal to the difference between the square of the sum of the second and third [of the proportionals] and the square of the sum of the second and first. The second and third proportionals are to be found.

Let *AB* and *BC* stand at right angles and connect *CA*, which is cut in half at *D*. From *D* as a center and at the distance *DA* or *DC* describe a circle. Extend *BA* indefinitely and from the point *C* draw a straight line cutting the extension of *BA* at *E* and the circumference at *F*, so that *FE* is equal to *AB*. From *A* erect a parallel to *BC* cutting *CE* at *G*. I say that *EA* is the second and *EG* the third [of the proportionals] being sought.

Let *AF* be subtended and let *AG* be extended to the circumference at *H*. Hence the triangles *GCH* and *FEA* have equal sides and equal angles, since the acute angles *AEF* and *HCG* are equal, the right angles *AFE* and *GHC* are equal, and the sides *CH* and *FE* are equal. So *EA* and *CG* are also equal. Moreover, *BA* is to *AE* as *CG* (i.e., *AE*) is to *GE*. Thus there are three proportionals, *BA*, *AE* or *CG*, and *GE*. Moreover *BE* is the sum of *BA* and *AE*, the first and second [of the proportionals]. And *CE* is the sum of *CG* and *GE*, the second and third. Hence the square of *CE* differs from the square of *BE* by the square of *CB*.

Given, therefore, *AB*, the first of three proportionals, and the straight line *BC*, the square of which is that by which the square of *EC*, the sum of the second and third, differs from the square of *EB*, the sum of the first and second, it has been discovered that *EA* (or *GC*) and *EG* are the second and third of the proportionals, as was to be done.

From this one may, in short,

> Construct four continuously proportional straight lines, the extremes of which are in double ratio.

It has been shown poristically[14] that if there are three proportional straight lines [and if] the square of the sum of the second and third differs

[14]See n. 12 supra p. 395.

from the square of the sum of the second and first by three times the square of the first, twice the first will be the fourth continued proportional in that series.[15]

Thus, assuming any first you choose and something that is three times the square of the first, the second and third will be found. In this series the fourth will be twice the first.

PROPOSITION VIII

If there is an isosceles triangle and a straight line leading from one end of the base to the [opposite] leg equal to that leg, the exterior angle formed by the base and the line drawn from the end of the base is three times either of the base angles of the isosceles triangle.

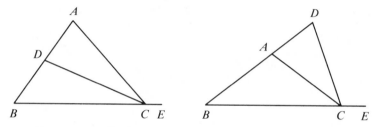

Let the triangle ABC have AB and AC as equal legs and from the angle ACB draw a straight line, CD, to the leg AB, extended if necessary, equal to the leg AB or the leg AC, and extend BC to E. I say that the angle DCE is three times the angle ACB or ABC.

Since the triangles BAC and DCA are isosceles, the angle ACB is equal to the angle ABC and the angle ADC to the angle DAC. Thus the angle ACB or ABC is one of the two parts by which two right angles exceed the angle BAC to the exterior angle of which the angle BDC is equal. Therefore the angle BDC consists of these two parts. The angle DCE, however, is the sum of the angle DBC and the angle BDC. Therefore the angle DCE is [the sum of] three parts and DCE is three times the angle ACB or ABC, as was to be shown.

[15]For example, if

$$1 : x = x : x^2$$

and

$$(x^2 + x)^2 - (x + 1)^2 = 3,$$

then

$$1 : x = x^2 : 2.$$

Proposition IX

To trisect a given angle.

Let *A* be the angle to be trisected.

From the center *B* describe a circle at any distance you choose, and let the diameter be *CBD*. Mark off the arc[16] *DE* which defines the size of the given angle and extend *DBC* indefinitely. Draw the straight line *EFG* cutting the extended diameter at *F* and the circumference at *G* so that *FG* is equal to *BC* or *BD*, the radius of the circle. I say that the angle *EFC* is one-third the angle *EBD*, that is, the given angle *A*, and that the arc[17] *GC* is one-third the amplitude [of the arc *ED*].

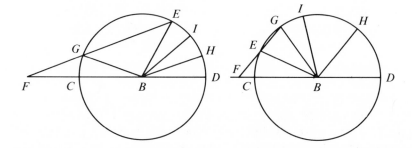

Let *G* [and] *B* be joined. Then the triangle *FGB* is isosceles. From *B*, one end of its base, draw *BE* equal to the leg *BG*. Hence[18] the angle *EBD* is triple the angle *GBF* or *GFB*. Moreover, the arc *GC* defines the size of the angle *GBF*. Accordingly, within the arc *DE* mark off the arcs *DH* and *HI* equal to the arc *CG* and draw the straight lines *BH* and *BI*. Therefore the angle *EBD*—that is, the given [angle] *A*—is trisected by the straight lines *BH* and *BI*, which is what was to be done.

---

[16] *circumferentia.*

[17] *arcum.*

[18] This is a long leap, but the gap can be bridged this way:

(1) *BGE*, the exterior angle of *BGF*, = *BFG* + *FBG* = 2*BFG*.

(2) *BGE* = *BEG* = 2*BFG*.

(3) *GBE* = two right angles − 4*GBF*.

(4) *GBD* also = two right angles − *GBF*.

(5) Therefore, *EBD* = two right angles − *GBE* − *GBF* or = two right angles − two right angles + 4*GBF* − *GBF* = 3*GBF*.

Proposition X

If there are three proportional straight lines, as the first is to the third so the sum of the squares of the first and second is to the sum of the squares of the second and third.

As the first [of three proportionals] is to the second, so the second is to the third. Consequently as the square of the first is to the square of the second, so the square of the second is to the square of the third and, by synaeresis, as the square of the first is to the square of the second, so the sum of the squares of the second and first is to the sum of the squares of the second and third. But as the square of the first is to the square of the second, so the first is to the third. Therefore as the first is to the third so the sum of the squares of the first and second is to the sum of the squares of the second and third, as was to be shown.

Proposition XI

If there are three proportional straight lines, as the first is to the sum of the first and third, so is the square of the second to the sum of the squares of the second and third.

As the first [of three proportionals] is to the third, so the square of the second is to the square of the third and, by synaeresis, as the first is to the sum of the first and third, so the square of the second is to the sum of the squares of the second and third.

Corollary

If there are three proportional straight lines, there are three solids constructed from them that are equal:

First, the solid product of the first and the sum of the squares of the second and third.
Second, the solid product of the third and the sum of the squares of the first and second.
Third, the solid product of the sum of the first and third and the square of the second.

It has been shown that the first is to the third as the sum of the squares of the first and second is to the sum of the squares of the second and third. The first solid proposed is the product of the extremes of [this] proportion and the second is the product of [its] means. Hence the first and second are equal.

It has likewise been shown that as the first is to the sum of the first and third so the square of the second is to the sum of the squares of the second and third. The first solid that has been proposed is again the product of the extremes of [this] proportion and the third is the product of [its] means. Hence the first and third are equal and therefore the third is also equal to the second.

PROPOSITION XII

If there are three proportional straight lines, the cube of the sum of the two extremes minus the solid product of this sum and the sum of the squares of the three is equal to the solid product of the same and the square of the second.

The square of the sum of the two extremes is equal to the square of each of the extremes plus twice the square of the mean. Hence the square of the sum of the two extremes minus the sum of the squares of all three is equal to the square of the mean or second, and the square of the sum of the two extremes minus the sum of the squares of all three is to the square of the second as that sum is to the same sum, viz., one is equal to the other. What has been proposed follows from resolution of the proportion.[19]

PROPOSITION XIII

If there are three proportional straight lines, the solid product of the first and the sum of the squares of the three minus the cube of the first is equal to the solid product of the first and the sum of the squares of the second and third.

The sum of the squares of the three minus the square of the first is the square of the second plus the square of the third. Hence the sum of the squares of the three minus the square of the first is to [the sum of the squares of] the second and third[20] as the first is to the first. In other words, one is equal to the other. What has been proposed follows from resolution of the proportion.

[19]I.e., if p, q and r are the three proportionals,

(1) $(p + r)^2 = p^2 + r^2 + 2q^2$

(2) $(p + r)^2 - (p^2 + q^2 + r^2) = q^2$

(3) $[(p + r)^2 - (p^2 + q^2 + r^2)] : q^2 = (p + r)^2 : (p + r)^2$

(4) $(p + r)^2 [(p + r)^2 - (p^2 + q^2 + r^2)] = (p + r)^2 q^2$

(5) $(p + r)^3 - (p + r)(p^2 + q^2 + r^2) = (p + r)q^2.$

[20]1646 has "is to the square of the second and third."

Proposition XIIII

If there are three proportional straight lines, the solid product of the third and the sum of the squares of all three minus the cube of the third is equal to the solid product of the third and the sum of the squares of the first and second.

The sum of the squares of all three minus the square of the third is equal to the square of the second plus the square of the first. Thus as the sum of the squares of the three minus the square of the third is to [the sum of] the squares of the second and first,[21] so is the third to the third. That is, one is equal to the other. What has been proposed follows from resolution of the proportion.

Corollary

Given three proportional straight lines, there are three affected solids constructed from them that are equal:

First, the cube of the sum of the first and third minus the solid product of this sum and the sum of the squares of the three.

Second, the solid product of the first and the sum of the squares of the three minus the cube of the first.

Third, the solid product of the third and the sum of the squares of the three minus the cube of the third.[22]

Since these solids are equal to those that are equal [to each other] under the preceding corollary, they are equal to each other.

Proposition XV

If two perpendiculars are dropped from the circumference of a circle to its diameter, one at the center, the other off center, and a straight line making an angle with the diameter equal to one-third of a right angle is drawn towards the center perpendicular from the point of incidence of the other perpendicular and another straight line is drawn from the point at which this construct cuts the center perpendicular to the angle [formed by the diameter and] the semicircle, three times the square of the latter is equal to the square of the off-center perpendicular plus the squares of the segments of

---

[21]1646 has "is to the square of the second and first."

[22]If p, q and r are the three proportionals, $(p + r)^3 - (p + q)(p^2 + q^2 + r^2) = p(p^2 + q^2 + r^2) - p^3 = r(p^2 + q^2 + r^2) - r^3$.

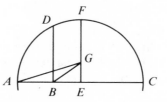

the diameter between which this perpendicular is a mean proportional.

Let *ABC* be the diameter of a circle from the circumference of which is dropped the perpendicular *DB* and let *AB* be the smaller segment [of the diameter], *BC* the greater and *E* the center. But *FE* is also dropped perpendicularly from the circumference and from *B* is drawn the straight line *BG* in such fashion that the angle *GBE* is equal to one-third of a right angle, whence *BG* is twice *GE*. Let *A* [and] *G* be joined. I say that

$$3AG^2 = DB^2 + AB^2 + BC^2.$$

Since

$$AB^2 = AE^2 + BE^2 - (2AE \times BE)$$

and

$$BC^2 = BE^2 + EC^2 + (2BE \times EC),$$

and *AE* and *EC* are equal, therefore

$$AB^2 + BC^2 = 2AE^2 + 2BE^2.$$

Add *DB²* to both. But

$$DB^2 + BE^2 = AE^2,{}^{23}$$

and therefore

$$AB^2 + BC^2 + DB^2 = 3AE^2 + BE^2.$$

Since *BG* was constructed equal to 2*GE*, *BE²* is 3*GE²*. Moreover

$$AE^2 + EG^2 = AG^2.$$

---

[23]This, of course, follows from the fact that the radius *AE* is equal to the radius *DE*, *DE* being the hypotenuse of the right triangle *DBE*.

Therefore

$$3AG^2 = DB^2 + AB^2 + BC^2,$$

as was to be demonstrated.

PROPOSITION XVI

If there are two individual isosceles triangles and the legs of one are equal to those of the other and the base angle of the second is equal to three times the base angle of the first, the cube of the base of the first minus three times the product of the base of the first and the square of the common leg is equal to the product of the base of the second and the square of the same leg.

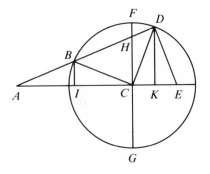

Let the first triangle be ABC having equal legs AB and BC. Since the second triangle is also isosceles and either of the base angles of this second triangle is three times the angle BAC or BCA and is necessarily less than a right angle, therefore either of the angles BAC and BCA is less than one-third of a right angle and the angle ABC is greater than a right angle. Let AB and AC be extended. From C to AB extended, draw CD equal to AB. Then from D to AC extended draw DE also equal to AB. So there are two isosceles triangles, ABC and CDE. But CD and DE, the legs of the second triangle, are equal to AB and BC, the equal legs of the first triangle. Moreover, just as either of the angles BAC and BCA is one part of two right angles, so the angle ABC [is equal to] two right angles minus those two parts, and the exterior angle of the angle ABC [is equal to] those two parts.[24] The angle ADC is equal to this exterior angle, since the angles DBC

[24] *Qualium autem uterque angulorum BAC, BCA est pars una, angulus ABC est duorum rectorum minus talibus duabus partibus, et angulus exterior anguli ABC duarum est illarum partium.* The grammar is confusing, but the sense is clear.

and *CDB* are equal on account of the equality of the legs *CD* and *CB*. The angle exterior to the angle *DCA*, moreover, is the sum of the angles *ADC* and *DAC*. Thus the second triangle is *CDE*, which is isosceles and has legs equal to the legs of *ABC*, the first triangle, and either of its base angles, namely *DCE* or *DEC*, is three times the angle *BAC* or *BCA*. I say, then, that

$$AC^3 - 3(AC \times AB^2) = (CE \times DC^2) \text{ or } (CE \times AB^2).$$

For let a circle be described at the distance *CB* or *CD* from *C*, its center, and let the diameter *FCG* cut *AE* perpendicularly at *C* and *AD* at *H*. Let *BI* and *DK* be drawn parallel to *FG*, cutting *AE* perpendicularly at *I* and *K*. Hence *AI* and *IC* are equal and *AC* is twice *AI*. So also *AB* and *BH* are equal, making *AH* twice *AB*. Likewise *CK* and *KE* are equal, making *CE* twice *CK*.

Moreover, CG^2 (that is, AB^2) is equal to $CH^2 + (FH \times HG)$ and, by conversion, $AB^2 - CH^2$ is equal to $FH \times HG$ (that is, to $BH \times HD$). Furthermore, CH^2 is equal to $AH^2 - AC^2$ and AH^2 is $4AB^2$. Hence

$$AC^2 - 3AB^2 = BH \times HD.$$

But

$$BH : HD = IC : CK$$

and

$$IC : CK = AC : CE,$$

since the latter terms are twice the former. Hence

$$AC : CE = BH : HD$$

and consequently *AC* is to *CE* as BH^2 (i.e., AB^2) is to $BH \times HD$—i.e., to AC^2—$3AB^2$. Thus, resolving this proportion,

$$AC^3 - 3(AC \times AB^2) = CE \times AB^2,$$

as was to be demonstrated.

Assuming that *Z* is any side of an equilateral triangle and that, therefore, each of the angles is one-third of two right angles,

$$A^3 - 3Z^2A = Z^3,$$

thus making *A* the base of an isosceles triangle the base angle of which is one-ninth of two right angles.

Let *Z* be 1 and *A* *x*. [Then]

$$x^3 - 3x = 1.$$

If Z is 100,000,000, these are the triangles:

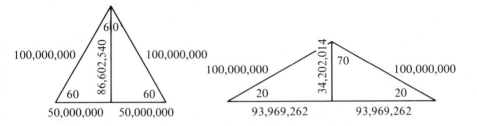

PROPOSITION XVII

If there are two individual isosceles triangles the legs of one of which are equal to those of the other and if the angle which is the difference between a base angle of the second and two right angles[25] is three times the base angle of the first, three times the product of the base of the first and the square of the common leg minus the cube of the base of the first is equal to the product of the base of the second and the square of the common leg.

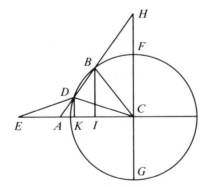

Let the first triangle be ABC, having AB and BC as its equal legs. Since the angle that is the difference between either of the base angles of the second triangle and two right angles is three times the angle BAC, it is necessarily greater than a right angle. Therefore either of the base angles, BAC or BCA, is greater than one-third of a right angle and the vertical angle ABC is less than a right angle. Hence draw CD into AB equal to AB.

[25] *Angulus autem, quem is qui est ad basin secundi relinquit e duobus rectis.*

Then from D to CA extended draw DE equal to AB. There are now two isosceles triangles, ABC and EDC, and DE and DC, the legs of the second triangle, are equal to the equal legs, AB and BC, of the first triangle. Just as either of the angles BAC and BCA is one part of two right angles, so the angle ABC is [the difference between] two right angles and the other two parts, and the angle exterior to the angle ABC [is equal to] these two parts and, since the angles DBC and CDB are equal on account of the equality of the legs CB and CD, the angle ADC is equal to it. The angle exterior to the angle DCA is the sum of the angles ADC and DAC. Thus the second triangle, CDE, is itself isosceles and has legs equal to the legs of the first triangle, ABC, and either of the base angles that remain when a base angle, DCE or DEC, is subtracted from two right angles is three times the angle BAC or BCA. I say, therefore, that

$$3(AC \times AB^2) - AC^3 = EC \times DC^2 = EC \times AB^2.$$

Describe a circle around C, its center, at the distance CB or CD and construct the diameter FCG cutting a continuation of EA perpendicularly at C and likewise AD, also continued, at H. Construct BI and DK parallel to FG and cutting [the extension of] AE perpendicularly at I and K. Therefore AI and IC are equal and AC is double AI. So also AB and BH are equal[26] and AH is double AB, and EK and KC are equal and EC is double EK. Moreover, CH^2 is equal to CF^2—that is, AB^2—plus $HF \times HG$ and, inverting,

$$CH^2 - AB^2 = HF \times HG = HB \times HD.^{27}$$

Furthermore,

$$CH^2 = AH^2 - AC^2$$

and AH^2 is equal to $4AB^2$. Hence

$$3AB^2 - AC^2 = BH \times HD.$$

But

$$HB : HD = CI : CK$$

and

$$CI : CK = CA : CE,$$

[26] The triangle HBC is isosceles, since the angle CHB equals the angle BCH: (1) (a) CHB equals IBA, IB having been constructed parallel to HC; (b) since IB bisects ABC and ABC equals $180° - 2BCA$, IB equals $90° - BCA$; (c) BCH also equals $90° - BCA$. (2) The two triangles HBC and BCA have BC as a common side. (3) But BC equals AB. Therefore (4) AB equals BH.

[27] This last follows from Proposition II of this book.

since the consequents are double the antecedents.[28] Therefore

$$CA : CE = HB : HD$$

and consequently CA is to CE as HB^2 (i.e., AB^2) is to $HB \times HD$ (i.e., $3AB^2 - AC^2$). Resolving this proportion,

$$3(AC \times AB^2) - AC^3 = EC \times AB^2,$$

as was to be shown.

Proposition XVIII

If there are two individual isosceles triangles, the legs of one being equal to those of the other and the base angle of the second being three times the base angle of the first, three times the product of the square of the common leg and one-half the base of the first plus or minus a length the square of which is equal to three times the height of the first when the cube of the same half of the base, thus enlarged or diminished, is subtracted from it, is equal to the product of the base of the second and the square of the leg.

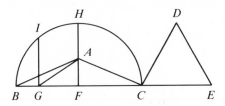

Let BAC be the first triangle, having equal legs AB and AC, and let CDE be the second, having equal legs DC and DE. Let AB and AC be equal to DC and DE, but let the angle DCE or DEC be three times the angle ABC or ACB. Erect AF, the altitude of the first triangle, and construct AG on the base facing toward B, [equal to] two times AF. Then either BF or FC becomes one-half the base and the square of GF is three times the square of AF, the altitude. Therefore BG is equal to BF minus the length GF, and GC is equal to FC plus the length GF. I say that

$$3(BG \times AB^2) - BG^3 = CE \times DC^2 = CE \times AB^2.$$

I say again that

$$3(GC \times AB^2) - GC^3 = CE \times DC^2 = CE \times AB^2.$$

[28] I.e., in $CI : CA = CK : CE$, the consequents are double the antecedents.

From the center F at a distance of BF or FC describe a circle and extend FA to the circumference at H. From the same circumference drop the straight line IG perpendicularly to the point G on the diameter. BG, GI and GC, therefore, are three proportionals. Since, moreover, AG is twice AF or, put otherwise, since the angle AGF is one-third of a right angle, therefore

$$3AB^2 = BG^2 + GI^2 + GC^2.\textbf{[29]}$$

Thus there are three affected solids that are equal:

First, $BC^3 + 3(BC \times AB^2)$
Second, $3(BG \times AB^2) - BG^3$
Third, $3(GC \times AB^2) - GC^3$.

But the first is equal to the product of CE and the square of AB, from the antepenultimate proposition. Therefore the second and third are equal to the product of CE and the square of AB. Whence the proposition is settled.

Proposition XIX

To extend the diameter of a circle so that the extension is to the radius plus the extension as the square of the radius is to the square of the extended diameter.

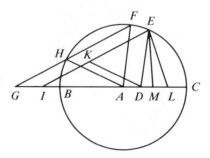

Describe a circle with A as its center and BAC its diameter and assume that CD is one-third of the diameter and the arc CE one-third of half the circumference or, put otherwise, that it is the arc of a hexagon. Then connect ED and draw the radius AF parallel to it. Draw FG from the point F to an extension of CB, cutting the circumference at H and such that

---

[29] I.e., $AB^2 = BF^2 + AF^2$ and $3AB^2 = 3BF^2 + GF^2$. But $BG^2 + GI^2 + GC^2$, when fully spelled out, equals $3BG^2 + 6(BG \times GF) + 4GF^2$, which is the same as $3BF^2 + GF^2$ when fully spelled out.

HG is equal to the radius *AB* or *AC*. Construct *EI* parallel to *FG*, cutting *CG* at *I*. I say that this construct is what is called for, for

$$IB : IA = AB^2 : IC^2.$$

Let *AH* be joined and draw *DK* parallel to it and on *BC* extended erect *EL* equal to *DE*. Since, therefore, *GH* and *HA*, the legs of the triangle *GHA*, are equal and *AF* has been drawn from *A*, a point on the base, equal to the leg *GH*, the angle *FAC* becomes three times the angle *HAG*. Moreover, the triangles *IKD* and *KDE* are similar to the triangles *GHA* and *HAF*, and *IKD* is an isosceles triangle. But the triangle *DEL* has also been constructed with equal legs and those legs, *DE* and *EL*, are equal to the legs *IK* and *KD*, and the angle *EDL* or *ELD* is three times the angle *KID* or *KDI*. So ID^3 minus three times the product of *ID* and IK^2 or minus three times the product of *ID* and DE^2 equals the product of *DL* and DE^2.

AD, moreover, is one-third the radius *AB* and when *EM* is dropped perpendicularly from *E* to the diameter *DM* becomes one-sixth the radius. Thus $3/4 \; AB^2$ will equal EM^2. Since

$$EM^2 + DM^2 = DE^2,$$

therefore

$$DE^2 = \frac{3}{4} AB^2 + \frac{1}{36} AB^2.$$

Likewise

$$AB^2 : DE^2 = 9 : 7$$

and thus $3DE^2$ is equal to $7/3 \; AB^2$, and the product of *DL* and DE^2 equals $7/27 \; AB^3$. Hence

$$ID^3 - \left(ID \times \frac{7}{3} AB^2 \right) = \frac{7}{27} AB^3.$$

Let this be the first conclusion.

Now multiply all these solids by 27. Then

$$27ID^3 - 63(ID \times AB^2) = 7AB^3.$$

Converting this equality to a proportion,

$$(9ID^2 - 21AB^2) : 7AB^2 = AB : 3ID.$$

But

$$ID^2 = IA^2 + AD^2 + 2(AD \times IA)$$

and AD is $1/3$ AB. Hence

$$9ID^2 = 9IA^2 + 6(IA \times AB) + AB^2.$$

Hence

$$[9IA^2 + 6(IA \times AB) - 20AB^2] : 7AB^2 = AB : (AB + 3IA).$$

Resolving this proportion, since the solid products permit division by 27,

$$IA^3 + (AB \times IA^2) - 2(IA \times AB^2) = AB^3.$$

Let this be the second conclusion.

Transform the equality into a proportion once more:

$$(IA - AB) : AB = AB^2 : [IA^2 + 2(IA \times AB)]$$

and, by diaeresis,

$$(IA - AB) : IA = AB^2 : [IA^2 + 2(IA \times AB) + AB^2]$$

and, by substitution,

$$IB : IA = AB^2 : IC^2,$$

which is what was to be demonstrated.[30]

From the first conclusion, if AB is 100,000,000 ID becomes 124,697,960.

Proposition XX

To construct an isosceles triangle such that the difference between the base and either of the legs is to the base as the square of the leg is to the square of the sum of the leg and base.

Let the described circle be set out with A as its center and BC as its diameter and extend CAB, the diameter, to D, so that

$$DB : DA = AB^2 : DC^2.$$

From D draw a straight line, DE, to the circumference equal to AB or AC and join AE. I say that the triangle DEA is what is being sought. The legs ED and EA are equal. Moreover, DB is the difference between the base DA and the leg AC or AB. DC is the sum of the base DA and the leg AC, that is AE. Hence an isosceles triangle, DEA, has been constructed and DB, the difference between the base and the leg AE or ED is to DA, the base, as the

---

[30]At this point 1646 carries an extensive "scholium" which virtually repeats what has gone before.

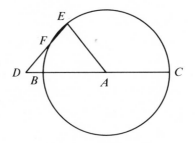

square of *EA* or *ED* is to the square of the sum of the base *DA* and the leg *EA*. This is what was to be done.

PROPOSITION XXI

> If there is an isosceles triangle and the difference between its base and either of its legs is to the base as the square of the leg is to the square of the sum of the leg and the base, a straight line drawn from one end of the base to the [opposite] leg, which is equal [in length] to the leg, will bisect the base angle.

Repeat the preceding construction and let *DE* cut the circle at *F* and join *A* [and] *F*. I say that *AF* bisects the angle *EAD*.
Since by hypothesis

$$DB : DA = AB^2 : DC^2,$$

therefore

$$DB : AB = (DA \times AB) : DC^2.$$

But *DB* is to *DE* or *AB* as *DF* is to *DC*.[31] Hence

$$DF : DC = (DA \times AB) : DC^2.$$

Consequently *DF* is to *AB* or *DE* as *DA* is to *DC* and, by subtraction,

$$DF : FE = DA : AC.$$

Hence the connecting line *EC* becomes parallel to *FA* and the angle *ECD* is equal to the angle *FAD*. But the angle *EAD* is twice the angle *ECD* since it is at the center while the latter is on the circumference. So the angle *EAD* is bisected by the straight line *AF*, as was to be shown.

[31]From Proposition II of this book.

PROPOSITION XXII

If there is an isosceles triangle and the straight line drawn from one end of the base to the [opposite] leg, equal [in length] to that leg, bisects the base angle, the vertical angle will be one and a half times either of the base angles.

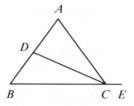

Let the triangle *ABC* have equal legs, *AB* and *AC*. When a straight line, *CD*, equal to the leg is drawn from the point *C* to the opposite leg, the angle *ACB* will be bisected. I say that the angle *BAC* is one and a half times the angle *ABC* or *ACB*.

Since the straight line *CD*, which is equal to the leg *AB* or the leg *CA*, is drawn from *C*, the end of the base of isosceles triangle *ABC*, the exterior angle *DCE* is three times the angle *ACB* or *ABC*.[32] Just as the angle *ABC* or *ACB* is of two parts, so the angle exterior to *DCB* is of six. The angle *DCA*, which is one-half of the angle *ACB*, is one [of these parts]; so also is the angle *DCB*. Hence the angle *DCE* and its exterior angle comprise seven parts. These, moreover, are equal to two right angles just as are the three angles of a triangle. Since, then, the angles *ABC* and *ACB*, whichever you please, are of two parts, the angle *BAC* is left with the remaining three. Therefore *BAC* is equal to one and a half times either the angle *ABC* or *ACB*, as was to be shown.

PROPOSITION XXIII

If there is an isosceles triangle with a vertical angle equal to one and a half times either of the base angles and a straight line is drawn from one end of the base to the [opposite] leg equal [in length] to that leg, thus creating another isosceles triangle one leg of which is the line that has been drawn cutting [a leg of the original triangle] and the other is the leg that has not been cut, either of the base angles in the second triangle will be three times the remaining angle.

---

[32] From Proposition VIII of this book.

Let the triangle *ABC* have its legs, *AB* and *AC*, equal and let the angle *BAC* be one and a half times either of the angles *ABC* and *ACB*. From *C*, one end of the base, draw the straight line *CD* to the leg *AB* equal to *AB* or *AC*. Then the triangle *ACD* is again isosceles and *CD* and *CA*, its legs, are equal. I say that either of the angles *ADC* or *DAC* in the triangle ACD will be three times the angle *DCA*.

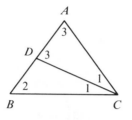

Since the angle *BAC* is one and a half times the angle *ABC* or *ACB*, therefore just as the angle *ABC* is made up of two parts, so *BAC* is made up of three. But the angle *ACB* also has two parts since it is equal to *ABC*. Hence the three angles of the triangle *ABC*—that is, two right angles— are counted as seven parts.

Since, moreover, the triangle *ACD* is also isosceles, having its leg *DC* equal to its leg *CA*, therefore just as the triangle *DAC* is counted as having three parts, so the angle *ADC* will have the same and, therefore, the angle *ACD* will have one since the two right angles count as seven [parts]. Hence in the triangle *ADC* either of the angles *DAC* or *ADC* is three times the remaining angle, *ACD*, which is what was to be demonstrated.

Proposition XXIV

To inscribe an equilateral and equiangular heptagon in a given circle.

Let the given circle have *A* as its center and *BAC* as its diameter. An equilateral and equiangular heptagon is to be inscribed in it.

Extend the diameter, *CB*, to *D* so that

$$DB : DA = AB^2 : DC^2$$

and draw *DE* across the circumference equal to the radius. I say that *EB* is the arc of a heptagon, that is, one-seventh of the whole circumference.

Let *DE* cut the circle at *F* and connect the radii *AE* and *AF*. The triangle *DEA*, therefore, is isosceles and is so constituted that the difference between the base and the leg is to the base as the square of the leg is to

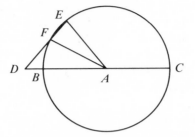

the square of the sum of the leg and the base. Hence the straight line *AF*, which is equal to the leg, bisects the base angle and, therefore, just as its two right angles have seven parts, so the angle *EAD* has two and, as the four right angles—that is, the whole circumference—have seven parts, so the angle *EAD* has one. But the amplitude of this angle, *EAD*, defines the arc *EB*. It subtends one-seventh [of the whole]. So the arc *EB* is one-seventh of the whole circumference and seven times this subtends [the whole]. Hence there has been inscribed in the given circle an equilateral and equiangular heptagon, which is what was to be done.

Alternatively

To inscribe an equilateral and equiangular heptagon in a given circle.

Let the given circle be *ABCDEFG*. An equilateral and equiangular heptagon is to be inscribed in *ABCDEFG*.

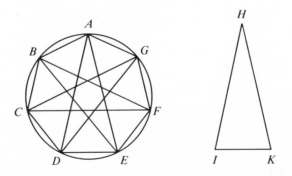

Construct an isosceles triangle, *HIK*, having the angles at *I* and *K* three times the remaining angle at *H*. Inscribe in the circle *ABCDEFGH* a triangle with the same angles as *HIK*. Let this be *ADE* and such that the angle *DAE* is equal to the angle at *H* and that *ADE* and *AED* are equal to those at *I* and *K*. Either *ADE* or *AED*, therefore, is triple the angle *DAE*. Hence either the arc *AD* or the arc *AE* will be triple the arc *DE* and one-third of the arc *AD* or *AE* will be equal to the arc *DE*. Let these thirds be *AB*, *BC*, *CD*, *AG*, *GF* and *FE* and [draw the chords that] subtend [them]. Hence, as was required, an equilateral and equiangular heptagon has been inscribed in a given circle.

Assume a hypotenuse of 100,000,000 and a right angle with seven parts. The right triangles having seven [parts] will be these:

Assuming, further, that *Z* is the leg of an isosceles triangle the vertical angle of which is one and a half times the base angle,

$$A^3 + ZA^2 - 2Z^2A = Z^3,$$

making *A* the base of this triangle.

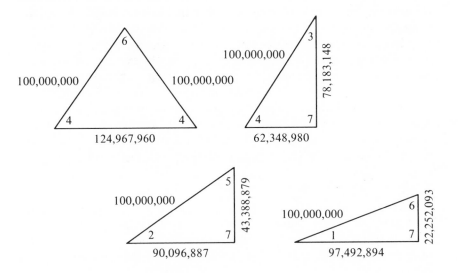

Stated in numbers, let *Z* be 1 and *A x*:

$$x^3 + x^2 - 2x = 1.$$

By reduction,

$$E^2 - 21Z^2E = 7Z^3$$

and *E* is the sum of the base of this triangle and one-third its leg.

Stated in numbers, let *Z* be 1 and *E x*:

$$x^3 - 21x = 7.$$

Proposition XXV—A General Corollary

It is generally true that problems otherwise insolvable in which cubes are equated to solids or fourth powers to plano-planes, with or without affections, can all be solved by constructing two mean continued proportionals between given terms or by sectioning angles into three equal parts.

It has been shown in the *Treatise on Understanding Equations* that equations of the fourth degree can be reduced to cubic equations, that cubics with quadratic affections can be reduced to cubics with linear affections, that cubics with linear affections can be reduced to pure cubics and, last, that cubics with negative linear affections can be reduced to pure cubics if the solid affecting the cube is subtracted from the cube and if one-third of the plane coefficient [which], with the linear term, [composes] the affecting solid is less than the square of one-half the length that results from dividing the affected cube by the aforesaid one-third.

In pure cubics, therefore—as, say, when the cube of the unknown, A, is given equal to B^2D—B and D are known to be the extremes in a series of four continued proportionals and A, which is being sought, is the second of them.

In cubics so affected by a negative linear term that one-third of the plane coefficient [which], with the linear term, [composes] the affecting term is greater than the square of one-half the length arising from division of the affected cube by the aforesaid one-third—as, say, when

$$A^3 - 3B^2A = 2B^2D$$

and B is greater than D—it is known that there are two isosceles triangles, the legs of one equal to those of the other, that the base angle of the second of these is three times the base angle of the first, and that the base of the second is D and the leg is B. The A that is being sought, moreover, is the base of the first.

Finally in cubes that are affected by being subtracted from an affecting solid, as (say) in

$$3B^2E - E^3 = 2B^2D,$$

the E that is being sought will, using the same construction as that set out in the preceding formula, be half the base of the first [triangle] plus or minus a length the square of which is equal to three times the square of the altitude of the first. This is because the leg of an isosceles triangle is always greater than one-half the base, as is clear [from the fact] that the perpendicular cuts the base in half. So the square of the leg is greater than the square of one-half [the base] by the square of the perpendicular.

Hence all cubic and biquadratic equations, however affected, that are not otherwise solvable can be explained in terms of two problems—one the discovery of two means between given [extremes], the other the sectioning of a given angle into three equal parts. This is very worth noting.

UNIVERSAL THEOREMS ON THE ANALYSIS OF ANGULAR SECTIONS[1]

with demonstrations by

Alexander Anderson

Theorem I

If there are three right triangles the acute angle of the first of which differs from the acute angle of the second by the acute angle of the third, the first being the largest of these, the sides of the third will have these likenesses:

The hypotenuse will be analogous to the product of the hypotenuses of the first and second.

The perpendicular will be analogous to the product of the perpendicular of the first and the base of the second minus the product of the perpendicular of the second and the base of the first.

The base [will be analogous] to the product of the bases of the first and second plus the product of their perpendiculars.

Call the angle subtended by what is known as the perpendicular the acute angle and call the angle subtended by the base the remainder of a right angle. The hypotenuse, clearly, is the side subtending the right angle.

---

[1]The title varies: 1615 has *Ad Angularium Sectionum Analyticen Theoremata* καθολικωτερα; 1646 has *Ad Angulares Sectiones Theoremata* καθολικωτερα.

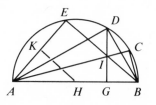

Let the three triangles be *AEB*, *ADB* and *ACB*, the bases of which are *AE*, *AD* and *AC* and the perpendiculars *EB*, *DB* and *CB*, and let *EB* cut the base *AC* at the point *I*. Drop the perpendicular *DG* to the straight line *AB*. Then *AD* will be to *DB* as *AE* is to *EI*—that is, to *EB* − *IB*— and

$$(DB \times AE) = (AD \times EB) - (AD \times IB).$$

Adding the product of *AD* and *IB* to both sides,

$$(DB \times AE) + (AD \times IB) = (AD \times EB).$$

Moreover,

$$AD:AB = CB:IB,$$

and the products of *AB* and *CB* and of *AD* and *IB* are equal. Therefore,

$$(DB \times AE) + (AB \times BC) = (AD \times EB).$$

Subtracting the product of *AE* and *DB* from both,

$$(AB \times BC) = (AD \times EB) - (AE \times DB).$$

Dividing these by *AB* there arises the length *BC* and

$$AB^2:[(AD \times EB) - (AE \times DB)] = AB:BC,$$

which was to be demonstrated.
    Again,

$$AG:AD = AE:AI,$$

and the product of *AD* and *AE* will be equal to that of *AG* and *AI*. Furthermore,

$$(AB \times AC) = (AG \times AI) + (AG \times IC) + (GB \times AC)$$

and

$$(GB \times AC) = (GB \times AI) + (GB \times IC).$$

Also,

$$(AG \times IC) + (GB \times IC) = (AB \times IC)$$

and, furthermore,

$$(AG \times AI) + (AB \times IC) + (GB \times AI) = (AB \times AC).$$

But

$$(GB \times AI) = (DB \times EB) - (DB \times IB),$$

since GB is to DB as EI—that is $EB - IB$—is to AI, and DB times IB is equal to AB times IC, since

$$IB:IC = AB:DB.$$

Therefore the product of AG and AI plus the product of AB and IC plus the product of EB and DB minus the product of AB and IC equals the product of AB and AC—i.e., the product of AG and AI or of AD and AE plus the product of DE and EB. Dividing these by AB, there arises the length AC and, therefore,

$$AB^2:[(AD \times AE) + (EB \times DB)] = AB:AC,$$

which was the second thing to be shown.

Scholium[2]

The import of the demonstration is this: If the hypotenuses of the triangles are different, as in the triangles AKH, ABD and ACB, [it is nonetheless true,] because of the similarity of the triangles [to those above], that

$$AB^2:[(AE \times AD) + (EB \times DB)]$$

$$= (AB \times AH):[(AD \times AK) + (DB \times KH)]$$

if

$$AB:AH = AE:AK = EB:KH.$$

Likewise,

$$AB^2:(AB \times AH)$$

$$= [(EB \times AD) - (DB \times AE)]:[(KH \times AD) - (DB \times AK)].$$

Let the perpendicular of the first triangle be 1 and its base 2. Let the perpendicular of the second triangle be 1 and its base 3. The perpendicular of the third will be analogous to 1 and its base to 7.

---

[2]Σχολιον

Theorem II

If there are three right triangles and the acute angle of the first of these plus the acute angle of the second is equal to the acute angle of the third, the sides of the third are like this:

The hypotenuse is analogous to the product of the hypotenuses of the first and second.

The perpendicular is analogous to the product of the perpendicular of the first and the base of the second plus the product of the perpendicular of the second and the base of the first.

The base [is analogous] to the product of the bases of the first and second minus the product of their perpendiculars.

Repeat the diagram for the preceding theorem in which

$$AG:AD = CB:IB$$

and the product of *AD* and *CB* is equal to the product of *AG* and *IB*. But

$$(AB \times EB) = (AG \times IB) + (AG \times IE) + (GB \times BE),$$

which last is the sum of the products of *GB* and *BI* and of *GB* and *IE*, and

$$AB:DB = AI:IE$$

and the product of *AB* and *IE* is equal to the product of *DB* and *AI*. But

$$(AB \times IE) = (AG \times IE) + (GB \times IE).$$

Adding the product of *GB* and *IB*—that is, the product of *DB* and *IC*, since *GB* is to *DB* as *IC* is to *IB*[3]—

$$(AG \times IE) + (GB \times IE) + (GB \times IB)$$

$$= (AI \times DB) + (IC \times DB) = DB \times AC.$$

Hence the product of *AG* and *IB*—that is, of *AD* and *CB*—plus the product of *DB* and *AC* will be equal to the product of *AB* and *EB*. Dividing through by *AB*,

$$AB^2:[(AD \times CB) + (DB \times AC)] = AB:EB,$$

which was to be demonstrated.

[3]This follows since (1) we have been given at the beginning $AG:AD = CB:IB$, whence (2) $AD:DG = IB:IC$. Therefore (3) $IC:IB = DG:AD$ and (4) from VI, 8, of the *Elements*, $GB:DB = DG:AD$. Hence (5) $IC:IB = GB:DB$.

Again, AB is to AD as AI—that is, $AC - IC$—is to AE, and

$$AB \times AE = (AD \times AC) - (AD \times IC).$$

But the product of AD and IC is equal to the product of CB and DB, for

$$AD:DB = CB:IC.$$

Therefore,

$$AB \times AE = (AD \times AC) - (CB \times DB)$$

and, dividing through by AB,

$$AB^2:[(AD \times AC) - (CB \times DB)] = AB:AE,$$

which was to be demonstrated.

Likewise, it is permissible for the hypotenuses of the triangles to be unequal, as has been noticed before.

Let the perpendicular of the first triangle be 1 and its base 7. Let the perpendicular of the second triangle be 1 and its base 3. The perpendicular of the third triangle will be analogous to 1 and its base to 2.

Theorem III [4]

If there are two right triangles the acute angle of the first of which is a fraction of the acute angle of the second, the sides of the second are like this:

The hypotenuse is analogous to a stipulated power[5] of the hypotenuse of the first. The power stipulated, moreover, corresponds to the grade of the multiple ratio [between the two angles]. It is a square if the ratio is double, a cube if it is triple, a fourth power if it is quadruple, a fifth power if it is quintuple, and so on to infinity.

[To find] the analogues of the sides around the right angle corresponding to the hypotenuse, construct an equally high power of a binomial root composed of the base and perpendicular of the first [triangle] and distribute the individual homogeneous products successively into two parts, the first of each being positive, the next negative, [and so on]. The base of the second triangle becomes the analogue of the first of these parts, the perpendicular the analogue of the second.

---

[4]So overjoyed was Viète with his discovery of this theorem that, when he set it out in his *Ad Problema, Quod Omnibus Mathematicis . . . Proposuit Adrianus Romanus Responsum* (1646, p. 315), he prefaced it with the words: "Cujus inventi laetitia adfectus, o Diva Melusinis, tibi oves centum pro una Pythagoraea immolavi."

[5]*similis potestati conditionariae.*

Thus in double ratio, the hypotenuse of the second is similar to the square of the hypotenuse of the first or, stated otherwise, to the sum of the squares of the sides around its right angle, the base to their difference, and the perpendicular to twice the product of the aforesaid sides.

In triple ratio, the hypotenuse of the second is similar to the cube of the first hypotenuse; the base to the cube of the first base minus three times the product of the first base and the square of the first perpendicular; and the perpendicular to three times the product of the first perpendicular and the square of the first base minus the cube of the perpendicular.

In quadruple ratio, the hypotenuse of the second is similar to the fourth power of the first hypotenuse; the base to the fourth power of the first base minus six times the product of the square of the perpendicular of the first and the square of the base of the same plus the fourth power of the perpendicular [of the first]; and the perpendicular to four times the product of the perpendicular of the first and the cube of its base minus four times the product of the base of the first and the cube[6] of the perpendicular of the same.

In quintuple ratio, the hypotenuse of the second is similar to the fifth power of the hypotenuse of the first; the base to the fifth power of the base of the first minus 10 times the product of the cube of the perpendicular of the first and the square of its base plus five times the product of the perpendicular of the first and the fourth power of its base; and the perpendicular to five times the product of the fourth power of the perpendicular of the first and its base minus 10 times the product of the square of the perpendicular and the cube of the base [of the first] plus the fifth power of the base of the same.

Given any right triangle you choose, let its hypotenuse be Z, its perpendicular B and its base D. From the demonstrations of the second theorem for a triangle of the double angle, since the double angle differs from its half by one-half, Z^2 will be to $D^2 - B^2$ as Z is to the base of the double-angle [triangle]. And from the same, Z^2 will be to $2\,DB$ as Z is to the perpendicular of the double-angle [triangle].

Again, Z^3 is to $D^3 - 3DB^2$ as Z is to the base of a triple-angle triangle and Z^3 is to $3D^2B - B^3$ as Z is to the perpendicular of the same triple-angle triangle.

And Z^4 is to $D^4 - 6D^2B^2 + B^4$ as Z is to the base of a quadruple-angle

[6]1615 omits this word.

triangle and Z^4 is to $4D^3B - 4B^3D$ as Z is to the perpendicular of the same quadruple-angle triangle.[7]

Again, 2^5 is to $D^5 - 10\,D^3B^2 + 5DB^4$ as Z is to the base of a quintuple-angle triangle and as Z^5 is to $5D^4B - 10D^2B^3 + B^5$ is to the perpendicular of the same quintuple-angle triangle.

Thus by multiplying the hypotenuses and sides around the right angles in accordance with the ratios already demonstrated, the homologues of multiple-angle triangles may be derived to infinity by the method just shown. This is very clear from the following table:[8]

Right Triangles

Degree of the Ratio	Hypotenuse	Sides Around the Right Angle		Hypotenuse	Base	Perpendicular
		Base	Perpendicular			
[Simple]	Z	D	B			
						Double Angle
Double	Z^2	D^2 $2DB$ B^2		Z^2	D^2 $-B^2$	$2DB$
						Triple Angle
Triple	Z^3	D^3 $3D^2B$ $3DB^2$ B^3		Z^3	D^3 $-3DB^2$	$3D^2B$ $-B^3$
						Quadruple Angle
Quadruple	Z^4	D^4 $4D^3B$ $6D^2B^2$ $4DB^3$ B^4 [9]		Z^4	D^4 $-6D^2B^2$ $+B^4$	$4D^3B$ $-4DB^3$
						Quintuple Angle
Quintuple	Z^5	D^5 $5D^4B$ $10D^3B^2$ $10D^2B^3$ $5DB^4$ B^5		Z^5	D^5 $-10D^3B^2$ $+5DB^4$ [10]	$5D^4B$ $-10D^2B^3$ $+B^5$

[Carrying] this progression to infinity will give the ratio of the sides [of any multiple-angle triangle] in [keeping with] the ratio of the [simple] angle to the multiple angle as prescribed. This is what was to be demonstrated.

[7]1646 adds at this point: Again, Z^5 is to $D^5 - 10D^3B^2 + 5DB^4$ as Z is to the base of a quintuple-angle triangle and to $5D^4B - 10D^2B^3 + B^5$ as Z is to the perpendicular of the same quintuple-angle triangle.

[8]The format of this table is somewhat altered from the formats used in 1615 and 1646.

[9]1615 omits this item.

[10]1615 has $5D^3B^4$.

Let the base of a given right triangle be 10 and its perpendicular 1, and let its acute angle be known as [the] simple [angle]:

The base of a double-angle triangle will be 99, its perpendicular 20.

The base of a triple-angle triangle will be 970, its perpendicular 299.

The base of a quadruple-angle triangle will be 9401, its perpendicular 3960.

The base of a quintuple-angle triangle will be 90,050, its perpendicular 49,001.

If it is impossible to subtract the [negative] factors [from the positive], it is clear that the multiple angle is obtuse; in this case the excess of these factors is nevertheless assigned to the side and the angle subtended will be known to be exterior to the multiple.

Alternatives to the Same
Adapted to Geometric Language

If there are any number of right triangles and the acute angle of the second is twice that of the first, the third three times, the fourth four times, the fifth five times, and so on in natural progression, the perpendicular of the first is the first of [a series of] proportionals, the base the second, and the same series may be continued [thus]:

In the second, the base will be to the perpendicular as the third [of the series] minus the first is to twice the second.

In the third, as the fourth minus three times the second is to three times the third minus the first.

In the fourth, as the fifth minus six times the third plus the first is to four times the fourth minus four times the second.

In the fifth, as the sixth minus 10 times the fourth plus five times the second is to five times the fifth minus 10 times the third plus the first.

In the sixth, as the seventh minus 15 times the fifth plus 15 times the third minus the first is to six times the sixth minus 20 times the fourth plus six times the second.

In the seventh, as the eighth minus 21 times the sixth plus 35 times the fourth minus seven times the second is to seven times the seventh minus 35 times the fifth plus 21 times the third minus the first.

And so on to infinity, dividing the successive proportionals into two parts in accordance with this series, making the first of each [part] positive, the next negative, and using such multipliers as is required by the order of the grades in the construction of powers from which these are derived.

All this is clear from inspection of the table set out above.

Theorem IIII

If beginning as a point on the circumference of a circle any number of equal segments are laid off and straight lines are drawn [from the beginning point] to the individual points marking the segments, as the shortest is to the one next to it, so any of the others above the shortest will be the sum of the two nearest to it.

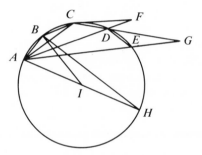

Let an arc[11] of a circle, AE be cut into any number of equal parts subtended by the straight lines AB, BC, CB and DE. Draw the straight lines AC, AD and AE. Draw[12] also the straight lines CF and DG equal to CA and DA. Then, because of the similarity of the isosceles triangles ABC, ACF and ADG,

$$AB:AC = AC:AF = AD:AG.$$

The straight line AF, moreover, is equal to AD [+] AB, for in the isosceles triangle ACF the angle CFA is equal to the angle CAF—that is, to the angle BAC—and the angle CDA is equal to twice the angle BAC since it comprehends a double arc. Hence the angle CDA is twice the angle CFD and is equal [to the sum of] the angles CFD and FCD. Thus the angles CFD

[11]*circumferentia.*
[12]1615 has *iungantur;* 1646 has *ducantur.*

and *FCD* are equal and the sides *CD* and *DF* are equal. But the side *CD* is equal to *AB* and, therefore, *FD* will be equal to *AB* and the straight line *AF* will be equal to the sum of *AD* and *AB*.

Similarly in the isosceles triangle *ADG*, the base angles *DAG* and *DGA* are equal. Thus the angle *DGA* is equal to the angle *CAD* and the external angle *DEA* of the triangle *DGE* is equal to three times the angle *CAD* or *DGE*, since it comprehends a triple arc. Therefore, just as the angle *DGE* is [made up] of one of [three] parts, so the angle *EDG* is [made up] of two. Thus the triangle *EDG* has the same angles as the triangle *ACD*[13] and the side *DE* is equal to the straight line *CD*. Therefore the side *EG* is equal to the side *CA* and the straight line *AG* is equal to the sum of *AC* and *AE*. Hence

$$AB:AC = AC:(AB + AD) = AD:(AC + AE^{14}),$$

and so on if there were more segments. This is what was to be demonstrated. Hence

Zetetic

To construct in a circle two arcs in a given multiple ratio, which ratio also holds between the squares of the straight lines by which the arcs are subtended.

Let the given circle be that which is given above, *ABH*, and let its diameter be *AH* and its radius *BI*. Construct the straight line *BH* and let the arcs *AB* and *AC* be in double ratio, *AB* and *AD* in triple, *AB* and *AE* in quadruple, and so on. Then

$$BI:BH = AB:AC$$

because of the similarity of the triangles *BIH* and *ABG*.[15] Hence $(BH \times AB)/BI$ will equal *AC* and

$$AB:\frac{BH \times AB}{BI} = \frac{BH \times AB}{BI}:\frac{BH^2 \times AB^2}{AB \times BI^2}.$$

Subtracting *AB* [from the last term] yields $[(BH^2 \times AB^2) - (AB^2 \times BI^2)]/(AB \times BI^2)$, that is $\{(BH^2 \times AB) - (BI^2 \times AB)\}/BI^2$, [which is]

---

[13]*Est itaque triangulum EDG aequiangulum triangulo ACD.*
[14]1615 has *CE*.
[15]1615 has *ABC*.

equal to AD from the preceding proposition. Therefore

$$BH^2:(BH^2 - BI^2) = AB:AD$$

or, since

$$AH:AB = AB:BK,$$

BK^2 will be AB^4/AH^2, $[(AB^2 \times AH^2) - AB^4]/AH^2$ will equal AK^2, and $[(4AB^2 \times AH^2) - 4AB^4]/AH^2$ will equal AC^2. From the preceding theorem, however, this is equal to $AB^2 + (AB \times AD)$. Subtracting AB^2 from both, $[(3AB^2 \times AH^2) - 4AB^4]/AH^2$ will equal $AB \times AD$ and, dividing by AB, $[(3AB^2 \times AH^2) - 4AB^4]/(AB \times AH^2)$—that is, $[(3AB \times AH^2) - 4AB^3]/AH^2$—will equal AD. Hence

$$AH^2:(3AH^2 - 4AB^2) = AB:AD.$$

Again, as

$$AH:BH = AB:AK,$$

making $(BH \times AB^{16})/AB$ equal to AK, whence $(BH \times AB)/AI$ will be equal to AC. However,

$$AB:\frac{BH \times AB}{AI} = \frac{BH \times AB}{AI}:\frac{BH^2 \times AB^2}{AB \times AI^2},$$

which last is $(BH^2 \times AB)/AI^2$. This minus AB is equal to $[(BH^2 \times AB) - (AI^2 \times AB)]/AI^2$ which, from the foregoing demonstrations, is AD. Moreover,

$$AB:\frac{BH \times AB}{AI} =$$

$$\frac{(BH^2 \times AB) - (AI^2 \times AB)}{AI^2}:\frac{(HB^3 \times AB^2) - (BH \times AI^2 \times AB^2)}{AB \times AI^3},$$

that is, $[BH^3 - (BH \times AI^2)]/(AI^3 \times AB)$.[17] Subtracting AC or

---

[16]1615 has $(BH \times AB)/AH$.
[17]This expression is confused in 1615.

$(BH \times AB)/AI$, that is

$$\frac{(BH^3 \times AB \times AI) - (BH \times AI^3 \times 2AB)}{AI^4}$$

or

$$\frac{(BH^3 \times AB) - (BH \times AI^2 \times 2AB)}{AI^3}$$

will equal AE. Hence

$$AI^3:[BH^3 - (2AB \times AI^2)] = AB:AE.$$

Other [arcs] in a given multiple ratio can also be constructed by the same method, as was to be done. To this also pertains the general analytical device for the squaring of lunes that Viète treats in the eighth book of the Variorum,[18] Chapter IX.

Theorem V

If beginning at one end of the diameter of a circle any number of equal arcs are laid off and straight lines are drawn from the other end to the terminal points of the equal arcs, the radius will be to the straight line drawn from the aforesaid end [of the diameter] nearest the diameter as any intermediate line is to the sum of the two lines nearest to itself in the same semicircle. And if the equal arcs so laid off are greater than a semicircle, the [ratio] is that of the shortest line to the difference between the two nearest to it.

Let there be a circle with AB as its diameter and P its center and let its circumference, beginning at the point B, be cut into any number of equal parts, BI, IH, HG, GF, FE, etc., to which are also equal BL, LM, MN and NO. From the other end of the diameter, A, draw the straight lines AI, AH, AG, AF, AE, etc., to the ends of the equal segments and connect the points BL, IL, IM, HM, HN, GN, GO, etc., by drawing [other] straight lines. These will be equal, one by one, to those that were drawn earlier from the point A, inasmuch as they subtend like numbers of equal segments, and they will cut the radius PB at the points P, Q, R, S, T, V and X. Just as PK, a straight line from the center, cuts BL, the shortest line, [in half] at a right

[18]I.e., the *Variorum de Rebus Mathematics Responsorum Liber VIII*, which appears at pp. 347ff of the 1646 *Opera Mathematica*.

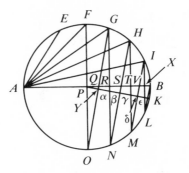

angle and also cuts [in half] at right angles the others that are parallel to
BL at the points Y, β and δ, so also it cuts GN, HM and IL at the points α, γ
and ϵ.[19]

Since the straight lines IL, HM, GN and FO connect points on both
sides equally distant from B, the end of the diameter, they will be
perpendicular to the diameter and

$$AB:AI = QO:OP = GQ:GR.^{20}$$

Therefore

$$GO:(OP + GR) = HN:(RN + HT).$$

So also for the [ratio of the] remaining intermediate [straight lines] to the
sums of the halves of the two nearest to them on either side.
    Likewise,

$$AB:AI = G\alpha:GY = \alpha N:N\beta.^{21}$$

Hence AB is to AI^{22} as the whole of GN is to the sum of the halves, GY and
$N\beta$, nearest to it on either side. So also HM is to the sum of the halves on
either side, $H\beta$ and $M\delta$, and so on for the others. As, moreover, any
intermediate is to the two halves nearest to it on either side, so twice the
intermediate is to the sum of the same. Therefore as the diameter is to the
line nearest the diameter, so twice an intermediate is to the sum of the two
nearest to it, and as the radius is to the line next to the diameter, so a simple

[19]So in 1646; 1615 omits the last clause and mixes α, γ and ϵ with the points at which PK
intersects the diagonals.
    [20]This is as it is given in the text. It is evident, however, that in pursuit of brevity,
Anderson slipped and that it should read: "$AB:AI = FO:GO$, and $QO:OP = GQ:GR$."
    [21]The remark in the preceding footnote is also applicable here. This should read:
"$AB:AI = OF:OG = GO:GN$, and $G\alpha:GY = \alpha N:N\beta$."
    [22]The text has BI.

intermediate is to the sum of the two next to it on either side, which is what was to be proven.

Let, secondly, the circumference[23] of a circle the diameter of which is *FC* be cut into equal parts, *FH*,[24] *AB*, *BD* and *DH*, which are greater than a semicircle and let the [equal] short lines, *BC* and *CD*, be inscribed in either semicircle. I say that as the radius is to a long subtend, so is *BC* to the difference between *AC* and *CD* or *CD* to the difference between *BC* and *CH*.

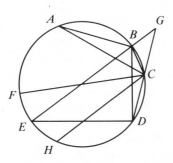

Let *AC* be subtended; make *BG* equal to *BC*, *DC* having been extended to *G*; prolong *GB* to *E*, [*BE* being a diameter]; and draw *ED*. Then the angle *BCG* (that is *BGC*[25]) will be equal to the angle *BED*[26] (that is, *BCA*, since it has been assumed that the arcs *BD* and *BA* are equal). The angles *BAC* and *BDC* are also equal and the sides *BG* and *BC* are equal by construction. Therefore *AC*[27] and *DG* will also be equal. However, since the angle *BCG* is equal to the angle *BED*, [the angle] formed [by the intersection of] a diameter and a long subtend, the radius will be to the long

---

[23]*peripheria.*

[24]The text has *FA*.

[25]The triangle *CBG* is isosceles by construction and the angles *BCG* and *BGC* are its base angles.

[26]The reasoning behind this statement would be clearer if Anderson had said *GED* rather than *BED* and had altered the order of his presentation. The reasoning, I think, is this:

(1) The triangles *ABC* and *BCD* are identical, since *BC* = *BG*, *AB* = *BD*, and the angles *BAC* and *BDC* are equal.

(2) Hence *AC* = *DG*.

(3) But the arc *AC* equals the arcs *AB* + *BC*, and the arc *DE* equals the arcs *DH* + *HE*.

(4) *AB* is given equal to *DH*, and *FE* equals *HE*, since *BD* + *DH* + *HE* (a semicirle) = *CD* + *DH* + *HF* (a semicircle) and *CD* = *BC* (by construction) and *BC* = *FE*.

(5) Therefore the triangle *GDE* is isosceles with *GED* and *EGD* as its base angles.

(6) Therefore the angle *GED* equals the angle *EGD* or *BGC*.

[27]1615 has *AG*.

subtend as *BC*, [a short subtend], is to *CG*, the difference between *AC* and *CD*, as was to be proven.[28] By the same method it can also be shown that *DC* is to the difference between *HC* and *CB* as the radius is to the longest of the produced lines.

Theorem VI

If beginning at one end of the diameter [of a circle] a number of equal arcs are laid off on the circumference and from the other end straight lines are drawn to the ends of the equal arcs so laid off, these lines are the bases of triangles that have the diameter as a common hypotenuse, and the base of the one closest to the diameter is known as the base of a single-angle triangle, that of the next as the base of a double-angle triangle, and so on in this order. The series of straight lines also constitute [a series of] continued proportionals, the first of which is equal to the radius, the second to the base of a single-angle triangle, and the progression of the other succeeding bases will be in the following order:

The third of the continued proportionals minus twice the first will be the base of the double-angle triangle; the fourth minus three times the second, the base of the triple-angle triangle; the fifth minus four times the third plus twice the first, the base of the quadruple-angle triangle; the sixth minus five times the fourth plus five times the second, the base of the quintuple-angle triangle; the seventh minus six times the fifth plus nine times the third minus twice the first, the base of the sextuple-angle triangle; the eighth minus seven times the sixth plus 14 times the fourth minus seven times the second, the base of the septuple-angle triangle; the ninth minus eight times the seventh plus 20 times the fifth minus 16 times the third plus twice the first, the base of the octuple-angle triangle; the tenth minus nine times the eighth plus 27 times the sixth minus 13 times the fourth plus nine times the second, the base of the nonuple-angle triangle; and so on to infinity.

A new affection is added to each odd place of the proportionals, negative following positive and positive fol-

---

[28]1615 and 1646 differ in their presentation of this last sentence. 1615 has: *ita BC ad CG (est enim angulus BCG aequalis angulo BED, quem facit quoque diameter cum subtensarum maxima.) differentiam ipsarum AC, CD quod erat demonstradum.* 1646 has: *ita BC ad CG differentiam ipsarum AC, CD. Est enim angulus BCG aequalis angulo BED, quem facit quoque diameter cum subtensarum maxima.*

lowing negative, and the proportionals themselves always alternate. The multipliers in the first affection increase by units, in the second by triangular numbers, in the third by pyramidal numbers, in the fourth by triangulo-triangular numbers, in the fifth by triangulo-pyramidal numbers. The increase does not start from 1 as in the development of a power but from 2.

Let the circumference of any semicircle be cut into as many parts as you please and let the radius be Z. From one end of the diameter construct straight lines to the section points, the first of these straight lines being B. Then from the preceding theorem Z will be to B as B is to the sum of the diameter and [the line] that follows next after B. This is B^2/Z which, when the diameter or twice the radius is subtracted from it, leaves $(B^2 - 2Z^2)/Z$ equal to the third. Then as Z is to B, so is $(B^2 - 2Z^2)/Z$ to the sum of the second and fourth and this, when B, the second, is subtracted from it, leaves $(B^3 - 3Z^2B)/Z^2$ equal to the fourth. Thus if the product of the second and last is divided by the *epanaphora* of Z—that is, by the grade next below the power—and the next preceding is subtracted from it, there emerge what are called the other proportional affections to infinity. So

$$\frac{B^4 - 4Z^2B^2 + 2Z^{429}}{Z^3}$$ will be equal to the fifth.

$$\frac{B^5 - 5Z^2B^3 + 5Z^4B}{Z^4}$$ will be equal to the sixth.

$$\frac{B^6 - 6Z^2B^4 + 9Z^4B^2 - 2Z^6}{Z^5}$$ [will be equal to] the seventh.

$$\frac{B^7 - 7Z^2B^5 + 14Z^4B^3 - 7Z^6B}{Z^6}$$ [will be equal to] the eighth.

$$\frac{B^8 - 8Z^2B^6 + 20Z^4B^4 - 16Z^6B^2 + 2Z^8}{Z^7}$$

[will be equal to] the ninth.

$$\frac{B^9 - 9Z^2B^7 + 27Z^4B^5 - 30Z^6B^3 + 9Z^8B}{Z^8}$$

[will be equal to] the tenth,

and so on, as was to be demonstrated.

[29] The middle term $(-4Z^2B^2)$ is followed in 1646 by an unexplainable and superfluous *sic*.

In familiar terms,[30] let the radius be 1 and the base of the first x. Then

$x^2 - 2$ will be the base of a double angle

$x^3 - 3x$ will be the base of a triple angle

$x^4 - 4x^2 + 2$ will be the base of a quadruple angle

$x^5 - 5x^3 + 5x$ will be the base of a quintuple angle

$x^6 - 6x^4 + 9x^2 - 2$ will be the base of a sextuple angle

$x^7 - 7x^5 + 14x^3 - 7x$[31] will be the base of a septuple angle

$x^8 - 8x^6 + 20x^4 - 16x^2 + 2$ will be the base of an octuple angle

$x^9 - 9x^7 + 27x^5 - 30x^3 + 9x$ will be the base of a nonuple angle.

Thus, as shown by the series in the following table, by continuously joining the root 2[32] [in each column] to the one standing next to it and by adding to this sum the number next to these [and so on], the remaining coefficients of the multiple affections can be created up to infinity.

Coefficients of the Affections

First (−)	Second (+)	Third (−)	Fourth (+)	Fifth (−)	Sixth (+)	Seventh (−)	Eighth (+)	Ninth (−)
2	Second							
3	(+)							
4	2	Third						
5	5	(−)						
6	9	2	Fourth					
7	14	7	(+)					
8	20	16	2	Fifth				
9	27	30	9	(−)				
10	35	50	25	2	Sixth			
11	44	77	55	11	(+)			
12	54	112	105	36	2	Seventh		
13	65	156	182	91	13	(−)		
14	77	210	294	196	49	2	Eighth	
15	90	275	450	378*	140	15	(+)	
16	104	352*	760*	672	336	64	2	Ninth
17	119	442	935	1122	714	204	17	(−)
18	135	546	1287	1882*	1386	540	81	2
19	152	665	1729	2817*	2508	1254	285*	19
20	170	800	2275	4104*	4390*	2640	825	100
21	189	952	2940	5833*	7207*	5148	2079	385

*These values have been recomputed in accordance with the formula of the text. Those given in 1615 and/or 1646 are different.

[30]*In notis.*

[31]1646 has $147x^3$.

[32]*radicem binarium.*

Theorem VII

If beginning at a point on the circumference of a circle a number of equal parts are laid off and straight lines are drawn from the same point to the termini of the equal arcs so laid off, a series of straight lines in continued proportion will be constituted, the first of which is equal to the shortest line drawn, the second to the next-to-shortest, and the remainder in the following order:

The third of the continued proportionals minus the first will be equal to the third; the fourth minus twice the second to the fourth; the fifth minus three times the third plus the first to the fifth; the sixth minus four times the fourth plus three times the second to the sixth; the seventh minus five times the fifth plus six times the third minus the first to the seventh; the eighth minus six times the sixth plus 10 times the fourth minus four times the second to the eighth; the ninth minus seven times the seventh plus 15 times the fifth minus 10 times the third plus the first to the ninth; the tenth minus eight times the eighth plus 21 times the sixth minus 20 times the fourth plus five times the second to the tenth; and so on to infinity, so that a new negative affection is added at each odd place of the proportionals, negative following positive and positive following negative. The proportionals themselves come alternately and the coefficients of the first affection increase by unity, of the second by triangular numbers, of the third by pyramidal numbers, of the fourth by triangulo-triangular numbers, of the fifth by triangulo-pyramidal numbers, beginning with unity as in the construction of powers.

Cut the circumference of a circle into a number of equal parts beginning at any assumed point and from it draw straight lines to the ends of the equal arcs. Let the shortest of these [lines] be Z and the next shortest B. Hence, from Theorem IIII, the first is to the second as the second is to the sum of the first and third. The third, therefore, will be $(B^2 - Z^2)/Z$. By the same method used in the preceding [theorem],

The fourth will be $\dfrac{B^3 - 2Z^2B}{Z^2}$

The fifth will be $\dfrac{B^4 - 3Z^2B^2 + Z^4}{Z^3}$

The sixth will be $\dfrac{B^5 - 4Z^2B^3 + 3Z^4B}{Z^4}$

The seventh will be $\dfrac{B^6 - 5Z^2B^4 + 6Z^4B^2 - Z^6}{Z^5}$

The eighth will be $\dfrac{B^7 - 6Z^2B^5 + 10Z^4B^3 - 4Z^6B}{Z^6}$

The ninth will be $\dfrac{B^8 - 7Z^2B^6 + 15Z^4B^4 - 10Z^6B^2 + Z^8}{Z^7}$

The tenth will be $\dfrac{B^9 - 8Z^2B^7 + 21Z^4B^5 - 20Z^6B^3 + 5Z^8B}{Z^8}$

By the same reasoning, also, other proportionals to infinity affected in the manner proposed may be derived equal to straight lines drawn in a circle, as was to be demonstrated.

In familiar terms, let the shortest [straight line] produced be 1, the second x. Then

$x^2 - 1$ will be equal to the third
$x^3 - 2x$ will be equal to the fourth
$x^4 - 3x^2 + 1$ will be equal to the fifth
$x^5 - 4x^3 + 3x$ will be equal to the sixth
$x^6 - 5x^4 + 6x^2 - 1$ will be equal to the seventh
$x^7 - 6x^5 + 10x^3 - 4x$ will be equal to the eighth
$x^8 - 7x^6 + 15x^4 - 10x^2 + 1$ will be equal to the ninth
$x^9 - 8x^7 + 21x^5 - 20x^3 + 5x$ will be equal to the tenth.

Thus by joining the root 1 to the term next to it and adding the sum to the next following, the remaining coefficients of the multiple affections can be created to infinity. These, if you wish, can easily be set up in a table in the manner presented by us under the preceding proposition.

Theorem VIII[33]

If beginning at one end of a diameter there are laid off along the circumference of a circle a number of equal parts and straight lines are drawn from the ends of the same diameter to the individual section points, the radius will be to the chord subtending one of the equal parts as any other straight line drawn from either end of the diameter, except the diameter itself or the line next to it, if they fall within these

[33]In the text this is labeled Theorem VII.

sections,[34] is to the difference between the two lines drawn from the other end of the diameter to the sections nearest to it on either side. Thus also the diameter itself, whether it falls within an equal section or not and[35] the one next to it falling within a section is the sum of the two lines from either end of the diameter to the two sections nearest to it on either side.

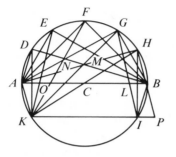

Describe a circle around the diameter AB, with its center at C, the circumference of which is divided into a number of equal parts, AD, DE, EF, FG, GH, HB and BI and draw straight lines from the points B and A to the individual sections. Assume also that AK is equal to AD and draw the straight lines HI, GI, GK, FK, EK, DK and AK. Let CH be the radius and let the straight line GI cut the diameter at the point L.

Since the straight line HI divides the angle BIL in half, it is perpendicular to the base. The triangle BIL is isosceles and similar to the triangle HCB. The triangle BLI is also similar to the triangle GAL, so the triangle GAL is isosceles and the sides GA and AL are equal. Moreover,

$$CH:HB = HB \text{ or } BI:BL,$$

BL being the difference between the sides AG and AB. Similarly, since the angles GBE and EKG are equal to the angle HCB (since they subtend double arcs on the circumference and in a single one at the center), the angles KEB and BGK are also equal to the angle CBH, they subtending equal arcs. The straight lines GK and EB intersect at M. The triangles EKM and GBM are similar to the triangle HCB, and

$$HC:HB = GB:GM,$$

GM being the difference between GK (that is HA, for they subtend equal arcs) and EK (that is AF, for they also subtend equal arcs). Likewise, the

---

[34]The meaning and relevance of this qualification is not clear.
[35]The text has *ei*, apparently a misprint for *et*.

straight lines FK[36] and DB intersect at the point N and the triangles FBN and DKN are isosceles and similar to the triangle HCB, and

$$HC:HB = FB:FN,$$

FN being the difference between the chords FK and DK, that is GA and EA, as above. Similarly the straight lines EK and AB intersect at the point O, and

$$HC:HB = EB:EO,$$

EO being the difference between the straight lines EK and AK, that is FA and DA. It can likewise be demonstrated that

$$HC:HB = GA:(FB \sim HB) = FA:(EB \sim GB) = EA:(DB \sim FB).$$

If HCK, KIP and HBP are protracted, the triangles HCB and HKP will be similar, for the angles HCB and HKP, the former at the center, the latter on the circumference, are equal and the angle CHB is common to both. Hence the remaining [angles] will be equal to each other. Therefore

$$CH:HB = HK:HP.$$

HP, however, is double HB, for the angle IBP is equal to the angle HKI and the angle BPI to the angle BHC. Therefore the triangle BIP is isosceles and the legs BP and BI—that is, BP and BH—are equal.

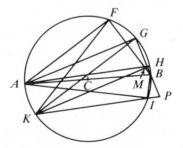

Now having drawn the straight lines GK, KP and GBP as above, let the diameter not run between the equal sections but let it intersect the circumference at the point B within a section. Since the arcs GAK and AGH are equal, AK and GH having been assumed to be equal segments, the chords AH and KG will also be equal. Hence, as before, the angle ABG[37] is equal to [the angle] that the chord of any equal arc makes with a

[36]1646 has EK.
[37]1615 has AGB.

diameter, and *GKP* is equal to a center angle. Thus the triangle *GKP* is isosceles and similar to that which comes from radii and a straight line subtending one of the equal segments. So the radius is to that subtend as *KG*—that is, *AH*—is to *GP*. *BP*, moreover, is equal to *BI*, for in the inscribed quadrilateral *KGBI* the exterior angles *PBI* and *BIP* are equal to the interior angles *GKI* and *KGB*. Therefore the triangle *BIP* is isosceles and similar to the triangle *GKP* and the sides *BI* and *BP* are equal. But as the radius is to the chord of an equal part, so also is *BH* to the difference between *AG* and *AI*. For the angle *BHK* is equal to that produced by the diameter and the chord of any equal segment, and the angle *HBF* is equal to the center angle of one segment[38] of the equal parts. Whence the triangle *BMH* will be isosceles and the triangle *FKM* will be similar to it, so that as the radius is to the chord of any equal segment, so *BH* is to *HM*, the difference between the straight lines *HK* and *MK*.[39] Moreover, *HK* is equal to *AI*, for the segments *AK* and *HI* are equal. Having added *KI* to both [these pairs of sides], *KIH* and *AKI* are equal. In addition, *KF* is equal to *AG*, for the segments *AK* and *FG* were assumed to be equal. Having added *AF* to both [these pairs of sides], *KAF* and *AFG* are equal. Likewise, [as the radius is to the chord of any equal segment], so *AG*[40] or *KF* is to *FM*, the difference between the straight lines *BF* and *BM* or *BH*, as was to be proven.

Theorem IX

Given right triangles with equal hypotenuses, the acute angle of the first of which is in fractional ratio with the acute angles of the other triangles in order, namely one-half the acute angle of the second, one-third that of the third, one-fourth that of the fourth, and so on, there will be constituted a series of straight lines in continued proportion, the first of which will be equal to one-half the hypotenuse and the second to the perpendicular of the first triangle[41] and this will be the equality between the succeeding continued proportionals and the bases and perpendiculars of the succeeding triangles:

Twice the first minus the third of the continued proportionals will be equal to the base of the second triangle.

[38]The text has *insistenti* which I read as probably a typographical error for *segmenti*.
[39]1646 has *KF*.
[40]1615 has *FG*.
[41]The text has "angle."

Three times the second minus the fourth will be equal to the perpendicular of the third triangle.

Twice the first minus four times the third plus the fifth will be equal to the base of the fourth triangle.

Five times the second minus five times the fourth plus the sixth will be equal to the perpendicular of the fifth triangle.

Twice the first minus nine times the third plus six times the fifth minus the seventh will be equal to the base of the sixth triangle.

Seven times the second minus 14 times the fourth plus seven times the sixth minus the eighth will be equal to the perpendicular of the seventh triangle.

Twice the first minus 16 times the third plus 20 times the fifth minus eight times the seventh plus the ninth will be equal to the base of the eighth triangle.

Nine times the second minus 30 times the fifth plus 27 times the sixth minus nine times the eighth plus the tenth will be equal to the perpendicular of the ninth triangle.

And so on to infinity, in reverse order from that set out in Theorem VI.

Let there be a semicircle like the one before, the circumference of which is cut into any number of equal parts and from the ends of the diameter let the sides of right triangles be drawn. Let the radius be X and let the perpendicular of a fractional triangle be B. Hence

$$X : B = B : \frac{B^2}{X}.$$

Subtracting [the last term] from the diameter, $2X$, leaves $(2X^2 - B^2)/X$, the base of the second triangle, according to the preceding theorem. This makes

$$X : B = \frac{2X^2 - B^2}{X} : \frac{2X^2 B - B^3}{X^2}.$$

Adding the last term to B, since the perpendiculars increase as the bases decrease, makes $(3X^2 B - B^3)/X^2$ equal to the perpendicular of the third triangle. Following the same method,

$$\frac{2X^4 - 4B^2 X^2 + B^4}{X^3}$$ will be the base of the fourth triangle.

$$\frac{5X^4B - 5B^3X^2 + B^5}{X^4}$$ will be the perpendicular of the fifth triangle.

$$\frac{2X^6 - 9X^4B^2 + 6X^2B^4 - B^6}{X^5}$$ will be the base of the sixth triangle.

$$\frac{7X^6B - 14X^4B^3 + 7X^2B^5 - B^7}{X^6}$$

will be the perpendicular of the seventh triangle.

$$\frac{2X^8 - 16X^6B^2 + 20X^4B^4 - 8X^2B^6 + B^8}{X^7}$$

will be the base of the eighth triangle.

$$\frac{9X^8B - 30X^6B^3 + 27X^4B^{5\,\textbf{42}} - 9X^2B^7 + B^9}{X^8}$$

will be the perpendicular of the ninth triangle,

and so on in the same progression to infinity, aided if you wish by the table of Theorem VI.

In familiar terms, let the first of the continued proportionals be 1, the common half hypotenuse of the right triangles, and let the second of the continued proportionals be x. Let this be known as the perpendicular of the triangle with a fractional angle.

$2 - x^2$ will equal the base
of the double-angle triangle.

$3x - x^3$ will equal the perpendicular
of the triple-angle triangle.

$2 - 4x^2 + x^4$ will equal the base
of the quadruple-angle triangle.

$5x - 5x^3 + x^5$ will equal the perpendicular
of the quintuple-angle triangle.

$2 - 9x^2 + 6x^4 - x^6$ will equal the base
of the sextuple-angle triangle.

$7x - 14x^3 + 7x^5 - x^7$ will equal the perpendicular
of the septuple-angle triangle.

421646 has $-27X^4B^5$.

$2 - 16x^2 + 20x^4 - 8x^6 + x^8$ will equal the base
of the octuple-angle triangle.

$9x - 30x^3 + 27x^5 - 9x^7 + x^9$ will equal the perpendicular
of the nonuple-angle triangle,

and so on in an order inverse to that of Theorem VI just as it has been set out there, except that the quality of the affections changes in each pair of cases.

Theorem X

If half the circumference of a circle is divided into a number of equal parts and straight lines are drawn from the end of the diameter to the points marking off the sections, the shortest of these will be to the diameter as the sum of the diameter, the shortest line and [a line] the square of which plus the square of the shortest line is equal to the square of the diameter is to twice the sum of all the straight lines.

Let a semicircle be divided into a number of equal parts at the points *A*, *B*, *C*, *D*, *E*, *F* and *G*, and from *A*, one end of the diameter, draw the straight lines *AB*, *AC*, *AD*, *AE*, *AF* and *AG* to these section points. Then divide the other semicircle into the same number of segments, *AN*, *NO*, *OP*, *PQ*, *QX* and *XG* and connect the opposite points beginning with the diameter by straight lines. These intersect the diameter at right angles. They are *BHN*, *CIO*, *DKP*, *ELQ* and *FMX*. Connect the alternate ends of these with the transverse lines *CRN*, *DSO*, *ETP*, *FVQ* and *GX*.

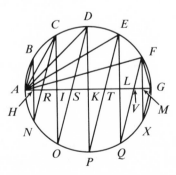

BN, therefore, will be equal to *CA*, *CN* to *AD*, *CO* to *AE* and *DO* to *AF*. Likewise the straight lines *EP*, *EQ*, *FQ* and *FX*, taken individually, can be shown to be equal to these and *GX* is equal to *BA*. Hence [the sum of] the straight lines *AB*, *BN*, *CN*, *CO*, *DO*, *DP*, *EP*, *EQ*, *FQ*, *FX* and *GX* is equal to twice [the sum of] *AB*, *AC*, *AD*, *AE* and *AF* plus the diameter *DP*

or *AG*. Add the diameter *AG* to each of these [sums] and all of the aforesaid [i.e., the first sum] plus the diameter AG will be equal to twice the sum of *AB, AC, AD, AE, AF* and *AG*.

However, as *AH* is to *HB*—that is, as *AB* or *GF* is to *FA*—so *HR* is to *HN*, *RI* to *IC*, *IS* to *IO*, *SK* to *KD*, *KT* to *KP*, *TL* to *LE*, *VL* to *LQ*, *VM* to *MF* and *GM* to *MX*. Hence, as *AB* is to *AF*, so *AG* is to the sum of all the perpendiculars on the diameter *AG* and, by permutation, as *AB* is to *AG*, so is *AF* is the sum of all of those perpendiculars.

Again, *AH* is to *AB*—that is, *FG* or *AB* is to *AG*—as *HR* is to *RN*, *RI* to *RC*,[43] *IS* to *SO*, *SK* to *SD*, *KT* to *TP*, *TL* to *TE*, *LV* to *VQ*, *VM* to *VF*, and *MG* to *GX*. Therefore, as *AB* is to *AG*, so all of *AH*, *RI*, etc. (that is *AG*) are to the sum of the transversals. Moreover, as *AB* is to *AG*, so *AF* is to all the perpendiculars. Hence as *AB* is to *AG* so the sum of *AF* and *AG* is to all the transversals and perpendiculars and, by composition, as *AB* is to *AG*, so the sum of the three, *AF*, *AG* and *AB*, is to the sum of all the perpendiculars, all the transversals and the straight line *AG*—that is (as has been demonstrated) to twice the sum of *AB, AC, AD, AE, AF* and *AG*, as was to be demonstrated.

Hence a mystery, heretofore understood by no one, either in arithmetic or in geometry, is explained by the analysis of angular sections.

PROBLEM I

Given numerically the ratio of the angles, to give the ratio of the sides.

This is clearly taught by Theorem III.

PROBLEM II

To construct one angle to another as one number is to another.

This can be solved by Theorems III, VI and IX, whether the ratio of the unequal [terms] is greater or less [than unity]. If the ratio of the inequality is greater [than unity], it can be solved by Theorems V and VIII.[44] Hence this corollary:

---

[43] 1615 has *RT*.

[44] *In ratione minoris majorisve inaequalitatis ex Theorematis 3, 6, & 9 satisfieri potest: at in majoris inaequalitatis ratione ex Theorematis 5 & 8.*

Corollary[45]

Since a straight line, not a diameter, inscribed in a circle subtends two arcs, one of which is less than half the circumference and the other of which is greater than half the circumference, the equation [stating the relation] between the chord subtending a segment of the smaller [arc] and the greater or smaller [arc] will also apply to the chord subtending a similar segment of the greater [arc] and to other chords subtending [certain] other arcs which, in their sweep, are the sum of the greater or smaller [of the foregoing] and even multiples [of the smaller].

Notwithstanding that this has been adverted to in Theorem VIII, if a segment greater than a semicircle is divided into equal parts, whether the diameter cuts at the section points or not, there is no change from the prescribed order or the nature of the affections pertaining to the perpendiculars or in the series of numerical coefficients. Thus in the second figure accompanying that theorem the sum of the chords *GB* and *BI* may be arrived at from the chord *AH*. Later on the difference between the chords drawn from the point *A* that are closest on both sides to the sections [drawn] from the point *I* can be derived from the difference between the said sum and the chord *GB*, earlier demonstrated—that is, from the chord *BI*. By this operation, therefore, what were there changed may now be restored.

But in the progression of the bases, when the equal segments are greater than a semicircle, the order of the homogeneous terms of affection, as shown in Theorem V, is reversed and the progression is like that set out in Theorem IX. If twice the ratio of either of the smallest chords in either semicircle to the difference of those on either side is changed, then the nature of the homogeneous terms is restored to the ratios of the intermediate term to the sum of those on both sides of it. This certainly ought to be clear enough from the formula of Theorem V. Hence appears the truth of this corollary.

[The following] problems pertaining to sections of given angles are derived from Theorems VI and IX, so that it may be seen how useful this work is. They may be extended *ad infinitum* in accordance with the reasoning there set out. Let this example be proposed:

---

[45] This corollary also appears verbatim in the *Responsum,* referred to n. 4 supra.

Exercise I[46]

To divide a given angle into three equal parts.

Assuming that X is the radius or semidiameter of a circle, B the chord subtending the angle to be divided and E the chord of one segment,

$$3X^2E - E^3 = X^2B$$

and E will have two values: (i) the chord of one-third the arc, (ii) the chord of one-third the remainder of the whole circle.

It has been shown that the equality [relating] the chord of the smaller or greater segment to the chord of part of the smaller segment is also applicable to the chord of a similar part of the larger segment.

Exercise II[47]

To divide a given angle into five equal parts.

Making the same assumptions as before,

$$5X^4E - 5X^2E^3 + E^5 = X^4B$$

[46]*Problemation I.* I have translated this as "exercise" to distinguish this series from the separate series of *problema* that precede and follow the corollary. The same "exercise" also appears in Viète's *Responsum,* n. 4 supra, as a *theoremation.* After setting out the corollary given above, Viète propounds it thus:

"Assume that X is the sine of 90° and B twice the sine of the angle to be divided. Let E be twice the sine of the segment. [If]

$$3X^2E - E^3 = X^2B,$$

E has two values: (i) twice the sine of one-third the angle; (ii) twice the sine of the difference between one-third the angle and one-third of two right angles.

"In familiar terms,

$$3x - x^3 = \sqrt{2}.$$

Assuming that 1 is the sine of 90°, $\sqrt{2}$ is twice the sine of 45°. Therefore x is twice the sine of 15° or it is twice the sine of 45°. Hence x is the binomial root $2 - \sqrt{2}$ or $\sqrt{2}$.

"[Or let]

$$3x - x^3 = 1.$$

Assuming that 1 is the sine of 90°, 1 becomes twice the sine of 30°. Therefore x is twice the sine of 10° or twice the sine of 50°. Hence x is

$$\frac{34,729,635,533,296}{100,000,000,000,000} \text{ or } \frac{153,208,888,623,795}{100,000,000,000,000}.\text{"}$$

[47]In the *Responsum* (n. 4 supra), the *theoremation* is stated thus:
"[If]

$$5X^4E - 5X^2E^3 + E^5 = X^4B,$$

and *E* will have three values: (i) the chord of one-fifth the arc, (ii) the chord of one-fifth the remaining circumference of the whole circle, (iii) the chord of an arc that is the sum of one-fifth the arc and two-fifths of the whole circle.

It is worth demonstrating this last by example for the uninitiated and those less practised in analysis.

Let a circle the diameter of which is *AB* be cut in unequal parts the greater of which is *BAG* and the smaller *BHG* and let one-fifth of the smaller segment be *BH*. To this add the segment *HGC* which equals two-fifths[48] of four right [angles]. The sum must not exceed a semicircle.

Five times the segment *BGC* will be equal to twice[49] the arc subtending four right angles—the full sweep around the point *K*[50]—plus the arc *BG*, and five times the assumed segment *BC* accounts for this sum. Let these five be set out: they will be the segments *BGC*, *CAD*, *DBE*, *EAF* and *FBG*. Thus it is the segment *BD* that will be left over if twice *BGC* is subtracted from a full circle [and *BD*] is twice *CA*, the remainder of the semicircle when *BGC* is subtracted from it. Therefore *EC* is equal to *BD*, since the straight lines *BC* and *CD* are equal to *CD* and *DE*, and this will be equal to double *CA*. Hence *EA* is triple *CA*.

E has three values: (i) twice the sine of one-fifth the angle, (ii) twice the sine of the difference between one-fifth the angle and one-fifth of two right angles, (iii) twice the sine of an angle that is the sum of one-fifth the angle and one-fifth of four right angles, provided this sum does not exceed 90°.

"[Let]

$$5x - 5x^3 + x^5 = 1.$$

Having assumed that 1 is the sine of 90°, 1 becomes twice the sine of 30°. Hence *x* is twice the sine of 6° or twice the sine of 30° or twice the sine of 78°. So *x* will be the trinomial root $9/4 - \sqrt{5/16} - \sqrt{15/8} + \sqrt{45/64}$, or 1, or the trinomial root $9/4 - \sqrt{5/16} + \sqrt{15/8} - \sqrt{45/64}$.

"[Let]

$$5x - 5x^3 + x^5 = \frac{68,401,028,665,134}{100,000,000,000,000}.$$

Having assumed that 1 is the sine of 90°, the given constant of the proposed equation is twice the sine of 20°. Therefore *x* is twice the sine of 4° or of 32° or of 76°. So *x* will be

$$\frac{13,951,294,748,825}{100,000,000,000,000} \text{ or } \frac{105,983,852,846,641}{100,000,000,000,000} \text{ or } \frac{194,059,145,255,109}{100,000,000,000,000} \text{,"}$$

[48] 1615 has "one-fifth."

[49] 1615 omits this word.

[50] 1615 has *sive integrae circulationi circa A punctum;* 1646 omits *integrae* and changes *A* to *K*.

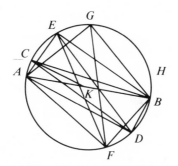

By the same reasoning, since the straight lines *CB* and *CD* are also equal to *ED* and *EF*, the segments *BD* and *DF* are equal, and *BF* will be equal to four times *CA*. Similarly the segments *GE* and *EC* are equal and *GA* will be equal to five times *CA*. Therefore the right triangle *ACB* will be a triangle of the simple angle, *BAD* of the double, *BAE* of the triple, *BAF* of the quadruple and *BGA* of the quintuple.

Assuming, therefore, that the radius is the first [in a series] of continued proportionals and *CB* is the second and that the series goes on, the straight line *GB*, according to Theorem VI, will be equal to the sixth minus five times the fourth plus five times the second.

In familiar terms, let *CK* be 1 and *CB* x. *GB* will be equal to $x^5 - 5x^3 + 5x$.

Exercise III[51]

To divide a given angle into seven equal parts.

Making the same suppositions as above,

$$7X^6E - 14X^4E^3 + 7X^2E^5 - E^7 = X^6B$$

[51]The corresponding *theoremation* in the *Responsum* (n. 4 supra) is this:
"[If]

$$7X^6E - 14X^4E^3 + 7X^2E^5 - E^7 = X^6B,$$

X has four values: (i) twice the sine of one-seventh the angle, (ii) twice the sine of the difference between one-seventh the angle and one seventh of two right angles, (iii) twice the sine of an angle that is the sum of one-seventh [the angle] and one-seventh of four right angles, (iiii) twice the sine of an angle that is the sum of the aforesaid difference and one-seventh of four right angles.
"[Let]

$$7x - 14x^3 + 7x^5 - x^7 = 1.$$

and E has four values: (i) the chord subtending one-seventh of an arc, (ii) the chord subtending one-seventh of the remainder of the circumference of the whole circle, (iii) the chord subtending an arc that is the sum of one-seventh [of the arc] and two-sevenths of the whole circle, (iiii) the chord subtending an arc that is the sum of one-seventh [of the arc] and four-sevenths of the whole circle.

This will be demonstrated thus. Let there be a circle with AB as its diameter, let CB be a subtending straight line and let BK be one-seventh of the arc CB. Add to this the arc KD equal to two-sevenths of the whole circumference and construct BD and DA. I say that seven times the angle DBA is equal to four right angles plus [the angle of] the arc ADC and, therefore, from Theorem VI, that the equality [governing the relation] between the straight lines BC and BK is also applicable to the terms BD and BC.

Let BD, DF, FI, IG, GE, EH and HC be equal and since seven times the arc DB measures off eight[52] right angles—i.e., twice the whole circumference of the circle AB, since the angles are measured along the circumference—plus the arc BC, therefore a continual marking off of DB seven times will end at the point C. And since the lines BD and DF have

---

Having assumed that 1 is the sine of 90°, 1 becomes twice the sine of 30°. Hence x is twice the sine of $4\frac{2}{7}$° or of $21\frac{3}{7}$° or of $55\frac{5}{7}$° or of $72\frac{6}{7}$°.

"And if

$$7x - 14x^3 + 7x^5 - x^7 = 2,$$

since 2 is twice the sine of a right angle, x becomes twice the sine of $12\frac{6}{7}$° or of $54\frac{2}{7}$°. So x will be 4,450,418,680/10,000,000,000, the side of a tessaradecahedron, of 18,019,377,358/10,000,000,000, a straight line the square of which plus the square of the side of a heptagon is equal to the square of the diameter."

[52]The text has "four" but this is impossible unless *quatuor rectos angulos* means "four straight angles," a permissible translation but one that would make *angulus rectus* here inconsistent with its clear meaning elsewhere.

been assumed to be equal, the arc *FB* will be twice *DA*, since *FB* is the complement of twice *DB* [in filling out] the whole circle.[53] Therefore the arc *DBI* is equal to the arc *FB*, since the straight lines *DF* and *FI* are equal to *BD* and *DF*. So the arc *ADI* is three times *AD*. Likewise, since the straight lines *IG* and *GE* are also equal to *DF* and *FI*, the arc *IE*[54] is twice *AD* and the whole of *ADBE* is equal to five times *AD* and the straight lines *EH* and *HC* are equal to the same [i.e., to *DF* and *FI*], wherefore the whole of *ADHEC* will be seven times *AD*. Hence, from Theorem VI, assuming that the radius *AL* is the first [of a series] of continued proportionals and *DB* the second and that the series is continued, the straight line *CB* will be equal to seven times the second minus 11 times the fourth plus seven times the sixth minus the eighth.

In familiar terms, let *AL* be 1 and *DB* x. Then

$$7x - 14x^3 + 7x^5 - x^7 = CB.$$

This equation will also be solved similarly by Theorem IIII.[55]

Now truly from the rules of Theorems V and VIII flow multiple roots for given problems up to infinity, as said above. Anyone who wishes an example should consult Viète's answer to Adriaen van Roomen's problem.[56]

PROBLEM III

To compute in commensurable numbers the straight lines subtending the arcs of a circle that are in arithmetic progresssion beginning with the one first inscribed as the largest or smallest and the one next to it as the second.

This operation can be deduced from Theorems VI, VII and IX where it is clearly set out and demonstrated.

---

[53]Stated more fully, since *BD* + *DA* makes a half circle and *DB* + *DF* + *FB* makes a whole circle—i.e., 2*BD* + *FB* makes a whole circle—*FB* must be twice *BD*.

[54]1615 has *BE*.

[55]The text has *de termino quarto*. I read *termino* as a misprint for *theorema*.

[56]See the *Responsum,* cited n. 4, p. 422 supra. The problem posed was that of finding the value of *x* in the proportion $x{:}45x - 3795x^3 + 95,634x^5 - 1,138,500x^7 + 7,811,375x^9 - 34,512,075x^{11} + 105,306,075x^{13} - 232,676,280x^{15} + 384,942,375x^{17} - 488,494,125x^{19} + 483,841,800x^{21} - 378,658,800x^{23} + 236,030,652x^{25} - 117,679,100x^{27} + 46,955,700x^{29} - 14,945,040x^{31} + 3,764,565x^{33} - 740,459x^{35} + 111,150x^{37} - 12,300x^{39} + 945x^{41} - 45x^{43} + 1x^{45}$, if the value of the second term is given. Viète found 23 possible answers.

Problem IIII

To find the sum of the lines subtending arcs of a circle that are in arithmetic progression beginning with an inscribed maximum and minimum.

This is shown in Theorem X.

Corollary

An analyst will fabricate, felicitously and surely, a mathematical table and, aided by these principles of analysis and having learned the method of solving all powers whatsoever, pure or affected, will check his fabrication.

To do so, he will first look into the perpendicular of one minute [of arc], which he can do with accuracy this way:

1. By sectioning a hypothetical line in extreme and mean ratio, he will obtain the perpendicular of 18°.[57]
2. By dividing this in five, he will discover the perpendicular of 3° 36'.
3. By trisectioning, he will be given the perpendicular of 20°.
4. And by trisecting this, the perpendicular of 6° 40'.
5. And by bisecting this, the perpendicular of 3° 20'.
6. From the difference between the perpendiculars of 3° 36' and 3° 20', he will be given the perpendicular of 16', per Theorem I.
7. Bisecting this will produce the perpendiculars of 8', 4', 2' and 1'.

   Then returning to angles in multiple ratio, others in commensurable numbers will be constructed in accordance with the rule of Theorem VI.

These fundamentals on angular sections, derived from the fount of pure analysis, from which an infinity of other corollaries can also be deduced by elegant reasoning, were first thought up and presented by the greatest mathematician in many a century, Francois Viète. He transmitted them to us without any demonstrations. My efforts have now fully and perfectly confirmed them from the principles of geometry. Accept them, worthy mathematicians, and be mindful of all that is good and fair.

---

[57]I.e., given $1:x = x:x^2$, and given also $x^2 + x = 1$, x will be found to be 2 sin 18°. As is clear, Viète's *latus hypotheticum* is sin 90°. In his *Canon Mathematicus* (Paris, 1579), he uses an expression which Ritter (biog., p. 50) translates "Sinus d'un droit ou hypothétique."